"John Baggett makes an important contribution to contemporary work on Jesus. His rich academic and professional experiences are reflected in these pages. Sound biblical study, solid theological reflection, and faithful application to personal and global concerns make this a valuable tool for personal and group enrichment. This is an important book for every pastor and lay interpreter of the Christian life and faith."

— DAVID HILTON
retired United Methodist minister
former District Superintendent
in Louisville Conference

"Baggett brings a vital, credible, and fully *human* historical Jesus to life through a combination of creative insight, solid biblical scholarship as illuminated by contributions from his field of cultural anthropology, and the touch of a skilled biographer. He invites and guides the reader not to look *at* Jesus as a lifeless dissected specimen under an analytical microscope but to look *with* Jesus at God and the world as Jesus saw them. . . . Demonstrates that 'the Jesus of history' and 'the Christ of faith' were — and are — one reality, the ultimate reality for believers then and now."

— MICHAEL MILLER
distinguished elder in the
Presbyterian Church (USA)

Seeing through the Eyes of Jesus

His Revolutionary View of Reality
and His Transcendent Significance for Faith

John Baggett

WILLIAM B. EERDMANS PUBLISHING COMPANY
GRAND RAPIDS, MICHIGAN / CAMBRIDGE, U.K.

Published 2008 by
Wm. B. Eerdmans Publishing Co.
2140 Oak Industrial Drive N.E., Grand Rapids, Michigan 49505 /
P.O. Box 163, Cambridge CB3 9PU U.K.
www.eerdmans.com

Printed in the United States of America

14 13 12 11 10 09 08   7 6 5 4 3 2 1

Library of Congress Cataloging-in-Publication Data

Baggett, John.
Seeing through the eyes of Jesus: his revolutionary view of reality
and his transcendent significance for faith / John Baggett.
        p.   cm.
Includes bibliographical references.
ISBN 978-0-8028-6340-9 (pbk.: alk. paper)
1. Jesus Christ — Person and offices.
2. Christianity — Philosophy.   I. Title.

BT203.B34   2008
232 — dc22
                                2008018549

CONTENTS

This book has been many years in the making. I trace its beginnings to conversations with my mother during my teenage years while my sister and I helped her wash and dry the dishes. These were often serious theological discussions during which we children were challenged to use our critical faculties to think about our faith and always to take the Bible seriously while not always taking it literally. Later, college classes in Old and New Testament at Kentucky Wesleyan College under professors Ed Beavin and Tom Rogers not only helped to shape my intellectual understanding of the Bible but my life of faith as well. Beavin's course on "The Prophets of Israel" was particularly influential in nurturing within me an enduring passion for justice for the stigmatized and oppressed in our society, and an appreciation for the prophetic and compassionate ministry of Jesus.

It was not until my seminary years at Vanderbilt Divinity School, however, that a long-term fascination with the Quest for the Historical Jesus was initiated. Under the mentoring of my Greek New Testament professor Leander Keck, I steeped myself in what has now been called the "Second Quest" for the historical Jesus. Vanderbilt professors Kendrick Grobel, Everett Tilson, Langdon Gilkey, Walter Harrelson, Gordon Kaufman, and others also contributed substantially to a life-shaping internal dialogue between theology, the Scriptures, my pastoral duties as a student pastor, and my personal life of faith. These scholarly giants laid the foundation without which this book could never have been written.

My understanding of Jesus' mission and ministry was also forged during my years of Chicago inner-city ministry, my participation in the civil rights movement, and my sojourn as a faculty member of the Ecumenical Institute. I shall always be indebted to Dean Joseph Matthews and my colleagues at the Institute, and to the theologians and esteemed thinkers we studied together, for key theological insights found throughout this work. While my subsequent personal theological journey has changed my own thinking considerably over the years, I cannot imagine this book without the Institute experience. Nor can I imagine it apart from my later experiences as an advocate for persons with mental illness and as a mental health administrator. My friends in the National Alliance for the Mentally Ill and professional Mental Health colleagues, unbeknown to them, have challenged me over many years to reshape not only my views on mental illness, but also, in the face of the needs of persons with profound disabilities, my theological insights and personal faith as well.

It is also important to mention my mentors and friends in the Anthropology and Religion Departments at the University of North Carolina at Chapel Hill, Dr. James Peacock and Dr. William Peck, who must be acknowledged with appreciation, not only for their guidance in the 1980s during my years of graduate study in Anthropology, but for their recent willingness to read and comment on the manuscript of this book.

With regard to the development of the manuscript, I am indebted above all others to Michael Miller and to Charles Sensel, fellow members of that informal association of Kentucky Wesleyan College alumni known as "The Second Floor Ministerial Association," for their many hours of reading, questioning, and commenting on the manuscript, and for their unfailing faith in this project and their tireless advocacy for its publication. It is impossible adequately to express my appreciation to these two friends for their labors. Other members of that group who read portions and gave encouragement must also be mentioned. They are: David Hilton, Phil and Sandy Hoy, Dewey Sanders, Alan Krauss, John Conn, Joe Roop, Rodney Dempsey, and James Jones.

Other good friends and colleagues who read various chapters and provided valuable suggestions were Terry and Lynn Stelle, the Rev. Jim Wilson, Dr. Geff Kelly, and Dr. Pat Kelley. I am also grateful to Rev. Ronald DeGinnaro for sharing some of his personal library with me at a critical point in the development of this work.

It is an honor to have been selected by William B. Eerdmans for the publication of this labor of love. It am particularly privileged to have become acquainted with William (Bill) Eerdmans, President of Eerdmans Publishing, whose suggestion to include a planned second book as Part II of this work was among the better advice I have received in this life. It has also been a pleasure to work with the capable editors of Eerdmans in the publishing process.

If this book speaks to educated thoughtful persons, both the religiously committed and the religiously curious, then it is in no small part due to the assistance of those mentioned above. If the book fails in any way, the responsibility for that failure lies with the author alone.

Finally, this work would never have come to fruition without the daily sacrifices, sincere questioning, insightful critique, and enthusiastic support of my wonderful wife, Diane Call Baggett. Without her assistance over the three years of the birthing of this book, it would not have come to be, and it is to her that *Seeing through the Eyes of Jesus* is dedicated.

INTRODUCTION

I was in my early twenties when I put on a pair of prescription glasses for the first time. It was an amazing experience. Suddenly objects were crisper and sharper. I could see clearly children playing in the park in front of my home. I could watch from my window the bustling activity on a Chicago street more than a block away. The world was filled with heretofore unseen details. Contrasts were deeper and colors appeared richer. I was mesmerized. I was looking at the same reality I had seen hundreds of times. Nothing was changed, but everything was transformed.

This book is intended for both the religiously committed and the religiously curious. It is an invitation to thoughtful readers from diverse backgrounds to view the realities of their lives through a unique and transforming set of eyes. It is an opportunity to see the particular relationships that constitute the experience of one's own personal reality today from the standpoint of a remarkable spiritual revolutionary who lived two millennia ago. Consequently, this book is about Jesus, the historical human being, and, at the same time, about the contemporary quest for spiritual consciousness.

This is also a book about the transcendent significance of that historical human being. It is an opportunity for thoughtful readers to cross a bridge over temporal and cultural chasms to see Jesus as his disciples and early followers saw him. It is an invitation to consider the implications of embracing Jesus' view of reality as ultimate reality and as the reality of one's own life. Consequently, this book is about the Christ of faith, and, at the same time, about the contemporary search for an authentic life of faith in a postmodern world.

One of my early teachers in New Testament liked to point out that there

1

are two ways to read the Bible.[1] The first is to read it critically, as one would study any historical or literary set of materials. The second is to read it devotionally, as sacred writings through which transcendent truth is revealed.[2] Many people believe that these two approaches are incompatible with one another. But I believe the challenge in our time is to live with the tension between these two methodologies and not to let one destroy the other.[3]

As a person trained in the social sciences and in the academic study of the Bible, I recognize that facts must be established using agreed upon methods of research designed to assure a maximum of objectivity. But, at the same time, as a cultural anthropologist with concentrations in the anthropology of religion, symbolic anthropology, and psychiatric anthropology, I understand that facts without human interpretation, meaning, and commitments are sterile and essentially useless.

As a person of faith, I value intellectual honesty and embrace the truths disclosed by evidence and methodology-based literary and historical criticism of the Bible. At the same time, I hold fast to the conviction, grounded in devotion, that God continues to reveal God's treasures through the earthen vessel of those writings.

In writing this book, I have sought to remain faithful to both ways of reading the Bible and to recognize and affirm the creative struggle between them. It is my hope that in doing so both scholarly understanding and faith understanding may be enriched.

1. I am indebted to my friend and former classmate Michael Miller for reminding me of the words of the late Dr. Thomas Rogers, a professor of religion at Kentucky Wesleyan College for many years, and for several related statements that follow. The distinction between the two ways of reading, of course, did not originate with Dr. Rogers and has been discussed and debated among theologians since post-Enlightenment biblical scholarship emerged. A particularly noteworthy example of thoughtful reflection on the relationship between the two approaches was written by Dietrich Bonhoeffer in 1925 when he was nineteen. It was titled "Paper on the Historical and Pneumatological Interpretation of Scripture" (in Bonhoeffer, 2003, pp. 285-89).

2. The first type is sometimes referred to as "academic biblical study" and the second as a "faith-based" reading and interpretation of Scripture. The second approach is what Bonhoeffer called "pneumatological" interpretation (2003) and I have similarly termed "spiritual" interpretation.

3. Bonhoeffer (2003) wrote: "None of us can return to a pre-critical time. Both methods are used side by side by any pneumatological interpreter" (p. 294). For a more extensive discussion of my understanding of the relationship between spiritual and academic biblical studies, see the Addendum to Part I at the end of this book.

Part I of this book is about the historical human being Jesus as evidenced by scholarly study of the historical and literary sources. But this is not yet another treatise on the historical Jesus as a lifeless, dissected specimen under an analytical microscope. It is rather an invitation to look *with* Jesus at God and the world as Jesus saw them, and to see and understand the relevance of that remarkable vision in one's own life and historical moment.

Part II of this book is about the Christ of faith as proclaimed by the earliest Christians and New Testament authors who employed extravagant metaphorical images to express Jesus' transcendent significance. But this is not yet another abstract academic discussion of propositions about Jesus' divinity. It is rather an opportunity to see Jesus as the pioneers of faith saw him, and to understand the implications of their vision for one's own life and faith in today's world.

While it is common in contemporary scholarship to distinguish between the Jesus of history and the Christ of faith, some may object that this methodological distinction, manifested in separate sections of this book, runs the risk of undermining the unity of the gospel. While I am keenly aware of this potential danger, I believe that the unity of God's good news for humankind is to be found in the shared reality of Jesus the human being and those who confess him to be the Christ, the Son of God. Grasping the unity of that vision for our time depends upon a willingness first to examine separately each view in depth.

Jesus was a human being.[4] Before those who knew him and those who learned from others about him came to believe in him as the Messiah, the Christ sent from God to save the world, he was a flesh and blood Jewish man from Nazareth of Galilee. Before the early Christian church confessed him to be their Lord, the Son of God and Savior, the eternal Word made flesh, and long before the faithful declared in creed that he was one of the three persons of the Holy Trinity, there was this man living in history. Jesus himself frequently referred to his own person as "this human being." He called himself *bar 'enash(a)* in Aramaic, which was rendered in Hebrew as *ben 'adam* and in Greek as *huios tou anthrōpos,* and which is translated into English as "son of man." The everyday meaning of this term in Jesus' world was "human being."

---

4. This assertion is intended as a statement of historical fact with which any reasonable contemporary historian or social scientist would agree. For Christians it is also an important theological statement. Christian orthodoxy has asserted since the Council of Chalcedon in 451 CE that Jesus was both fully human and fully divine.

Jesus was a "son of Adam," a member of the human race. In the community he initiated, even this phrase would very soon become a metaphor of faith in his transcendent significance.[5] But in the beginning, this Jewish man identified himself not as a member of his particular remarkable ethnic group, nor as a superhuman figure transcending the limitations of human existence, but as a mortal member of humanity.[6] Within a very few years that mortality would be recorded dramatically in the accounts of his passion.

5. In their present form the Gospel accounts probably use "Son of Man" as a title for the Messiah. But a careful reading reveals that the Gospels have three types of passages in which the "son of man" language is used. The first type, which almost certainly goes back to Jesus, used the language in sayings about human beings in general and as a circumlocution for the first-person pronoun. (An example would be Matt. 8:20.) The second type used the term in predictions of suffering, and these passages probably have their roots in words of Jesus in which "son of man," while still meaning "human being" and used as a circumlocution for the first-person pronoun, appears to take on a significance associated with Jesus as a prophet and "Messiah contrary to expectations." (An example would be Mark 8:31.) The predictive nature of these passages probably was strengthened by the post-resurrection community as to detail; but their basic message of a prophet destined to suffer, and a mission that had Messianic significance, most likely originated with Jesus. Jesus may have adopted the "son of man" way of speaking about himself from the fact that Yahweh, according to the book of Ezekiel, addressed the prophet Ezekiel as "son of man." The frequent usage in Ezekiel is that of God speaking his word directly to a human being. It is entirely possible that Jesus also used the "son of man" reference because he felt himself addressed by God in the same way as Ezekiel. Such a usage was consistent with Jesus' conscious role as a prophet, one who, as other prophets, was destined to suffer and die. The third type of "son of man" passage is clearly titular and is intended to refer to Jesus' transcendent significance. This type is associated with the apocalyptic vision of Daniel that "one like a son of man" appeared on the clouds of heaven (Dan. 7:13). This usage in the Gospels probably was a later reinterpretation of Jesus' "son of man" language by the early church based on the post-resurrection identification of Jesus as this "one like a son of man" and the belief that the apocalypse was at hand. (An example would be Mark 13:26.)

6. Because Jesus showed up in history a male I have chosen to use male pronouns for his historical person. Because Jesus used a male metaphor, *Abba,* to refer to God I have also kept male pronouns for the God of his understanding. In some other places in the text I have again chosen for efficiency male pronouns because to do otherwise would be linguistically awkward and would detract from the flow of the text, though the meaning is intended to apply across genders. I realize and regret that this usage may be troublesome to those who are attempting to overcome centuries of male bias and discrimination toward females in Christianity. I trust that I have made clear in the text, however, that for Jesus there appears to have been no distinction of status between male and female, as demonstrated by his female disciples and his vision of the Messianic banquet. I also confess that I probably have not done justice to the feminine qualities of God in this work though I certainly embrace them.

4

Jesus the human being was an event in history, made up of words, deeds, and those peculiar social interactions that are combinations of words and deeds, verbal exchanges characterized by "challenge and response." The latter refers to a serious social game well known in the Middle East and Mediterranean cultures, societies with an ancient and pervasive preoccupation with honor and shame.[7] The Gospels document that Jesus experienced the testing of his honor during sharp verbal exchanges with his contemporaries on a number of occasions.[8] Jesus, as all human beings, dealt with such personal and social challenges of his life. He breathed the same air, drank the same water, and absorbed the same culture as his Galilean and Judean neighbors. He faced the everyday problems of living in the world and in a particular society. The Jesus story, as portrayed in the Gospels and the writings of the early church, is about the significance of this human being. But before all of that was Jesus the human being.

Any treatment of Jesus that focuses on his full humanity is likely to generate concerns on the part of sincere Christians that Jesus is being reduced to a "mere man."[9] While acknowledging that the importance of Jesus for faith

7. See the discussions of "honor and shame" in chapters IV and V, and those of "challenge and response" in chapters VI and VII. Drawing upon contemporary anthropological studies of Mediterranean societies, along with classical studies and biblical scholarship, a significant consensus has emerged across disciplines that identifies *honor* as an ancient core cultural value believed to be in limited supply in a conflict-preoccupied region. See Hanson (1996), Malina (2001), Gilmore (1987), Malina and Neyrey (1988), and Neyrey (1988) and (1999) for background on the cultural preoccupation of the region with "honor and shame" and "challenge and response" social exchanges.

8. A classic example is found in Mark 12:13-17, the challenge concerning the paying of taxes.

9. This reduction of Jesus to a "mere man" has been the pagan and secular view of Jesus throughout history. Assertion of Jesus' divinity consequently has seemed to be more of a priority to the established church than emphasizing Jesus' humanity. Enlightenment and nineteenth-century liberal portraits of Jesus, which focused on the humanity of Jesus, notwithstanding, Christianity almost always has focused on the divinity and neglected the human side of the equation. That seems especially true in our own time. Much contemporary Christian preaching and theology tends to eclipse the human Jesus to the extent that it effectively undermines belief in his full humanity. The Jesus proclaimed in many pulpits in our time is more like a pagan god, a half-man and half-god hero, than the fully human and fully divine Jesus confessed by the early church. The question today is: "If we still believe Jesus was both fully human and fully divine, then what do we mean by that assertion and what relevance does that meaning have for our real lives?" Part I of this book seeks to recover for our time the reality behind the fully human part of this paradoxical confession. Part II of

could be trivialized by a *cynical* or purely *reductionist* focus on his humanity, I believe that the significance of Jesus for people of faith, or for people in general, can be clarified and enhanced by a study of Jesus the human being undertaken responsibly and respectfully. If persons confess that Jesus has decisive significance for the way they understand and live their lives, then surely it makes all the difference whether they genuinely perceive the way in which he understood and lived his.

Furthermore, thoughtful Christians also will understand that arguably there is as great, if not greater, risk that neglect of Jesus' humanity can result in reducing him to a "mere myth." When theology about Jesus is cut off from the life and faith of Jesus the human being, that theology is in danger of becoming irrelevant to our own human lives and our own struggles with the problems of existence. Or, perhaps even more troubling, Christian communities may be tempted to provide religious sanction for attitudes and behaviors foreign and contrary to the spirit of Jesus the human being.

Understanding the reality of Jesus the human being is of vital relevance for understanding the significance of Jesus in our own lives. But achieving such understanding is deeply complicated by three facts. The first has to do with the nature of the texts themselves, the second with historical and cultural context, and the third with the reality that a human being is not an object, but a self.

The first fact is that the Gospel sources were written to convince their readers of Jesus' transcendent significance, not to provide historians with objective information about his life. This fact presents us with a serious dilemma. We cannot begin to see through the eyes of Jesus until we first determine, with a significant degree of probability, which things written about his human life were the theological constructions of the evangelists and their sources and which were the words and social interactions of Jesus himself. Overcoming this problem involves relying upon the best scholarship available to examine the texts and to make reasonable judgments about historicity. A common starting point is the attempt to distinguish between the textual material that speaks to the significance of Jesus for the early church, and that which probably provides earlier data about his words, deeds, and relationships.[10] The

---

this book attempts to recover for our time the reality behind the Christian belief in the divine significance of this human life as proclaimed in the transcendent metaphors of the New Testament writers.

10. I would emphasize that it is a *starting* point and not an ending point. While the dis-

task then becomes much like an archeological dig, for the texts contain layers of meaning from different periods of their transmission, beginning with Jesus and the earliest oral traditions, through later interpretive redactions, to the Gospel authors themselves.

What I have attempted to do in this book is to rely on those passages, for the most part, for which there is fairly wide agreement among mainstream scholars that the texts probably reflect either what Jesus actually or approximately said or did. I am, however, somewhat less skeptical about what we can know about the historical Jesus than many mainstream scholars. Such confidence is rooted in studies of the psychology of memory and the dynamics of religious cults, as well as personal experiences. Disciples and followers of charismatic leaders retain and recall specific words and actions of those leaders for decades. The same phenomena of vivid memories occur when ordinary folk can recall in great detail interactions with celebrities. This intensification of memory increases even more when such encounters happen under circumstances of crisis. The consensus of contemporary scholars is that the Gospel writers were not eyewitnesses, and probably did not receive their materials directly from eyewitnesses. Nevertheless, many of the traditions behind the earliest sources represent emotionally charged experiences of followers of Jesus who knew him personally, if only for a brief encounter. The presumption of such emotionally charged experiences behind the textual tradition allows me to find historical authenticity at times where others remain doubtful.[11] In those cases where I have departed significantly in my historical determinations from mainstream scholarship, I have attempted to explain my reasons for doing so in the notes.

The second fact complicating our understanding is that we live today in a very different historical and cultural context than did Jesus. Many difficulties

---

tinction between the "Jesus of history" and the "Christ of faith" is an essential one for any study of Jesus the human being, it is complicated by the fact that Jesus no doubt had a self-understanding of the transcendent significance of his own life and mission. Given the likelihood of some degree of congruence between that self-understanding and the post-resurrection faith, separating the former from later interpretive material is probably the most difficult challenge facing any scholar engaged in a "quest for the historical Jesus."

11. For more discussion of the principle of emotionally charged memory, see the Addendum to Part I. Admittedly, this principle does little more than provide a counter to the extreme skepticism of those who consider everything suspect because the tradition keepers and Gospel writers were "biased." But when taken seriously it shifts significantly the burden of proof to the skeptics, particularly with regard to units of text where there is no clear consensus.

in understanding the Jesus of history are related to the problem that we have an inadequate knowledge of the unconscious and taken-for-granted assumptions of his social world. Every society has cultural preoccupations and stylized patterns of behavior that help to explain why indigenous people think and act as they do. The interchanges between Jesus and his contemporaries are manifestations of such motifs and cultural patterns. In the chapters that follow, a number of cultural keys, such as "peril and refuge," "honor and shame," "challenge and response," and "blessing and curse," will be explored as means to illuminating various passages.[12]

Jesus, of course, was not simply a product of his culture. He was a remarkable innovator whose vision altered the course of human history. It is therefore necessary to see not only how Jesus was influenced by his culture, but also how he adapted it, questioned it, and attempted to redefine its vision of reality.

Most selves live unquestioningly in the reality they learned from their families, their teachers, and their neighbors. They participate unquestioningly in the conventional understandings of their times and places in history. It is possible to gain a significant knowledge of such persons by studying their cultural and historical contexts. One does not need to know much about their particularity to understand who they are. But sometimes an innovator comes along. Occasionally, a unique self takes the building blocks of his or her personal and social reality and rearranges them. Innovators, often for inexplicable reasons, come to view reality differently from their neighbors. They observe the same phenomena as their contemporaries, but they construct what is initially an idiosyncratic view of those phenomena that becomes their reality. In science, Copernicus, Galileo, Newton, and Einstein come to mind. In the realm of religion, Moses, Buddha, Jesus, and Mohammed are obvious examples.[13]

The "aha!" experience, which is an inexplicable inspiration resulting in a different way of viewing reality, can, and often does, happen to ordinary people. Such events can be life changing for an individual, but usually have

12. For discussions of "peril and refuge," see chapter II; for "honor and shame," see chapters IV and V; for "challenge and response," see chapters VI and VII; for "blessing and curse," see chapter IV.

13. That Jesus was a remarkable innovator and represented a decisive historical and cultural turning point should be obvious to all reasonable persons. Of course, Jesus' role in history and in the Christian community means far more than that for persons of faith as we explore in Part II. See note 9 above.

little ripple effects on others. On the other hand, the great turning points in history can be attributed to such "aha!" experiences.

The human being Jesus represents such a turning point in history. In order to explore the life of this particular innovative person, it is necessary, as with any historical figure, to place him in his historical and cultural context. Then it is necessary to determine his relationship to that context. Such contextual clarity, whether of culture mirrored or of culture challenged, is essential for any accurate picture of Jesus the human being and of his view of reality.

Cultural knowledge, however, is only the first step to understanding. We must also look deeper to grasp the human commonalities across time and culture latent within those assumptions that often appear foreign to our own experience. To see through the eyes of Jesus is not to bring the cultural assumptions of another time and place and try to force them kicking and screaming into our time and place. It is rather to grasp the universal depth human and spiritual truth of the way in which Jesus viewed reality within our own historical and cultural experience.

While the task of reconstructing a human being's view of reality is extremely challenging, it is far less daunting than attempting to write a biography.[14] There is much we will never be able to know about the sequential

---

14. I am in agreement with many of Johnson's (1997) objections to a number of the current historical studies of Jesus. I am not, however, as alarmed by the dangers of the quest for the historical Jesus as are some critics. The "quest" is justified and necessary, in my opinion, when the focus is on renewing our vision of the fully human Jesus of history. It remains questionable, both historically and for faith, when studies produce reductionistic results that can distort that vision. Many of the contemporary scholars engaged in the "third quest for the historical Jesus," including some of the more traditional contributors, call to mind the "Parable of the Blind Men and the Elephant" popularized by nineteenth-century poet John Godfrey Saxe. When one scholar sees Jesus as a kind of countercultural philosopher, another sees him as a Jewish rabbi, another as a protesting peasant revolutionary, another as a kind of shamanic healer, another as apocalyptic prophet, and still another as intentional suffering savior, these interpreters of historical data are similar to the blind men who thought the elephant to be like a wall, spear, snake, tree, fan, or rope. These perceptions of Jesus are not entirely incorrect. They are pointing to important and even essential truths about Jesus the human being. But most of the portraits, unfortunately, are so *reductionistic* as to be almost totally misleading. This does not mean, however, that these scholars' insights and work should be dismissed out of hand. On the contrary, it is important to learn from those persons who have devoted their lives to the research that underlies their works, to affirm their labors, and to incorporate many of their contributions into a more comprehensive framework. I am indebted throughout this work for a number of insights from a wide range of scholars who have substantial disagreements with one another.

events of Jesus' life, and probably there will be room always for disagreement about particular words and deeds. We are fortunate, however, that we can discern, with a significant degree of confidence, key elements of his cultural context and the fundamental nature of his relationships with certain of his contemporaries, and those relationships reveal with substantial clarity his view of reality.

This leads us to the third fact complicating our task. A human being is not an object to be examined. A human being is a self to be understood. And, as the nineteenth-century philosopher Søren Kierkegaard articulated so profoundly, the self is a bundle of relationships.[15] To understand other human beings, both now and historically, it is necessary to enter into their constructs of reality, the way in which they view and understand their own bundles of relationships, and the way in which they order, unify, and make sense of the chaos of their own lives. We live in relation to our families, our work, our neighbors, our "in-groups," and our "out-groups." We live in relation to the weather, to the pain we feel when we touch a hot stove, and to the pleasure we feel when we eat tasty food. But, as Kierkegaard also pointed out, we live as well in relation to that mysterious Power that is responsible for our being in existence and for the particular set of relationships that make up the self that we are. Some may call that mysterious reality "fate," some "luck," others "the way life is," and still others "God." Such names imply relationship, and the relationship we have with that ultimate reality shapes all our other relationships. Jesus called that reality *Abba.*

I have therefore chosen to structure Part I of this book around Jesus' significant relationships and to explore them within their cultural context, beginning with his relationship with *Abba,* the God of his understanding, and then with key groups of his neighbors. My objective is to look at the selfhood of Jesus as a "bundle of relationships," each of which reveals a critical aspect of his revolutionary view of reality. It is his intimate relationship with *Abba* that both creates and discloses the profound spirituality that permeates his entire view of life.[16] As we investigate in a series of chapters his relationships

15. See Kierkegaard (1980, chapter 1).

16. By spirituality I am referring to relationships with the realities of life and other human beings centered in and determined by a primary relationship with the transcendent or with the god or gods of one's understanding. For Jesus, this primary relationship was with *Abba,* the God of his understanding. In this work I use *spirit* and *spiritual* in several related ways. Jesus and his contemporaries believed the spirit world impacted their daily lives (see particularly chapter III). That world was made up of spirit beings, demons and angels, Sa-

with the desert, the disabled, the destitute, the despised, the devout, the despots, and the disciples, the revolutionary implications of his perspective come into focus.

These first eight chapters clarify Jesus' view of reality as a radical understanding of the compassionate relation of God toward humankind and the revolutionary implications of this perception for relations among human beings. Jesus' own response to this vision was one of hope, compassion, inclusiveness, tolerance, social responsibility, and self-sacrifice.

Jesus, as is true of each human being, was a unique and unrepeatable event in history. But what was it about this particular unique human being that generated extraordinary metaphors of ultimate significance and commitments, even unto death, of those who came to believe in him and follow his way? What was there about this particular human being that so altered those who knew him that all subsequent human history was forever changed?

Following Jesus' death by crucifixion, a substantial number of disciples and followers experienced Jesus as alive, as having been raised from the dead. What had been speculations and intimations of the transcendent significance of Jesus' life during his Galilean ministry and final days in Jerusalem had become utterly destroyed hopes with his crucifixion. But their shared post-crucifixion experiences "resurrected" those hopes and provided for Jesus' band of followers overwhelming confirmation of what they had suspected for a long time — that Jesus was far more than a mere human being.

But how was such a thing to be understood? How was it to be appropriated in the lives of those who had come to believe? Which human words could possibly express the awesome mysteries of transcendent reality? The New Testament community did what every culture tends to do when attempting to express that which goes beyond ordinary human experience. They identified a number of powerful religious metaphors found in their historic tradition, along with selected others from the neighboring cultures with which they interacted, and reformulated those symbols in an attempt to express the inexpressible. These were metaphors that already possessed transcendent associations, and were intended by the early church to express the overwhelming conviction that their experience of Jesus was an experi-

---

tan, and Yahweh, or God, who manifested himself as the "Holy Spirit." In speaking of the spirit world or spirit revolution, I use lowercase (spirit). I have chosen to use the capitalized *Spirit* only when it refers to the Holy Spirit.

ence of God and God's transforming activity in their own lives and in history. To understand these expressions of faith in Jesus and the reality behind the Christian belief in the divine significance of this human life as proclaimed in the transcendent metaphors of the New Testament writers is the intent of Part II of this book.

We have seen that the work of discerning Jesus the historical human being amidst the post-resurrection claims about his transcendent significance in the biblical sources is a complex challenge. Because it is those very claims we examine in Part II, we are no longer concerned with digging behind the textual sources but with comprehending the faith they proclaim. Yet, in facing this new challenge, we encounter a similar set of difficulties that burden the work of understanding the ancient symbolic power and contemporary meaning and relevance of the extravagant metaphors of that post-resurrection faith. The first problem is the limited ability of language to express the transcendent, the second is the all too prevalent tendency to assume that the only type of truth is literal truth, and the third is that these religious symbols come to us as culturally alien concepts.

In the first place, metaphors always come from the world of finite experience and are ultimately incapable of expressing adequately that which transcends human experience. Metaphors are integral to human consciousness. They facilitate the discovery and the creation of meaning.[17] They are unconsciously used in culturally conditioned ways in many contexts every day, shaping our views of life, relationships, and social interactions.[18] We speak, for example, of being "up" or "down" without being consciously aware that we are using spatial metaphors to describe emotional moods. Metaphors are also the poet's essential instruments for capturing and eliciting human emotions and the physicist's necessary tools for describing and teaching the mysteries of the universe. Such metaphors expand our understanding far beyond the objects we observe and the names we give them. The expressions "love's gentle breath" and "black holes in space" allow us to experience understanding otherwise beyond our grasp.

It is not surprising, then, that when human beings have experiences of unexpected moments of spiritual awareness, of awe, of fear and fascination, of altered states of consciousness, and when they experience inexplicable en-

17. This was the focus of philosopher Paul Ricoeur's *The Rule of Metaphor: Multi-Disciplinary Studies of the Creation of Meaning of Language* (1975).

18. Lakoff and Johnson (1980).

counters with otherness, that they struggle to speak of these things by using metaphors. But no matter how enlightening the metaphors, these figures of speech are never able to describe accurately and adequately the transcendent reality toward which they point. That is simply because no language has the capacity to express the inexpressible.

The ancient Israelites were very much aware that one could not reduce the divine to something worldly. The ways of the Creator were beyond human comprehension.[19] Even the sacred name of the Deity could not be spoken.[20] Images of God were forbidden.[21] But metaphors were not only permitted, they flourished. God was spoken of as Lord, King, Potter, Maker, Judge, Shield, Shepherd, Keeper, Rock, Refuge, Shelter, and Deliverer, to name some of the better known titles. Each of these metaphors expressed aspects of Israel's understanding of God and God's relationship to God's people.

When earthly metaphors, taken from the experience of nature and human society, are used to express transcendent reality they become *transcendent metaphors*. Transcendent metaphors are intended to point beyond themselves to transcendent truth, but can never objectify and possess that truth. Only in faith and spiritual experience can that truth be seen, and even then, it is seen imperfectly, as if one were looking at "a poor reflection in a mirror."[22] Metaphors, though essential to human understanding and creative thought, are always limited in their adequacy.

Furthermore, because metaphors involve a comparison of two phenomena from differing realms of experience, they invariably have associations that can mislead. One only needs to think of the cruelty of a tyrant king such as Herod the Great to grasp the risk of applying monarchical language to the Deity.

The implications of this insight are important for our task. As various metaphors that were used by the earliest Christians to speak of the transcendent significance of Jesus are considered, it will be necessary to discern, with the assistance of contextual clues, those aspects of the comparisons that are fruitful, and those that have a tendency to mislead. And, just as in Part I we

---

19. Pss. 139:6; 145:3; Rom. 11:33-36.

20. The name *Yahweh* is found more than six thousand times in the Hebrew Bible. Out of the desire scrupulously to avoid using the name in vain, as the third commandment required, it became established practice to substitute 'Adonai, which is usually translated "Lord" when reading the text.

21. Exod. 20:4.

22. 1 Cor. 13:12.

look at a variety of Jesus' relationships, it also will be prudent for us to consider in Part II a number of diverse metaphors. That will assist us in discerning the ways in which an array of differing metaphors not only reveal transcendent truth, but are able to correct one another so as to prevent misunderstanding.

In the second place, metaphors, and transcendent metaphors particularly, are often misinterpreted as concrete literal statements rather than as symbols that point to a very different kind of reality. Jesus used a number of metaphors and symbolic narratives taken from the everyday experience of those around him to point to transcendent meaning. The ability of those metaphors and narratives to transform those who heard them, however, depended on the capacities of hearers to be open to the relational and spiritual realities to which the metaphorical expressions pointed. They could only transform the lives of "those who had ears to hear."

Nicodemus, according to John's account, was a rabbi, a person so well schooled in religious knowledge that he was a respected teacher of others and presumably a powerful leader and member of the prestigious Sanhedrin, the supreme Council of Jewish priests.[23] One would think that such a man would have had no difficulty understanding a transcendent metaphor. Yet, in the Gospel account, Nicodemus had difficulty hearing Jesus' message because he was trapped in a literal way of thinking.

When Jesus used the metaphor of human birth in order to point to the radical spiritual transformation that is a prerequisite for authentically experiencing new life in the reality of God's love, Nicodemus was confounded. That an adult human being could once again enter his mother's womb to be reborn was an absurd idea. Because Nicodemus assumed that the only kind of truth was concrete factual truth, he was unable to understand the existential spiritual truth of the metaphor. And because he struggled to understand it literally, he was at risk of missing out altogether on the spiritual reality to which it pointed. He was distracted by the question of how the metaphor could be true, rather than grasping the question of what the transcendent spiritual meaning of the metaphor was.

The post-resurrection followers of Jesus also used highly intentional metaphorical language in order to point to the transcendent significance of Jesus' life, death, and resurrection. They spoke of Jesus as the Christ (or Messiah), the Son of David, the Son of Man, the Son of God, Emmanuel, the

---

23. John 3:1-21. That Nicodemus belonged to the Sanhedrin is implied by John 7:50-52.

Holy One, the Suffering Servant, the Lamb of God, the Great High Priest, the King of the Jews, the King of Kings, the Lord of Lords, the Advocate (or Comforter), the Alpha and Omega, the Savior, the I AM, the Word (or *Logos*), and many more. And they also expressed themselves in metaphorical narratives that gave dramatic form to these designations of transcendent honor. These stories declared, for example, that it is Jesus, and by implication not Caesar, who is the true Son of God.[24] And it is Jesus, not the Roman god Bacchus, who is the true God of wine, for it is Jesus alone who has the power to transform life into eternal life.[25]

The initial question these symbols were designed to address was not "how" Jesus is God, a question the church would struggle over for centuries, but "Who is this human being Jesus?" and "What is his transcendent significance?"[26] Whenever Jesus' followers, while reflecting on these symbolic titles, later became obsessed with the "how" rather than the "who," the literal meaning rather than transcendent significance, they have been at risk of falling into the Nicodemus syndrome. By remaining trapped in concrete thinking and being preoccupied with the wrong questions, they have often missed the authentic reality of what it means to confess the divinity of Jesus.

When transcendent metaphors are made literal, either they become nonsense or they become graven images. John's Gospel, which contains a plethora of metaphors and metaphorical narratives pointing to the transcendent significance of Jesus, warns with the Nicodemus story that these symbolic expressions are not to be taken literally but as symbols of spiritual realities. To reify them, as if they themselves were the reality to which they are intended to point, could be a fatal error.

Consequently, great care must be taken in the interpretive enterprise to assure that that we do not fall into the trap of investing these symbolic ex-

---

24. "Son of God" was a title that had been used for the king of Israel (Ps. 2:7) and had Messianic significance in the time of Jesus. But it also appeared on Roman inscriptions referring to Emperors Augustus, Tiberius, Nero, Titus, and Domitian. See Mowery (2002). In Luke 1:32, 35, an angel delivers the word to Mary that Jesus will be the Son of the Most High, the Son of God.

25. Bacchus was the Roman god of wine, while Dionysus was the Greek version. There were elaborate cultic rituals and beliefs associated with these pagan deities in classical times. John 2:1-11 and John 15 use god of wine symbolism to point to the transcendent significance of Jesus. See the discussion in chapter XIV of this book.

26. See Bonhoeffer (1960, pp. 30-33) for a discussion of the critical point that the Christological question is not "How?" but "Who?"

pressions with the notion that they express concrete rather than transcendent truth. We must avoid the temptation to treat these symbols as historical facts in order that we might genuinely open ourselves to the existential and spiritual relevance that they have for our lives. The task of elucidating the transcendent significance of Jesus for our own time and culture must remain paramount. These symbols are the clay jars that contain the treasure. They are not the treasure itself. And it is the treasure we must seek.

In the third place, those of us, who live many centuries later, find that the transcendent metaphors of the New Testament largely come to us today as alien concepts. Just as it is impossible to understand the social interactions of Jesus the human being apart from relevant cultural concepts, neither can we understand the metaphors of Jesus' transcendent significance apart from their social framework. Even when we approach metaphors with awareness of the limitations of symbolic language and are mentally and devotionally open to their existential and spiritual meanings, we may still miss the transforming power of those symbols if we do not understand the cultural presuppositions that surround them.

The symbols that were seized upon and reinterpreted to illuminate the transcendent significance of Jesus were familiar ones for the early Christians. They had profound meaning in the ancient Jewish and Mediterranean cultures. Because we live in a different time and culture, they have lost much of their richness and power as windows to transcendent reality.

Because the metaphors are alien to our culture, many secular persons have understood them superficially as primitive relics of an ancient worldview, and have dismissed them as "mere metaphors" or "mere myths." Christians, on the other hand, while often having little knowledge of the background of these metaphors, are familiar with them, but too often have seen them primarily as propositions requiring assent. They are thought to be statements that should be accepted authoritatively as concrete assertions that must be believed in order to be a Christian. This type of familiarity with what remain alien concepts, along with the problem of literalism discussed above, has contributed to the endurance of a very popular form of "salvation by works," the "works" being the considerable human effort required to believe with the mind certain statements culturally conditioned rational minds find incredible. For many today, even the belief in "salvation by grace through faith" has become a proposition to be believed, rather than a spiritual and relational reality.

It should not be surprising, then, that the extravagant metaphors used by early Christians to appropriate and understand the significance of Jesus in their lives can become unnecessary stumbling blocks for both nonbelievers and believers today.

It is not the metaphors, but the reality the metaphors are pointing toward, that is our subject matter. But here is the rub. We can only get to that subject matter by way of these same metaphors. That will require careful examination of their social and anthropological contexts and the taken-for-granted assumptions that were associated with these symbolic expressions in New Testament times. For example, it is important to understand the power and exchange relationships between benefactors and patrons in ancient Mediterranean culture, in order to clarify the relationship between the Deity and humankind implied in calling Jesus Lord.[27] And it will be helpful to understand the pervasive symbolic power and meaning of blood sacrifice in the ancient world in order to begin to grasp what it means to speak today of Jesus as our Redeemer.[28]

But anthropological context is not the end of the matter. We will also need to discover, sometimes with explanations, and sometimes with the assistance of new metaphors, ways to express for our postmodern world the meaning and significance of the early Christian faith in the transcendent significance of Jesus.

In order to accomplish this, Part II is structured around six key organizing titles pointing to the transcendent work of Jesus. As we explore Jesus as the Revolutionary Hero, the Revealing Word, the Redeeming Sacrifice, the Reconciling Savior, the Reigning Lord, and the Resurrected Life, along with the New Testament titles of honor associated with these roles, the transcendent significance of Jesus for faith today should begin to become transparent.

Moreover, the reality to which the symbols of Jesus' transcendent significance ultimately point should be clarified for the reader as none other than the same revolutionary view we encountered in Part I, reality as seen through the eyes of Jesus the human being. To see through the eyes of Jesus is to be confronted with an existential question: Is this reality, which discloses the distorted and delusional nature of all other constructed realities, the one and only reality that I am willing to embrace and in which I desire to live my life? Or, to use New Testament language, "Is Jesus my Christ?" The concluding chapter invites the reader to consider what it might mean to see

---

27. See Neyrey (1994) and (2005) and chapter XIII of this book.
28. See discussion in chapter XI of this book.

his or her own reality through the eyes of Jesus, and to live in that reality as a person of faith in today's world.

Many books have been written about Jesus and his significance for humankind. Over the past two decades, a whole new set of works has been produced with widely varying conclusions. In addition to the notes for each chapter, the Addendum to Part I provides additional information for those interested in the methodology used to establish historical probability.

I have written these pages in the hope that thoughtful readers will be able to try on, as it were, the lens through which Jesus viewed reality. I invite readers not only to look at Jesus' world through that lens, but to look at their own reality as well. But let readers be warned in advance — in doing so, nothing may be changed, but everything could be transformed.

PART I

Seeing through the Eyes of Jesus

CHAPTER I

Jesus and *Abba*

I t is never easy to see through the eyes of another. To view reality as a contemporary friend sees it is difficult enough. To see the world through the eyes of one who lived in a distant time and place is immensely more challenging. More difficult still is the task of grasping across history and culture the spiritual reality of such a person. Yet that is where our journey must begin, for before we can see Jesus' relationships with others as he saw them, it is necessary to understand the way in which his primary relationship with the God of his understanding shaped the way he viewed all of life.

The God of Jesus' Youth

We have no reliable information about the childhood and youth of Jesus except what we can infer from the common experience of typical young males growing up in first-century Galilee.[1] It seems safe to say, since Jesus knew the

---

1. Luke's account of Jesus in the Temple (Luke 2:41-52) is thought by many scholars to be a narrative construct. (See Addendum to Part I for discussion of *Differing Dimensions of Truth*.) A large number of stories about Jesus' childhood, not included in the canonical Gospels, circulated in the second century, most of which were absurd demonstrations of the child's supernatural powers. Luke's story is remarkable in its reserve, however. It is not out of the question that the kernel of this story was a family story kept alive by Jesus' family and shared with followers after his death and resurrection. While it may be rather far-fetched that he would have been instructing the scribes at that age, the element of authenticity in the story might be that Jesus' family was observant of the required festivals and that Jesus was

Scriptures and often quoted them during the time of his ministry, that he went to the local synagogue school.[2] It is likely that he was educated in his hometown of Nazareth, though he could have walked four miles or more to a synagogue located in the city of Sepphoris, or perhaps to another nearby location.[3] Synagogues of that period operated both elementary schools and secondary schools. All Jewish children were expected to attend elementary school from the age of five until the age of twelve or thirteen. Their teachers probably were local scholars in the Law, known as scribes, and lay members of the sect of the Pharisees.[4]

---

one of those gifted young scholars in the local synagogue who would have been a qualified candidate for secondary education. The tension in the story is understandable due to the missing child and worried parents, but it also could be indicative of the tension between a family that needed their coming-of-age child to go to work and his inclination to follow the path of scholarship.

2. I have benefited significantly in the discussion of Jesus' training in these paragraphs from David Biven's *Jerusalem Perspective Article: Jesus Education* (© 1987-2004) at www .jerusalemperspective.com. A similar approach taken by Meier (1991) also has been useful. A number of scholars have questioned whether or not the *Mishnah* descriptions of Jewish education that are relied upon by Biven and others (for example, *Avot* 5:21) were in practice at the time of Jesus. While the text of the *Mishnah* may be as late as a hundred years after Jesus, there is no good reason to doubt that the basic practices described there were in place well before the time of Jesus. The first-century Jewish historian Josephus (*Against Apion* 1.60) indicates, for example, that Jews prided themselves on the education of their children. Jesus' extensive knowledge of the Scriptures and his ability to debate their meaning perhaps is best explained by accepting the probability that such schools were in place well before he was born.

3. Sepphoris (also known as Zippori) has been excavated as well as attested to by non-biblical sources as the capital of Galilee until about 18 CE. It was burned and destroyed in 4 BCE and rebuilt during the time of Jesus' childhood. It is a mystery why the city is not referred to at all in the Gospels. Jesus chose to make his home base for his ministry Capernaum on the Sea of Galilee rather than Sepphoris. It has been suggested that he might have wanted to avoid both Sepphoris and Tiberius as unsafe due to their importance to Herod Antipas. Sepphoris was a Jewish city with a Gentile presence and Hellenistic influence. There is controversy concerning the degree of Greek cultural influence and the possible impact of that culture upon Jesus.

4. The extent of Pharisee presence in Galilee during Jesus' lifetime is controversial. Some scholars have concluded that the Pharisees did not have a strong presence there until after the destruction of the Second Temple in 70 CE, and that the references to Pharisees in the controversies of Jesus in the Gospels represent the tension between the Jesus movement and the Pharisees sometime after that date. While the destruction of the Second Temple no doubt preceded a significant increase in the numbers and the influence of Pharisees in Jewish communities outside Jerusalem, it is likely that there was at least a modest presence in

Following a coming of age ritual, involving a blessing from a child's fa-ther indicating that he was now of the age of responsibility, most young men were expected to quit school, begin work, and contribute to their meager family incomes. Students, however, who showed exceptional promise, and where family means made it possible, could continue to study at the second-ary school together with adults who devoted their spare time to the study of the Torah. Occasionally an outstanding secondary student would leave home to go and study with a famous teacher. Because Jesus was portrayed in the Gospels as able to quote Scripture spontaneously and to debate effec-tively, skills most often learned in those days in post-elementary education, it is possible that Jesus spent his entire youth and young adulthood engaged in such learning.

It is more likely, however, considering the modest circumstances of his birth family, that Jesus' formal education ended at his "coming of age."[5] As-suming he applied himself, his knowledge of Scripture would have been sub-stantial by that time. Elementary students were required to memorize the sa-cred texts through group recitation and individual repetition. Jesus would have been well rehearsed in reciting passages from the Torah, the prophets, and the psalms by the time he went to work in his father's trade.

If in fact he followed in the footsteps of his father Joseph, he became a craftsman, probably a "construction worker," around age thirteen, and his "education" was a very different one than that of the scholar.[6] His education

---

Galilee during Jesus' lifetime, particularly of local laity who sought to live according to the rules of the sect.

5. If there is historical authenticity in the accusation in John 7:15 that Jesus had not "studied," it would support this conclusion. The charge did not mean that Jesus was illiter-ate, or had not attended elementary school, but that he had not spent several years of ad-vanced study with an established teacher, most of whom were located in Jerusalem at the time.

6. In Mark 6:3 Jesus is referred to in Greek as a *tekton*. While *tekton* is usually translated "carpenter" or "wood worker," it probably more accurately is translated "artisan," "crafts-man," or "builder." It is the same word that is used for those who built houses and public buildings out of stone. I have chosen to speak of Jesus as a "construction worker" as an ap-proximate translation of how he probably made a living prior to his ministry. In the second century it was believed he made plows and yokes from wood. While this is certainly possible, that belief probably was derived from Jesus' sayings about plows and yokes. It should be noted that Jesus also spoke about houses built on sand or rock. Just as likely is the possibility, given Jesus' later use of Capernaum as a headquarters for his ministry and his close relation-ship with the fishermen of that town, that in his early years Jesus had been a boat builder and repairer.

consisted of carpentry and artisan skills, and the life experiences of a trained laborer in an oppressed region consisting largely of working poor and destitute people.

Regardless of the amount of formal and informal education Jesus might have received, it is also likely that his home engaged in regular study of the Torah.[7]

> These commandments that I give you today are to be upon your hearts. Impress them on your children. Talk about them when you sit at home and when you walk along the road, when you lie down and when you get up. Tie them as symbols on your hands and bind them on your foreheads. Write them on the doorframes of your houses and on your gates. (Deut. 6:6-9)[8]

Jesus also would have participated in the religious observances of his household. These likely would have included family attendance at some, if not all, of the seasonal festivals in Jerusalem, Sabbath worship at the local synagogue, and daily recitation of the *Sh'ma* upon rising in the morning and retiring at night:

> Hear O Israel: The Lord our God, the Lord is one. Love the Lord your God with all your heart, and with all your soul, and with all your strength. (Deut. 6:4-5)

And Jesus' parents no doubt also taught their children through example and instruction the purity rules that typically were practiced at home with regard to food and meals.

The God of Jesus' youth was the God of creation, of the patriarchs, of Moses and the exodus community, the God of the covenant with Israel, and the God of the prophets who pronounced judgment on Israel for its viola-

---

7. Some homes may have had one or more scrolls of particular books that had been handed down across generations in their possession to facilitate family study. Most homes likely would have had phylacteries, or small black boxes containing mini-scrolls with passages of the Torah, which also could be attached to clothing to be worn by the pious (Matt. 23:5). The common people probably believed that having such items at home or on their person provided protective benefit.

8. Except where otherwise noted Bible quotations are from the NIV. The chief exceptions are my own translations of words, phrases, or entire passages indicated by the notation "altered." In those instances, my translation appears in italics.

tion of that covenant. He was the Holy God whose Name was so sacred it could not be uttered. Jesus surely also was exposed to the God of mercy in Hosea, Jeremiah, and the "suffering servant" in what we now call Second Isaiah, and this knowledge would become decisive for him later.[9] But the prophets of mercy likely were eclipsed in his early training, because, in the religious atmosphere of the synagogue of Jesus' day, God was primarily the Lawgiver. God's Law consisted not simply of ethical commandments, but also of the complex laws of ritual purity and sacrifice recorded in the Torah and all the traditions handed down by the elders who interpreted that Law. Jesus would have been taught that keeping this Law in all its intricacies was essential to receiving God's blessing, and that failing to do so would result in God's terrible judgment.

The God of Jesus' youth, we therefore can reasonably suppose, was a Holy Being, a righteous and judging God, associated with long-ago deeds and holy places, yet requiring daily acknowledgment and obedience to his Law. This God likely would strike awe in the heart of any boy who struggled with the possibility that he might not fully observe every specific requirement of the Law.[10]

God as *Abba*

If Jesus had remained simply a product of his religious upbringing and training it is unlikely the world ever would have heard of him or been changed because of him. At some point, however, probably around the time of his baptism by John, Jesus' understanding of God underwent a radical transformation from one informed by his training to one informed by his own charismatic experience. The radical nature of this transformation is re-

9. The term *Second Isaiah* refers to the scholarly consensus that the book of Isaiah was composed in two distinct periods of history. The earlier material is found in chapters 1–39, and is often called First Isaiah. Chapters 40–55 are widely referred to as Second Isaiah. The remainder of the book is now referred to as Third Isaiah. Each of these sections is an edited collection that probably represents multiple authors. Second Isaiah contains the well-known theme of the "suffering servant" of God.

10. Of course, we have no way of knowing this to be true for Jesus, but if it was otherwise, then surely Jesus would need to have experienced an alternate, untraditional, atypical education and family upbringing, and that seems unlikely for the son of a craftsman worker who lived in the village of Nazareth.

flected in Jesus' words to his disciples about what is necessary in order to begin such a journey of understanding.

> I tell you the truth, anyone who will not receive the kingdom of God like a little child will never enter it. (Mark 10:15)[11]

The understanding and experience of the reality of God and of spirit existence is so dramatically different from conventional wisdoms and religious experiences that to enter that realm, according to Jesus, demands a total and complete starting over. All prior assumptions and taken-for-granted truths, all beliefs about God and humankind's relation to God, must be set aside, all attitudes and opinions must be released, for the kingdom of God is only knowable to those who are open and prepared for a startlingly new vision and experience.[12]

Child of the Father

Symbols are seldom one-dimensional, but have multiple levels of meanings. So it is with the symbol of becoming a child. Not only is it a metaphor for the prerequisite condition for beginning the spirit journey; it also is a sign of the radically new relationship with God that is entered when that journey begins. For one does not simply become like a child, one comes to understand oneself *as* a child. The wonder underlying Jesus' metaphor is that this

11. That these words originate with Jesus is highly probable, but the interpretation of similar passages in the Synoptics (Matt. 18:1-4; Mark 9:33-37; Luke 9:46-48) related to greatness and humility is almost certainly a later interpretive application (see Addendum to Part I, *Differing Dimensions of Truth,* and discussion of historical and literary levels in *Methods for Establishing Historical Authenticity*) in the context of leadership struggles in the earliest post-Easter Christian community, though it is not impossible that Jesus used the same symbol (child) for more than one lesson. Crossan (1991) has argued that the child symbolism is not an example of humility for disciples as conventionally understood, but one that radically proclaims that the kingdom is a kingdom of "nobodies." The child symbol could have multiple meanings, but I have concluded that the primary meaning for Jesus was that of a new beginning in which a radically new orientation in consciousness occurs. It is interesting to note in passing that psychotherapist Carl Jung (1958) included the "child" as an archetype of the human unconscious related to new beginnings.

12. In John's Gospel this meaning of radically starting over is underscored by the rebirthing image in Jesus' words to Nicodemus: "no one can see the kingdom of God unless he is born again" (John 3:3b).

child is not an orphan in this world, but knows the self to be the loved and cared-for child who has entered into relationship with God as parent.

Jesus knew this dual meaning of becoming a child, because that is what he experienced with his baptism and during the time of his temptation and spiritual preparation in the desert.[13] Jesus had to rethink his life and understanding in response to the preaching of John the Baptist and his baptismal experience.[14]

> As Jesus was coming up out of the water, he saw heaven being torn open and the Spirit descending on him like a dove. And a voice came from heaven: "You are my Son, whom I love; with you I am well pleased." (Mark 1:10-11)[15]

The end result was that Jesus grasped, at the depths of his being, his relationship as a child of God, son of the Father.[16] This relationship was so ex-

13. For reasons of emphasis and artistic style, I frequently have used unqualified language in these chapters to speak of what Jesus knew, thought, or did. Of course, every statement about Jesus is an interpretive speculation based on limited evidence that is open to a variety of interpretations. I trust the reader to assume that all such statements should be taken as my educated opinion.

14. While the account of Jesus' baptism in Mark (1:9-11) generally is seen as a narrative interpretation of the significance of the historical event, rather than a literal opening of the heavens, the descent of the Spirit in the form of a dove, and a voice speaking, this symbolic language could be based upon Jesus' own experience of and reflection upon that event. Literary critics long have held that Jesus' baptism by John is rooted in fact, as it later became an embarrassment to be explained and would have served no purpose as a creation of the early church. At some point Jesus began to understand and experience himself in a Father and Son relationship to Yahweh. It is reasonable to speculate that Jesus reflected on an ecstatic possession of the Spirit that occurred with baptism, an experience that partly could have consisted of hearing a voice, and that Jesus experienced a moment of epiphany in which he grasped that he was in fact a very specially loved son of Yahweh. The hearing of voices, while associated with persons who have serious mental illness, is a fairly common phenomenon that occurs cross-culturally in normal individuals, particularly when in religious trance (American Psychiatric Association, 2000, p. 300; Oztürk in Kiev, 1964, p. 349).

15. A number of scholars have concluded that Ps. 2:7b, "You are my Son, today I have become your Father," may well have been the earliest form of the words from heaven. These words may have been changed during the transmission of the narrative to avoid the idea that the event was an "adoption." If that is the case, the words of Ps. 2:7b strengthen the likelihood that the baptism altered Jesus' understanding of God and his relationship to God as *Abba*. But, as all of the Synoptic Gospels record the revelation that Jesus was God's very loved son, the words of the psalm are by no means necessary for my point.

16. The Gospel writers and the early church interpreted the "son" language to be a reve-

traordinarily intimate that Jesus would address and refer to God from that point forward as *Abba,* the colloquial and mundane Aramaic name for a male Jewish parent.[17] Jesus' use of *Abba* as the name with which he consistently addressed and referred to God is the key to understanding the primary relationship of his life.

In first-century Galilee, the family culture was "father centered." Families were *patrilineal,* which means that descent was traced through fathers.[18] Families were also *patrilocal.* The eldest son, as the heir, usually lived and raised his family in the father's house. The other adult male children and their families were expected to live nearby, often in a dwelling sharing a courtyard with the father's home. Within this family network, the father, along with the mother, was to be honored and respected, but the father was the undisputed head of the household.

In most families, a special bond existed between the father and his male children, especially the eldest.[19] Fathers generally had great affection for

---

lation of Messiahship. In the Messianic climate of the time it is likely that Jesus also understood his baptism as a Messianic anointing, though it initially may have been perceived as a prophetic anointing similar to the anointing of Elisha the prophet (1 Kings 19:16). Certainly, as discussed in this chapter, being a beloved son of *Abba* strongly influenced Jesus' grasp of his own mission. But the significance of the revelation of being a Son of the Father was far more than the birth of Messianic consciousness. For Jesus, it was a revelation of the nature of God himself, and ultimately the revelation of a very untraditional notion of Messiahship. Jesus appears to have carried out his mission with the understanding that he was the first of many to find himself in a relationship to Yahweh as Father.

17. Jeremias (1965) suggested that *Abba* may have originated with baby talk in which "ab ba" was a kind of babbling noise made by an infant much as "da da" later becomes "Daddy" and then "Dad" in our experience, and thus connotes intimacy. Jeremias later called this argument "a piece of inadmissible naivety" (1967, p. 63). Of course, it is impossible to know which came first, the name or the infant effort to express itself. Be that as it may, the important issue is usage, not origin. *Abba,* or some form of this Aramaic utterance, was both what children *of all ages* called their male parent and how they addressed him. It was, then, by common usage, often an intimate and informal address and referent (a conclusion that in no way depends on Jeremias's earlier speculation).

18. See Malina (2001, chapter 5) for a more detailed discussion of kinship practices in New Testament times.

19. The affection of fathers for sons is portrayed dramatically in the patriarchal accounts of Abraham and Isaac (Gen. 22:2), Jacob and Joseph (Gen. 37:3), and the grief of David over the slaying of Absalom (2 Sam. 18:33). By tradition, the eldest son was to inherit a double portion of the father's estate (Deut. 21:15-17; Isa. 61:7), receive the paternal blessing (Gen. 27), and succeed the father in authority (Gen. 27:29; 2 Kings 2:9).

their sons and saw them as their personal legacy. A male child potentially could be a source of great pride or of great shame. As Jesus' parable of the prodigal son shows, for a son to leave his home of origin was a troubling and sorrowful event, while the return of a son to his father's house was a time of great rejoicing.[20]

Both the Hebrew and Greek words for "father" carried a dual meaning in popular culture.[21] *Father* routinely meant one's male parent. But the same word also could be used to speak of a male ancestor, particularly the founding male ancestor.[22] Jewish people spoke of "Father Abraham" to identify their ethnic identity. It is highly likely that the Aramaic *Abba* also had this double meaning.

Although it was relatively rare, God had been, on occasion, referred to in Scripture as "Father."[23] This was usually in the context of the Creator, the benevolent transcendent founding ancestor, who, in potter fashion, was believed to have formed the first man from clay.[24] The metaphor of "Father" also came to be associated with the divine authority and protection of King David and his lineage, for the king of Israel was honored by being referred to as God's "son."[25] And God, as the implementer of justice,

20. Luke 15:11-32.

21. The Hebrew word was *'ab;* the Greek was *patēr.*

22. Josh. 24:3; Luke 1:73; 16:24; John 8:53, 56; Acts 7:2; Rom. 4:12.

23. Despite the fact that there are a few sparse incidences of usage prior to or contemporary with Jesus that are frequently referenced as evidence that Jesus' use of "Father" for the Deity was not unique, I am still convinced with Jeremias (1965) that such passages are quite different from Jesus' very personal use of *Abba.* Furthermore, one naturally would expect that there are poetic metaphors used by the writers in a patriarchal culture that describe the relation between Yahweh and the people, or Yahweh and their king, as Father and offspring. What is unique about Jesus' usage is the intimate, informal, and consistent titular usage of *Abba* found nowhere else in the literature before him. By consistent usage I refer not only to Mark 14:36, where *"Abba,* Father" occurs, but to the many places where Jesus' Aramaic word for "father," some form of *Abba,* has been translated by the tradition and the Gospel writers into Greek. (It is a broad consensus among scholars that Jesus spoke in Aramaic rather than Greek.) I believe Jesus' usage of *Abba* is also supported by the utterance of *Abba* by Paul in Gal. 4:6 and Rom. 8:15 well before the Gospels were written. I am further convinced of this special and consistent usage by the fact that the image of the parent-child relationship as descriptive of the relationship between human beings and God was evidently central to Jesus' message as discussed here and in subsequent chapters.

24. Deut. 2:6; Mal. 2:10.

25. 2 Sam. 7:14; Ps. 2:7. This led in post-Davidic times to the understanding that the Messiah as king was a "son" of God.

had been described by a psalmist as a "father to the fatherless and a defender of widows."[26]

Jesus, no doubt, was familiar with such passages, and his understanding of God was almost certainly shaped by them. But Jesus' usage of the Aramaic *Abba* went well beyond this previous metaphoric usage. For Jesus, *Abba* was a direct address, implying a relationship of respectful but intimate affection. *Abba* carried with it the connotation of the informality and trust of a child addressing his male parent, and the affection of an adult son providing care for his aging father. What is remarkable about Jesus' usage is the intimate, informal, and consistent titular usage of *Abba* found nowhere else in the literature before him.

To many contemporary religiously observant countrymen, the use of the intimate and mundane address of *Abba* for the Holy God, Yahweh, whose Name was so sacred that it could not be spoken, would have been unthinkable, if not blasphemous.[27] To be sure, unlike the idea of "father" in our modern democratic and child-centered families, *Abba*, in first-century Galilee, was used in the context of a patriarchal society in which a father's authority was virtually unquestioned in the home. A Galilean father was entitled to the highest respect and obedience, and was to be honored by his sons, as required by the commandment, for an entire lifetime.

Nevertheless, Jesus' use of *Abba* for the deity was a scandalous usage in its informality. And there can be no doubt that Jesus' use of the term was quite intentional. The fact that Jesus used this address for the mighty God of creation, for the God of Abraham, Isaac, and Jacob, for the God of Moses and the prophets, is, in a spiritual sense, revolutionary. It was an outward expression of the revolution of the spirit that had transformed his life. His relationship to his own life and to God had been altered radically at the very core of his personality. At the heart of this change was an intimate, direct, intense personal relationship with God, which is symbolized in the word *Abba*.

---

26. Ps. 68:5.

27. In Mark 14:53-65 and John 10:22-42 Jesus was charged with blasphemy as justification for his crucifixion. In Mark it appears that the alleged blasphemy is Jesus' claim to be the Messiah, *the Son of the Blessed One.* In John it is the claim that the *Son* is one with the *Father.* While calling God *Abba* would not have met the legal definition of blasphemy, I am suggesting that it would have deeply offended some religious sensibilities.

A Broker-less Relationship

This relationship, unlike access to Yahweh in traditional thought and practice, was broker-less.[28] We are familiar with the broker image in real estate and the trading of stocks and bonds. In most real estate and stock trading the buyer and seller do not deal directly with one another, but negotiate transactions through brokers. In religious terms, the transactions between gods and the people traditionally occur with the brokerage of the priesthood. This brokerage takes the form of performance of religious rituals and instruction of the laity in the moral and ritual behavior that is required to please the gods. First-century Jews understood that in order to please Yahweh and to receive Yahweh's blessing, the Law as interpreted by the religious leaders had to be obeyed. Between every ordinary Jew and Yahweh was the brokerage of the priests, the scribes, and the Law.

There was, however, another tradition within Judaism in which certain common citizens were called by Yahweh to be his voice. These were *nabi,* the prophets who received instruction directly from Yahweh, usually in the form of ecstatic visions, and who pronounced God's judgments and mercies with the confident proclamation, "Thus says the Lord." These prophets experienced their calling in relation to the covenant between Israel and Yahweh and their pronouncements were directed to the national circumstances of their times. These voices proclaimed that Israel's blessing as God's chosen people was in danger, or already eclipsed, because of their sin, but Yahweh's mercy was still available, offering new opportunities for repentance and righteousness.

When John the Baptist appeared in the wilderness by the Jordan preaching a baptism for the forgiveness of sins, he was widely understood to be such a prophet. The appearance of this wilderness ascetic with a message of the kingdom of God and of repentance gave the people the hope that deliverance of the Holy Land from hundreds of years of foreign intervention and oppression was at hand. The people came in great numbers to the Jordan to experience this rite of repentance for their participation in the collective guilt that had brought so much trouble to their homeland. Jesus was among them.[29]

---

28. While the broker-less concept is not new as a focus of Protestant theology, I have found Crossan (1991) informative for my own thinking. He employs the metaphor "brokerless kingdom" as a key to understanding Jesus' message and ministry.

29. The reader who is puzzled by the idea that Jesus participated in an act of repentance

It was not long, however, until Jesus began to preach in Galilee a message substantially different from that of John. Just as John no doubt experienced a broker-less relationship to Yahweh who had called him to his mission, so Jesus experienced himself as one who directly had been given his own role, mission, and message by Yahweh. Central to his unique and innovative message was the reality that Yahweh had presented himself to Jesus as *Abba*.[30]

> All things have been committed to me by my Father. No one knows who the Son is except the Father, and no one knows who the Father is except the Son and those to whom the Son chooses to reveal him. (Luke 10:22)

For Jesus, then, having been introduced to Yahweh as his "Father," there is no intermediary, no broker, not even the one who baptized him, who mediates between Yahweh and himself. The reality of Jesus is that his identity is defined by the relationship he has with God. That relationship is like that of a child who is nurtured, cared for, protected, and trained by a strict but loving father. Such a relationship is of its very nature direct and unmediated. And, for Jesus, it was a relationship sustained by a conscious and constant life of prayer.

---

should remember that repentance certainly may be a turning from sin, but it also can mean regret that leads to change, even a "guiltless turning," a changing of one's mind and direction. In the Old Testament God is said to have repented (NIV translates "grieved") when God had regret for appointing Saul king (1 Sam. 15:11). And in Ps. 106:45 God is said to have repented (NIV translates "relented") out of his great love when he heard the cry of his covenanted people. The prophets generally assumed that God would repent if the people would repent (see, for example, Jer. 18:8 and 26:13). It also may be relevant to remember that Jesus the human being said to the rich young ruler, "Why do you call me good? No one is good — except God alone" (Luke 18:19). While we have no way of knowing his precise reasons for coming to be baptized, we can say with great assurance that the baptism of Jesus was a decisive *turning* point in his life.

30. See notes 17 and 23 above. It is almost certain that the usage of *Abba* (frequently translated *patēr*) originated with Jesus. Not only do the oldest traditions contain this language, there is no other reasonable explanation for this usage coming into being. I am further convinced that the Lord's Prayer as found in Luke is an emotionally charged memory that originates with Jesus and was a part of his invitation to the disciples to enter into the son-Father relationship.

An Approachable Awesome God

That Jesus was a man of prayer there can be little doubt. The Gospel writers portray him as going apart from the crowds and from the disciples to pray, particularly at critical junctures in his ministry.[31] He would even spend all night in prayer.[32] Jesus is also described as instructing his followers concerning prayer. Prayer for Jesus is private and not for show (Matt. 6:5-6; 6:12), simple and direct (Matt. 6:7, 9-13; Luke 11:2-4; 18:10-14), persistent (Luke 18:1), trusting (Matt. 7:7-8; 21:22, Mark 11:24; Luke 11:9-11), and forgiving (Matt. 5:44; Mark 11:25; Luke 11:4). Specific prayers attributed to Jesus illustrate these themes.

> I praise you, Father, Lord of heaven and earth, because you have hidden these things from the wise and learned, and revealed them to little children. Yes, Father, for this was your good pleasure. (Luke 10:21)

> Father,
> hallowed be your name,
> your kingdom come.
> Give us each day our daily bread.
> Forgive us our sins,
> for we also forgive everyone who sins against us.
> And lead us not into temptation. (Luke 11:2b-4)[33]

Both of these prayers begin with the combined use of the informal address, "Father," with a formal indication that the identity of the one addressed is Yahweh, whose Name is so holy that it cannot be spoken, and who is the Ruler of heaven and earth.[34] The paradox of the approachable and in-

---

31. Mark 1:35; 6:46; 14:32; Matt. 14:23; 26:36; Luke 5:16; 6:12; 9:18; 9:28; 11:1; 22:41. While many of these passages are narrative transitions constructed by the Gospel writers, they no doubt reflect an accurate memory tradition of Jesus as one who frequently and particularly at times of great difficulty turned in private solitude to *Abba* in prayer.

32. Luke 6:12.

33. Matthew's version contains the last line of this model prayer as do some ancient manuscripts of Luke, but it is generally accepted that Luke's original version did not contain it.

34. These prayers are very likely to have come from Jesus' lips in very similar language to that narrated. The first prayer is rejected as originating with Jesus by many scholars because it has the style of Johannine theological discourse, which should be dated much later

timate, yet awesome and almighty God is more than a salutation; it is fundamental to Jesus' understanding and experience. While the relationship of child to Father is at the heart of the matter, it is equally critical to understand that God as *Abba* is not only in charge of the son, as any good Galilean father would have been, but this Father is in charge of the universe as well. *Abba* is not just Jesus' Father; *Abba* is *our* Father, *everyone's* Father.

Abba "in Charge"

If the first key to understanding Jesus' relationship with God is *Abba,* the second equally important key is that for Jesus, "God is in charge." God, *Abba,* as Yahweh, the Creator God, is the one who makes life the way it is, and there are things about "the way life is" that we cannot understand or change. We cannot have life on our own terms.

Who of you by worrying can add a single hour to his life? (Luke 12:25)

We are finite beings. The very nature of being human is to be homeless in this world.[35]

---

and is not consistent with the linguistic style of the more likely sayings of Jesus. To this, however, Jeremias (1965) and others have argued on linguistic grounds that this passage, along with the accompanying word to the disciples quoted above, could well be rooted in the earliest strata of Semitic tradition and its Johannine feel is the result of translation issues. Furthermore, the passage is from Q and must be dated much earlier than the Johannine literature. Jeremias suggests that this may well be the authentic seed from which the Johannine literature eventually developed in full flower. The Lord's Prayer as found in Luke and Matthew also has been questioned by some Jesus Seminar members and others on the basis that it represents a liturgical tradition developed in the early church that was attributed to Jesus. Crossan (1991) is skeptical, arguing that had Jesus taught a specific prayer it would have been more widely and consistently attested. The stark simplicity, brevity, and directness of this prayer, however, along with the principle of *memory enhanced by emotionally significant experience,* argue for words very much like these to have originated with Jesus. The exact wording may well have been remembered differently by different followers in different church communities.

35. Q places this saying in the context of a potential disciple being told that following Jesus means he will become homeless. I suggest that this is a later adaptation of a Jesus saying that stood by itself as an aphorism of the human condition. It is similar to "dust thou art."

Foxes have holes and birds of the air have nests, but *a human being* has no place to lay his head. (Luke 9:58; altered)[36]

In other words, life is just plain insecure. If a human being believes that he can secure his life by ensuring his future through the accumulation of wealth, he is a fool.

But God said to him, "You fool, this very night your life will be demanded of you." (Luke 12:20a)

The Father's Care

Jesus grasped in a profound way that we human beings are not in charge of the universe. In the midst of his lucidity about reality, Jesus trusted God to govern the world with his fatherly care. Because we are Yahweh's children and he is our "Father," there is no need to be anxious about one's life.

Therefore I tell you, do not worry about your life, what you will eat; or about your body, what you will wear. Life is more than food, and the body more than clothes. Consider the ravens: They do not sow or reap, they have no storeroom or barn; yet God feeds them. And how much more valuable you are than birds! (Luke 12:22b-24)[37]

See how the lilies of the field grow. They do not labor or spin. Yet I tell you that not even Solomon in all his splendor was dressed like one of these. If that is how God clothes the grass of the field, which is here today and to-morrow is thrown into the fire, will he not much more clothe you, O you of little faith? (Matt. 6:28b-30)

Your Father knows what you need before you ask him. (Matt. 6:8b)

---

36. I have translated the usual "son of man" language in this passage as "a human be-ing," which captures what I believe to be Jesus' intent. While this passage could have been a reference to himself as a "homeless" prophet, as some have suggested, it is more likely that Jesus intended a teaching designed to underscore human finitude.

37. While I have relied for the most part on the NIV translation for Q (those units of text recorded by both Matthew and Luke and believed to have come from a common source), I have been influenced by Powelson and Riegert (1999) in my determination of which Gospel is more likely to better reflect that source in particular instances.

> Which of you, if his son asks for bread, will give him a stone? Or if he asks for a fish, will give him a snake? If you, then, though you are evil, know how to give good gifts to your children, how much more will your Father in heaven give good gifts to those who ask him! (Matt. 7:9-11)

Jesus' confidence in the everyday care of God is not in the prophetic voice of one addressing the collective Jewish people as a nation about issues of great national interest. Rather, it is in the voice of a Spirit-filled man who is speaking to individuals about their relationship with a personal and caring fatherly God. What was remarkable about this message was that this loving God of all creation, contrary to expectations, was specifically and actively in charge of the lives of ordinary, individual "nobodies."[38] And these individuals were being invited to trust God, as they once, as small children, trusted their fathers, to care for them. Individuals were being called to abandon the futile quest to find security in personal righteousness or material things and to participate instead in the reality of the secure relationship between trusting child and awesome caring parent.

In Jesus' teachings, God's care for his individual children is rooted in God's compassionate nature. It is not a compassion that is directed simply to a collective group; it is a loving-kindness aimed toward every individual in that group.[39] And this concern and compassion of God toward individual persons is found in the great lengths God is willing to go to rescue them from danger and his joy when they are returned to safety.

> Suppose one of you has a hundred sheep and loses one of them. Does he not leave the ninety-nine in the open country and go after the lost sheep until he finds it? And when he finds it, he joyfully puts it on his shoulders and goes home. Then he calls his friends and neighbors together and says, "Rejoice with me; I have found my lost sheep." (Luke 15:4-6)

---

38. I am indebted to Crossan (1991) for the insight that children, particularly peasant ones, were considered "nobodies" in New Testament times. Over against Crossan's use of this notion to support his view of Jesus as social revolutionary, however, is the emphasis on childhood education in Jewish culture (see note 2 above). I take it to be self-evident that all peasants of that period, particularly the destitute, were "nobodies" by virtue of the fact that they were not aristocrats. My point in this chapter is that the symbol of the child reveals an important dimension of Jesus' view of reality, namely the fact that there are no "nobodies" in the eyes of God.

39. Matt. 10:29-31.

God's extravagant love for his children is also to be seen in the joy with which he embraces and absolves them when, after they have separated themselves from him and allowed their self-wills to run riot, they return and ask his forgiveness.

> But while he was still a long way off, his father saw him and was filled with compassion for him; he ran to his son, threw his arms around him and kissed him.
>
> The son said to him, "Father, I have sinned against heaven and against you. I am no longer worthy to be called your son."
>
> But the father said to his servants, "Quick! Bring the best robe and put it on him. Put a ring on his finger and sandals on his feet. Bring the fattened calf and kill it. Let's have a feast and celebrate. For this son of mine was dead and is alive again; he was lost and is found." So they began to celebrate. (Luke 15:20b-24)

This message of the radical love and care of God for individual "nobodies" must have come to Jesus' hearers as an unexpected one amidst a stratified culture where personality was group oriented, and where the longing for national deliverance and restoration was often expressed in cosmic and collective terms.[40]

A Kingdom Contrary to Expectations

If Yahweh as merciful "Father" taking care of individual "nobodies" was contrary to the expectations of Jesus' contemporaries, then *Abba's manner* of being in charge was equally contrary to expectations.[41] The conventional view

---

40. See Malina (2001, chapter 2) regarding the "group-oriented personality" in the region. I certainly agree with this view of group-centeredness as a cultural phenomenon. My point here is that Jesus represents a remarkable break with that orientation. In Jesus' view, the honor and dignity of individuals is not determined by the group or one's place in stratified society. One should not, however, anachronistically read Jesus' focus on individuals as synonymous with the emphasis on autonomous individualism and self-reliance in contemporary American society. Jesus' focus is on God's relationship to each of God's children, and their reliance on him.

41. I have used the metaphor of "God being in charge" as a paraphrase of Jesus' use of "kingdom of God" and as an attempt to clarify Jesus' relationship of daily trust in *Abba's* care as well as the presently manifested aspect of his vision (see note 44 below).

of Jesus' contemporaries was that God had abandoned his people. Yahweh had allowed Satan and demonic forces to rule because of human sin. The cruel oppression of heathen emperors, malicious kings, and their armies had taken place because of the unfaithfulness of the people to the covenant. God had removed his care and protection and was no longer in charge. Demonic powers now had the upper hand.

But the people also believed that God would not turn his back on his people forever. God would not allow this awful suffering of his people to continue without intervening. A time of reckoning was coming. At some point in the future, perhaps soon, God would defeat the spiritual and human powers of cruelty. The most popular vision of deliverance was that a Messiah, someone descended from King David and anointed by God for this purpose, would appear on the scene, raise an army that would destroy the enemies of Zion, and restore the kingdom of Israel to all its glory. Some hoped to become freedom fighters who would join the Messiah in the final battle with their enemies and reap the rewards of victory.[42] When that happened, so they hoped, all the circumstances of life would be changed and the people would once again experience God in charge, protecting and pouring out his blessings upon them.

Jesus shared with many of his contemporaries a number of common elements in his understanding of the future vision of the kingdom of God.[43] Jesus no doubt believed in a final day of accountability and shared in the hope for an age to come in which injustice would end and all things would be made right. But there were also significant differences between Jesus' view and that of his contemporaries. Jesus had experienced the personal truth that when he turned his will and life over to the care of Yahweh as *Abba,* he had entered into a relationship with God that was an arrival *in the present* of that reign.[44] That relationship allowed him to see that the Father, who is

42. This popular vision was clearly expressed in *Psalms of Solomon* 17:23-51. See Acts 5:34-39 for failed Messianic revolutions. The first-century Jewish historian Josephus also recorded these and several other examples (as in *Jewish War* 2.8; *Antiquities* 18.1). Also see chapters II and VII below for further discussions of Messianic expectations.

43. This is discussed more completely in subsequent chapters.

44. Borg (1994), Crossan (1991), and others have concluded that the kingdom of God Jesus proclaimed was sapiential (divine wisdom for the present age) rather than apocalyptic. The vision of a sapiential kingdom was also present in the wisdom literature of the time. The Wisdom of Solomon (Apocrypha) and the works of the first-century Jewish philosopher Philo provide examples. God's kingdom is seen as a kingdom in which the eternal Wisdom

Yahweh, is in charge *now.* But his present sovereignty is hidden from all except those children who see with the eyes of faith.

> The kingdom of God does not come with your careful observation, nor will people say, "Here it is," or "There it is," because the kingdom of God is within you. (Luke 17:20b-21)

> The knowledge of the secrets of the kingdom of heaven has been given to you, but not to them. (Matt. 13:11)

Jesus and the ordinary individuals around him experienced God being in charge, and, with the eyes of those whose perceptions of reality had been transformed, could see God's amazing providential care at work in their own lives.

> Again he said, "What shall we say the kingdom of God is like, or what parable shall we use to describe it? It is like a mustard seed, which is the smallest seed you plant in the ground. Yet when planted it grows and becomes the largest of all garden plants, with such big branches that the birds of the air can perch in its shade." (Mark 4:30-32)

> Again he asked, "What shall I compare the kingdom of God to? It is like yeast that a woman took and mixed into a large amount of flour until it worked all through the dough." (Luke 13:20-21)

---

of God is already present in those who are enlightened. From my perspective, "enlightenment" can be a relevant and useful metaphor for the significance of the revelation of Yahweh as *Abba.* But while there can be no doubt that Jesus proclaimed the kingdom as a present reality, and that present reality was the focus of his preaching, it is difficult to reconcile the apocalyptic vision of the earliest church with that perspective unless it is a both/and matter rather than either/or. In other words, it is probable that Jesus believed the kingdom is present now to faith, that he was focused on that reality, that he thought it futile and probably unfaithful to look for signs and try to predict times. Nevertheless, he also believed with John the Baptist and many of his contemporaries that the kingdom he experienced would become manifest to all on the final Day of Judgment, and that the situation was urgent because one has no way of knowing when it will occur. The final apocalypse became a major focus of the early church, including the Synoptic writers, because the post-resurrection community faced potential annihilation from intense persecution, and saw in the resurrection a sign of the end. In 2 Thessalonians Paul addressed the problem of the delay of the final apocalypse. Several decades later, the Gospel of John represented a refocusing and elaboration of the sapiential message in a time when it was becoming clear that the "coming again" had evidently been *indefinitely* delayed.

Jesus described the kingdom of God, the activity of "God being in charge," as a catalytic and mysterious activity in which something tiny or hidden, and seemingly insignificant, produces remarkable results. It is all the more remarkable because it is that which is impure, such as leaven in a loaf of bread, or undesirable, such as mustard weed growing in a field of crops, that produces an amazing transformation. Contrary to expectations, God's reign is not easily observable. It is not scheduled to *begin* at some future point with a cataclysmic event. Neither is it dependent on the purity of human beings. For "God's being in charge" is *already* a spiritual reality amidst the ritually unclean and social outcasts of Galilee.

Those who were unable to see with the eyes of faith could only see evidence that God could not yet be in charge. The Romans continued to rule. Herod was as cruel as ever. Disasters destroyed. The hungry, destitute, and disabled continued to live lives of desperation. Human suffering and death were ever present. Surely it was absurd to think that God was in charge now. Yet, that is precisely what Jesus believed. In a world of great tragedy it was no doubt all too easy for many to dismiss Jesus as hopelessly naïve. A careful examination of Jesus' sayings and parables, however, clearly demonstrates that the one who sent his followers into the world to "be as shrewd as snakes" had no illusions about "the way life is."[45]

The Lucidity of Jesus

Growing up in Galilee, and being taught the Scriptures and history of the Jewish people, Jesus would have understood tragedy. When he was approximately two years old he may have been too young to understand, but his family and all the people of Nazareth would have seen the smoke of the burning city Sepphoris four miles away and the crosses that lined the road. Judas, son of Ezekias, led a revolt that year against the Romans and was defeated. The rebels were crucified and the city was burned to the ground.[46] Stories of the horrors of this time would have been shared frequently and would have impressed deeply any child growing up in Nazareth.

45. Matt. 10:16. They were instructed in the same saying to be as "innocent as doves." Consequently, the saying not only suggests lucidity and carefulness in interacting with a world filled with predators, but also that they should be grounded all the while in an honest and childlike trust in God as *Abba*.

46. See Acts 5:37 and Josephus (*Jewish War* 2.117-18; *Antiquities* 18.1-10).

Stories of tragedy also would have circulated through Galilee about events in Jerusalem and Judea. A year before the burning of Sepphoris, Herod the Great had burned alive a group of protestors who had dared to destroy the golden eagle that the king had placed at the entrance to the Temple in Jerusalem.[47] Violent open rebellion followed in which blood flowed on both sides. Jesus also would have been well educated in the wars of the Maccabean period and the Jewish heroes who were martyred in those struggles.[48]

Stories of traumatic historical events aside, Jesus would not have been able to escape awareness of the daily tragedies of an oppressed people under the burdens of heavy taxation, extreme poverty, the daily personal and shameful indignities of a subjected people, and a remarkably high incidence of ill persons believed to be victims of demon possession. It was a world filled with victims whose suffering was increased by a culture that blamed victims themselves for their misfortune.

The feeble attempts to displace the fears generated by such a world through explanations that blamed tragedy's victims were no different in Jesus' time than they are in our own. Blaming victims always has been a way for human beings to try to be in charge of their own lives while evading responsibility for their neighbors. If people are good, the judgmental suppose, bad things would not happen to them. And when bad things happen to others, so the thinking goes, it is of little or no concern, for those people deserve what they receive.

Lucid people, on the other hand, always have understood that tragedy often happens in significant disproportion to people's sins. Likewise, good fortune often occurs disproportionately to those who have done little or nothing to deserve it. Not only do bad things happen to good people; good things happen to bad ones as well.

> Or those eighteen who died when the tower in Siloam fell on them — do you think they were more guilty than all the others living in Jerusalem? I tell you no! (Luke 13:4-5a)

> Neither this man nor his parents sinned. (John 9:3a)

47. See Josephus (*Jewish War* 1.651-55; *Antiquities* 17.149-67).

48. The Maccabees were a family that provided religious, political, and military leadership during the second and first centuries BCE. It was a period noted for its bloody conflicts and intrigue.

41

He causes his sun to rise on the evil and the good, and sends rain on the righteous and the unrighteous. (Matt. 5:45b)

But if this is "the way life is," and Jesus was in no way naïve about the nature of reality, how is one to understand what Jesus meant when he spoke of God's fatherly care for persons in this world? How does one grasp the meaning of Jesus' faith that God, as *Abba*, is *already in charge, now?*

The Meaning of "Abba in Charge" *Now*

Jesus' message that "God is in charge now" certainly included the idea that God has great power and authority, and that those under that authority are accountable to God. But it did not naïvely mean that God is in immediate and complete "control" of all that occurs. Contrary to popular expectations, "God being in charge now" did not mean a suspension of "the way life is," for such a suspension would effectively mean the final end of the age, the end of existence, as human beings know it. "God is in charge now," but the fundamental nature of existence has not yet changed. There remains randomness in nature and choice in human affairs. The sun continues to shine and the rain continues to fall on both the just and unjust, and human beings continue to be accountable for their intentional behaviors. That is "the way life is."

Jesus' view of the nature of God's kingdom was that the present creation as humans experience it, "the way life is," is itself a manifestation of "God being in charge now," as is the work of God's Spirit in the lives of God's "children." Consequently, Jesus' message of the kingdom of God was a call to submit to "God being in charge now," which was both *a call to face and accept reality* and, at the same time, *a call to submit to the care and guidance of God's Spirit.*

Jesus as Spirit Revolutionary

The idea of the kingdom of God has always been revolutionary and subversive from the standpoint of the kings of this world and their political, religious, and economic establishments. Open rebellion and sedition with the intent of restoring God's rule on earth had a long and bloody history in the Holy Land. The proponents of such radical change were dangerous and generally were dealt with swiftly and mercilessly. Even discourse about the passive longing for the coming of divine intervention and ultimate overthrow of the kingdoms of this world was experienced as subversive of loyalty toward those kingdoms and a threat to their ultimate peace.

The kingdom of God as Jesus understood it was also revolutionary. But it was a very different kind of revolution. This mysterious reality was first and foremost a spiritual revolution. This revolution was about redefining and transforming the individual's relationships to God and then to neighbor. For Jesus, the political situation was not the real problem, and taking up arms against it was not the solution. In fact, none of the external circumstances of life constituted the basic human problem. That problem was to be found in people's relationship to the realities of their lives. Jesus saw that the fundamental human problem was the fact that people were not living in the realities of their situation in the world as God intended, in relation to him as their Father.

Unlike many religious leaders throughout history, however, Jesus' radical spirituality did not lead him to espouse a path of escape from the world and avoidance of responsibility for its evils. In fact, the spirit revolution he envisioned was far more radical in its implications for society and for changing history than any of the conventional Messianic visions of his time. His was not a revolution aimed at rearranging the seats of privilege and power, but one devoted to nothing less than the transformation of the world through the transformation of the spiritual and interpersonal relationships of human beings. But those around Jesus did not share this revolutionary view. They believed that if God would fix their external problems, everything would be fine. Jesus was well aware of their manner of relating to life. He had been tempted to view it that way himself.

Tempted by Other Visions

At his baptism Jesus was seized by the Holy Spirit. This was a profound experience of the intrusion of the spiritual world into his personal world. He appears to have entered an altered state of consciousness for an extended period of time.[49] As has been reported in anthropological accounts of similar

49. The temptation story in its present form is usually interpreted as Jesus' rejection of the misuse of his power as Son of God and Messiah and thus a construct of the early com-

spirit journeys in many cultures, Jesus did not eat during that altered state, and it is likely that he did not experience much rest. He went on a journey of altered consciousness that involved cycles of ordeals. He was overwhelmed by awe, by fear and fascination with the numinous revelation of reality that never could adequately be put into words.

> Then Jesus was led by the Spirit into the desert to be tempted by the devil. After fasting forty days and forty nights, he was hungry. The tempter came to him and said, "If you are the Son of God, tell these stones to become bread."
>
> Jesus answered, "It is written: 'Man does not live on bread alone, but on every word that comes from the mouth of God.'"
>
> Then the devil took him to the holy city and had him stand on the highest point of the temple. "If you are the Son of God," he said, "throw yourself down. For it is written:
>
> 'He will command his angels concerning you,
> and they will lift you up in their hands,
> so that you will not strike your foot against a stone.'"
>
> Jesus answered him, "It is also written: 'Do not put the Lord your God to the test.'" (Matt. 4:1-7)

Jesus probably shared with his disciples during his ministry the stories of the ordeals he experienced when on his spirit journey following his baptism. Immediately upon being overwhelmed by the revelation that he was *Abba's* beloved son, Jesus was tempted to obtain proof for that assertion.[50]

That temptation first came in the form of an image. Many of the stones in the desert where Jesus traveled on his spirit journey are similar in shape

---

munity that may have been important for catechesis. I am convinced along with Borg (1987, p. 41) and others that there is a core memory here (later redacted for pedagogical purposes), shared by Jesus with his followers, of his initiation into his spirit journey. Together with the baptism, the basic elements of an initiatory rite of a traditional shaman or healer are present. Even a spirit creature (common in anthropological accounts) in the form of a dove is recorded. The dove symbolism is indicative of the Spirit as it fluttered above chaos in the creation, the messenger of good news in the flood myth, and the innocent sacrificial offering for sin used by the poor in the Temple worship of the time.

50. The temptation story no doubt also reflects the larger issue of the nature of the Messianic mission, but as narrated, it speaks to a deeply personal struggle during Jesus' post-baptismal spirit journey with the potential for unfaith following the revelation of Jesus' "Sonship."

and size to loaves of bread. Famished from his fast, alone and without food, Jesus looked at the bread-like stones. As he did so, he was overtaken by the obsessive thought that if the revelation to him that he was *Abba's* extravagantly loved child was really true, he surely possessed the magical power to change his physical circumstances; he could turn one of these stones into bread and immediately satisfy his hunger. And if that act was successful, then he would have a sign, proof that the revelation was really true.

But what if he were not successful? Would that mean the revelation of being a loved son was not true? At that moment Jesus appears to have had another thought. He recalled the words of Deuteronomy 8:3, which again assured him of the validity of his experience as son of *Abba.* Human beings have more than physical needs. Their greatest need is to be restored to the relationships for which God has created them. That had already happened to Jesus. It was the only miracle he needed.

But that was not the end of the matter. Temptations can be persistent. The desire to seek certitude for the revelation of his relationship with *Abba* then came to him in an even more dramatic form. He found himself preoccupied with a passage from the Psalms that could be interpreted to mean that God's care for his child included the ability to escape, with the miraculous intervention of God's angels, the limitations of human existence, particularly suffering and death.[51] Jesus knew at the moment it occurred to him that this was a temptation of Satan, the great spiritual Deceiver. For Jesus knew, as we all know, the consequences of leaping off a high tower, regardless of one's righteousness or relationship with God. He also knew that Scripture could be used to justify actions totally opposed to God's intentions for humankind.

Jesus appears to have understood at that point of his journey a profound reality. Contrary to expectations, God's care was not to be seen as rescue *from* "the way life is." God's care was to be seen as rescue *in the midst* of "the way life is." Jesus found the guidance he needed once again to ward off the temptation to test the validity of his experience of being God's compassionately loved son. He was assisted by the words of yet a different verse of Scripture. It was a verse that reminded him not to test God.[52] One was not to

51. Ps. 91:11-12. The fact that Jesus' brother James was reported killed by being thrown from the pinnacle of the Temple (Eusebius, *Ecclesiastical History*) may have influenced the particular form of this temptation in the tradition, although it is also possible that this temptation influenced the tradition about James. Or could it have been an ironic coincidence?

52. Deut. 6:16.

try to prove God's compassionate care, but to trust it in the midst of the challenges of one's unique journey as a human being. One was not to try to escape the limitations of "the way life is," but to embrace reality and live in it as God's creation.

The eyes of Jesus saw that divine care comes as guidance amidst the treacherous difficulties of life. Sometimes such guidance provides direction that leads one away from danger, while at other times it leads one through the dark valley of suffering and death while providing comfort and support for the journey. Such guidance is the only miraculous sign one needs. Jesus would be guided by this insight throughout his own journey and it became a central focus of his message to others. But before that, there was another temptation that had to be faced.

> Again, the devil took him to a very high mountain and showed him all the kingdoms of the world and their splendor. "All this I will give you," he said, "If you will bow down and worship me."
>
> Jesus said to him, "Away from me, Satan! For it is written: 'Worship the Lord your God, and serve him only.'" (Matt. 4:8-10)

The final temptation Jesus experienced in the desert was not about seeking the certitude that he really was God's loved son. He had already passed that test. What was required was faith, not certitude. Nor was it about escaping the realities of life as God had created them. He had passed that test also. What was required was acceptance, not illusions. The final temptation took a different direction. It was about consciously and intentionally turning his back on his relationship with God for one with Satan, the spirit of darkness, the personification of evil.

Jesus understood that he could choose to walk away from the revelation of his relationship with *Abba* and the calling of his baptism. In his spirit trance, he journeyed to a high mountain and there he saw all the kingdoms of power and wealth of this world before him. He realized, at a profound level of his being, his own potential greatness and that his calling to serve God was not being forced upon him. There was another path available. He had the power of choice. He could use his God-given talents to acquire wealth, status, and power instead. Surely he could convince his countrymen that he was the Messiah they were expecting, defeat Herod and the Romans, and become king; and then he could go on to become the new Caesar ruling over the entire world. Perhaps Jesus even thought that if he cut that deal with the devil he could do a lot of good for people as their ruler. Would that not be a softer and easier way than the path toward which God was leading him? The images were grandiose, but at that moment it all must have seemed possible.

The devil had tempted Jesus with the vision that he could control his own universe, that he could have life on his own terms as a human being, changing rocks into bread, leaping without harm from tall buildings, and controlling the world and all its inhabitants for his own purposes. But then, everything Jesus had learned as a child and everything he had learned on his present spirit journey converged in the words from Scripture that came to his assistance at that moment. Recalling the imperative of Deuteronomy 6:13 to worship and serve God alone, Jesus made his choice. He surrendered to the reality that it is God and God alone who is in charge of the universe. He chose to submit to God's being in charge of his life. He chose to live out his life as the beloved son of *Abba* that he was. He chose the vocation that God had chosen for him.

But the temptations had not only been about his personal struggle; they also had clarified his mission in history. His revolution would not be a revolution to rescue people from "the way life is," or even to achieve power so he could alleviate their problems. Rather, his vocation would be a spirit revolution, addressing the relationships of human beings to their God and with their neighbors. When, finally, Jesus' time of intense journey to the spirit world was ended, he was fatigued, hungry, and fundamentally changed.

Jesus and the Will of God

Jesus began his ministry under the power and guidance of the Spirit. He understood himself to be called not simply to obey the Law as one more good and proper Jew, but to obey the radical will of God for his particular life as it unfolded each day. Each day he sought in prayer to determine how to manifest his devotion to *Abba,* to love him with all his heart, soul, and mind, and his neighbor as himself, as the daily circumstances of life and the needs of the neighbor confronted him. His was a life in constant contact with *Abba.* He turned to *Abba* for guidance. He sought God's direction for what he was to say; where he was to say it; to whom he was to speak it; and how he was to respond to interruptions. He felt himself led to proceed from one location to another, and received wisdom regarding his interactions with the crowds, the disciples, and his adversaries.

The transformation Jesus experienced in his own life led him to believe that access to the reign of God, in which the caring, merciful *Abba* was in charge of his life, had become not just a reality for himself, but a possibility for all. God is not just in relationship with oneself as *Abba,* but is in relationship to other selves as *Abba* as well, and the joy of that relationship is open to everyone.

A relationship with God in which one child is forgiven is a relationship in which that forgiven child forgives other children. A relationship with God, which is that of a child, recognizes the love that God has for another child, even when the other insults with a backhand to the right cheek or persecutes. A relationship with God, which is that of a child, treats other children with the same respect that God has for them. To be in relationship with God is to imitate God in one's own relationships.

> *Be compassionate as your Father is compassionate.*
> Do not judge and you will not be judged.
> Do not condemn, and you will not be condemned.
> Forgive and you will be forgiven. (Luke 6:36-37; altered)[53]

One cannot grasp the reality of Jesus and his relationship with the Father, unless one also understands his relationship with the neighbor. It was the unity of his obedience to God and his responsiveness to the needs of his neighbors that compelled him to leave the isolation of the desert and to expend his life energies among the people of the Galilean oasis. There he ministered to the destitute, the sick, the disabled, the outcasts, and the unclean. It was Jesus' uncompromising commitment to love his neighbor as *Abba* loved the neighbor that drove Jesus to risk his own life in the mission to which his Father, the God of heaven and earth, had called him.

---

53. It is clear to most scholars that Luke reflects Q in using the Greek *oiktirmon,* which usually is translated "merciful" and here is translated "compassionate." Matthew not only has changed "compassionate" to "perfect" (Greek *telios*) here, but also has inserted the notion into the Markan narrative of the rich young man in Matt. 19:21.

CHAPTER II

Jesus and the Desert

I n the fifteenth year of the reign of Tiberius Caesar, 28-29 CE, a prophet
named John, clothed in camel's hair and a leather girdle around his waist,
living off the land by eating locusts and wild honey, appeared in the desert
on the other side of the Jordan from Judea. This wild-looking man came
preaching a baptism of repentance.

> John said to the crowds coming out to be baptized by him, "You brood of
> vipers! Who warned you to flee from the coming wrath? Produce fruit in
> keeping with repentance. And do not begin to say to yourselves, 'We have
> Abraham as our father.' For I tell you that out of these stones God can
> raise up children for Abraham. The ax is already at the root of the trees,
> and every tree that does not produce good fruit will be cut down and
> thrown into the fire." (Luke 3:7-11)

It was a message of impending doom. Those who came to hear him
were chastised for their wickedness. John told them they were as dangerously
evil as a mass of squirming offspring of poisonous snakes trying to escape
from a brush fire. He sternly warned them to repent truly and to change
their evil ways. Abraham's children could not depend on their ethnic birth-
right to save them from the fiery judgment. That was a dangerous illusion. If
these citizens of the land were to escape the wrath to come, they needed genuinely to change their hearts and to demonstrate that change in their behaviors. They were like fruit trees that were barren and useless, good only for
burning. If they did not begin to bear fruit soon, by leaving their wicked

ways and living an ethical life, they would be destroyed in the fiery judgment. And there was not much time. They needed to repent and be baptized *right now*. Already the divine axe was taking aim at the root of the tree. It was ready to swing and cut them all down. Already Yahweh was prepared to destroy them in his angry judgment.

As word spread about this prophet, a steady stream of indigenous humanity came to the Jordan to hear his message and to receive his baptism. Galileans were among them and one of them was a man in his early thirties named Jesus. Why did the citizens of Jerusalem, Judea, and Galilee interrupt their daily lives and leave their cities and villages to journey to the Jordan on the edge of the desert? Why did they subject themselves to his punishing diatribes and hell-fire preaching? Why did they come to hear this strange character and be immersed in the Jordan River by him?

A Culture of Peril and Refuge

Since human beings first settled in what is now the Middle East, the desert has influenced profoundly both the ecology and the collective psyche of the people of that region. The desert-oasis environment of the Middle East is psychologically reflected in a "peril and refuge" pattern of culture that pervades all aspects of the region's social relationships.[1] Such patterns of culture are not only pervasive, but tend also to have persisted from archaic times.[2] The desert, or wilderness, was widely understood in the ancient Middle East to be a place of great danger. The desert around the Dead Sea into which the Jordan flows has only two inches of rain per year. It is a wilderness covered with small rocks, with extreme temperatures, and with sudden blinding and blasting dust storms. It is an environment where one could perish quickly without water. In Jesus' day it was also the home of wild animals and dangerous spirits.

Any wilderness reminded the Jewish people of the desert experiences of Moses and their ancestors. The desert wilderness of Sinai was the location of the awesome and holy revelation from Yahweh to Moses, the deliverance of the tablets of law, and the area where their ancestors were miraculously fed and sustained for forty years. The desert was a sacred but terrifying place

1. I am indebted to anthropologist John Gulick (1983) for this important insight.
2. See Benedict (1934).

where one might struggle with Satan or be possessed by the Spirit of Yahweh.

If deserts are places of peril, oases are places of refuge. Oases are interruptions to the barrenness of the desert containing fertile lands, precious life-giving water, and nourishing vegetation. In the Middle East, oases are frequently in the form of fertile river valleys, where ancient civilizations began and over which countless wars have been waged. They also are found along the banks of lakes, such as the Sea of Galilee, and around ancient wells and watering holes.

Within the cultural preoccupation of the region with peril and refuge, it is taken for granted that within every peril there is some refuge, and within every refuge there is some peril.[3] Accordingly, there are oases in every desert and serpents in every Eden.

For those who live in or near deserts, water is a symbol of life and of cleanness. It quenches the thirst and washes away the sandy grime that sticks mercilessly to the skin. Water also symbolizes spiritual purity. As the body is cleaned by bathing, so is one spiritually cleansed in sacred rituals of water purification. The ancient Hebrews escaped Egypt through the parting of the waters of the sea. Forty years later they entered the land of promise by crossing the River Jordan. Legend held that centuries later the prophet Elijah was transported to heaven after the waters of the Jordan had been parted.[4] Water and refuge, passing through water and deliverance, ritual bathing and purification, all were deeply entrenched in the Jewish psyche by the time of John the Baptist.

Land of Oppression

When John the Baptist began his ministry, Tiberius Caesar was the Roman emperor, while the administrator of Judea, including Jerusalem, was the Gentile Roman Pontius Pilate. The Roman administrator of Galilee was Herod Antipas, son of Herod the Great who had died in 4 BCE after a cruel and oppressive reign over a region that included both Galilee and Judea. Life was hard for ordinary people under Roman and Herodian rule. The major-

---

3. This paradox almost appears to be the relation of yin to yang in Eastern thought. But the tension here is not one of harmonious tension, but rather borders on paranoia.

4. 2 Kings 2:7-12.

ity of people in Judea and Galilee were very poor and heavily taxed.[5] While the fertile lands of Galilee provided a decent living for landowners, most natives of the region were poor tenant farmers and laborers. These were the working poor who lived harsh and simple lives close to the margin between poverty and destitution. A significant percentage of persons, including many widows, divorced single women, the sick, and the disabled, lived in extreme poverty.[6] Partly due to such poverty, malnourishment, disease, and emotional distress were widespread.

Judean communities were occupied by Roman legions whose presence reminded the people daily of the indignities suffered by a chosen people who had been ruled by foreign governments, with only brief exceptions, for hundreds of years. Herod in Galilee also had soldiers at his disposal, recruited and conscripted from the local population. These soldiers were known for practicing extortion to supplement their meager pay. Throughout the region there were architectural reminders of the Roman presence and foreign cultural intrusion. The lavish lifestyles of the Roman authorities and their appointed kings, supported by the technology of the time, stood in sharp contrast to the subsistence economy and burdened lives of the people of the land.

Movements of Hope

The shame that goes with oppression, poverty, and foreign cultural encroachment often has created intense apocalyptic expectations across time and cultures. Such expectations have been labeled *millennial* because of their frequent association with the sects that arose in Europe as the first millennium of Christianity approached. Anthropologists have documented the fact that conquest and subjugation of a traditional society will sometimes

---

5. I discuss these conditions in greater detail in subsequent chapters, particularly chapter IV.

6. The degree of poverty in the region is controversial among some scholars. Some argue that the fertile land of Galilee and the benefits of Greek culture and Pax Romana made the area comparatively prosperous. Others point out that the economic system, which existed primarily for the purpose of providing tribute to Rome, was an oppressive environment that over time accumulated wealth in the hands of a few and increased poverty among the masses. The fact that Jesus focused much of his ministry on the poor and developed a large following is important evidence supporting the idea that poverty was widespread.

erupt in a millennial movement such as the cargo cults of World War II New Guinea and parts of Melanesia, or the Ghost Dance movement of the late nineteenth-century Native Americans.[7]

These movements share similar beliefs concerning a new age that they believe will dawn soon in which the cultic adherents will be blessed with a utopian existence. The new age is sometimes envisioned as a return to the conditions of a primordial paradise that will come through intervention from the gods or spirits. The movements generally are led by charismatic prophets who draw upon traditional mythology and symbolism in the creative construction of the utopian vision. It is often believed that the new age will be ushered in by certain activities of the prophet and his followers, although, in some cases, the new age is simply expected to come at an appointed time.

In most millennial movements, the new age, as wonderful as it is believed to be, will not come without a time of intense suffering. Its birth is to be accompanied by a time of crisis in which the members of the movement are purified and protected while their enemies are destroyed.

Study of these cults across cultures makes it possible to see common conditions that sometimes give rise to such movements. They frequently appear to be the response of a group that not only has been conquered by an alien culture, but is also under extreme pressure to adopt foreign ways.[8] Such movements appear related to the contrast between the technology and affluence of the occupying force and the technology and subsistence economy of

---

7. See Wallace (1956) and Worsley (1967), among others. Wallace uses the term *revitalization movements*. Two Ghost Dance religions arose among the Native Americans of the Western territories in the late nineteenth century. Prophetic visions involved the end of the existing world, the ousting of the white intruders, the return of dead relatives, and the restoration of the buffalo, their nations, and their cultural values. Warriors of the cults wore "ghost shirts," which they believed were bulletproof, into battle. Cargo cults broke out among remote tribes during the early twentieth century and during World War II in New Guinea and Melanesia in response to the intrusion of European culture. Wild trance dancing and belief that ancestors would soon return to bring an abundance of European-type goods characterized the cargo cults.

8. While this is characteristic of many situations, it is not always the case as David Koresh and the Waco cult illustrate. This movement did not fit the anthropological model of cultural intrusion, in the usual sense, although Koresh, no doubt, saw the "government" as a corruption of this world compared with the "purity" of his cult. The Koresh cult does lend itself to a psychological interpretation with regard to the personality makeup of persons vulnerable to cult recruitment.

the natives. Millennial movements are dramatic responses to what are very real threats to cherished traditions and cultural values. They are profoundly spiritual in concept and experience, and, at the same time, politically and economically subversive.

Given the foreign occupation and threat of syncretism, it is not surprising that similar movements arose in first-century Galilee and Judea. There were rich symbolic traditions to draw upon in the construction of their apocalyptic visions.

> "See, I will send my messenger, who will prepare the way before me. Then suddenly the Lord you are seeking will come to his temple; the messenger of the covenant, whom you desire, will come," says the Lord Almighty. (Mal. 3:1)

> See, I will send the prophet Elijah before that great and dreadful day of the Lord comes. He will turn the hearts of the fathers to their children, and the hearts of the children to their fathers, or else I will come and strike the land with a curse." (Mal. 4:5-6)

Based upon such prophecies, there was widespread popular belief among the Jews of Jesus' day that the prophet Elijah, who had lived more than eight hundred years earlier, would return to prepare the way for the Messiah. The Messiah, in turn, would usher in the new age, for the old order would be destroyed and purified in the fire of Yahweh's wrath, and the faithful would rule the earth with justice and mercy. All nations would honor Yahweh and make pilgrimage to worship him in Jerusalem.

The Desert Ascetics

Elijah was a powerful legendary heroic figure in the popular imagination associated with Yahweh's fiery judgment. It was Elijah who had called down fire from heaven and defeated the prophets of Baal (1 Kings 18:36-38). It was he who challenged King Ahaziah and again called down fire, this time upon the king's soldiers (2 Kings 1:2-17). And it was this prophet who passionately had rebuked a king for false witness and murder of an innocent man (1 Kings 21).

Elijah was a prophet associated with the desert. He had been clothed as a desert hermit, with only a garment of hair and a leather belt around his waist (2 Kings 1:8). And it was said that he was miraculously fed in the desert by ravens (1 Kings 17:1-6). Elijah was also a prophet associated with the waters of the Jordan River and their sacred significance (2 Kings 2:8).

John as the Coming of Elijah

When John the Baptist appeared in the wilderness near the Jordan wearing clothes made of camel's hair and a leather belt, word probably spread like wildfire that Elijah had indeed returned. For John, this almost certainly was not a case of mistaken identity. His appearance and message made it clear that this prophet of the desert understood and presented himself as one possessed by the spirit of the returned Elijah. It was in Elijah's spirit that John proclaimed a message of apocalyptic divine fire that would defeat the pagan enemies and their false gods and bring final victory to all those who shared with others and treated them justly.

> The word of God came to John son of Zechariah in the desert.[9] He went into all the country around the Jordan, preaching a baptism of repentance for the forgiveness of sins. As is written in the book of the words of Isaiah the prophet:
>
> > "A voice of one calling in the desert,
> > Prepare a way for the Lord
> > Make straight paths for him." (Luke 3:2b-4)
>
> "What should we do then?" the crowd asked.
> John answered, "The man with two tunics should share with him who has none, and the one who has food should do the same."
> Tax collectors also came to be baptized. "Teacher," they asked, "what should we do?"

---

9. Is it coincidence that John's father is named Zechariah, a prophet of the apocalyptic age? Some have suggested this name, along with his mother's name, Elizabeth, are narrative constructions of Luke (see Addendum to Part I, discussion on *Differing Dimensions of Truth* and literary construction), as was John's birth story. It is also true that Jewish children were often named after famous heroic ancestors, just as they are in most cultures. In the Middle East, as among Native Americans, one's name carried with it strong connotations of personal qualities and destiny that reminded one of the spiritual reality of the self.

"Don't collect any more than you are required to," he told them.

Then some soldiers asked him, "And what should we do?"

He replied, "Don't extort money and don't accuse people falsely — be content with your pay." (Luke 3:10-14)

And people came out to the edge of the desert, to the very Jordan where Joshua had led the people out of the desert crossing into the Promised Land, and where Elijah was said to have ascended into heaven, in order to be baptized by John.

John entered the waters and immersed those who came in a baptismal rite of purification.[10] Ritual "washings" for the purposes of purification were common practice in Judaism.[11] Law and tradition required that people wash themselves in relation to a number of contexts.[12] Ritual washing was required of priests before entering the sanctuary and before sacrifice.[13] Homes of the religiously compliant sometimes kept large jars of water for the purpose of ritual washing and bathing.[14] Communities also provided for the rituals. Both natural and constructed pools for bathing were located at various sites, particularly in Jerusalem, where ritual bathing of hands and feet was required for entrance to the Temple.[15] Self-administered washings occurred for most people in relation to meals, sexual contact, postmenstrual cleansing, and purification from contact contamination with unclean persons and the dead. These daily and occasional uses of water for purification were acts of obedience to God's requirement to be holy.

John's rite of cleansing, on the other hand, appears to have been unique in a number of respects. His baptisms probably were intended as one-time events. They were not self-administered, but performed by the desert prophet in preparation for the final judgment. John clearly was convinced that the final judgment would come so soon that those who were then living needed to undergo radical preparation for it.

10. The word translated baptism *(baptizō)* means "to dip or immerse." It also implied "washing."

11. Mark 7:2-4.

12. See 2 Sam. 12:20; Lev. 14:8; 15:5, 11, 16, 18; Num. 19:11-12, 17, 19; Deut. 21:6-9; Ezek. 16:4 for examples.

13. Exod. 30:7-21.

14. John 2:6.

15. John 5:2. According to Crossan and Reed (2001) over three hundred ritual bathing pools from the Roman period have been identified by archeologists in the Jewish homeland (p. 209).

I baptize you with water for repentance. But after me will come one who is more powerful than I, whose sandals I am not fit to carry. He will baptize you with the Holy Spirit and with fire. His winnowing fork is in his hand, and he will clear his threshing floor, gathering his wheat into the barn and burning up the chaff with unquenchable fire. (Matt. 3:11-12)

John's ministry of baptism, then, was the prophetic ministry of preparation for impending final judgment, which he evidently believed would be accomplished by the Messiah. There was no distinction between the time of judgment and the time of the Messiah in John's preaching. That time would be like the threshing of grain, in which wind separates the wheat from the chaff and the chaff is burned in a fire.[16] This was to be the Messiah's baptism with the Holy Spirit and with fire that was to come. For John's Messiah was the one who would wield the winnowing pitchfork in that final separation. On that terrible day, the Spirit of Yahweh, the "Wind of God," would gather, like good grain, those who had been baptized with water and truly had repented. The remaining, those who had refused to repent, would, like chaff, be cast into the eternal fire.

John's vision was one of a sudden cosmic final day that would set all things right by destroying evildoers and by saving the just. Similar to the millennial movements of later centuries, his movement was taking place in the final days before that end and the new utopian beginning were expected. He declared that the ritual of baptism should be accompanied by genuine repentance and just living. This was the way to escape from the eternal fires and to ensure one's place in the age to come. Some of John's converts became disciples who lived ascetic lives as he did and assisted John with his work. Most probably returned to their homes to live morally holy lives until judgment day.

John's lifestyle and his message were profound expressions of the peril and refuge, desert and oasis, cultural preoccupation of the region. John's baptism offered refuge from the peril of the wrath to come.

The Essene Community

This "holy man" who baptized his countrymen with water was not, however, the only one in the desert region during that era to live an ascetic life, prac-

---

16. The Greek word *pneuma* refers both to spirit and to wind. That is also true for the Hebrew word *ruach*.

tice water purification, and seek to prepare for a final day of judgment. There probably were a number of such individual desert ascetics through the years.[17] And near where John baptized was a substantial desert community of people who were John's contemporaries and who were also preparing for the wrath to come.

About thirty miles from the place where John baptized in the Jordan was the wilderness ascetic Qumran religious community known as Essenes.[18] Much is now known about this religious order due to the discovery of the Dead Sea Scrolls in 1947 in caves near the Dead Sea. The writings discovered there were the sacred scrolls that guided this desert community.[19]

The sect was founded by devout temple priests in 152 BCE because Jonathan Maccabee assumed the role of high priest. Jonathan was considered by the traditional priestly community not to be descended from the correct hereditary line to function as high priest. In protest, the group withdrew from the Temple and Jerusalem and built a complex of buildings in the desert. There they lived under a strict set of communal rules, including celibacy, poverty, and obedience to the community elders. A leader of the community, referred to only as the Teacher of Righteousness, was responsible for many of the beliefs. While this group had been persecuted in its early years, and had been devastated by an earthquake in 31 BCE, Qumran was a thriving community during the lifetimes of John the Baptist and Jesus.[20] The community was later destroyed by the Romans during the Jewish wars of 66-70 CE.

17. A few years after John another ascetic wise man lived in the desert and practiced water purification. In the year 56-57 CE, approximately a quarter century after John the Baptist's death, the first-century Jewish historian Josephus, during his late teens, became the devoted disciple of a man named Bannus. Josephus described him as one "who dwelt in the wilderness, wearing only such clothing as trees provided, feeding on such things as grew of themselves, and using frequent ablutions of cold water, by day and night, for purity's sake." Josephus left Bannus when he was nineteen years of age to become a Pharisee (Josephus, *Life* 10-12).

18. The overwhelming consensus among scholars is that Qumran was an Essene community. Some who practiced the Essene life lived in Jerusalem, including some married members. There are those who believe the Qumran community represented a different sect from the Essenes. If so, they represented one more example of an ascetic group practicing rituals of water purification.

19. For an excellent source on the Dead Sea Scrolls and the Essenes, see Vermes (1999).

20. There is no hard evidence to support the theories that John or Jesus, or both, spent time in the Essene community. A highly controversial hypothesis by Eisenman (2004) that the Teacher of Righteousness was James the brother of Jesus has not been widely supported, largely because the relevant scrolls have been given earlier dates.

The Dead Sea Scrolls and archeology have clarified that a theology of apocalyptic visions, asceticism, purification by ritual cleansing, and ethical behavior was alive and well in the desert near the Jordan in the first century.[21] Based upon their interpretation of Scripture, the Essenes had a unique vision of the advent of the Messianic age. The scrolls reveal that the sect believed in two Messiahs. One Messiah was to be a warrior from the Davidic line who would defeat their pagan conquerors; the other was from the priestly line of Aaron. As the Essene community was a priestly order, it is not surprising that the priestly Messiah was expected to be supreme while the warrior Messiah would play a secondary role in the age to come. The sect anticipated that the ascendancy of the Messianic priest would result in the Temple being restored to its rightful grandeur and authentic practices, and that the new age would be accompanied by a great feast.

The Essenes awaited the coming of the new age on the edge of the desert where Joshua and the Israelites had camped in anticipation of entering the Promised Land. The life they chose as appropriate for such waiting was that of asceticism. This was a monastic order divided into classes of priests, Levites, and laymen, each with prescribed roles. Initiates underwent extensive instruction, which emphasized obedience to the rule of the order. Initiation took place in an annual baptism ceremony in which the baptized were made pure by the Holy Spirit. This rite was the first of many ablutions and baptisms required of members to assure purity.

For the Essenes, daily life was a struggle against the evil demons ruled by Belial, the Prince of Darkness. These demons were already at war with God's heavenly angels under the leadership of the Angel of Truth, the Prince of Lights.[22] The members devoted themselves to strict ethical behavior and sought to purify their hearts and minds in relation to God and their community. While pessimistic about the ability of human beings to resist evil in this age, they had great confidence that these cosmic spirits of darkness would soon be defeated in the ultimate apocalyptic battle. The Essenes were also certain that their ascetic community of the faithful would be the remnant that would be placed in charge of the Temple and the world.

21. Archeologist Shimon Gibson excavated a cave in 1999 that might have been used by John the Baptist. The cave contained a large bathing pool that was probably constructed and used in later centuries. The cave had drawings that indicate it to have been a shrine to the Baptist.

22. Belial was the name for Satan in the Dead Sea Scrolls. It probably has the same linguistic root as Beelzebub.

The Essenes shared with their contemporaries a belief that the advent of this Messianic age would be preceded by the forerunner predicted by the prophets. There is no evidence, however, that they embraced John the Baptist as that forerunner.

John and the Essenes

John the Baptist had several things in common with the Qumran community. He too camped on the edge of the desert awaiting the coming of the Messiah. John had disciples who shared in his ascetic lifestyle. He and his disciples were known for their fasting and austere existence. John's preaching of repentance presumes pessimism about the sinful nature of human beings. His vision of the Messianic age was one associated with the burning of the wicked in a great conflagration. At the center of his message was a baptism that cleansed people from their sins. He exhorted those baptized to live an ethical life in relation to their neighbors in order to "flee from the wrath to come." John believed in the Holy Spirit, and undoubtedly believed in evil spirits as well.

Despite the similarities, however, there were significant differences. John was certainly no Essene. His message clearly proclaimed a single Messiah, one who would destroy the wicked and usher in the new age. His ascetic style was that of the individual desert hermit, rather than the communal desert cloister. Most significantly, his baptism was not an initiation for the religious elite into a secretive sect, requiring poverty, chastity, and obedience within a community rule. It was rather a baptism for the common people, for the tax collectors and socially ostracized, for the forgiveness of their sins. It was a call to ethical behavior, not in a society of purity, but in the everyday world of give and take. Tax collectors were not told to resign and take up the religious life, but to collect only what was owed. Soldiers were not told to leave the army, but to quit harassing and extorting people.

The Essenes clearly were focused on hereditary rights. Their order had been founded on a protest against a priest with the wrong ancestry. They saw themselves as the true Israel, the faithful and true descendants of Abraham who would restore the priesthood to its proper hereditary line and participate in a new covenant. For John, salvation was not based upon heredity, but upon the good fruits of one's life. The circumcised children of Abraham had become so sinful that they too needed to undergo baptism just as Gentile proselytes were required to do following conversion to Judaism.[23] Jew and Gentile were equally unclean. John particularly understood himself as preparing the way for a kingdom of the common people and undesirables, unclean sinners, including tax collectors, soldiers, and prostitutes.

John was also unique among individual prophets of the desert. With all the ritual purifications going on, only John became known as "the Baptist." And, as far as we know, John was the only desert prophet of the period to dedicate himself to preparing the masses for the apocalypse, rather than devoting himself and a small elite group of followers to personal purity in expectation of that event.

Jesus and John

So the people came in droves from the countryside, from villages and city backstreets to be baptized by John for the forgiveness of sins. They came because they were weary of poverty, harassment, humiliation, discrimination, illness, and the injustices of a foreign-occupied and -subjected land. They came, as well, because they experienced the heavy burden of their own failure to live as they had been taught that God and the Law of God intended. They came because they longed for forgiveness from all their sins. They came because they had hope for a better life for themselves and a better world to come. It was as one of the common people from Galilee that the craftsman construction worker from Nazareth came to be baptized.[24] It was to be a decisive event in the life of Jesus.

Jesus probably entered the water naked, as did the others, symbolic of the unclothed, innocent, and pure state of Eden.[25] There he was immersed in

23. The practice of ritual cleansing by immersion for proselytes is referred to in rabbinical literature, particularly *Yebam* 46-47. It remains controversial whether the practice was well established prior to the destruction of the Temple, but it seems reasonable to assume so.

24. There is no reason to believe that John recognized Jesus either as a kinsman or as the Messiah on this occasion. While the Gospels have John witnessing to Jesus as the Messiah, and Luke's narrative has them as kinsmen, the question John sends to Jesus from his prison cell implies no personal knowledge of Jesus, nor any preconceived belief about him. Most mainstream scholars regard the birth story and baptismal confessions of John in the Gospels as narrative constructs (see Addendum to Part I, *Differing Dimensions of Truth*, for discussion of literary truth versus literal truth) while John's question from prison almost certainly reflects a remembered event.

25. That people were baptized naked was the assumption of the early church fathers.

the waters of the Jordan. He did not baptize himself. He was baptized by John. After Jesus left the water, he spent time in prayer, probably somewhere nearby in solitude. The entire episode appears to have been an overwhelming and transforming religious experience. It was not long afterward that Jesus began his own prophetic ministry, one that was both complementary and contrasting to the ministry of the Baptist.

Complementary Roles

That Jesus and John were complementary in their ministries is foreshadowed in Luke's narrative that identifies the two men as kin to one another.[26] Luke's birth narrative, modeled on Abraham and Sarah, is a metaphor for the fact that John and Jesus were remarkable, Spirit-filled kindred souls. Both shared a vision of a Day of Reckoning when God would judge the world and the wicked and faithless would be destroyed.[27]

Jesus' ministry was also complementary to John's because both John and Jesus shared a mutual audience: the common people, the poor, the outcasts, the ritually nonobservant, and the flagrantly sinful. Jesus also had great appreciation for John's role in history.

> The Law and the Prophets were proclaimed until John. Since that time, the good news of the kingdom of God is being preached, and everyone is forcing his way into it. (Luke 16:16)

> Jesus began to speak to the crowd about John: "What did you go out into the desert to see? A reed swayed by the wind? If not, what did you go out to see? A man dressed in fine clothes? No, those who wear expensive clothes and indulge in luxury are in palaces. But what did you go out to see? A prophet? Yes, I tell you, and more than a prophet. This is the one about whom it is written:
>
> > 'I will send my messenger ahead of you,
> > who will prepare your way before you.'" (Luke 7:24b-28)

26. Many scholars believe the Luke birth narrative is a construct (see Addendum to Part I, *Differing Dimensions of Truth,* for discussion of literary truth versus literal truth) based upon the Genesis narrative concerning Abraham and Sarah and the claim of kinship with Jesus a literary device. See note 9 above.

27. See, for example, Matt. 13:24-30.

Ultimately, John and Jesus shared the same fate. They each became martyrs for their respective prophetic messages and deeds.

Contrasting Ministries

But Jesus was not just complementary to John; he also represented a clear contrast to the Baptist. That contrast is not simply that Jesus was greater than John, which the early church fervently believed and portrayed the Baptist as also believing. Rather, Jesus was significantly different from John in his self-understanding, his theology, and his behavior.

Jesus shared with John the vision of a final judgment with its division of humankind. Jesus appears to have appropriated John's language about harvests, winnowing, barren fruit trees, and fire. But Jesus, unlike John, focused his message not on the doom to come, but on the good news of what was already happening in the present. His was a ministry devoted to the present opportunity to enter a trusting relationship with *Abba* as ruler of one's life and the possibility of beginning to experience now the wondrous life that was promised for the age to come. John emphasized God's wrath; Jesus was consumed with God's compassion.

Jesus understood that the kingdom of God was not just near; it was already here. For the Baptist, the kingdom of God was in the future. Human beings were still living in the old era of wickedness and would have to go through many apocalyptic terrors before they could enjoy that kingdom. But Jesus believed that he and his followers now lived between the "no longer" of the old era, when Satan and the demonic powers were allowed to inflict misery and suffering on God's children, and the "not yet" of the final destruction of those powers and the setting right of things on the final Day of Judgment.[28] This "in between time" was not just a time of fearfully watching and waiting for the final crisis while evil continued to have its way. The new age

28. I first heard the image "between the no longer and the not yet" in a lecture by the late Joseph W. Matthews of the Ecumenical Institute in Chicago sometime in the early 1960s. It referred in that context to the human existential reality in which the past is *no longer* and the *not yet* future is being created by present decisions, and the intentional decision of a few, the church dynamic in history, to "lay down their lives on behalf of all humankind between the 'no longer and not yet.'" Matthews may have appropriated the terms from Bultmann (1951, p. 322), where existence in faith is spoken of as a movement between "no longer" and "not yet."

of God's reign had already begun and was spreading quietly and rapidly. Its signs were everywhere to be seen, for those with eyes to see. This was an exciting time in which boldness was required. People were not just being saved from the wrath to come, they were experiencing joyful new lives as those who had not only repented of their sins, but had found their rightful place in *Abba's* care and guidance.

Furthermore, in contrast to John, the Essenes, and other apocalyptic prophets of the era, Jesus' view of the judgment was one that was contrary to popular expectations in a number of dramatic respects. Not the least of these surprises was Jesus' announcement that those who assumed they had some advantage due to their status as religious insiders were going to be shocked.

So the last will be first, and the first will be last. (Matt. 20:16a)

I say to you that many will come from the east and the west, and will take their places at the feast with Abraham, Isaac and Jacob in the kingdom of heaven. But the subjects of the kingdom will be thrown outside, into the darkness, where there will be weeping and gnashing of teeth. (Matt. 8:11-12)

Those who thought their lifetime of obedience to the Torah would result in greater reward in the new age than latecomers to a life of faith were to be confounded by the compassion of God.

For the kingdom of heaven is like a landowner who went out early in the morning to hire men to work in his vineyard. He agreed to pay them a denarius for the day and sent them into his vineyard. About the third hour he went out and saw others standing in the marketplace doing nothing. He told them, "You also go and work in my vineyard, and I will pay you whatever is right." So they went.

He went out again about the sixth hour and the ninth hour and did the same thing. About the eleventh hour he went out and found still others standing around. He asked them, "Why have you been standing here all day long doing nothing?"

"Because no one has hired us," they answered.

He said to them, "You also go and work in my vineyard."

When evening came, the owner of the vineyard said to his foreman, "Call the workers and pay them their wages, beginning with the last ones hired and going on to the first."

The workers who were hired about the eleventh hour came and each received a denarius. So when those came who were hired first, they expected to receive more. But each one of them also received a denarius. When they received it, they began to grumble against the landowner. "These men who were hired last worked only one hour," they said, "and you have made them equal to us who have borne the burden of the work and the heat of the day."

But he answered one of them, "Friend, I am not being unfair to you. Didn't you agree to work for a denarius? Take your pay and go. I want to give the man who was hired last the same as I gave you. Don't I have the right to do what I want with my own money? Or are you envious because I am generous?" (Matt. 20:1-15)

Assumptions about the benefactors of the new age being those who have supposedly achieved religious superiority are delusional. It is not the self-righteously pure, but the genuinely compassionate who will be blessed.

Then the King will say to those on his right, "Come you who are blessed by my Father; take your inheritance, the kingdom prepared for you since the creation of the world. For I was hungry and you gave me something to eat, I was thirsty and you gave me something to drink, I was a stranger and you invited me in. I needed clothes and you clothed me, I was sick and you looked after me, I was in prison and you came to visit me."

Then the righteous will answer him, "Lord, when did we see you hungry and feed you, or thirsty and give you something to drink? When did we see you a stranger and invite you in, or needing clothes and clothe you? When did we see you sick or in prison and go to visit you?"

The King will reply, "I tell you the truth, whatever you did for one of the least of these brothers of mine, you did for me." (Matt. 25:34-45)

This final judgment based on the generous compassion of God and the compassionate behavior of human beings was a very different kind of final judgment than the Baptist anticipated.

Compassion was, for Jesus, the centerpiece of his ministry. Both John and Jesus ministered to the outcasts, but John simply baptized them without discrimination. Jesus, on the other hand, reached out to them like a shepherd for lost sheep. He went to their communities and homes, broke bread with them, touched the unclean among them, healed them of their illnesses, and pronounced forgiveness for their sins.

John chose the desert and the desert way of asceticism for his prophetic ministry of preparing for impending judgment and doom. In contrast, Jesus chose the oasis, the fertile land around the Sea of Galilee, to proclaim *Abba's* compassionate care and victory over evil, and to celebrate robustly this good news with the ordinary people of the land.

Jesus the Unexpected One

Because it was Jesus' conviction that *Abba's* reign was already underway in his own life and the lives of his followers, Jesus rejected the life-denying ascetic way of the desert, choosing rather to embrace and celebrate reality, as he perceived it.

> To what, then, can I compare the people of this generation? What are they like? They are like children sitting in the marketplace and calling out to each other:
>
> > "We played the flute for you,
> >   and you did not dance;
> > we sang a dirge,
> >   and you did not cry."
>
> For John the Baptist came neither eating bread nor drinking wine, and you say, "He has a demon." *This human being* came eating and drinking, and you say, "Here is a glutton and a drunkard, a friend of tax collectors and 'sinners.'" But wisdom is proved right by all her children. (Luke 7:31-35; altered)[29]

> Now John's disciples and the Pharisees were fasting. Some people came and asked Jesus. "How is it that John's disciples and the disciples of the Pharisees are fasting, but yours are not?"
>
> Jesus answered, "How can the guests of the bridegroom fast while he is with them? They cannot, so long as they have him with them." (Mark 2:18-19)

29. The reference to "wisdom and her children" can be interpreted to say that Jesus considered himself to be a child of "Sophia" or "Wisdom" and that he and other children of "Sophia" were being proved correct, despite expectations to the contrary, by the wondrous deeds of Jesus' ministry. Some scholars have concluded that Jesus' self-understanding was that of a sage, or teacher of wisdom. I find no difficulty with that interpretation as long as it is seen as one among several self-images that were important to Jesus.

Jesus rejected the ascetic life because the great Messianic wedding banquet had already begun. The reign of God was already present. People were entering into a spirit relationship with *Abba* and that was occasion for celebration both in heaven and on earth. The great banquet was a banquet at whose table were the common people, the religiously nonobservant, the tax collectors, and the outcasts.

Jesus' role and identity in that new reality was also unexpected.

> "John the Baptist sent us to you to ask, 'Are you the one who was to come, or should we expect someone else?'"
>
> So he replied to the messengers, "Go back and report to John what you have seen and heard: The blind receive sight, the lame walk, those who have leprosy are cured, the deaf hear, the dead are raised, and *the destitute are given good news. How deserving of honor is anyone who does not dishonor me.*" (Luke 7:20b, 22-23; altered)

No doubt, these acts were understood by Jesus as foreshadows of the final victory of Yahweh over the demonic forces. But, more important, Jesus' compassionate and miraculous ministry was understood by him as a set of signs of the already present Messianic age. Jesus' historic role in this Messianic drama was not the popularly expected one based on prophecies from Zechariah, Malachi, and Daniel. Jesus' role was based upon the vision of the prophet Isaiah, whose picture of the Day of the Lord was one of good news, of healing and liberation for the diseased and imprisoned, accompanied by celebration and hope for the coming of that Day.[30]

As he sat in prison, awaiting his fate, John probably was puzzled and bewildered by Jesus' answer.[31] Jesus' words certainly implied Messianic activity. This was a man who, by the power of the Holy Spirit, was accomplishing mighty deeds, as Elijah had done and as Isaiah had prophesied. On the other hand, these words did not unambiguously answer for John the question of whether Jesus was the Messiah. Here was no fiery figure with a pitchfork of judgment in his hand as John and many prophets before him had predicted. Here was a man of compassion and of peace. Could this "*no* Messiah" be *the* Messiah? Was Judgment Day near or not?

Perhaps equally puzzling to the desert ascetic would have been reports that Jesus enjoyed sharing good food and wine with his friends and that he

30. See Luke 4:18-19; Isa. 61:1-2.

31. Matthew provides the setting of this passage from Q as a question sent from prison.

and his followers engaged in massive picnics and outdoor feasts. Contrary to expectations for the Messiah, it was rumored that Jesus was a glutton and a drunkard. While such slander was no doubt generated by Jesus' enemies, the half-truth in those lies lay in the fact that Jesus' lifestyle was one in which he made no secret of the fact that he enjoyed feasting with his followers and the people of the land. His way was a life-affirming one based upon confidence in the goodness of God's creation, the reality of God's presence, and compassionate care for ordinary people living ordinary lives.

Jesus understood quite well that his own Messianic mission did not provide signs of the reign of God that would convince the unbelieving. Nor did he know or pretend to know when the final setting right of things would come.

> But understand this: If the owner of the house had known at what hour the thief was coming, he would not have let his house be broken into. (Luke 12:39)

Jesus compared the coming Day of the Lord to a thief in the night. The very nature of such home intrusions was their unexpectedness.[32] It was just as impossible to know when the final crisis would occur as it was to anticipate just when one's house would be robbed. But, even more significant than the uncertainty of timing of the end time for Jesus was his assertion that people would not even be able to see the arrival of "God being in charge" when it happened.[33] For John the Baptist, the arrival of God's kingdom, by necessity, would have coincided with the terrible Day of Judgment. That was the conventional expectation. But Jesus saw that the arrival of God's reign and the Day of Judgment are not synonymous. The final judgment would surely occur at some point in God's own time, but God's reign had already arrived, not in a cataclysmic moment of destruction, but in the miraculous restoration of ordinary "nobodies" to life as *Abba* intended it to be.

---

32. While the early church probably emphasized watchfulness, Jesus probably, as Paul, in 1 Thess. 5:2, used the "thief" metaphor primarily as a disclaimer about the ability of human beings to discern the timing of the Day of the Lord.

33. Luke 17:20-21.

Preparation and Celebration

John the Baptist, the prophet of desert asceticism and apocalyptic doom, would not likely have found in Jesus' response to his query anything that convinced him that Jesus was the "one who is to come." It raised more questions than it answered. From the perspective of Jesus and his disciples, however, it was understood that John had prepared the way for Jesus' ministry. It was John who had been Yahweh's instrument bringing Jesus to his own baptism, which led to his subsequent testing in the wilderness. It was John's harsh message of God's intolerance for wickedness that laid the groundwork for Jesus' remarkable ministry of *Abba*'s compassion, preaching the good news, healing the sick, casting out demons, and raising the dead.

It was not long after that final exchange of messages between John and Jesus that Herod ordered the beheading of John. John's death was surely experienced by his disciples and by the common people who had been baptized by him as one more disappointment in a long line of dashed hopes. The new age did not come with John's death. But hope does not die easily. By that time a new prophet was on the scene in Galilee, casting out demons, healing the sick, and raising the dead.

John's imprisonment and death undoubtedly made a vivid impact on Jesus. It may have convinced him that his own ministry would ultimately end in death as well. Despite that ominous vision, the eyes of Jesus could see, as he ministered to those in need, the exciting reality that life was already a banquet and the time had already come to begin to celebrate the defeat of the forces of evil. So, for now, there were people to be taught, demons to be exorcised, illness and disability to be healed, and sinners to be rescued. *Abba* had urgent business for him to be about.

CHAPTER III

Jesus and the Disabled

A s a young man in Galilee, Jesus was familiar with the reality of illnesses, injuries, and disabilities common to the region. Life expectancy was less than half what it is today in Western societies.[1] Nutrition deficits were common among the poor. While the Romans addressed some of the sanitation needs of the cities by constructing aqueducts, by modern standards the general Galilean populace was exposed to a number of risks with regard to its drinking water and sewage, particularly in the villages. Jesus' contemporaries suffered from a wide range of disorders. They experienced their share of parasites, such as head lice and tapeworms. Though relatively rare among Jews of that time, some are known to have had tuberculosis and tumors. Various skin diseases with symptoms of rashes, scales, and sores were plentiful. Those suffering from them were known as lepers, though the specific disease identified as leprosy in the modern world was rare. Conditions that involved a discharge, such as a menstrual flow or male genital emission, were serious concerns in the purity-conscious environment.[2] Viral and bacterial infections also were well known and sometimes devastated whole villages.

Of particular note were the disabled, those with seizure disorders, paralysis of body parts, deafness, blindness, muteness, and psychosis. Such conditions were tragic for those with these conditions and for their families. Disabilities limited and sometimes eliminated the economic productivity of persons and their capacities to contribute to family support. They also

1. I am indebted to Zias (2002) for the following discussion of disease in ancient Israel.
2. See Lev. 15.

placed huge burdens on other family members, neighbors, and family friends who exerted and often exhausted their own physical and spiritual energy in assuring safety and care.

Sickness and Stigma

As in other times and places, first-century Galilean society profoundly stigmatized the sick and disabled. Societies generally are suspicious of those who, because of illness, cannot fulfill their responsibilities. The ill and disabled frequently are believed to be malingering, using sickness as an excuse to avoid responsibility and work. Their conditions are often thought to be either the fault of themselves or their parents. This idea of fault may be based on the notion that the individual or a near family member has offended an ancestor, has desecrated a sacred object, or has otherwise offended the gods.[3] Galileans in Jesus' day believed that sin, the failure to keep God's Law, was the reason for disease and disability.[4] While the book of Job had called the logic of that idea into question centuries earlier, it continued to be a deeply ingrained belief.

Even in our own culture, people often believe that if they are "good," nothing really bad will happen to them. When something does, they struggle to determine what they have done wrong. In Jesus' culture, this natural tendency was reinforced by the accusing fingers of those who sought to be superior in the eyes of God, themselves, and others through fanatical and meticulous observance of the Law, as they understood it. The tragedy of being sick and disabled, particularly for those with chronic conditions, was therefore compounded by the shame of knowing that neighbors, and especially those who were held in esteem for their religious status, judged and blamed the victims themselves for their conditions.

Not only was causation of these unfortunate conditions explained in terms of sin, but the persons themselves also were considered impure as long as the conditions persisted. Even when healed, such persons were still thought to be polluted until they had been ritually purified. Righteous peo-

---

3. This blaming phenomenon is also known in the modern world. Until relatively recently, psychodynamic family blame theories were widely held by mental health professionals with regard to mental illnesses in North America.

4. See John 9:1-2.

ple were particularly concerned about contamination from those with skin conditions. Such persons were required to humiliate themselves by keeping their hair unkempt, wearing torn clothes, and shouting out, "Unclean! Unclean!" when anyone approached them. If the condition was chronic, they were required to live in isolation from others. Persons who had bodily discharges were also considered impure, and contact with them meant ritual cleansing was needed as well. Those with fever, epilepsy, paralysis, muteness (aphonia), deafness, blindness, or psychosis were considered to be possessed by unclean spirits. Thus, every condition of sickness and disability was a sign of sinfulness, impurity, and danger.

Because all shared in this view of the world, it must be assumed that the victims did as well, though a very few, like the author of Job before them, may have questioned whether their sin was in any way proportional to their suffering. Most of the unfortunate, no doubt, understandably internalized the guilt and shame their society projected upon them.

Jesus as Compassionate Healer

What was Jesus' relationship with these sick and disabled persons and their families? Jesus did not see them as strange, worthless human beings whose presence was a danger and an offense to the sensibilities of respectable folk, as did many of his contemporaries. Jesus saw them as *Abba's* children suffering in body, mind, and spirit. He empathized with them, felt great compassion for them, and reached out to help them.

> That evening after sunset the people brought to Jesus all the sick and demon-possessed. The whole town gathered at the door, and Jesus healed many who had various diseases. (Mark 1:32-34a)

At some point, very early in his ministry, Jesus realized that through the power of the Holy Spirit, which he experienced as having taken control of his life, he had received the gift of healing.[5] Jesus understood that his calling included the role of bringing free healing to those suffering from disease and disabilities. His God-given gift was to be used on behalf of "the least of these," God's children and society's outcasts. The one who told the parable of

5. Less than twenty-five years after Jesus' ministry the apostle Paul would write to the Corinthian congregation concerning the gifts of the Spirit (1 Cor. 12:1-11).

the talents was himself the example of a good and faithful servant who does not waste his gifts.[6]

The Search for a Cure

Those afflicted with these disorders, along with their families and caretakers, saw, in Jesus, hope for an end to pain, misery, exhausting burden, guilt, and shame. Once word about Jesus began to spread concerning one or two successful healings, it is understandable that a substantial number of persons with these conditions came, or were brought by family and friends, to Jesus to be healed.[7]

The natural and rationalistic medicine associated with Hippocrates had been around the Greek and Roman world for over four hundred years by the time of Jesus.[8] This tradition denied the role of spiritual agents in illness and healing, looked for natural causes, and believed in physician interventions consistent with the theory of natural causation. All diseases, as theorized by Hippocrates, were related to the four bodily fluids that might not be functioning properly. Interventions involved herbal and chemical concoctions along with the use of leeches and similar cures for diseases of the blood and other bodily fluids. No doubt there were physicians who practiced this type of medicine in the cities in and near Galilee.

Along with these practitioners of Greek and Roman medicine were a substantial number of traditional folk healers who practiced near the boundary between Jewish religion and pagan magic. As did native healers in other times and places, they related illness to spiritual forces. Anthropologists have identified five types of folk explanations for illness: soul loss, breach of taboo, disease sorcery, object intrusion, and spirit intrusion.[9] How one explains the causes of disease is directly related to how a healer goes about curing a disease. In the case of disease sorcery, the effects of a curse must be removed by the correct ritual. In the case of object intrusion, the healer must magically remove the foreign object from the body of the ill individual. In the case of spirit intrusion, the harmful spirit must be exorcised.

6. Matt. 25:14-30.
7. See Mark 1:32-34; Mark 3:7-12; Matt. 12:15; Luke 6:17-19; Mark 6:53-56; Matt. 14:34-36; Matt. 15:29-31.
8. See Hippocrates, *On Ancient Medicine*.
9. Murphy (1964).

First-century Galilean culture primarily believed in spirit intrusion. As in other cultures, alternative beliefs also were present. Some of the folk healers practicing in and around Galilee were primarily herbalists using potions and applications, while others relied on ancient magical knowledge. Their skills were learned from mentors who passed along the secrets of the trade. Like most of their counterparts in other cultures, they commonly were paid for their services, whether in coin or in barter.

The woman who touched Jesus' garment was said to have visited many physicians.

> A large crowd followed and pressed around him. And a woman was there who had been subject to bleeding for twelve years. She had suffered a great deal under the care of many doctors and had spent all she had, yet instead of getting better she grew worse. When she heard about Jesus, she came up behind him in the crowd and touched his cloak, because she thought, "If I just touch his clothes, I will be healed." Immediately her bleeding stopped and she felt in her body that she was freed from her suffering. (Mark 5:24b-29)

As happens today among those with treatment-resistant chronic conditions, this woman "shopped" for a cure among the different types of healers. In chronic misery, anemic, and in pain, she had spent all her financial resources on physician fees, without success. Although treated by many healers, she had only gotten worse. Like so many who are chronically sick, and the burdened families who often assist them, she cared little about the theory behind the healing process. As is common among such persons in third world countries today, she went from physician to physician, regardless of orientation, desperately seeking a cure.[10] She came and tried to touch Jesus because he had a growing reputation as an effective healer.

Jesus' Reputation as a Healer

That Jesus was a healer with a reputation for extraordinary success is an established historical fact.[11] The Jewish historian Josephus refers to Jesus as "a

10. See Janzen (1978).

11. The overwhelming consensus among scholars from various disciplines supports this conclusion. Of course, there are extreme skeptics who continue to dispute that we can know

doer of wonderful deeds."[12] The Gospel writers incorporate several summaries of healing activities into their narratives that suggest extensive healing activity. We know that Jesus attracted large crowds of people during his ministry. This was likely due to his reputation as a healer, though undoubtedly he was an effective teacher as well.

The strongest evidence that Jesus was a successful healer is to be found in the fact that his adversaries did not challenge the results of his efforts, or dismiss him as a failure. Had he not been successful they would have ignored him as someone who did not have to be taken seriously. But far from ignoring him, they found it necessary to try to discredit him by accusing him of sorcery.[13]

> And the teachers of the law who came down from Jerusalem said, "He is possessed by Beelzebub! By the Prince of Demons he is driving out demons."
>
> So Jesus called them and spoke to them in parables: "How can Satan drive out Satan? If a kingdom is divided against itself, that kingdom cannot stand. If a house is divided against itself, that house cannot stand. And if Satan opposes himself and is divided, he cannot stand; his end has come. In fact, no one can enter a strong man's house and carry off his possessions unless he first ties up the strong man. Then he can rob his house." (Mark 3:22-27)

The Prince of Demons was called Beelzebub by Jesus' accusers. This name was a local popular title for the head demon that was also known by many as Satan. The name Beelzebub was probably derived from Baal, the

anything about Jesus, or who question his historical existence, but when the vast majority of historians and other scholars apply the same criteria to Jesus as to other ancient historical figures they conclude that we can know a few basic facts. Among these is the fact that he had a reputation as a great healer. The historicity of any particular healing story is more controversial. While acknowledging a revision process in the oral tradition period that tended to increase the marvel of these narrated events, thus making them *less* believable for moderns, I am convinced that several original healings are recoverable and represent emotionally charged memories that remained strong for decades. These recoverable accounts are representative generally of the types of healings Jesus performed successfully and of his methods.

12. *Antiquities* 18.63f. While Josephus's reference to Jesus was obviously edited by later Christian scribes, most scholars believe that the original text is relatively transparent and is consistent with Josephus's style elsewhere. See Barrett (1956); Crossan (1991).

13. Most scholars argue that these accusations, as other negative ideas about Jesus, would not have been a later creation and therefore originated during Jesus' ministry.

god of the Canaanites defeated by the prophet Elijah. Jesus' adversaries explained his success as a healer by reference to his being possessed by the Prince of Demons. They attempted to discredit him by classifying him as an evil magician, who practiced sorcery by the power and authority of the chief demon responsible for wreaking misery and havoc upon the earth.[14] Jesus' response was both profound and amusing. Jesus pointed out that the accusation was faulty in its logic and in the human experience of conflict. Satan would not be trying to cast out his own demons and thereby destroy his own kingdom. On the other hand, the fact that Jesus was successful in casting out demons was pointed to as evidence that the Holy Spirit of God was at work in his healing, that God's reign had already begun, and that Satan's defeat was sure.

Understanding Jesus' Healings Today

Jesus' relationship with the sick and disabled presents certain special difficulties for those who would understand this relationship two thousand years later. To his contemporaries, this relationship involved the demonstration of wondrous power. Jesus is described in the Gospels as casting out demons that had entered the victims and caused these terrible conditions. For those who live in and take for granted a modern worldview of natural causation, the idea of demon intrusion is problematic. Before we can adequately explore the relationship between Jesus and these suffering souls, it is necessary to engage in a dialogue between our own knowledge of illness and healing, and the worldview in which Jesus did his mighty deeds.

There always has been something profoundly mysterious about illness and healing. People have attempted to understand since the dawn of consciousness the reasons for their illnesses and to explain why some recover and others do not. Even in the world of modern medicine and natural causation we often are bewildered by the unexpected loss of health or amazed by the unexpected recovery.

14. In so doing, they also attempt to undermine the idea that Jesus may be the returned Elijah, for they are essentially accusing him of being one of the priests of Baal.

Demon Intrusion and Conversion Disorder

Jesus and his neighbors shared a common understanding of illnesses and disabilities as caused by demon intrusion. While the priestly Sadducees in Jerusalem did not believe in angels or demons, the Pharisees, the Essenes, and almost all other first-century Jews did.[15] There were hints of such beliefs going back to very early traditions, particularly among the common people, but a theology proper of angels and demons emerged under Persian influence during the exile of the sixth century BCE and continued in postexilic times.[16] Much of Judaism underwent a significant transformation from the radical monotheism that denied the existence of such beings or relegated them to impotence, to a modified monotheism, influenced by Zoroastrian dualistic mythology, which gave these beings significant roles in their lives and national destiny, albeit as ultimately subservient to Yahweh. The popular belief in Jesus' day was that Yahweh was allowing the rebellious Prince of Demons, who was served by all the specific troublemaking demons, to cause suffering because of the sins of God's people. In the age to come, however, these demons would lose their power to do harm and would be cast into the apocalyptic fire.

These troublemaking demons were known by the types of trouble they created. They were the agents of disease, disability, natural disasters, and misfortunes in general. For example, a "dumb" demon would cause a man to be unable to speak.[17] In some cases a demon might have a specific name, as in the case of "Legion" that possessed the Gerasene man who lived in a graveyard in a Gentile community about six miles southeast of the Sea of Galilee.[18]

Even when exorcized, a demon remained dangerous. There was a risk that it would return and even bring additional demons with it.

When an evil spirit comes out of a man, it goes through arid places seeking rest and does not find it. Then it says, "I will return to the house I left."

15. For the Sadducees, see Acts 23:8. The Dead Sea Scrolls contain numerous examples of Essene belief in angels and demons.

16. Belief in angels and demons is reflected in the apocryphal and pseudepigraphal writings (for example, Tobit, 2 Esdras, 1 Enoch, and *The Testaments of the Twelve Patriarchs*).

17. Mark 9:25.

18. Some scholars regard this narrative as a parable about Jesus, Gentiles, and Roman legions and not as historical event. Even so, the core story may represent an authentic healing of a psychotic who lived in a cemetery.

When it arrives, it finds the house unoccupied, swept clean and put in order. Then it goes and takes with it seven other spirits more wicked than itself, and they go in and live there. And the final condition of that man is worse than the first. (Matt. 12:43-45a)

This perceived risk of multiple spirit intrusion was a way of understanding a universal phenomenon. In modern terms, it remains a mystery that people with serious disorders can sometimes experience periods of complete remission from symptoms only to be made much worse than before by a later, and perhaps more virulent, onslaught of the disease.

The disability conditions that were considered to be caused by demon intrusion were likely to have been numerous in Galilee. Psychiatrists understand today that blindness, muteness, deafness, paralysis, seizures, and hallucinations are often the result of neurological disease. But they also know that these same symptoms can exist without any known neurological problem. They can be manifestations of what psychiatry today calls conversion disorders. The term *conversion disorder* is rooted in the theory that unconscious psychological conflicts are sometimes "converted" into a bodily illness in which an emotional problem is externalized as a physical symptom. This process is thought to assist the unconscious with concealment of the psychological conflict, but at the same time it is symbolic of the conflict. For example, blindness may be symbolic of the unconscious unwillingness to "see" an unpleasant and undesirable reality. While this theoretical process remains hypothetical in modern psychiatry, a diagnosis of conversion disorder means that *no known neurological or medical causation is discoverable.* Unlike the neurologically impaired, the prognosis for those with conversion disorder is usually good. Many spontaneously respond in a relatively short time. A few less fortunate victims may have conditions that last for years. This disorder is more common in rural populations, in individuals of lower socioeconomic status, and in developing third world countries. It is not unreasonable to assume a relatively high rate of conversion disorder in the social and political environment of first-century Galilee.[19] It is important to understand that persons with these disorders are truly disabled. The blind can-

19. Rates of the disorder are very difficult to establish. According to *DSM-IV* (American Psychological Association, 2000), they range in North America from 11 per 100,000 to 500 per 100,000. Mental health centers report up to 3 percent of all patients have conversion disorder. Medical surgical hospital studies show a range of 1 percent to 14 percent. In distressed third world countries the percentages are likely to be much higher.

not see and the deaf cannot hear. Their subjective experiences are no different than those with neurological impairments.

While we have no way of knowing for sure that some of those who were healed by Jesus had what we today would call conversion disorders, it is suggestive that of the relatively few specific accounts of healings in the Gospels, many of them are consistent with the symptoms of this modern diagnosis. Those of us who live within a worldview that expressly rejects the causation of illness and disability as spirit intrusion nevertheless can comprehend how a person might be involuntarily overwhelmed and "possessed" by an emotional response to a personal crisis that leaves that person blind, deaf, aphonic, hallucinating, paralyzed, or subject to seizures. We might be able to understand further how both psychiatrist and folk healer could be successful in treating such disorders.

Of course, these same symptoms frequently do have neurological causes. Various diseases are also the result of microorganisms, immune failure, and genetic propensities. We know today that people often become ill and die because of these conditions. Could Jesus have been the successful agent of healing, without the aid of modern medicine, in some of these more difficult cases as well?

Jesus understood himself to be filled with God's Spirit, which had bestowed upon him the gift of healing. He experienced the power of the Spirit working through him miraculously to relieve suffering manifested in a broad range of diseases. Moreover, some of the disabilities he healed appear to have been chronic lifelong conditions.[20] It is likely, if such healings occurred today, that many witnesses would also consider them to be genuine miracles.

Even in a world of "medical miracles" there remains something about illness and healing that is beyond our ability to understand. Why does one person experience remission from a deadly cancer, while another with the same disease dies? Why does one person with serious heart damage go into congestive heart failure and die, while another with an equally damaged

---

20. See Luke 13:10-13 and Mark 5:25-34 for examples. John's Gospel narrates that the paralytic in John 5 and the blind man in John 9 were long-term seriously disabled persons who only could have been healed by dramatic, unexpected divine intervention. While many scholars have seen these persons in John's Gospel as examples of the tendency to heighten over time the miraculous nature of the healings reported in Mark, one cannot rule out the possibility that these stories are based upon earlier traditions and personal knowledge of the unprecedented dramatic nature of those healing events.

heart "miraculously" recovers? How does the healing process really work? What factors increase the odds of "spontaneous remission and recovery"?

There are hypotheses that seek to answer these questions, but in some ways, the more medical science seeks to understand the healing process, the more mysterious it appears to be. This mysteriousness almost always impresses itself on a patient, who, after receiving a debilitating and perhaps fatal prognosis, subsequently experiences a "spontaneous recovery." Such patients often believe that their recoveries are miraculous. Frequently they will speak of the power of prayer, or the gift of God's healing. Sometimes they simply are filled with awe. "Spontaneous recoveries" are by definition exceptions to the rule. They do not lend themselves to statistically based scientific study. But they do happen and they remind us that there is something about the healing process that remains mysterious. The success of Jesus as a healer was as awesome and mysterious for his contemporaries as today's unexpected "cures," with or without medical assistance, are for us.

Jesus and Folk Methods

Jesus, of course, was not the only local healer who has ever had a reputation for success. Jesus' healing activity was similar to those of many others across ages and cultures.[21] Every society has its native or folk healers, some of whom gain a reputation among the people for their effectiveness.[22] They are known by a variety of terms, such as *shaman, medicine man, holy man, magician,* and *sorcerer.* Many are women. Sometimes they function as both spiritual leader and bodily healer. In some cultures there is strong competition between the priestly leaders who ritually facilitate healing at the officially sanctioned temples and shrines and the lay healers who rely on their own relationships with the spirit world to diagnose and cure diseases. Some healers are practicing herbalists, others are well trained in magical incantations and gifted in sleight-of-hand, and still others have developed the capacity to slip easily into the altered state that they experience as the spirit world.

In every culture there are some healers who are not well respected, but there are always well known healers who are held in high esteem. Hanina ben

---

21. Philostratus's *Life of Apollonius of Tyana* has similar summaries of people coming from all over the country, in that case Greece, to seek healing from Apollonius.

22. See Kiev (1964); Torrey (1972); Eliade (1964); Kleinman (1979), for examples.

Dosa, like Jesus, lived in the first century prior to the destruction of the Temple. The rabbinical tradition reports a number of healing miracles by this wonder worker.[23] However foreign to our worldview and understanding of causation and cure the works of such native healers are, there is every reason to believe that, if they have possessed a reputation among their contemporaries for success, then they have been instrumental in at least some recoveries.

Again, the techniques used by healers are directly related to their theories of causation. At first glance, one sees some interesting similarities between Jesus' techniques and those found in various other folk healing traditions. For example, Jesus sometimes used the power of touch. He took Simon Peter's feverish mother-in-law by the hand and helped her to rise.[24] He also touched a man with a serious skin disease.

> A man with leprosy came to him and begged him on his knees, "If you are willing, you can make me clean."
>
> Filled with compassion, Jesus reached out his hand and touched the man. "I am willing," he said. "Be clean!" Immediately the leprosy left him and he was cured. (Mark 1:40-42)

Living alone, away from others, allowed only to wear torn clothes and to keep his hair unkempt, always warning others with the shout of "Unclean, Unclean," as required by Leviticus 13:45-46, this man's life was miserable. The narrator tells us that Jesus was filled with compassion for the leper. The demonstration of that compassion was Jesus' willingness to reach out his hand and touch this untouchable man. This was a remarkable act. In touching the man with the skin disease, Jesus himself was considered to be unclean and in need of ritual purification. It was a scandalous act that signaled the triumph of inclusive compassion over exclusive purity. It is difficult to imagine how this man who was starving for affection must have felt when Jesus reached out and touched him. There is something primordial about the need for human touch.

While Jesus, as portrayed in the healing narratives, did not always have physical contact with those he healed, he is said to have done so on a number of occasions. In addition to the leper, Jesus also touched Peter's mother-in-law (Mark 1:29-31), Jairus's daughter (Mark 5:21-24a, 38-42), a deaf mute (Mark 7:31-37), the blind man of Bethsaida (Mark 8:22-26), the coffin of a

23. Vermes (1981).
24. Mark 1:29-31.

widow's son at Nain (Luke 7:11-17), the crippled woman (Luke 13:10-17), the man with dropsy (Luke 14:1-6), and the man born blind (John 9:1-7). In addition, Jesus' garment was touched by the woman with a vaginal hemorrhage, a woman considered to be unclean (Mark 5:25-30).

Touch has always played an important role in healing. Most healers employ physical touch at some point in the healing process, even if it is incidental to a physical exam. Modern research has demonstrated that touch therapy by nursing personnel, therapeutic massage, and affectionate touch by family and friends promote healing and recovery.[25]

In addition to touch, Jesus is reported to have used his own saliva, which he rubbed on the eyes of the blind (Mark 8:22-26) and placed on the tongue of the deaf mute (Mark 7:31-37) during the healing event. On these occasions, Jesus accompanied his touch with verbal orders to the demons. Such commands may have been formulaic wording, as the Aramaic words are retained and translated in the otherwise Greek narrative. To the deaf and mute man he said, *"Ephphatha!"* which means "Be opened!" To Jairus's daughter, who was believed already to be dead, Jesus said, *"Talitha koum,"* which means "Little girl, I say to you, get up!"

Later, the apostle Peter also used formulaic command and touch to heal a crippled man at the temple.[26] The combination of touch and formulaic words is characteristic of much folk healing.

Evidently, however, Jesus did not always touch the person being healed. On some occasions he is reported simply to have used his verbal authority to order the demon out of its victim, sometimes accomplishing his purpose from a considerable distance. It is difficult to know if these differences are related to methodologies for differing conditions, or simply differences arising in narrative transmission. Either way, it is clear that Jesus' healings were in some respects similar in form to those of many folk healers.

Failure and Faith

There is one more significant way that Jesus' healings were similar to those of folk healers. Jesus was not always successful. A hint of this may be found

25. While research on touch remains controversial, the evidence for its effectiveness is persuasive enough that a number of schools of nursing have incorporated touch therapy into their curricula.

26. Acts 3:1-10.

in Mark 1:32-34, where Mark writes that the people brought to Jesus *all* the sick and demon-possessed and that Jesus healed *many*. More to the point is the account of Jesus' visit to his hometown.

> He could not do any miracles there, except lay his hands on a few sick people and heal them. And he was amazed at their lack of faith. (Mark 6:5-6a)

The reason for the failure is explained as lack of faith, and this lack of faith in this case was related to the truism that a prophet is without honor in his own home.[27] The people knew Jesus as local craftsman and construction worker, and as a member of a local family. They knew his mother, his brothers, James, Joseph, Judas, Simon, and his sisters. Nazareth was a village with a likely population of two hundred to four hundred.[28] As in most small towns everyone knew a great deal about his or her neighbors. They were unwilling to believe this person they knew so well could be a great prophet and could perform mighty deeds.

Even in modern medicine, the "lack of faith" explanation has a kind of validity. A high degree of confidence in the healer and his method, and willingness to cooperate with it, are essential to the success of engaging the ill person's desire and stimulating his or her immune system in the healing process. If prescribed medicines have efficacious benefits, then failure to take them contributes to bad outcomes. But even when prescribed treatments have no intrinsic value, there may be benefit for those who comply. Research on placebos, those harmless non-therapeutic pills that are given in clinical trials to determine the effectiveness of new drugs, has demonstrated the "placebo effect." Many who take the non-active pills show improvement due to the expectation that they are taking efficacious drugs. It is their "faith" in the drugs and the healer who gives these medications to them that is believed to account for this difference. Likewise, a lack of confidence in a healer and the chosen treatment significantly reduces desirable outcomes.

27. Lack of faith is a common explanation for the failure of folk healings. It is not the inadequacy of the healer, but the failure of the sick to have faith that is seen at the root of the problem. This is consistent with the rationalizations of the medicine man or woman who instructs the ill person to engage in some ritual activity, and when the cure does not occur, explains the failure as disobedience in properly carrying out the instructions. Of course, people today do not always carry out physician orders or complete their regimen of medications. Some patients develop a reputation among physicians as noncompliant and therefore responsible for their poor outcomes.

28. Crossan and Reed (2001) base this estimate on archeological evidence.

As important as "faith" may be to healing, our worldview of illness and healing understands today that "lack of faith" is a limited explanation for failure.[29] Faith is important to recovery, but it is never a guarantee.

Some disorders are treatable, but not curable. Some are curable but treatment resistant. We do not always know why one person responds to treatment, and another does not. Frequently, an initial treatment does not bring about the desired result.

> They came to Bethsaida, and some people brought a blind man and begged Jesus to touch him. He took the blind man by the hand and led him outside the village. When he had spit on the man's eyes and put his hands on him Jesus asked, "Do you see anything?"
>
> He looked up and said, "I see people, they look like trees walking around."
>
> Once more Jesus put his hands on the man's eyes. Then his eyes were opened, his sight restored, and he saw everything clearly. Jesus sent him home, saying, "Don't go into the village." (Mark 8:22-26)

Here Jesus was involved in a healing in which the patient indicated that his sight was only partially restored. The images of men were "like trees walking." With an additional effort this problem was fixed. But this healing illustrates the treatment-resistant nature of some conditions. It is reasonable to assume that Jesus, as is true of all healers, had outcomes in some cases that were less than those desired.[30]

---

29. Just as no one really is expected to grow a severed limb through folk healing, we would expect many people today with serious disabilities and debilitating conditions to be beyond restoration. Most of us know persons in our midst who are blind, paralyzed, deaf, aphonic, psychotic, or seizure disordered. We know persons who have been diagnosed with diseases of the body and brain who, to the best of our knowledge, are going to live with their disorders until they die. While there is much we do not know about the healing process, and occasionally there are surprising recoveries, it would be cruel to suggest that the reason for their continued conditions is a "lack of faith." The attribution of "lack of faith" is another form of faulting the victim, a variation on the belief that such suffering is caused by sin. The appropriate "faith" response of an individual with a disorder that is beyond the capability of modern medicine to cure is to adapt to a way of life that includes living and coping with a disability. It is not to engage in a fruitless struggle to obtain the necessary "faith" to secure a miracle.

30. It is clear that the man had once been able to see. Otherwise he would not have been able to recognize and describe what he saw. We do not know how or when he lost his sight. This well could be a case of what we today would call a conversion disorder. Be that as it may,

While not always successful, Jesus nonetheless had a reputation as an extraordinary healer who did what others had been unable to do. Obviously, many sick and disabled persons were healed and restored as a result of Jesus' ministry. To what is such success attributable? The psychiatrist E. Fuller Torrey has identified four commonalities that are important to the success of the healing of illnesses rooted in the problems of living that are true both of modern mental health professionals and traditional healers.[31] These commonalities include a healer with therapeutic personal qualities, an ill person with expectations for healing accompanied by emotional arousal, a naming of the problem arising from a shared worldview, and a resulting sense of mastery in the person being healed.

When we consider Jesus' healing ministry we see that he was compassionate and empathetic; he was willing to interact with the "unclean" seeker personally, physically, and respectfully. Jesus was a charismatic speaker with behaviors that appeared to be the fulfillment of divinely inspired Scriptures and suggestive of ancient prophets. The sick and disabled came with strongly felt expectations and excitement over the belief that this man could and would heal them. And Jesus and they had a shared and deeply held belief that these disorders were intruding demons and that one who had the gift of Yahweh's spirit was more powerful than these intruders. Finally, these persons experienced themselves as having been liberated from these demonic forces and once again able to be in control of their own lives and to engage in life as normal people.

Healings as Signs of Abba's Reign

In studying the anthropological literature, however, some important differences between Jesus and many indigenous healers are evident. While most healers gain materially from their work, Jesus did not. He practiced free healing available to all who came in faith. While many healers engage in elaborate rituals and recite mysterious incantations, Jesus' approach was brief and efficient. The closest he came to the use of formulas was the use of

---

the use of spittle and touch was consistent with expectations from a folk healer, which would have caused the blind man, who could not see what Jesus was doing, to have confidence that the act of healing would be successful.

31. Torrey (1972).

a few brief commands to the demons. His healings are remarkable for their conciseness and efficiency. For many healers, sleight-of-hand magic is a necessary part of the ritual of healing in order to secure the necessary confidence in the healer and his ritual. For example, sleight-of-hand "surgery" is a technique handed down from healer to healer where object intrusion is considered a cause of illness. Jesus did not engage in such tricks.

These differences may lie largely in the uniqueness of Jewish religion and culture. Healing in a culture whose tradition is that of a radical monotheism that is uncomfortable with magic is going to be quite different in its formal manifestations from healing in polytheistic and pantheistic environments. On the other hand, Jesus' method may be rooted more in his personal message and mission than in cultural motifs. That is almost certainly true of the offering of free healing to all.

Furthermore, the healings of Jesus cannot be separated from the historical context of his mission to declare and demonstrate that *Abba's* reign was already present. Jesus was living between the "no longer" of the reign of Satan and his demons, and the "not yet" of the final defeat of those powers and the fullness of Yahweh's reign. His healings were both compassionate demonstrations of God's love for outcasts and the inclusive nature of the new age, and signs that these blessings were already available in the here and now.

These were not unambiguous signs, however. They did not have the power to convince those who refused or were unable to believe. They were subject not only to the interpretation of witchcraft, casting out demons by the power of Satan, but to other explanations as well.

> As soon as they left the synagogue, they went with James and John to the home of Simon and Andrew. Simon's mother-in-law was in bed with a fever, and they told Jesus about her. So he went to her, took her hand and helped her up. The fever left her and she began to wait on them. (Mark 1:29-31)

We have no way of knowing what kind of fever the woman had, nor how high it was. Was it due to an infection, or was it perhaps a symptom of emotional distress? Was there something about the presence of Jesus' touch that broke the fever? Did having her sons home and being visited have an effect on the outcome? Or was it coincidental that the fever broke at that moment?[32]

32. See also John 4:46b-47, 49-53 for another example of a marvelous deed that could be interpreted as coincidence.

It is understood by many persons of faith that there are no coincidences. What others see as coincidence, are, to the eyes of faith, miraculous events. To his followers, this story is about Jesus' miraculous power to heal. Believers were convinced that Jesus had such power. Some persons today believe that such a healing is an example of a paranormal ability. There are many others today who believe that prayers frequently can assist those suffering from disease with recovery. Anecdotes about the power of such prayers are common not only among believers, but among a growing number of healthcare professionals as well.[33]

Cynics however, probably thought Jesus was just lucky. Perhaps he happened to be at the right place at the right time. That has always been the way of the miraculous. Alternative explanations are available. Whether by explanation of coincidence or collusion with Satan, Jesus could be dismissed by those who chose to do so. To those who, like Jesus, believed in the compassion of God, and who knew themselves to be empowered by the indwelling of his Spirit, these events were no accidents. God's love was being demonstrated as the demonic agents of pain and suffering were cast out and defeated. For the eyes of faith, this was a sign that believers were already experiencing the reign of God. Extraordinary healing miracles allowed them to see the everyday miracles that God was working in their mundane lives.

Healing and Forgiveness

The reality of God's love and acceptance into his new realm was also demonstrated by the fact that Jesus connected healing to his role as declarer of the forgiveness of sins available to these social outcasts.

> A few days later, when Jesus again entered Capernaum, the people heard he had come home. So many gathered that there was no room left, not even outside the door, and he preached the word to them. Some men came bringing to him a paralytic, carried by four of them. Since they could not get him to Jesus because of the crowd, they made an opening in the roof above Jesus and, after digging through it, lowered the mat the paralytic was lying on. When Jesus saw their faith, he said to the paralytic, "Son, your sins are forgiven."

33. Dorsey (1997).

Now some teachers of the law were sitting there, thinking to themselves, "Why does this fellow talk like that? He's blaspheming! Who can forgive sins but God alone?"

Immediately Jesus knew in his spirit that this was what they were thinking in their hearts, and he said to them, "Why are you thinking these things? Which is easier to say to the paralytic, 'Your sins are forgiven,' or to say, 'Get up, take your mat and walk'? But that you may know that the Son of Man has authority on earth to forgive sins. . . ." He said to the paralytic, "I tell you, get up, take your mat and go home." He got up, took his mat and walked out in full view of them all. This amazed everyone and they praised God, saying, "We have never seen anything like this." (Mark 2:1-12)

While everyone was amazed at the healing, it is clear that the message Jesus wanted to communicate was the forgiveness of sins. Shamed and blamed, stigmatized by the prevailing belief that his paralysis was caused by his sins, the paralytic needed not only physical healing, but also spiritual healing. He needed to know that all his real or perceived transgressions of the Law, all disobediences to God, were in a word, absolved and wiped clean.

The setting for this healing was Jesus' home in Capernaum. We do not know whether it was actually Jesus' house, or someone else's home, such as Simon Peter's, where Jesus stayed when in town. Word had spread that Jesus was home and people had gathered with excitement to hear him teach. What was he teaching that day? He could have been telling parables about the extravagant compassion of *Abba* and his willingness to give good gifts to his children. He could have been talking about the relationship between man's willingness to forgive others and God's forgiveness. We do not know. But when Jesus looked up and saw that some men had dug through the roof of the home and made a hole large enough to be lowering through it a paralyzed man on his pallet, he was not upset, as some might have been, about the damage to the house. He responded, instead, with appreciation for the determination and faith of the paralyzed man and his helpers. But instead of doing the expected thing and immediately healing the man, Jesus pronounced forgiveness of his sins.

We do not know how old the man was. Since Jesus addressed him affectionately as "son," he may have been a young man with paralysis. Or he, like the paralytic in John's Gospel, could have spent many years on his pallet.[34]

34. John 5:5.

He probably was full grown, as it took four men to assist him. In any case, the use of "son" suggests that Jesus regarded the man with empathy, as he would his own son.

This quality of empathy undoubtedly was critical to the success of Jesus as a healer. Research has shown that the quality of empathy is far more important for obtaining good outcomes in mental health settings than theoretical orientation and training.[35] Did Jesus' empathy and human sensitivity permit him to perceive an inner struggle that lay behind the paralysis? Did he, as many folk healers who enter a town with prior knowledge of their subjects, already have some knowledge of this man? Had he made a prior assessment of the paralytic's spiritual as well as physical condition? Or did he have the ability to "read" a person's eyes, body language, and affect and understand what was going on inside him?

What we do know is that he surprised everyone by pronouncing that the man's sins, his history of straying from and defying God's will, were forgiven. The word for "forgiven" literally means "sent away." Just as demons are cast out and sent packing, so the spiritual presence and power of a lifetime of sins is banished by Jesus' command.

Does Jesus' forgiving word mean that he believed the popular notion that disability was caused by sin? If we are to believe the Gospel of John, Jesus rejected that idea.

> As he went along, he saw a man blind from birth. His disciples asked him, "Rabbi, who sinned, this man or his parents, that he was born blind?"
> "Neither this man nor his parents sinned," said Jesus. (John 9:1-3a)

The notion that disability is punishment for sin appears inconsistent with Jesus' teachings and actions. Both the sun and the rain, whether as benevolent producers of crops, scorching drought, or torrential flood, make no distinction between the just and the unjust. But Jesus surely recognized that the connection between sin and personal suffering was deeply entrenched in people's consciousness. In non-neurological paralysis, a form of conversion disorder, we understand today that there are psychological and spiritual aspects to the symptoms. Did Jesus suspect that the paralytic needed to set aside some terrible burden before healing was possible? Perhaps there was a shameful deed in his past. Or maybe he had been unable to get beyond some

35. Strupp and Hadley (1980).

tragic personal or family secret. Had some traumatic event become an unconscious excuse not to take responsibility for his life and behavior, or an excuse for the lack of courage to deal with his problems and those of his family? Whatever Jesus perceived, he believed that, at least in this particular case, forgiveness was a prerequisite to recovery.

While Jesus' ministry was different in significant ways from that of John the Baptist, his message continued to share with John's this central theme of forgiveness. Forgiveness of sins accomplishes two critical things. First, it restores a person who has become estranged from God, who experiences God as enemy and judge, or as remote and irrelevant, to the intimate relationship of a child and a loving father. Second, it restores a person who has estranged himself from others, because of sin, shame, and guilt, to the human community. While not everyone in the community might be willing to forgive wrongs that have harmed them, the forgiven person has the newly found capacity to make amends and to demonstrate a level of social responsibility that allows the community as a whole socially to reintegrate the individual. This capacity is made possible by the experience that accompanies forgiveness, of liberation from the need to justify past behavior and to perpetuate it into the future. Such social reintegration is also a critical component and result of most folk healing.[36] For Jesus, forgiveness was the gateway to experiencing *Abba's* loving care and the spiritual willingness to turn one's will and life over to him.

Jesus did not simply forgive the paralytic and send him on his way. He commanded the man to rise and pick up his pallet and go home. He was not content with only addressing the man's spiritual needs. He was concerned with the whole person, for he knew that *Abba* in his compassion did not want this man to continue through life with paralysis and the miserable existence of spending his days on a foul pallet.

This is a key to understanding Jesus' relationship with the sick and disabled outcasts. They were not unworthy of the love of God and humankind because they were possessed by demons, nor were they being punished for their sins. They were, instead, God's beloved children, who were victims of powers beyond their control. As human beings, they were also sinners in need of forgiveness. They were people; they were suffering physically and socially, and God wanted to end their suffering. In being willing to see them when they were invisible to others; to touch them when others believed

36. Turner (1967).

them polluted; to speak with them when others ignored them; and to bring healing and forgiveness to them when others heaped blame and shame upon them; he restored them to their humanity and their rightful status as children of *Abba*.

Healings as Windows to the Spirit

As we have said, modern psychiatry understands that non-neurologically based disabilities may be symbolic of underlying psycho-social-spiritual problems. Jesus, too, may have seen these disabilities as signs, or metaphors, of common spiritual problems, not only of the disabled, but of physically whole persons as well.

> Can a blind man lead a blind man? Will they not both fall into a pit? (Luke 6:39b)

> Do you still not see or understand? Are your hearts hardened? Do you have eyes but fail to see, and ears and fail to hear? (Mark 8:17b-18)

From this perspective, the blind may be symbolic of those who cannot see God's true activity in the world, the deaf symbolic of those who shut their ears to God's word, paralytics symbolic of those unable to commit to discipleship. If Jesus understood these conditions as both physical human suffering and spiritual metaphors, then his healings were also signs of God's persistent efforts to break through human resistance to God's invitation to his kingdom. They were signs that God was able to reach out and heal people's spiritual blindness, spiritual deafness, and spiritual paralysis if they were willing to become as children and receive an entirely new orientation.

Jesus urgently desired for those who dismissed his healings, whether as sorcery or coincidence, to be able to "see" them as signs of the presence and power of the Holy Spirit demonstrating *Abba's* compassion; to "hear" the announcement that God's reign was already present and being fulfilled in inclusive joyful association; and to be able to overcome doubt and indecision and decide to follow him.

Jesus was a spirit revolutionary. He did not understand his role as that of a Messiah who would challenge the reigning worldly authorities politically and militarily. He understood himself as a man chosen by God to inau-

gurate a revolution of the spirit, a transformation of the relationship between humans and God and of the relationship of human beings with one
another. Neither did Jesus understand his mission as a folk healer. While a
compassionate healer with extraordinary insight, talent, and willingness to
sacrifice his energies for the sick and disabled, healing was not his vocation.
His entire life was an expending of himself on behalf of others, in order to
invite them to enter the reality of God's reign. Using his God-given gifts to
relieve the suffering of sickness and disability was a dramatic way in which
he could demonstrate *Abba's* compassion for all and the reality of the reign
of God, present and future, in which victory over the demonic powers that
bring suffering to humankind is already present.

Abba loves his children and does not want them to suffer. He is not just
worried about their souls. He is concerned about them as persons, and
therefore about their bodies and minds as well. That is why Jesus offered free
healing to all. *Abba* loves his children, grieves over their spiritual wandering,
their despair that they cannot have life on their own terms, and the evil and
cruelty in their hearts toward others; and he wants them to leave all that behind and participate in the great banquet, the abundant life, he has prepared
for them. That is why Jesus offered free forgiveness to all.

The eyes of Jesus could see the wholeness of those with broken bodies
and the brokenness of those whose bodies were whole. The possibility of
healing was not only available to the sick and disabled; it was available to the
most disreputable of sinful men and women.

CHAPTER IV

Jesus and the Destitute

M ost chronically ill and disabled persons in first-century Galilee were made destitute by their conditions. Unable to support themselves, they were forced to become beggars. In his healing ministry Jesus demonstrated *Abba's* extravagant compassion for these disabled and ritually impure individuals.

The disabled were not, however, the only ones who were recipients of Jesus' ministry of compassion. There were other more able-bodied persons who were also destitute. Like those who were disabled, these desperate individuals had lost most, if not all, ties to their families and home communities. They tended to be homeless wanderers going from one place to another depending on the generosity of those from whom they begged. They stationed themselves at prominent intersections of commerce, along the access routes to the markets, outside the gates of the homes of the wealthy, near the synagogues, and close to the Temple. They usually were filthy, malodorous, and wearing torn and soiled clothing. Their presence was impossible to ignore, though many passersby no doubt pretended to do so.

Rich Man, Poor Man, Beggar Man

Distinctions among gender, age, kinship, ethnicity, nationality, wealth, occupation, and moral character are important in all cultures. Jesus' homeland was no exception. Specific social rules, which defined appropriate behaviors and locations for interactions between persons according to various distinctions, were well understood parts of the social fabric of the time. This was particularly true of the social roles implicit in the economic pecking order. In order to understand Jesus' relationship with those on the bottom rung of the social ladder, it is necessary to visualize the contrast between the life-styles and social realities of the destitute and powerless on the one hand and those of the rich and powerful on the other.

> Jesus sat down opposite the place where the offerings were put and watched the crowd putting their money into the temple treasury. Many rich people threw in large amounts. But a *destitute* widow came and put in two very small copper coins, worth only a fraction of a penny.
>
> Calling his disciples to him, Jesus said, "I tell you the truth, this poor widow has put more into the treasury than all the others. They gave out of their wealth; but she, out of her poverty, put in everything — all she had to live on." (Mark 12:41-44; altered)

Jesus used this incident to contrast the rich aristocrats and the destitute widow.[1] The difference was dramatic. These contributors to the Temple's treasury resided at opposite ends of the social ladder. The aristocrats had great wealth, while the widow had less than she needed for survival. The aristocrats' gifts involved no sacrifice at all; the widow gave everything she had for her own sustenance. It was a contrast revealing a fundamental un-fairness in Jesus' world. His observation was probably at least as much about the fundamental injustice of a religious system that required so little of the rich and so much from the destitute, as it was praise for the woman's sacri-fice and devotion.[2]

Be that as it may, there were two distinct classes of people in Jesus' world, the rich and the poor.[3] Within each of those classes there were two subclasses. Among the rich there were some who were the super rich of their

---

1. The Greek word *ptōchos*, which is usually translated "poor," I have translated as "des-titute." The Greek word for poor was *penēs*. *Ptōchos* was used for beggars and others who lived below the subsistence level. See Neyrey (2002).

2. This passage, like so many of Jesus' sayings, has multiple meanings. While Jesus' words are appropriately interpreted as praise for the woman's sacrifice, and as an example of total devotion, they were also a criticism of the established Temple system (as discussed in chapter VI), along with criticism of the attachment of aristocrats to their wealth (as dis-cussed later in this chapter).

3. I am indebted to Neyrey (2002) and Harland (2002) for a number of points in the following discussion.

day and whose wealth and status far exceeded the wealth of the typically rich. The emperor's family and the kings appointed over various territories became the super rich due to the tribute they received. The wealthy included those descended from aristocrats, those who had managed to acquire large tracts of land, a few highly successful merchants and traders, and the priestly families responsible for the operations of the Temple. There were also two subclasses among the poor. The poor included the working poor, or the peasants, and the extremely poor, or the destitute. The peasants were small landowners who managed to support themselves at a subsistence level; tenants who worked the land of wealthy landowners and paid rent; and a variety of landless workers, including slaves, servants, wage laborers, day laborers, craftsmen, and fishermen. Jesus and his disciples came from this working-poor peasant class.[4] These citizens of Galilee lived at a subsistence level. At the extreme level of poverty were the destitute, an underclass living below a subsistence level, who primarily survived by begging.

A Great Chasm

Nothing similar to our modern middle class existed in Jesus' world. A tremendous social and economic gap separated ordinary poor people and the aristocracy. An even greater gap existed between the very rich and the destitute.

> There was a rich man who was dressed in purple and fine linen and lived in luxury every day. At his gate was laid a beggar named Lazarus, covered with sores and longing to eat what fell from the rich man's table. Even the dogs came and licked his sores.
>
> The time came when the beggar died and the angels carried him to Abraham's side. The rich man also died and was buried. In hell, where he was in torment, he looked up and saw Abraham far away, with Lazarus by his side. So he called to him, "Father Abraham, have pity on me and send Lazarus to dip the tip of his finger in water and cool my tongue, because I am in agony in this fire."

4. While many writers continue to describe Jesus and his family as middle class, they fail to understand that a carpenter, or more appropriately a construction worker or builder, was lower in social rank than a poor farmer (Crossan, 1994). Furthermore, it is entirely inappropriate to speak of a middle class in first-century Galilee. The social space between a poor peasant and a rich aristocrat was a vast and virtually unpopulated distance.

But Abraham replied, "Son, remember that in your lifetime you received your good things, while Lazarus received bad things, but now he is comforted here and you are in agony. And besides all this, between us and you a great chasm has been fixed, so that those who want to go from here to you cannot, nor can anyone cross over from there to us." (Luke 16:19-26)

In this parable of the rich man and Lazarus, the rich man is described as dressed in an outer garment of purple and undergarments of fine linen, clothes that only the wealthiest could afford.[5] This man of wealth lived in constant luxury. In dramatic contrast, lying at the gate of his palace was a beggar named Lazarus whose destitution was accompanied by shamefully unclean sores licked by dogs that were considered unclean animals. Lazarus was so hungry that he gladly would have eaten any crumbs and scraps that fell to the floor from the rich man's table. The parable then describes these two characters in the afterlife. The rich man is tormented by the fires of hell, and longs for a water-cooled finger on his tongue, just as Lazarus had longed to taste a bite of table scraps in his earthly life. And in the afterlife, Lazarus enjoys Paradise with the founding ancestor and recipient of the covenant, Abraham, just as the rich man had enjoyed his pleasurable existence on earth. Between the two is a great chasm that can never be crossed. This chasm of the afterlife mirrors the chasm between the rich man in his earthly paradise and the beggar in his earthly torment. The social distance between these two classes in Jesus' world was so great, and so static, that moving from one to the other was, to most people, unimaginable.

One could sometimes move, however, from being rich to becoming very rich, by shrewd investments and dealings. In the aristocratic agrarian economy of the Galilee ruled by Herod Antipas, the primary social roles of the aristocrats, as in other territories of the Roman Empire, were tax collection, estate oversight, and warfare. Such aristocrats, along with the retainer class

---

5. Lazarus was a common name. Many scholars, however, identify the Lazarus who died in this parable with the Lazarus of John 11:1-44, a name that is also identified with Mary and Martha, names of characters featured in another story in Luke 10:38-42. The Lazarus of this parable, and the Lazarus who was raised, have in common the name, the fact that they died, and the idea that Lazarus might return from the dead. Thus the story of John is seen as an elaboration on and development of the themes of the parable in the context of Jesus' power to raise the dead. It is left to the imagination of those familiar with both stories as to whether Lazarus did then go and speak to the five brothers of the rich man (Luke 16:27-31) about the mortal danger of their wealth.

that managed these functions, made up less than 10 percent of the population.[6] These wealthy citizens competed for the honors associated with the tax system, the accumulation of property, and military status. Filling out the 10 percent on the top rungs of the social ladder was the priestly class, which also lived in relative luxury due to the tithes and offerings that poured into the Temple's treasury from far and wide.[7]

Political appointments were awarded for political loyalty or distinguished military service, or could be purchased through bribery; they generally were followed by an increase in wealth, due to benefits associated with tax collection. Through frugal saving, prudent lending, and exploitation of natural and human resources, the modestly wealthy also could increase their net worth.

Downward movement was more common, however, than upward movement. Wealth could be squandered. A man born rich could descend through poverty to destitution.

> There was a man who had two sons. The younger one said to his father, "Father, give me my share of the estate." So he divided his property between them.
>
> Not long after that, the younger son got together all he had, set off for a distant country and there squandered his wealth in wild living. After he had spent everything, there was a severe famine in that whole country, and he began to be in need. So he went and hired himself out to a citizen of that country, who sent him to his fields to feed pigs. He longed to fill his stomach with the pods that the pigs were eating, but no one gave him anything. (Luke 15:11b-16)

In this parable of the lost son, the young man, like many children of wealth in other times and places, wasted his inheritance on debauchery. His imprudence was highlighted when the country in which he was living it up was stricken by a famine, and he had nothing saved for the emergency. Jesus' Jewish followers understood with amusement the total destitution, shame, and humiliation that the lost son in the parable experienced due to his fool-

6. Neyrey (2002) says that the monarch and aristocratic families made up 1 to 2 percent of the population and the retainer class, including tax collectors, police, scribes, priests, and the like, made up 5 to 7 percent.

7. This was particularly true of the high priest families, who often bought their positions from the Roman procurators in order to reap the benefits. See Achtemeier, "Priests" (1996).

ish debauchery. What could be of greater shame for a formerly wealthy Jewish lad than to become so destitute that he had to work for a non-Jewish foreigner, tend filthy and ritually impure pigs, and become so hungry that he was forced to beg for some of the ritually impure feed intended for those swine?

The lost son's destitution was a direct consequence of his own behavior. Jesus' listeners no doubt believed the son deserved his shame. Poverty conventionally was seen as the natural consequence of a lazy and hedonistic life.[8]

Of course, not all sin leads to destitution and not all destitution is caused by sin. Although Jesus' contemporaries considered destitution as evidence of sin, particularly those who were wealthy and liked to believe that their success was a reward for their virtue, reality was more complicated. Just as sin was not the cause of the blindness of the man born with that disability (John 9:1-3), so there were other destitute people who were not to blame for their misery. Among the destitute were undoubtedly some whose personal choices had brought about their desperate conditions. But many were victims of an exploitive economic system and personal bad fortune.

Debt and Taxes

It was even easier for a poor peasant to descend into destitution than for a rich man to fall. To show up in life poor in first-century Galilee was to find oneself exploited, for the poor had no ability to influence taxation, tenancy, servitude, or lending policies.

It is estimated that, when taxes in all their forms were counted, the tax rate for peasant farmers was equivalent to a third of what they produced.[9] While some peasants owned small tracts of land, many were rent-paying tenant farmers. The products grown by various farmers included wheat, barley, millet, rice, onions, garlic, leeks, squashes, cabbages, radishes, beets, olives, grapes, figs, dates, and beans. Farmers also raised cows, oxen, lambs, and goats, although these were rarely slaughtered for food, but were kept for their by-products and, in the case of oxen, for their labor.[10] Tilling the land with primitive tools and hard physical labor was a life-wearying way to make

8. See Prov. 10:4; 21:17; 13:18.
9. Oakman (1995).
10. Harland (2002).

a living. Even in good years only a small portion of what was produced was available for consumption. In addition to taxes, a portion of the harvest of all farmers had to be set aside for seeding the following year's crops. The Temple in Jerusalem was entitled to a tenth of everything. Landowners claimed their share for rent. The cumulative effects of taxes, trade tolls, rents, and the inevitable occurrence of poor crop years meant that there was little left for the peasant and his family.

Many peasants also lived in a cycle of increasing debt accompanied by usurious interest, and had no hope of ever paying off the loans.[11] Those who owned small family farms passed down to them by previous generations frequently became landless because of their debt. It was from these landless peasants that not only tenant farmers and day laborers came, but the skilled craftsmen emerged. A weaver, who previously had made cloth for the use of his farming family, now did so for others in order to eke out a living.[12] It is quite conceivable that Jesus' father or grandfather had lost the family land as a result of indebtedness, and was forced to take up the trade of builder instead. Be that as it may, indebtedness was a huge problem for the peasant population. It could and often did lead to destitution.

There were also many widows and other single women who lived below the poverty line of the day. Since the Torah was interpreted to allow a man to divorce a woman for any reason, some of these single females were essentially abandoned women who had been divorced by husbands who had grown tired of them. Still others among the destitute were victims of natural and personal disasters. Thus, while there were some like the lost son, whose own folly brought about his destitution, many of the destitute were victims of exploitation, illness, disability, widowhood, divorce, and other misfortunes.

"How Deserving of Honor are the Destitute"

What, then, was Jesus' relationship to the destitute? It was one of profound respect.

---

11. While usury was forbidden by the Torah (in fact, charging any interest at all was prohibited), it was common practice.

12. The craftsmen likely were lower on the economic ladder than tenant farmers, but probably slightly higher than the day laborers. See Crossan (1994).

How deserving of honor are the destitute, for God's kingdom belongs to you. (Luke 6:20; altered)

How deserving of honor are you who hunger now, for you will be satisfied. How deserving of honor are you who weep now, for you will laugh. (Luke 6:21; altered)

How deserving of honor are you when men hate you, when they exclude you and disparage you. (Luke 6:22a; altered)

Jesus did not say that the "poor" are "blessed" as most English translations indicate. He said that the "destitute," those with nothing and reduced to beggary, are "deserving of honor."[13] Because they are destitute, they are also hungry and perpetually sad. And because they dwell at the bottom of the social ladder, unclean "nobodies," total outcasts, they are victims of hatred, discrimination, and shameful insults.[14] At the top of the social pyramid of the times was the extravagantly wealthy emperor of Rome, to whom belonged such honor that he was considered by many of his loyal subjects (though not by the monotheistic Judeans) to be a god. At the bottom of the social pyramid were the destitute, who were so low they were regarded as less than human. Slaves, servants, peasant farmers, laborers, and craftsmen were poor, and considered inferior by the elite. They had to work hard, suffer indignity, and seldom were able to accumulate even a small amount of savings. But they preserved some honor, despite their lack of means, if they could remain self-supporting and deal honestly with their peers. The destitute had

13. As Crossan (1991) has pointed out, there was a tendency early on, as illustrated by Matthew's change to the destitute "in spirit," to attenuate the radical nature of this blessing. Hanson (1996) has argued persuasively for a translation that clarifies that these makarisms (honor statements usually referred to as beatitudes) are common literary devices of the region expressing social values in the form of declarations of honor. They are the opposite of declarations of rebuke and shame, which also are common. Hanson points out that the beatitudes of Matthew 5 and the woes of Matthew 23 are literary brackets around the ministry of Jesus. The honor statements in Matthew 5 are counterbalanced by the shame statements in Matthew 23. The intensity of the preoccupation with matters of honor and shame is difficult for the modern Westerner adequately to appreciate.

14. The text of Luke 6:22b, which associates this blessing with those who are persecuted for the name (Christian), was an application of these words to the experience of early Christian persecution. As spoken by Jesus the three blessings in Luke 6:20-21 are all addressed to the same destitute and despised outcasts at the extreme bottom of the social pyramid.

nothing, except distress, misery, and dependence on the generosity of others.[15] They had nothing, that is, except shame.

Jesus, then, said that the destitute, the dregs of society, who were despised and looked down upon by everyone else, including the poor, and who were perpetually hungry and sad, were the recipients of *Abba's* favor. As such, they did not deserve the shame that was projected upon them by others, but were entitled to honor and respect instead.

Honor and Shame

In order to understand Jesus' remarkable words bestowing honor on the destitute it is important to understand their cultural context. Anthropologists have identified the tension between honor and shame as a cultural motif and preoccupation among all Mediterranean societies, including Israel, across time and space.[16] Honor is the esteem that others bestow upon one for a feeling of importance and worth. One may have or gain honor because of birth, inheritance of wealth, success in accumulating riches, military valor, athletic victory, occupational achievement, or reputation for ethical or religious superiority, as well as through a variety of other means depending on the context. Shame is associated with the lack of or loss of honor. Honor and shame operate within the notion of limited good. Limited good is the idea that there are not enough good things to go around, so that one can increase the good for oneself only at the expense of others. Honor is therefore assumed to exist in limited quantity. In Jesus' world, honor was a greatly desired treasure in very limited supply.

In Mediterranean societies, shame and honor have struggled with each other for many centuries, on both personal and national levels, in the context of constant conflict. The desire to protect or seize honor frequently has involved persons in lying, deceit, and treachery. The patriarchal stories in Genesis are filled with examples of such struggles.[17] The higher one's honor, the

15. Aristophanes in approximately 388 BCE contrasted poverty and beggary in his final comedy, *Plutus*. Poverty "has to scrape and to screw" but "will in nothing be lacking." The beggar "alone has naught of his own."

16. Pitt-Rivers (1966); Foster (1972); Peristiany (1965). I am also indebted to Hagedorn and Neyrey (1998); Hanson (1996) and (1997); Neyrey (1999); and Malina (2001) for the discussion of honor and shame that follows.

17. Cain and Abel; Jacob and Esau; Joseph and his brothers; Dinah and the Shechemites are only a few examples.

more at risk is the life. A saying within the region is that lightning strikes the highest mountain and the tallest tree.[18] Those at the top are in danger of being toppled and shamed by either those below or by the fates or gods. Those who are higher on the ladder of honor must scheme constantly so as not to be replaced by those below and at the same time they must be careful not to offend the gods. Social structures are designed and established through the exercise of wealth and power to protect the interests of the haves and to fend off the threat of the have-nots. These social structures place a crushing weight upon those who are at the bottom of the social pecking order.

Blessing and Curse

Along with the culture of peril and refuge, of perpetual conflict and a pervasive struggle between honor and shame, "blessing and curse" are also symbolic themes in the world of the Middle East, both modern and ancient.[19] Words, particularly those that are formulated as pronouncements of blessing or curse delivered by one in authority, are considered to have powers of their own. They are often seen as efficacious even when the evidence suggests otherwise.[20] Once delivered, such words cannot be revoked any more than a person throwing a rock can interrupt its flight while it is hurtling toward its target. However, their effects may sometimes be attenuated and ultimately annulled through divine intervention. That is why ritual and prayer are particularly important when a curse is believed to exist. It is taken for granted that words uttered by one with appropriate authority can have the power to heal or to kill. Promises are particularly powerful and it is shameful to break them.

18. Horace's *Ode* 2.10.1-12 uses the image "tis the tops of mountains that the lightning strikes" as an argument for practicing the "golden mean." See also, for example, Aeschylus, *Agamemnon* 456-58 and Herodotus 7.10.

19. Hanson (1996).

20. During the invasion of Iraq in 2003, Westerners were amused and confounded by the optimistic reports of the Iraqi information minister that bore no resemblance to the reports of the Western press concerning the progress of the war. An almost identical scenario was played out by Radio Cairo during the Egyptian-Israeli war decades earlier. Westerners are prone to dismiss this phenomenon as the product of an inept propaganda effort. But when it is examined within the framework of the cultural phenomenon of "words of power," the reports, while deceitful, are seen as attempts to maintain honor in the midst of shame and to influence the outcome, not so much militarily as in terms of preserving honor.

In many ways the Torah's theme was that of blessing and curse amidst Yahweh's faithful promises and Israel's unfaithfulness. The blessing of the "good" creation, followed by sin, resulting in curse, was played out again and again. From the blessing of the garden, man and woman were evicted. The earth was polluted by sin, but then was washed clean by the flood; a rainbow was given as a sign of the promise that such a great flood would not happen again. Abraham was promised that his descendants would be a great nation, yet they became slaves in Egypt. Escaping from Egypt with divine assistance and promised a land flowing with milk and honey, they spent forty years wandering in the desert. Finally given victory in the conquest of Canaan, and the establishment of a great nation, they were overrun and exiled. Again and again, the promise of blessing is realized, followed by sin, and then by the effects of the curse for the sinning.

The destitute in Jesus' day were considered by most people to be suffering because of Yahweh's curse. This curse was because of sin, their own, their parents', or their ancestors'. In a culture that highly prized honor, and generally feared shame more than death, those who were destitute were shamed by all.[21] This shame was generally internalized, as all such shame tends to be, as self-loathing and guilt, regardless of whether the shamed one bore any personal responsibility for his or her circumstances.

What usually are seen as statements of blessing by Jesus upon the poor, the hungry, and the sad, are in fact words of power from "one who speaks with authority" declaring the destitute not only shameless, but deserving of honor.[22] The destitute are deserving of honor because they are human be-

---

21. See Prov. 14:20; 19:12.

22. Hanson (1996) argues, on linguistic and usage grounds, that makarisms (beatitudes) are not "words of power," as blessings and curses spoken as words of power are usually from an authority figure, a king, priest, or father, and unlike words of power, are in the form of a challenge and response dialogue. Makarisms may be spoken by anyone and generally state conventional social values of what is honorable and what is shameful. While I would agree that makarisms are different from and not as powerful as formal and ritualized blessings and curses from the mouths of authority figures in Middle Eastern culture, I would argue that less formal stylized makarisms, when spoken by "one who speaks with authority," are nevertheless words of power. In other words, there are differing levels of power in words, but all words have power. This is also true in our own culture to some degree, as words of an authority on a particular subject illustrate, but it is of particular significance in the Middle East, where all words bear great weight as social currency. Makarisms from the mouth of a great healer and teacher carry considerable weight, and when they challenge conventional wisdom, they have great power to evoke change. The outcome of such

ings who are recipients of God's compassion. The hungry are deserving of honor because they have already been invited to the great Messianic banquet where they will have the best seats. Those who weep are deserving of honor for they are promised "this too shall pass." A time of honor, great feasting, joy, healing, and vindication for those who have suffered has already begun and soon will be fully realized.

The destitute are not the recipients of Yahweh's curse; they are the recipients of Yahweh's compassion. This is the good news that Jesus preaches to the destitute. It is this good news to the destitute that is one of the signs that Yahweh's reign already has begun.[23]

> The Spirit of the Lord is on me, because he has anointed me to preach good news to the *destitute*. (Luke 4:18a; altered)

Because so many chronically ill and disabled are also destitute, the ministry of preaching to the destitute is one with that of healing the sick. Both activities are to announce and demonstrate the awesome compassion of *Abba*. This mission of compassion is manifested in Jesus' declaration that the long-expected realm of Yahweh is in fact a radical reordering and transformation of the present manifestations of honor and shame, a new order that is already in progress. Jesus does not call into question honor and shame as categories of meaning. Instead, he uses them as a dramatic challenge to his hearers to reorient their understanding of reality.

By appealing to the honor of Yahweh, the God of all creation who is so Holy that his Name is not to be spoken, Jesus calls upon his hearers radically to change their ideas of who is deserving of honor. Almost everyone took for granted that wealth and power were synonymous with honor. But only Yahweh can rightfully bestow honor. Yahweh chooses to hear the cry of the destitute, the disabled, the hungry, the depressed, to receive them as his children, and to declare that he is their *Abba*. He loves them, cares about them, and has prepared a place of honor for them at his heavenly banquet. All who hear this message are called upon to "be compassionate as *Abba* is compassionate." If those who hear Jesus' message of compassion enter this new orientation, they too are deserving of honor.

---

makarisms is not that of material change, as in a blessing for prosperity, but a psychosocial change from a position and self-understanding of shame to that of honor.

23. Luke 7:22-23.

Charity and Compassion

Honoring the destitute is a far more radical notion than giving gifts to the needy. Certainly the idea that Yahweh expects charity for the extremely poor did not originate with Jesus. Despite the shame associated with being destitute, there was an ancient tradition in Israel that charity toward the poor was a way of achieving honor while neglect of the poor was shameful.[24]

The Ideal of Charity

Charity for the poor as an ideal was rooted in the experience of Egyptian slavery and wilderness wandering, and the realization that God had provided out of his bounty for the destitute Israelites by leading them into "a land flowing with milk and honey."[25] Thus Yahweh required that the poor be given assistance as a requirement of the covenant. The prophets rebuked the nations of Judah and Israel for their neglect and exploitation of the needy.

> The Lord enters his judgment against the elders and leaders of his
>   people:
> "It is you who have ruined my vineyard; the plunder from the poor is
>   in your houses.
> What do you mean by crushing my people and grinding the faces of
>   the poor?" declares the Lord. (Isa. 3:14-15)

> They sell the righteous for silver, and the needy for a pair of sandals.
> They trample the heads of the poor as upon dust of the ground and
>   deny justice to the oppressed. (Amos 2:6b-7a)

The Torah provided for relief of the poor by requiring that every seventh year the land be left unplowed and unused so that the poor could benefit from whatever grew upon it that season (Exod. 23:11). During the other years farmers were not to harvest the very edges of the fields or harvest a second time so that the poor would be able to glean (Lev. 19:9-10). The debts of the poor were to be cancelled during the seventh year as well (Deut. 15:1-2).

24. See Prov. 14:21; 14:31; 28:27.
25. See Pss. 68:5; 68:10.

These requirements of charity for the poor, while widely ignored and neglected, were the taken-for-granted moral requirements in Jesus' day. When Jesus and his disciples gleaned ears of grain on their journeys, as men of poverty they were not rebuked for stealing (Mark 2:23). They were exercising their right as those living a life of poverty under the Law. The rebuke came for violating the Sabbath.

While the poor were often exploited and oppressed throughout the history of the Israelites, it was understood that such behavior was wrong and a violation of Yahweh's requirement to treat the poor with justice. The great prophets fervently had condemned those guilty of burdening the poor.

Compassion and Forgiveness

Jesus, however, went even further. He believed that an empathetic response to the neediest of neighbors was key to the very nature of *Abba* and his judgment of humankind.

> Then the King will say to those on his right, "Come you who are blessed by my Father; take your inheritance, the kingdom prepared for you since the creation of the world. For I was hungry and you gave me something to eat, I was thirsty and you gave me something to drink, I was a stranger and you invited me in. I needed clothes and you clothed me, I was sick and you looked after me, I was in prison and you came to visit me."
>
> Then the righteous will answer him, "Lord, when did we see you hungry and feed you, or thirsty and give you something to drink? When did we see you a stranger and invite you in, or needing clothes and clothe you? When did we see you sick or in prison and go to visit you?"
>
> The King will reply, "I tell you the truth, whatever you did for one of the least of these brothers of mine, you did for me." (Matt. 25:34-40)

The relationship between those who are to receive honor in the kingdom of God and those in great need presented in this parable is that of empathy. It is loving-kindness for those whom God honors with his loving-kindness. To treat the destitute with respect and dignity by responding in compassion to their need was to honor God.

The surprise of the compassionate ones at being so honored is also an important part of the parable. Responding in compassion to a needy neighbor was not to be done as a public act of charity, but, quietly, without fanfare, and without the desire for recognition.

> Be careful not to do your "acts of righteousness" before men, to be seen by them. If you do, you will have no reward from your Father in heaven.
>
> So when you give to the needy, do not announce it with trumpets, as the hypocrites do in the synagogues and on the streets, to be honored by men. I tell you the truth, they have their reward in full. But when you give to the needy, do not let your left hand know what your right hand is doing, so that your giving may be in secret. Then your Father, who sees what is done in secret, will reward you. (Matt. 6:1-4)

Giving to the needy is not about the need of the giver to feel good about himself or herself or superior to the recipient or others who might not give as generously. It is about treating one's needy neighbor with empathy, dignity, and respect as one would want to be treated if in similar circumstances.

Likewise, in the realm of God, where *Abba* is in charge, debts are to be forgiven, for his children are to treat each other as they have been treated by him.

> Therefore the kingdom of heaven is like a king who wanted to settle accounts with his servants. As he began the settlement, a man who owed him ten thousand talents was brought to him. Since he was not able to pay, the master ordered that he and his wife and his children and all that he had be sold to repay the debt.
>
> The servant fell on his knees before him. "Be patient with me," he begged, "and I will pay back everything." The servant's master took pity on him, canceled the debt and let him go.
>
> But when the servant went out, he found one of his fellow servants who owed him a hundred denarii. He grabbed him and began to choke him. "Pay back what you owe me!" he demanded.
>
> His fellow servant fell to his knees and begged him, "Be patient with me, and I will pay you back."
>
> But he refused. Instead, he went off and had the man thrown into prison until he could pay the debt. When the other servants saw what had happened, they were greatly distressed and went and told their master everything that had happened.
>
> The master called the servant in. "You wicked servant," he said, "I cancelled all that debt of yours because you begged me to. Shouldn't you

have had mercy on your fellow servant just as I had on you?" In anger his master turned him over to the jailers to be tortured, until he should pay back all he owed. (Matt. 18:23-34)

Debt was symbolic of the entrenched system of exploitation of the poor by the wealthy. The inability to pay back debts accounted for the descent of many of the poor into destitution. Forgiveness of the debts of a debtor who asked for more time to pay was an act of great compassion. It is unlikely that it happened very often. Its significance can only be appreciated in the light of the natural attachment to money and affluence characteristic of the rich.

A certain ruler asked him, "Good teacher, what must I do to inherit eternal life?"

"Why do you call me good?" Jesus answered. "No one is good — except God alone. You know the commandments: 'Do not commit adultery, do not murder, do not steal, do not give false testimony, honor your father and mother.'"

"All these I have kept since I was a boy," he said.

When Jesus heard this, he said to him, "You still lack one thing. Sell everything you have and give to the *destitute,* and you will have treasure in heaven. Then come, follow me."

When he heard this he became very sad, because he was a man of great wealth. (Luke 18:18-23; altered)

Jesus looked around and said to his disciples, "How hard it is for the rich to enter the Kingdom of God!"

The disciples were amazed at his words, but Jesus said again, "Children, how hard it is to enter the Kingdom of God! It is easier for a *big rope* to go through the eye of a needle than for a rich man to enter the kingdom of God."

The disciples were even more amazed, and said to each other, "Who then can be saved?"

Jesus looked at them and said, "With man this is impossible, but not with God; all things are possible with God." (Mark 10:23-27; altered)[26]

26. While most translations say "camel," literally translating the Greek *kamēlos,* it seems more likely that in the Aramaic *gamla,* which can mean either camel or a particular kind of rope, the allusion referred to the name of a big rope likely made of camel's hair. This type of rope probably was used, among other purposes, to tie large boats to docks. It would have been laughable for someone to attempt to thread one of these massive ropes through the eye

Jesus understood the wealthy to be at a substantial disadvantage when it came to Yahweh's kingdom. Their attachment to possessions and an affluent lifestyle was a stumbling block. That was particularly true of aristocrats who took advantage of the poor by foreclosing on their property when debts were not paid in a timely manner. Even when not overtly participating in such seizing of assets, those who enjoyed their treasures in this life participated passively in perpetuating the desperate conditions of the destitute. In a world of limited good, Jesus believed God's honor to be offended because some of his children lived in luxury while others were reduced to malnutrition and homelessness. In order to receive the blessings of the new age, one had to be willing to forgo the privileges of wealth in this world, be compassionate toward and generous with the needy, and, if unable to achieve detachment from worldly goods and empathy for the destitute while affluent, then be willing to divest oneself of wealth and become destitute as well.[27]

The Advantage of Having Nothing

In this world, the rich hold an overwhelming advantage over the destitute. In the realm of God, the world of the Spirit, the destitute hold an overwhelming advantage over the rich.

> The one who received the seed that fell among thorns is the man who hears the word, but the worries of this life and the deceitfulness of wealth choke it, making it unfruitful. (Matt. 13:22)[28]

---

of a needle used by fishermen in mending their nets. It would have been so impossible as to be ludicrous. See Lamsa (1940, xxiv and note on Matt. 19:24). While this translation generally has been ignored or rejected by textual experts, I am persuaded by the contextual significance of this saying for fishermen and the natural logic of the analogy, as well as by the linguistic possibility. This translation in no way waters down the "impossibility" point that Jesus made along with his assertion to the disciples that with God all things are possible.

27. While Jesus required the rich man to give up all he had, it is clear that not every one of means was required to make such a radical sacrifice. There were women who supported his movement out of the wealth of their aristocratic positions. Zacchaeus gave away half, not all, of his acquired wealth. Johnson (1981) has argued that Luke-Acts has different models for sharing based on the individual's slavery to his or her own possessions.

28. While the interpretation of the parable of the seeds probably is a later redaction, it is possible that Jesus used the parable more than once, and explained it on one or more oc-

Wealth is deceitful and places those who have it at a disadvantage when it comes to responding to Jesus' message about the kingdom. Wealth has a way of becoming one's master.

> No one can serve two masters. Either he will hate the one and love the other, or he will be devoted to the one and despise the other. You cannot serve both God and money. (Matt. 6:24)

One whose life is caught up in acquiring, enjoying, and keeping wealth and the material things it provides is seriously disabled when it comes to participating in a spiritual and status-free kingdom. In fact, as the stories of the rich man and Lazarus and the rich fool suggest, such a lifestyle is not only a handicap; it places one in mortal danger.

In contrast, the ability of the destitute to empathize with and be compassionate toward their suffering brothers and to experience God's care for themselves and others is unhindered by attachments to the things of this world. Leaving everything to participate in the ministry of Jesus was also much less of a problem for those who had nothing to begin with than it was for wealthy would-be followers.

In Jesus' parable of the lost son, the son "hits bottom" and comes to his senses. In order to perceive the world as *Abba* perceives it, there is an advantage, though no guarantee, for those who have "hit bottom." This is true whether one is destitute because of one's debauchery and foolishness or is the innocent victim of circumstances beyond one's control. When one no longer has anything to lose and all pride and pretensions have been stripped away, then the pathway to surrender to the care and will of God is a far greater possibility than when one has reason to be proud and self-satisfied.

Just as disabilities symbolized the spiritual handicaps of the able-bodied, so destitution symbolized the spiritual impoverishment of those whose worldly attachments prevented them from entering God's realm.

---

casions in a similar fashion. At any rate, the symbolism of the thorns as placing those who have wealth at a disadvantage in receiving Jesus' message is an interpretation consistent with his overall message concerning the rich.

Breaking the Cycle of Retribution

Debt also had symbolic as well as literal significance. Debt symbolized sin. The indebtedness of the poor being driven toward destitution was symbolic of unrepented sin driving the proud toward hardness of heart.

In the context of a cultural preoccupation with honor and shame, when one person wronged another, the victim's honor was diminished and a social debt was created. Retaliation was considered obligatory in order to reestablish one's own honor. Retaliation created a new victim and a reciprocal obligation for revenge. In the lands surrounding the Mediterranean, families, tribes, ethnic groups, and nations have perpetuated feuds of honor and shame for generations. When a person's, or group's, honor has been diminished by another, it creates a social debt, a debt that has to be repaid if honor is to be reestablished. Thus, according to the social obligations of Jesus' world, if someone struck another on the right cheek, an act of disrespect as well as physical harm, then one was obligated to strike back in kind.[29] This system of reciprocity codified in the Torah was as old as the Code of Hammurabi and had its parallels in Roman law as well.[30]

The assumption that a wrong created a social debt was also applied to wrongs committed against Yahweh. Sins against God required payment. This generally occurred through sin offerings and temple sacrifices, most often during the prescribed festivals. But Jesus' message was that God's merciful compassion would abolish the "debt" incurred by sin. Such free and broker-less absolution, however, carried with it obligation. The forgiven were required to forgive others. An outward sign of this could be the forgiveness of any monetary debt. But the parable of the debtor, who would not forgive debt, was less about money than it was about honor and shame. The servant dishonored his master when he failed to imitate the generosity of his master in relation to another servant. The master was forced to recover his honor by punishing the ungrateful servant. The intent of the parable was to underscore that forgiveness from Yahweh requires that Yahweh be honored by the replication of his compassion. The requirement was not simply related to monetary matters; it was the demand to break the cycle of retaliation

29. Lev. 24:19-20.

30. Exact reciprocity, however, only existed among social equals in these legal systems. For example, if a slave or servant suffered the loss of an eye by the hand of his master, then the master was required to set him free (Exod. 21:26). The master was allowed to keep his own eye.

and revenge by forgiving wrongs to self that were committed by others, including those associated with humiliation and shame.

> You have heard that it was said, "Eye for eye, and tooth for tooth." But I tell you, Do not resist an evil person. If someone strikes you on the right cheek, turn to him the other also. And if someone wants to sue you and take your tunic, let him have your cloak as well. If someone forces you to go one mile, go with him two miles. Give to the one who asks you, and do not turn away from the one who wants to borrow from you. (Matt. 5:38-42)

Not only were Jesus' followers to break the cycle of retaliation, they were to share their resources with those who asked and to lend to those who needed to borrow. If a needy person asked to borrow money, it was to be loaned without interest and without concern for whether it should be repaid.[31] Radical charity was required of those who had great possessions. In the context of honor and shame, sharing wealth with the destitute and extending forgiveness toward those who had wronged and offended, were dramatic expressions that radically undercut the established meanings of honor and shame. Both actions were recognition and acceptance of the humanity, dignity, and honor in the eyes of God of those the world believed were deserving of disrespect, maltreatment, and shame. For Jesus, justice and compassion for the destitute was not so much a matter of social obligation, as a matter of social and human value.

Not by Bread Alone

Within the context of human value, however, there could be legitimate uses of wealth other than sharing with the poor.

> While he was in Bethany, reclining at the table in the home of a man known as Simon the Leper, a woman came with an alabaster jar of very expensive perfume, made of pure nard. She broke the jar and poured the perfume on his head.

---

31. The Torah (Exod. 22:25; Deut. 23:20; Lev. 25:35-38) forbade charging interest for loans. This prohibition was widely ignored (Prov. 28:8; Ezek. 18:8; Matt. 25:27; Luke 19:23). The Gospel of Thomas 95 probably recalls a genuine saying of Jesus, "If you have money, don't lend it at interest."

Some of those present were saying indignantly to one another, "Why this waste of perfume? It could have been sold for more than a year's wages and the money given to the destitute." And they rebuked her harshly.

"Leave her alone," said Jesus. "Why are you bothering her? She has done a beautiful thing to me. The *destitute* you will always have with you, and you can help them any time you want. But you will not always have me. She poured perfume on my body beforehand to prepare for my burial. I tell you the truth, wherever the gospel is preached throughout the world, what she has done will also be told, in memory of her." (Mark 14:3-9; altered)

While those present rebuked and shamed the woman for her extraordinary waste of wealth that could have been used to assist the destitute, Jesus praised her for her extravagant gesture of honor to him, an anointing that Mark reports Jesus interpreted as preparation for his destined burial.

Jesus' praise for this extravagant symbolic act is only understood if one grasps that Jesus did not see his mission in terms of redistribution of wealth. He was a spirit revolutionary who saw his mission as transforming the human spirit in its relationships between God and neighbor, and neighbor and neighbor. Just as the destitute are deserving of honor, so this woman deserved to be honored, for in her honoring of Jesus, she anointed the one who proclaimed and demonstrated the extravagant compassion of God.

Jesus' mission was the reorientation of society on earth, in anticipation of the age to come, consistent with the compassionate will of *Abba*. Responding to the needs of the destitute is analogous to healing the sick. The bodies of the needy are not neglected in a pious desire to save their souls. It is important to feed the hungry, but not as a charitable act meant to impress others with how righteous one is. Feeding the hungry is not just about food.

The devil said to him, "If you are the Son of God, tell this stone to become bread."

Jesus answered. "It is written: 'Man does not live on bread alone.'" (Luke 4:3-4)

People need bread to live, but feeding them is only part of ministering to their needs. Those whom God honors are those whose response to the needs of their neighbors is an outward indication of recognizing the humanity, dignity, and honor in the eyes of *Abba* of those on the receiving end. The destitute are *Abba*'s beloved children. Jesus' relationship to the destitute bestowed human dignity in the forms of food, forgiveness, and the declaration that they were favored by *Abba* and therefore deserving of honor.

Jesus' relationship with the destitute goes far beyond charity. Those who live in the shame of destitution are to be treated with the same respect, dignity, and honor as family or wealthy friends.

> When you give a luncheon or dinner, do not invite your friends, your brothers or relatives, or your rich neighbors; if you do, they may invite you back and so you will be repaid. But when you give a banquet, invite the destitute, the crippled, the lame, the blind, and you will be blessed. (Luke 14:12b-14a)

The destitute are to be invited into one's home and treated as honored guests. It is in the social intimacy of breaking bread and sharing a meal together at the same table that one honors the destitute as *Abba* will honor them at the great Messianic banquet. Just as the cycle of negative social reciprocity is broken through forgiveness, so also entertaining the destitute breaks the positive but self-serving cycle of obligations created by commensality, the social sharing of food.

By honoring the destitute in one's home and sharing one's resources in social intimacy, the status-free and compassionate realm of God is demonstrated. The outsiders become insiders and the barriers that separate the two are destroyed. Archaic patterns of honor and shame that maintain division, discord, oppression, and discrimination are overcome. The breaking of bread symbolizes the brokenness of human social divisions, and eating the bread symbolizes the healing of that brokenness. This is the radical vision of Jesus. It is a vision that is subversive of the entire social fabric that depends upon distinctions of wealth as honor and poverty as shame.

But beyond the material aspects of this way of viewing existence are the spiritual realities. The hunger in the bellies of the destitute is symbolic of the hunger in the souls of all those searching for a right relationship with God and neighbor. Breaking bread with the destitute is symbolic of the spiritual community that occurs when those who have opened their hearts to *Abba*'s compassion come together. It is a foretaste of the heavenly banquet in the world to come. This heavenly banquet is not only prepared for the disabled and destitute, but also for the despised — hated tax collectors, prostitutes, half-breeds, and foreigners.

CHAPTER V

Jesus and the Despised

The disabled and the destitute in first-century Galilee were the victims of prejudice, discrimination, and scorn. They were avoided, marginalized, neglected, and made to feel useless. Peasants were also victims of discrimination by wealthy citizens and devout Jews. Many "people of the land" were too burdened by daily cares and unschooled in the Torah to be ritually and religiously compliant.[1] The devout considered the majority of peasants to be ritually impure and looked down upon them as ignorant and unworthy. If a nonobservant peasant came in contact with a devout Jew, or touched any part of his clothing or personal property, ritual cleansing was required.

In spite of the unkindness and humiliating nature of this kind of social ostracizing, these persons on the bottom rungs of the social ladder were seldom hated by their neighbors just because they were considered unclean. There were some people, however, who were almost always despised by both devout Jews and peasants. These included tax collectors, prostitutes, Samaritans, and foreigners.

1. The 'am ha'aretz is a term used in the Hebrew Bible for ordinary citizens, generally the peasant class. In rabbinic literature it was used for both the unlearned and otherwise noncompliant Jew. In the *Babylonian Talmud: Tractate Tohoroth* (oral rabbinic traditions collected and composed approximately 200 CE), noncompliant Jews were considered unclean, as was anything touched by them. In the Greek New Testament *ochlos* is used for a crowd of common people, but also could connote contempt for the ignorant multitude. The Greek adjective *hamartōlos* is generally translated "sinner" and can mean "ritually unclean," but most often refers to persons guilty of wickedness and stained by certain immoral behaviors. It literally means "missing the mark." Tax collectors and prostitutes are described as *hamartōloi*.

A Friend of Tax Collectors

Tax collectors were thought to be particularly despicable. The tax collection system in the Roman Empire of the first century was designed to assure maximum compliance. In the regions ruled by Pontius Pilate and Herod Antipas the responsibility for collecting taxes from residents usually lay with wealthy and politically connected Gentiles.[2] They were responsible for the head tax, the land tax, requisitions for support of the occupying forces, and tolls on goods brought to market. Fishermen, such as Simon and Andrew, paid a tax to have the privilege of fishing in one area of the Sea of Galilee, they paid toll taxes at collection points along the road to market, and when they sold their catch they paid a "sales tax." Tax collectors were personally responsible for paying the government. They were allowed under the system to collect more than they were responsible for paying and to keep the "profit," a system that led to widespread abuse.

The Despised Profession

Aristocratic "tax farmers" did not dirty their hands with the actual work of assessing and collecting, but employed local people to do it for them. They would purposely hire persons who were cruel and merciless. The local tax collectors would sometimes in turn hire other disreputable people to assist them. Tax collectors, at every level, were notoriously corrupt and known for their ability to find ways to collect more than was owed the government. As they were allowed to keep any excess amounts, many became quite wealthy. These local collectors were usually literate, kept detailed tax records, and were ruthless in pursuing unpaid claims.

The first-century Jewish philosopher Philo described the public's perception of tax collectors as "enemies and destroyers."[3] Some of that feeling no doubt was due to the resentment that has been present toward taxation throughout history, a resentment that was intensified in this case by the fact that a despised foreign government was responsible for relieving the people of their hard-earned resources. The common folk saw little public benefit

2. I am indebted to Hanson (1997) and Neyrey (2002) for a number of points in this discussion.

3. Philo, *Special Laws* 1.143.

from their taxes; rather, they were painfully aware that their hard-earned resources were allowing tax collectors to live in luxury. But hatred toward tax collectors was made even worse by the unscrupulous dishonesty and cruelty of the methods by which these despised persons extorted payment from the people. Philo tells a disturbing story of a tax collector who chased down those who got behind in their payments, threatened their families, and publicly tortured them when they were unable to pay.[4] It is no wonder that Jesus' contemporaries despised tax collectors.

When tax collectors came to John the Baptist in the wilderness near the Jordan, he exhorted them to stop collecting more than the required amount. John challenged them to change their ways. Jesus went even further in his dealings with these despised persons.

> Now *this human being* came eating and drinking, and you say, "Here is a glutton and a drunkard, a friend of tax collectors and sinners." (Luke 7:34; altered)

Obviously, hanging out with despised tax collectors was not a way to become popular. But Jesus did not challenge those who accused him of being a friend of these despicable people. He appears to have accepted the idea as a badge of honor.

> As he walked along, he saw Levi son of Alphaeus sitting at the tax collector's booth. "Follow me," Jesus told him, and Levi got up and followed him.
>
> While Jesus was having dinner at Levi's house, many tax collectors and "sinners" were eating with him and his disciples, for there were many who followed him.
>
> When the teachers of the law who were Pharisees saw him eating with the "sinners" and tax collectors, they asked his disciples: "Why does he eat with tax collectors and 'sinners'?"
>
> On hearing this, Jesus said to them, "It is not the healthy who need a doctor, but the sick. I have not come to call the righteous, but sinners." (Mark 2:14-17)

Jesus not only went to Levi's house for dinner, but we are told that there were many tax collectors and other transgressors present. Although Levi evi-

---

4. Philo, *Special Laws* 3.30.159-63.

dently became a disciple, one can presume that Jesus was eating with several such disreputable characters who never did change their ways.[5] Jesus clearly recognized tax collectors as unrighteous men devoted to their corrupt lives. These were not simply nonobservant Jews who were decent but they were ritually unclean persons. The tax collectors were guilty of both disobedience to the Law of Yahweh and cruelty toward Yahweh's children. They were not simply guilty of sin; they were agents of evil.[6] They were not only local representatives of the hated imperial occupying forces, draining desperately needed material resources for the benefit of the luxurious lives of foreigners; they were traitors to their Jewish heritage and their created humanity, exploiting fellow countrymen to feed their own greed.

In the worldview of Jesus' time, when people were subjected to great suffering, they were said to experience evil. Satan was the evil one, because he was the chief spirit who ruled over the demons that wreaked havoc and caused suffering upon the earth.[7] Likewise, an evil person was one who inflicted cruelty and suffering on others. This does not mean that such persons were incapable of kindness. Evil persons usually have been kind to friends and family.

> For if you love those who love you, what reward will you get? Are not even the tax collectors doing that? (Matt. 5:46)

In referring to the tax collectors as loving those who loved them, Jesus was making the dramatic point that even evildoers, shameful characters without a shred of honor, express affection and good will toward family and friends. As history has shown many times over, such "loving" people can be capable

---

5. The name of the tax collector in the first Gospel is Matthew (Matt. 9:9). It is not clear why the name is different. It may be because the brother of Alphaeus had a double name, as did Simon Peter. It also may be that the author of Matthew edited Mark's account in the light of another tradition about a tax collector named Matthew. Levi was a common name, but it was ironic that one named for the patriarch of the priestly tribe devoted to holiness was a profane tax collector.

6. When sin, as understood in the biblical tradition, leads to "hardness of heart," it wreaks evil and causes innocent suffering. It is not synonymous, however, with evil. Sin is disobedience to God. Evil is that which causes suffering and cruelty. Much sin, while disobedient, does not rise to the level of evil. Mother Teresa's sin cannot be reasonably compared to Adolf Hitler's evil. One prays for forgiveness of sins, but prays to be delivered from evil and evil ones.

7. See articles on "Satan" and "evil" in Achtemeier (1996).

of inflicting cruel suffering upon those not emotionally close to them.[8] These same persons usually have lived in the illusion that they were good people, because they were good fathers, sons, or friends. They have lived frequently by a code of honor that allowed them to compartmentalize their cruelty as a kind of necessary unpleasantness, though secretly many of them no doubt found pleasure in it. The tax collectors of Jesus' day were considered by most people to be such evil men deserving of divine punishment.

Repentance and Acceptance

> Two men went up to the temple to pray, one a Pharisee and the other a tax collector. The Pharisee stood up and prayed about himself: "God, I thank you that I am not like other men — robbers, evildoers, adulterers — or even like this tax collector. I fast twice a week and give a tenth of all I get."
>
> But the tax collector stood at a distance. He would not even look up to heaven, but beat his breast and said, "God, have mercy on me, a sinner."
>
> I tell you that this man, rather than the other, went home justified before God. For everyone who exalts himself will be humbled, and he who humbles himself will be exalted. (Luke 18:10-14)

The Pharisee in Jesus' story contrasted his "holy" life free of committing crimes, free of inflicting suffering, free of sexual transgressions, and filled with observance of required fasts and tithes, with that of the tax collector, a truly evil man. The Pharisee believed that God was bound to be far more pleased with his own life of righteousness than with the one who made a shameful living being cruel to fellow countrymen. In the presence of the tax collector it was easy for the Pharisee to feel superior.

The tax collector, on the other hand, experienced so much guilt and shame for his way of life that he felt unworthy to look heavenward, in God's direction. He pounded his chest with remorse and begged God to have mercy on him, a man guilty of great wickedness. Jesus praised this attitude of sincere and genuine repentance and declared that this evil man, not the

---

8. One only needs to think of lynch mobs and church bombers during the days of racial segregation in the United States or Nazi officials responsible for the death camps of World War II Europe to understand the point. For the most part, those engaged in such horrors demonstrated kindness and affection toward their families and comrades, as well as belief in the righteousness of their causes.

one who bragged to God about his good life, was the recipient of mercy and a right relationship. The despised tax collector who humbled himself in repentance experienced a relationship with *Abba* as his accepted child.

Jesus perceived himself as called to be the spiritual physician of the despised souls who were deeply entrenched in sin and preoccupied with doing evil. Jesus understood himself as a man in mission, doing the will of *Abba*, searching out these "lost sheep," and calling them to genuine repentance and a new relationship with *Abba*. To be "lost" is to be unable to find one's own way back home or to safety. That is why Jesus did not wait in the desert like John for people to come to him. Like the shepherd in his parable, he went searching for those who were lost wherever they were. That is why he broke bread with Levi and his associates, at the risk of his own reputation.

Jesus' association with tax collectors was in no way an endorsement of their dishonest and ruthless practices. It was a demonstration of *Abba*'s extravagant and merciful compassion toward those who had "missed the mark" widely. In doing so, Jesus not only reached out in mercy, but demanded accountability.

Making Amends

Being restored to a right relationship with God was not a simple matter for one who had acquired great wealth by extorting others. It required not only repentance but also a willingness to make amends for wrongs done.

> Jesus entered Jericho and was passing through. A man was there by the name of Zacchaeus; he was a chief tax collector and was wealthy. He wanted to see who Jesus was, but being a short man he could not, because of the crowd. So he ran ahead and climbed a sycamore-fig tree to see him, since Jesus was coming that way.
>
> When Jesus reached the spot, he looked up and said to him, "Zacchaeus, come down immediately. I must stay at your house today." So he came down at once and welcomed him gladly.
>
> All the people saw this and began to mutter. "He has gone to be the guest of a 'sinner.'"
>
> But Zacchaeus stood up and said to the Lord, "Look, Lord! Here and now I give half of my possessions to the poor, and if I have cheated anybody out of anything, I will pay back four times the amount."

Jesus said to him, "Today salvation has come to this house, because this man, too, is a son of Abraham. For *this human being* came to seek and to save what was lost." (Luke 19:1-10; altered)

Perched in a tree, visible for all to see, the notorious, powerful, and hated chief tax collector would have been recognized by most of those on the scene. Perhaps someone pointed him out to Jesus. We do not know for sure how Jesus knew his name. But we do know that Jesus called him by name, told the tax collector to climb down out of the tree, and invited himself to Zacchaeus's house for dinner. Jesus' relationship to the despised tax collectors was dramatized by his entering their homes, taking a place beside their tables, and breaking bread with them. These were particularly scandalous events, given the notoriety of such a disreputable man of power.

The tendency to stereotype is universal. It may be particularly prevalent as a cultural manifestation in the Middle East.[9] While stereotyping prejudges individuals, and as such can be cruel and unfair, it also can be useful in defining levels of safe social interactions for groups confronted by potentially dangerous outsiders. There may have been tax collectors in Jesus' day who were exceptions to the stereotype of cruelty, but it was a well understood fact that tax collectors as a rule represented treacherous social interactions. Any personal information obtained by a tax collector could be used for the purpose of exploitation and extortion. Wise people recoiled from tax collectors, much as most people do from snakes, whether they are poisonous or not. It was best for a Jewish citizen to keep a low profile around such a tax collector. But not only did Jesus fail to avoid tax collectors, he went home with them and had dinner.

Local tax collectors, though Jews, were considered by the public to have become as Gentiles. That is, they associated with non-Jews, they worked for the foreign authorities, they acted immorally as was the stereotype of Gentiles, and they exploited and victimized the Jewish people as non-Jews had done for centuries. So when Jesus said that Zacchaeus was also "a son of

9. Gulick (1983) describes the highly judgmental stereotypes of "nomad," "peasant," and "city dweller" in the modern Middle East. It appears to me that judgmental stereotyping has extended to many social categories in the region for many centuries. "In-group" depreciation of "out-groups" has been practiced widely and is an integral part of the culture of peril and refuge, as the designations tax collector, Samaritan, Pharisee, Sadducee, and Gentile or foreigner imply. While such stereotyping is found in all cultures, it seems particularly intense in the Middle East.

Abraham," it was a remarkable statement. Zacchaeus had been restored to his place of honor as one destined to feast with Abraham at the great banquet in the world to come.

Jesus heaped this praise and honor on Zacchaeus because the little tax collector had become a "little *big* man" by demonstrating his sincere repentance and making amends for his wrongdoing. It was not enough, in this instance, to beat one's chest and humbly pray for mercy, as important as that was for a first step; it was necessary to make restitution, to right the wrongs where possible, and to demonstrate compassion as the recipient of God's compassion.

So Zacchaeus, in an extraordinary act of repentance, gave half of his wealth to the destitute. With what was left, he declared his intention to make fourfold restitution to anyone he had cheated. In Exodus 22:1-4, a thief was required to make restitution for stealing another man's livestock. If a sheep had been stolen and was alive when discovered, the thief had to give the owner two sheep. If the sheep had been slaughtered or sold, the thief was required to give the owner four sheep. Defrauding someone under Roman law required fourfold restoration. While required by law, Zacchaeus's amends were totally voluntary, as he was in no danger of being prosecuted for his crimes, and no law required him to give half his goods to the destitute. When carried out, these amends more than likely would have impoverished the tax collector before he could complete them.

Making amends was not simply a matter of justice under the law, it was a necessary enterprise for Zacchaeus's salvation. When Jesus remarked, "Today salvation has come to this house," he was affirming the necessity of making amends in order to be truly free from the power of the sin and evil that dominated the relationships the tax collector had with others.[10] To continue to enjoy the benefits of his evil life at the expense of others would have become an insurmountable obstacle to a right relationship with *Abba*. Jesus delighted because *Abba* delighted in this lost sinner whose relationships with God and neighbor were transformed.

Jesus clearly preferred the company of despised tax collectors and other "sinners" to that of persons who believed themselves morally and religiously superior. To Jesus' religious contemporaries, sin was failure to obey the many

---

10. Those with long-term recovery from addictive diseases through twelve-step programs often testify to the importance of the steps dealing with amends in releasing them from the power of their addictions.

laws found in the Torah as interpreted by scholars in the Law. Their view of humanity made an important distinction between sinners and the righteous. Righteous people obeyed the Law. Sinners violated the Law. It was that simple. But Jesus, who found inspiration in the prophetic tradition, had a different understanding.

> The Lord says: "These people come near to me with their mouth and honor me with their lips, but their hearts are far from me. Their worship of me is made up only of rules taught by men." (Isa. 29:13)

The Pharisee, who prayed his proud and self-congratulatory prayer, was dishonest in his heart. His self-deceptions did not permit him to acknowledge the extent of his own sinfulness. The tax collector was guilty of theft by fraud many times over, but had no illusions about his status before God. The illusion of righteousness, the unwillingness to get honest with oneself about one's motives and one's judgmental and cruel attitudes, is a much more insidious and ultimately dangerous kind of sin. All are sinners, but there is more hope for the self-aware and flagrant sinner than for the one that self-deceives and attempts to deceive others into thinking he is not a sinner at all. Such a "non-sinner" must first experience the crisis of having the trumped-up illusion of righteousness broken before he can be delivered from the unrighteousness in his heart.

Prostitutes and Other Flagrant Sinners

In addition to tax collectors there were other lost sheep who had strayed far from home, but who were recipients of Jesus' demonstration of *Abba's* compassion.

> Jesus said to them, "I tell you the truth, the tax collectors and the prostitutes are entering the kingdom of God ahead of you." (Matt. 21:31b)

The Shameful Profession

As was true of the tax collectors, prostitutes in Jesus' day had no illusions about their sinfulness. Prostitution had long been equated with wickedness.

> Do not degrade your daughter by making her a prostitute, or the land will turn to prostitution and be filled with wickedness. (Lev. 19:29)

In Mediterranean culture, honor and shame were particularly associated with sex and gender issues.[11] The virtue of wives and sisters was the primary marker of honor, while the loss of virtue was a shameful event requiring severe retribution. Women who were not virgins at marriage, or committed adultery after marriage, or were divorced, were considered impure. Prostitution was believed to be so ritually unclean that earnings from the trade could not be brought to the Temple as offerings.[12] Priests were forbidden to marry prostitutes;[13]and if a priest's daughter entered the profession, the Law required she be burned to death.[14] When the eighth-century BCE prophet Amos predicted doom for the priest of Bethel, it included the prophecy that his wife would become a prostitute in the city.[15]

Despite this condemnation and abhorrence of prostitution, it was a widely accepted fact of life throughout the history of Israel. Both male and female prostitution were practiced.[16] Some prostitutes became quite famous. The mighty warrior Jephthah was the child of a prostitute.[17] A prostitute in the city of Jericho named Rahab provided shelter to Joshua's spies prior to the attack on that city during the conquest of Canaan.[18] She is listed in the genealogy of Jesus found in Matthew (1:5), as is at least one other woman tainted by scandal.[19]

Both Rahab and the mother of Jephthah illustrate the ability of Yahweh to accomplish his will despite the sin of his children. They were nevertheless despised sinners. Prostitutes along with tax collectors were singled out by Jesus as notorious examples of wickedness who, though rebellious toward

---

11. Gilmore (1987).

12. Deut. 23:18.

13. Lev. 21:7.

14. Lev. 21:9.

15. Amos 7:17.

16. In the Hebrew Bible sacred prostitutes (Hebrew *qedeshah*), both male and female, were a part of the Canaanite fertility cult. The availability of religiously sanctioned extramarital sex enticed Jews to the ceremonies worshiping the fertility gods. This practice became a metaphor in the prophetic literature for Israel's much broader unfaithful relationship with Yahweh (Judg. 8:33; Ezek. 16).

17. Judg. 11:1.

18. Josh. 2.

19. Matt. 1:6 refers to Uriah's wife (Bathsheba) as the mother of Solomon.

Abba prior to responding to Jesus' ministry, would be welcomed at God's great banquet before those who promised to do God's will, but failed to do it.

A Place at the Table

While Jesus was accused of associating with prostitutes along with tax collectors and other sinners, there is only one story of a possible interaction between Jesus and a prostitute in the Gospels.[20]

> Now one of the Pharisees invited Jesus to have dinner with him, so he went to the Pharisee's house and reclined at the table. When a woman who had lived a sinful life in that town learned that Jesus was eating at the Pharisee's house, she brought an alabaster jar of perfume, and as she stood behind him at his feet weeping, she began to wet his feet with her tears. Then she wiped them with her hair, kissed them and poured perfume on them. When the Pharisee who had invited him saw this, he said to himself, "If this man were a prophet, he would know who is touching him and what kind of woman she is — that she is a sinner."

20. Luke 7:36-47 has some common elements with the story of the woman in Mark 14:3-9 discussed in the previous chapter. In both stories perfume is poured on Jesus while at dinner with a man named Simon and the stories share the somewhat remarkable fact of a woman present at a male dinner. This has led a number of scholars to conclude that these are variations on the same story, with Luke, who does not use Mark's story here, either rewriting the story for his purposes or relying on a tradition that had already reworked it. There are significant differences, however, between Luke's story and Mark's story. In Mark, Jesus' head is anointed while in Luke it is his feet. In Mark, the issues are wasted wealth that could have been given to the poor and the anointing of Jesus for burial. In Luke the issues are that the woman is a "sinner," the mercy of God in forgiving her many sins, and the extent of her gratitude. In Mark, Simon is a leper and in Luke a Pharisee. The Gospel of John added to the confusion by combining the two stories and incorporating Lazarus's family. It is most likely that these were two different stories in the pre-Gospel tradition. The first story, essentially used by Mark, was about perfume and the poor. The second did not originally have anything about perfume in it. It was about a woman with a bad reputation, tears, and wiping the tears from Jesus' feet with her hair. Luke's story reads quite naturally without the perfume. In the oral transmission of the story over time the latter story "borrowed" the perfume from the first story, a very natural confusion and embellishment, given the similar settings. It is reasonable to conclude that without the perfume, the stories are really quite independent accounts of different occasions.

Jesus answered him, "Simon, I have something to tell you."

"Tell me, teacher," he said.

"Two men owed money to a certain moneylender. One owed him five hundred denarii, and the other fifty. Neither of them had the money to pay him back, so he cancelled the debts of both. Now which of them will love him more?"

Simon replied, "I suppose the one who had the bigger debt cancelled."

"You have judged correctly," Jesus said.

Then he turned toward the woman and said to Simon, "Do you see this woman? I came into your house. You did not give me any water for my feet, but she wet my feet with her tears and wiped them with her hair. You did not give me a kiss, but this woman, from the time I entered, has not stopped kissing my feet. You did not put oil on my head, but she has poured perfume on my feet. Therefore, I tell you, her many sins have been forgiven — for she loved much. But he who has been forgiven little loves little." (Luke 7:36-47)

Simon the Pharisee had invited Jesus to his house for dinner.[21] Jesus was reclining beside the table prepared with food, as was the custom. A woman entered the house, stood behind Jesus, and cried so hard that Jesus' feet became wet from her tears. The woman began to wipe Jesus' feet with her hair. She was described as living a life devoted to sin. It is probable that she was a prostitute.[22] Simon the Pharisee no doubt was not happy the woman was in his house. She was an uninvited guest.

Crowds seemed to follow Jesus constantly, providing him little privacy. This woman probably had followed Jesus inside along with some of the

---

21. Luke may have borrowed the name Simon from Mark's similar story of Simon the leper and given it to an unnamed Pharisee here, but Simon was a common name in Jesus' world. There were many men who were named Simon as well as many named John, James, Judas, and the like, and Jesus for that matter.

22. The woman in the story is not specifically identified as a prostitute, but she is identified as a sinner, one devoted to a sinful life. The Greek word for prostitute was *pornē* and was used in Matt. 21:31 but not here. It is clear, however, from this context that the woman had a very bad reputation that was well known in the town. A woman's honor or shame was virtually synonymous with her sexual reputation. It is likely that she was a prostitute, but she may have been a well-known adulterer. Given the shame involved in associating with "wicked" women, and the tendency of the tradition to protect Jesus from negative attributions, the story may have been softened from prostitute to sinner during its transmission.

crowd from the town who had pushed their way into the house and who were watching the men eat. Because she was a woman devoted to sin, and particularly if she supported herself as a prostitute, everything she touched in Simon's house was made ritually unclean. That included Jesus, who was sharing bread with the Pharisee. Simon was made so uncomfortable by the whole event that he evidently became hostile toward Jesus. Simon is reported to have questioned in his thoughts whether Jesus could be a prophet, because he assumed that Jesus did not know that this woman was a notorious sinner. Had he known, Simon reasoned, Jesus certainly would not have let her do to him what she was doing. Any prophet worth his salt would have recognized her "type" and not allowed himself to be touched in that way.

Jesus had no difficulty reading what was going on with his host. Jesus knew all about this woman's reputation. Jesus, in his sage-like way, turned to Simon and told him a brief parable about forgiveness of debts in which one debtor was forgiven a much larger debt than another. Then Jesus got Simon reluctantly to admit that the one who had the larger debt forgiven would love the moneylender more. Jesus then turned toward the woman, still speaking to Simon the Pharisee, and compared her behavior with that of his host.

"Do you see this woman?" Jesus asked. The question implied that Simon had never really "seen" this woman. For Simon, this was not a person, a human being, and a child of Abraham; this was a stereotype of gender and shamefulness. Jesus then pointed out that the woman, unlike Simon his host, had washed his feet and kissed him. In the context of honor and shame, Jesus had reclined at Simon's table to eat, and no member of that household, no servant or family member, and certainly not Simon himself, had paid Jesus the respect due a guest by washing his feet.

In the dusty lands of the region, it did not take long for sandaled feet to become caked with sandy grime. An important gesture of honor was to wash the feet of a guest prior to the beginning of the meal. Though usually carried out by the person of lowest status in the household, if no one else was available the task would have fallen to the host. It was also a symbol of respect to be greeted with a kiss by a family member, dear friend, or devoted follower.[23] Simon did not greet Jesus with a kiss. Jesus' message to Simon the Pharisee was clear. It was not the woman who was shameful; it was Simon who had

---

23. The "kiss" evidently became a standard greeting of Christians in the early church (Acts 20:37; Rom. 16:16; 1 Cor. 16:20; 2 Cor. 13:12; 1 Thess. 5:26; 1 Peter 5:14).

behaved shamefully because he had failed to honor Jesus with socially important gestures of courtesy.

The woman was showing her love and gratitude toward a man who had treated her with the respect due a child of *Abba*. Jesus understood that those despised by their neighbors were special recipients of God's compassion. It is likely that sometime prior to entering Simon's house, Jesus had met the woman, had a life-altering dialogue with her, and had pronounced absolution on her sins, as Jesus told his host at the meal that her sins had already been forgiven.[24] The woman's emotional response to the spirit transformation that had occurred upon that occasion was to weep over Jesus' feet. Then, perhaps in embarrassment over the fact that she had gotten his feet wet, she wiped them with her hair, then impulsively kissed them in gratitude.

Jesus' relationship to notorious sinners such as this woman was first to see her as a child of *Abba*, to interact with her in such a way as to reveal God's compassion toward her, not to be embarrassed or ashamed to be in her presence or to be the object of her public affection. This was a remarkable relationship in a male-dominated society with severe censure of female sexual shame. While women did not eat with men, and this woman was particularly not welcome at Simon the Pharisee's table, Jesus welcomed and praised her. Jesus understood that this woman, along with many tax collectors and prostitutes, would be given places of honor at God's great banquet to come. In fact, that banquet had already begun.

Tax collectors and prostitutes were two of the most despised professions. There were other professions that also were seen as despicable by many of the people. These included gamblers who used dice, organizers of games of chance, moneylenders who practiced usury, merchants dealing with produce raised during the Sabbatical year, and shepherds, among others.[25] It is safe to assume that Jesus had the same compassionate, empathetic, and respectful relationship with people engaged in these professions as he did with tax collectors and prostitutes.

---

24. John's Gospel records two such encounters with women of shame, the Samaritan woman in John 4 and the woman caught in adultery in John 8. Although the latter was probably a late addition to John, it may well have been a story that circulated independently from the time of Jesus.

25. Jeremias (1979, pp. 359-76).

Samaritans and Gentiles

The despised in Jesus' day also included the unorthodox outsiders and foreigners. Jews particularly despised Samaritans. Samaria was a political territory that lay between Judea, in which was the holy city of Jerusalem, and Galilee, a northern regional country of Jews who also looked to Jerusalem as their spiritual home.[26] Samaria was the central hill country of the once united kingdom of Israel that had been settled by the tribes descended from the patriarch Joseph. It had been a part of the Northern Kingdom of Israel, after the country's division at the death of Solomon, and prior to the Assyrian and Babylonian assaults.

Ethnic Enmity

Following the Assyrian conquest in 722 BCE some twenty-seven thousand Israelites of Samaria were deported. Many of them went to live in Jerusalem. Foreign colonists subsequently settled the region and many intermarried with the local population. Following the return of the exiled community to Jerusalem under the Persians around 521 BCE, Israelite descendants from the region of Samaria offered to assist with the rebuilding of the Temple at Jerusalem. Their offer was rejected due to the fanatical ethnic purity doctrines of the priestly leadership of the returned exiles, who considered them half-breeds at best. This rejection undoubtedly helped create a legacy of animosity between Samaritans and Jews. Political tensions over the years between the Jewish regions and the Samaritan region were also strained, with military incursions occurring from time to time across the borders in each direction.

While many and various peoples lived in the region of Samaria, those who were called Samaritans usually were those citizens of that area who practiced a form of Israelite religion that had evolved as a parallel development to Judaism over several centuries. It had common roots with Judaism, but was distinctive in a number of critical ways. Samaritans believed that Yahweh had designated Mt. Gerizim, located in the central hill country near the city of Samaria, from which the region was named, as the location where proper worship and sacrifice were to take place. Samaritans also believed

---

26. I am indebted to Meier (2000) for a number of points in this discussion about Samaritans. See also articles on "Samaria" and "Samaritan" in Achtemeier (1996).

that the Scriptures were limited to the Pentateuch, the first five books of the Hebrew Bible. Samaritans did not share in the belief of most Jews that the books of the prophets and the wisdom writings were sacred. Certainly the Pharisaic traditions that were being developed to interpret the Torah would have been considered worthless by the Samaritans.

Jews typically despised Samaritans. They were considered impure in race and heretical in belief. It is safe to say that Samaritans also despised Jews, and it was probably to avoid conflict with angry Samaritans that Galilean Jews usually avoided traveling through Samaria to Jerusalem, although that was considered a more efficient route.

> These twelve Jesus sent out with the following instructions: "Do not go among the Gentiles or enter any town of the Samaritans." (Matt. 10:5)[27]

Going outside the confines of the Jewish territories was dangerous and represented a challenge for which the twelve were not yet prepared. Jesus evidently did make minor excursions into Samaria accompanied by the disciples.

> And he sent messengers on ahead, who went into a Samaritan village to get things ready for him, but the people there did not welcome him, because he was heading for Jerusalem. When the disciples James and John saw this, they asked, "Lord, do you want us to call fire down from heaven to destroy them?" But Jesus turned and rebuked them and they went to another village. (Luke 9:52-56)[28]

27. Meier (2000) and other scholars believe that this passage is likely a construction of either Matthew or a source unique to Matthew (see Addendum to Part I for discussion of *Differing Dimensions of Truth* and literary construction). It is consistent with the author's theme of Jesus as the new Jewish Moses. While I agree that it is unlikely that these words were actually spoken by Jesus and are inconsistent with his inclusiveness, they are consistent with a general caution and high level of risk for Jews entering areas outside the Jewish boundaries. If Jesus said something similar to the twelve, it was probably not for the reasons Matthew implies, but as wise counsel to those in training.

28. This may be a constructed passage (see Addendum to Part I for discussion of *Differing Dimensions of Truth* and literary construction) reflecting a time when the early church was active in Samaria, but the rejection of Jesus by Samaritans in a passage used by Luke argues for authenticity, given Luke's consistent theme of mission to the Gentiles in the Luke-Acts complex. While this is a passage of rejection similar to those in other parts of Luke's work, it does not fit Luke's schema of rejection by the Jews and acceptance by Gentiles. I consider it supportive evidence of Jesus' willingness to carry his message, albeit in a very limited way during his lifetime, to the Samaritans, and by implication to the Gentiles.

The Samaritan village wanted no part of a group of Jews traveling through their country to get to Jerusalem, which, for them, was the location of an illegitimate temple. The Samaritans probably despised such pilgrimages of Jews. Their rejection of Jesus may have not been personal at all. But the disciples of Jesus took it quite personally.

James and John, who were called sons of thunder,[29] were disciples with a reputation as hotheads. The notion of calling down fire from heaven on a village reflected a memory of Elijah's curse on the soldiers of the ancient king of Samaria.[30] So the disciples wanted also to call down fire from heaven on these contemporary people of Samaria. These Samaritans had offended the honor of Jesus and his disciples, by refusing to let them stay in their village. The disciples were so furious they wanted to destroy the village and all who dwelled in it. Jesus rebuked them.

To comprehend the depth of suspicion and hatred held by Jews toward Samaritans, it is helpful to understand the cultural biases implicit in and unconsciously presupposed by the priestly law. That which was considered unclean in the dietary law was the marginal creature.[31] In order to be considered clean and kosher, an animal needed to conform to its class. Fish with scales, for example, were considered whole and edible. But eels and non-scaly fish were considered to be marginal and therefore unclean, for they did not fit the prototype of scaly creatures that used fins for locomotion in the water. Four-legged creatures with hands in front like crocodiles and mice did not fit the prototype of four-legged creatures with proper feet for walking and were considered unclean. The list of such distinctions was extensive.[32] Likewise, in human relations, only those who fit the Jewish prototype were considered sons of Abraham. Samaritans did not conform to their class, either. They were neither Jew nor Gentile. The Samaritans were unclean, for they were anomalous. They were both ethnically and doctrinally marginal from the Jewish perspective. Samaritans probably felt the same way about Jews.[33]

---

29. Mark 3:17.

30. 2 Kings 1:10.

31. See Douglas (1966, chapter 3).

32. See Lev. 11.

33. Many of the bases for stereotypes on both sides were more about propaganda than historical fact. This includes the biased references to Samaria and Samaritans in Josephus. Each of the religious/ethnic groups rewrote their histories to their own advantages. The point here is not that the prejudices were justified in any way, but that they existed and were virulent.

A Compassionate Samaritan

Jesus rebuked his disciples for wanting to destroy the Samaritan village. That in itself is remarkable, given the level of hostility between the groups. But Jesus' attitude toward the Samaritans was far more revolutionary than that.

> A man was going down from Jerusalem to Jericho, when he fell into the hands of robbers. They stripped him of his clothes, beat him and went away, leaving him half dead. A priest happened to be going down the same road, and when he saw the man, he passed by on the other side. So too, a Levite, when he came to the place and saw him, passed by on the other side. But a Samaritan, as he traveled came where the man was; and when he saw him, he took pity on him. He went to him and bandaged his wounds, pouring on oil and wine. Then he put the man on his own donkey, took him to an inn and took care of him. The next day he took out two silver coins and gave them to the innkeeper. "Look after him," he said, "and when I return, I will reimburse you for any extra expense you may have."
>
> Which of these three do you think was a neighbor to the man who fell into the hands of robbers? (Luke 10:30b-36)

The revolutionary nature of the parable, which throughout the current era has been called the "parable of the good Samaritan," has been virtually lost. To the modern reader "good" and "Samaritan" are practically synonymous, because the Samaritan is seen as an example of compassion and generosity toward a stranger in need. But for a first-century Jew the juxtaposition of "good" and "Samaritan" would have been virtually unthinkable.

The Jews who listened to Jesus preach would not have been surprised at the priest and Levite who avoided the injured man. In a dangerous land where anyone traveling from one populated place to another was subject to attack by bandits, Jesus' hearers would have immediately identified with the victim. There were few people who did not at least know someone who had been so victimized. While Jews observed their religion and attended the festivals in Jerusalem, there was little respect for the priestly class who managed and presided over Temple worship. They were generally considered to be corrupt collaborators with the occupying forces who lived affluently off the required temple tithes. Jesus' audiences would have smiled and chuckled knowingly when they heard that these religious professionals, obsessed with their own personal purity and having a cowardly concern for their own safety, would not come to the aid of a man who had been made unclean through injury, bloodiness, and near death.[34] But they would have gasped with shock when the hero of the story turned out to be a hated Samaritan. As was true for so many stories that Jesus told, this one had a surprise ending that challenged to the core the presuppositions and attitudes of his hearers.

It was a half-breed, a foreigner, and a hated heretic who demonstrated for all to understand what it meant to love one's neighbor. To be sure, the subpoint of the story was that the neighbor is anyone who is in need. But the main point of the story was that God makes no distinction between Jew and Samaritan. It did not matter that the Samaritan did not have a pure ancestry, or hold the "right" beliefs, or perform the "right" rituals in the "right" places. What mattered was that he treated another human being in need, presumably in his case a Jewish outsider, with compassion and generosity. He loved God by loving his neighbor in need, and the clear implication was that God approved. This was the revolutionary view of Jesus. All the debates over differences of beliefs and practices between these two religious traditions were suddenly irrelevant. All of the fears and grudges creating ethnic hostility were foolishness. What was relevant was the need of the neighbor and the courage, compassion, and generosity to respond to that need.

On another occasion a different Samaritan was held up as a positive example as the only leper among ten that returned to give thanks.[35] And the Gospel of John reports an extensive encounter with a Samaritan woman with a bad reputation.[36]

The Gospel of John also says that Jesus himself was accused of being a Samaritan.[37] This amounted to calling Jesus a dirty name. It was intended as slander, a means of discrediting the charismatic man. Coming from the

34. The priest and the Levite avoided the victim because, under purity laws, if he were dead they would have had to undergo ritual purification for a week.

35. Luke 17:16. This entire story is thought to be a construct by a number of scholars (see Addendum to Part I for discussion of *Differing Dimensions of Truth* and literary construction). Nevertheless, it may well authentically reflect incidental contact between Jesus and Samaritans. I have concluded, regardless of the authenticity of every Samaritan reference, that Jesus' attitude toward Samaritans was well known among early Christians.

36. John 4:1-42 probably contains a core story that dates back to Jesus, though it has been put to extensive theological purposes by the Gospel writer.

37. John 8:48. Many scholars attribute this accusation to later tradition, as it probably reflects the conflict between Jews and Christians in the latter part of the first century. It may have been a later development of the accusations found in Mark 3.

mouth of Jews who hated Samaritans it said that Jesus was a heretic of questionable birth and probably in league with Satan.[38] Of course, it was not true. Jesus was a Galilean Jew, not a Samaritan. It was an ironically appropriate designation, however, in the light of Jesus' story of the "good Samaritan." Jesus' entire ministry was the embodiment of compassion and generosity toward those in need, the disabled, the destitute, and the despised.

Gentiles in Need

In addition to Samaria and the Samaritans, the Gospels record several excursions of Jesus into Gentile territories and encounters with despised Gentiles. Devout Jews strongly believed that they should remain separate from non-Jews. Gentiles were considered responsible for most of the troubles of the Israelites throughout their perilous history. From Egyptian slavery, to Assyrian conquest and Babylonian captivity, to Greek and Roman empires and attempts to impose foreign culture and pagan compliance, Gentiles were believed to be dangerous, immoral, and perpetrators of evil. To be sure, there were "God-fearers," Gentiles who believed in the God of Israel and its ethical teachings, but who did not comply with circumcision and the purity laws. These Gentiles were generally respected by the Jews. But they were still Gentiles, kept at a distance from the holy sanctuary of the Temple in Jerusalem, and kept as well at a distance from their marriage-eligible daughters and sons. Despite the fact that there were some "good foreigners," Gentiles stereotypically were associated with pollution, political oppression, and religious persecution, not without considerable justification. Travel to Gentile territories was therefore discouraged, and when it occurred it was considered contaminating.

> Jesus left that place and went to the vicinity of Tyre. He entered a house and did not want anyone to know it; yet he could not keep his presence secret. In fact, as soon as she heard about him a woman whose daughter was possessed by an evil spirit came and fell at his feet. The woman was a Greek, born in Syrian Phoenicia. She begged Jesus to drive the demon out of her daughter.

38. There may be a suggestion in the accusation of Jesus being a magician like the Simon Magus of Acts 8:9-13. Magicians popularly were believed to obtain their powers from demonic forces.

"First let the children eat all they want," he told her, "for it is not right to take the children's bread and toss it to their dogs."

"Yes, Lord," she replied, "but even the dogs under the table eat the children's crumbs."

Then he told her. "For such a reply, you may go; the demon has left your daughter."

She went home and found her child lying on the bed, and the demon gone. (Mark 7:24-30)

Tyre was an ancient city located on the shores of the Mediterranean Sea in the Roman province of Syria and the historic region of Phoenicia northwest of Galilee. Tyre was a little more than thirty miles from Capernaum, where Jesus centered his ministry. The city of Tyre was a leading commercial port and was populated by a variety of ethnic Gentile groups. Mark reports that people both came to Jesus from that region and that Jesus visited it.[39]

The woman in this story is identified as a Greek who was born in the Syrian Phoenician region. To the typical chauvinistic Jew of the time she was a despised pagan. Furthermore, she was not identified as a God-fearer, a Gentile who believed in the Jewish deity and practiced Jewish morality without following all the purity rules. She came to Jesus for one reason. She was desperate to find a cure for her daughter. In the dialogue we see Jesus challenging the woman, who responds in a way that Jesus approves. Jesus' challenge, which to us may seem to be uncharacteristically depreciating, is not intended to degrade but to evoke consciousness. Both parties in the dialogue understood that they represented two very different worlds. That reality had to be acknowledged. Jesus challenged her to indicate why he should use his powers of healing for a pagan. Her response, as self-deprecating as it appears to have been, was simply that even a pagan is as deserving of compassion as dogs are of crumbs from the table.

Jesus was delighted with her response, for though she was not a Jew and probably had very limited knowledge of Jewish ways, she implicitly knew that her life and her daughter's life were valuable and worthy of compassion and healing. Jesus healed her daughter. We are not told whether the woman

---

39. See Mark 3:8. While Mark, as a number of scholars have suggested, may have constructed his Gospel so as to give the impression there was greater contact with Gentiles by Jesus than actually occurred, references to particular cities and regions, as well as specific individual Gentiles, represent a relevant emotionally significant early church memory of Jesus' ministry.

became a follower of Jesus or not. And that is the point. Jesus' relationship to those in need, even despised pagans, was about being a compassionate neighbor. It was not always about enlisting them in his cause.

> Then Jesus left the vicinity of Tyre and went through Sidon, down to the Sea of Galilee and into the region of the Decapolis. There some people brought to him a man who was deaf and could hardly talk, and they begged him to place his hand on the man. (Mark 7:31-32)

> Jesus and his disciples went on to the villages around Caesarea Philippi. (Mark 8:27)

Sidon was another important seacoast city of Syrian Phoenicia, lying about twenty miles north of Tyre. Decapolis ("ten cities") was a region east of Samaria and Galilee. It was there that Jesus was reported to have healed a deaf and nearly mute person. This man was almost certainly a foreigner as well. Aside from the location there is no difference in Jesus' relationship to this disabled man and his relationship to disabled Galilean Jews. Jesus' view of reality included the belief that Gentiles were also children of *Abba*. They were not to be despised as foreigners, but loved and ministered to as those whom Yahweh had also created and loved. While he evidently hoped to stir the children of Abraham to see reality as he saw it, and then with their help to enlighten the Gentiles, Jesus nevertheless carried his message to Gentile communities, and responded in compassion to despised foreigners in need of his healing.

Whether, then, Jesus was interacting with the disabled, the destitute, or despised tax collectors, prostitutes, Samaritans, and pagan Gentiles, he was the compassionate neighbor, living out *Abba's* compassion for all his children. The Gospel of Luke even reports that this compassion extended to the thieves who were crucified next to him.[40] The eyes of Jesus did not view the evil, the immoral, and the despised in terms of the popular stereotypes and

---

40. Luke 23:40-43. Many scholars consider this to have been a creation of Luke (see Addendum to Part I for discussion of *Differing Dimensions of Truth* and literary construction), but it may have been a part of Luke's special source that included substantial material about compassion. A number of scholars consider this and other details about the final hours of Jesus on the cross as legendary, as it is unlikely there were any credible witnesses close enough to hear what Jesus was saying. It is nevertheless consistent with Jesus' relationship with those who were despised, and it is by no means certain that there were not witnesses who later transmitted vivid details of the crucifixion.

distinctions of superiority and inferiority of the day; the eyes of Jesus always saw others, regardless of their shortcomings, as human beings, fellow children of Adam, and loved by God.

Such an unconventional way of viewing reality and such a radical rejection of conventional separatism accompanied by meal celebrations of the inclusiveness of God's banquet, by a popular charismatic healer and teacher, was bound to generate serious adversaries. Chief among these were the devout, the purity-conscious Pharisees and the priestly Sadducees.

CHAPTER VI

Jesus and the Devout

J esus' inclusive and compassionate view of the relations between God and humankind found popular support among the disabled, the destitute, the despised, and many of the "people of the land." It also generated fierce opposition from those devoted to the conventional religious vision of holiness achieved through personal purity.

The Pharisee Party

The Pharisees were the acknowledged leaders of the established Jewish piety of the period, and while numbering only about six thousand at the time of Jesus, were a common sight in all the villages and cities of Galilee.[1] Their

---

1. Scholars differ widely on the presence of Pharisees in Galilee prior to the destruction of the Second Temple in 70 CE. Skepticism is based upon the lack of archeological synagogue evidence for the pre-Temple period and the known dispersion from Jerusalem of religious leadership following the Temple's devastation, including significant settlement of Galilee at that time. It is further argued that the conflict between the Pharisees and the Christians following 70 CE resulted in the controversies of that later period being projected by the Gospel writers back to Jesus' ministry. But synagogues often met in the courtyards of ordinary homes, and given the Pharisaic mission to make observance of their purity code universal, a mission that had existed for almost two centuries prior to the beginning of Jesus' ministry, I find no reason to assume anachronism when the Gospels refer to Pharisees in the cities and villages of Galilee. The Pharisees had long before established a synagogue system to assist with their mission. Their scribes were the recognized religious leaders and experts in the Law who were relied upon in synagogue gatherings by the time Jesus came into conflict with

natural rivals, the Sadducees, a priestly sect based in the Temple at Jerusalem, were widely disliked, but many Pharisees were respected among the people of both the countryside and cities for their fervent rejection of foreign culture and obsessive devotion to traditional values. Conventional contemporary Jewish thought considered them models of proper Jewish piety.[2] They were the founders and architects of the local education system through a synagogue program that in theory set out to train every Jewish male in the intricacies of observance of the Law of Moses. Jesus himself almost certainly was a benefactor of their synagogue education. Yet, it was in opposition to the members of these religiously devoted Pharisees that Jesus most clearly defined his own unique orientation to reality.

> Another time he went into the synagogue, and a man with a shriveled hand was there. Some of them were looking for a reason to accuse Jesus, so they watched him closely to see if he would heal him on the Sabbath. Jesus said to the man with the shriveled hand, "Stand up in front of everyone."
>
> Then Jesus asked them, "Which is lawful on the Sabbath: to do good or to do evil, to save life or to kill?" But they remained silent.
>
> He looked around at them in anger and, deeply distressed at their stubborn hearts, said to the man, "Stretch out your hand." He stretched it out, and his hand was completely restored. Then the Pharisees went out and began to plot with the Herodians how they might kill Jesus. (Mark 3:1-6)

Who were these devout Pharisees who wanted to discredit Jesus and believed it wrong to heal on the Sabbath? And why were they so angry that they wanted to kill him?[3]

---

them. As indicated in this chapter, Jesus' relationship with the Pharisees was complex and there were different perspectives within Pharisaism. But there is every reason to believe, given the strong differences between Jesus' orientation and that of members of the Pharisee sect, that his conflicts with them over his vision of the kingdom of God occurred frequently during his ministry and foreshadowed conflicts within Judaism about the significance of Jesus and related purity issues in the years following his crucifixion.

2. I am indebted to the "Pharisees" article by Kohler (2002a) and the "Pharisees" article in Achtemeier (1996) for much of the background that follows.

3. Much has been written about the unfair stereotyping of Pharisees in the Gospels (see, for example, Varner, 1998). It is true that for each of the Gospel writers the Pharisees tend to be villainous *dramatis personae*, though each writer handles their dramatic roles

The name Pharisee is believed to derive from the Hebrew word *perusim* and means "separate ones." Members of the sect were known for their strict rules concerning separation from unclean persons, places, and things, for the sake of purity. The roots of their movement probably date to the period of the reforms of Ezra and Nehemiah around 400 BCE. The Pharisees emerged as a distinctive Jewish sect during the revolt of the Maccabees against the Seleucid rulers of Syria (166-160 BCE).[4]

By the time of Herod Antipas and Pontius Pilate, the Pharisees were the successors of those who had created an identity of religious and patriotic devotion over almost two centuries. It was an identity forged within a community that experienced foreign oppression, cultural intrusion, wars of rebellion, persecution, threats of genocide, and loss of identity through assimilation. The sect defined its role in this environment as the true interpreters of the Mosaic Law, defenders of that faith, keepers of the covenant, and teachers and proselytizers devoted to the survival and triumph of that faith over all its challenges. They understood themselves to be the guardians of a sacred tradition paid for by the blood of heroes and martyrs, and that tradition required of them radical obedience to its precepts. By the reign of Herod the Great, their movement had learned to survive by avoiding direct confrontation with the foreign rulers and with the social status quo, while continuing to provide a clear alternative to assimilation and Greco-Roman enculturation.

Devout Pharisees during the first half of the first century shared this common heritage, but they were not all poured from the same mold. A small number of them became highly influential members of Herod's ruling party

---

somewhat differently. Members of the sect are used in the Gospels as literary devices to clarify the distinction between Jesus' message and the Pharisaic perspective, a viewpoint that emerged after the destruction of the Second Temple as the predominant perspective of Judaism. The fact that the Gospel dialogues have been used by many Christians as justification for anti-Semitism is reprehensible from both a moral and a historical perspective. The historical Jesus was engaged in a debate within Judaism for its soul and direction, but the attitude that he brought to that debate was the spirit of the compassion of *Abba* for *all* his children. It is important, however, not to underestimate the intensity of the disagreement at the time, and the almost certain fact that some Pharisees were so angry with Jesus that they wanted him dead, and that shortly after his death Pharisees such as Saul of Tarsus were "righteously" participating in killing Christians. The differences were real and the feelings were intense.

4. The earliest reference to the Pharisees is found in Josephus, *Antiquities* 13.9, where they are described as an established sect around 145 BCE.

and actively involved in the Sanhedrin, the Jewish council of leadership located in Jerusalem. Most Pharisees, however, were not politically connected. They were scattered throughout the land, running the synagogues and recruiting new members for their movement. The leadership consisted of their scribes, the teachers of the Law, who were considered experts in the Law of Moses and the traditions of their elders. The majority of Pharisees were laypeople, who practiced trades and engaged in commerce. They belonged to a number of schools with differing versions of the Pharisee vision and lifestyle. These schools could be quite zealous in their disagreements with one another. The two that were most famous were the Jerusalem schools of two teachers, Shammai and Hillel.[5] While Hillel was considered more flexible and less rigid than Shammai, both sects were passionate in their pursuit of holiness. These factions engaged in extensive debates concerning the correct means of achieving ritual purity.

A Preoccupation with Holiness

Every human society has cultural preoccupations and core values.[6] The core value of the priestly tradition of Judaism was "holiness."[7]

> The Lord said to Moses, "Speak to the entire assembly of Israel and say to them: 'Be holy because I, the Lord your God, am holy.'" (Lev. 19:1-2)

This preoccupation with holiness developed in response to serious threats to the survival of Jewish identity. It emerged, from a wider set of competing values, as the obsessive focus that defined all other values during the Babylonian exile of the sixth century BCE. The Judean Babylonian and post-Babylonian leadership, especially the priestly families, realized that cultural and ethnic assimilation would likely mean the end of everything Jew-

---

5. The *Mishnah,* compiled by the rabbis around 200 CE, is the source of our knowledge of these schools. While this late date of composition raises historical doubts, I find the conclusion by Meier (2000) and others that these were likely to have been Pharisee sects that existed during the first century convincing.

6. Anthropologist Ruth Benedict developed the idea of core values in her classic work *Patterns of Culture* (1934). Another anthropologist, Mary Douglas, later analyzed "holiness" as a core value of ancient Judaism in her often quoted *Purity and Danger* (1966).

7. The following discussion of purity mapping is indebted to Neyrey (1988a).

ish. At stake was the covenant itself, and the loss forevermore of its promised blessing. Distinctive aspects of Jewish identity, especially traditional practices associated with Temple sacrifices, were codified into holiness rules. Sacred books containing the ancient stories and traditions were radically edited, probably shortly after the return from exile, to conform to the holiness perspective.[8] These edited books became the written authority whereby the threatened Jewish minority was able to preserve its distinctiveness for generations to come. Whether in the alien culture of Babylon, or the foreign-dominated environment of Judea, the holiness code provided a means for the people to remain distinct from their neighbors.

The priestly account of creation in the first chapter of Genesis, which dates to this period, is the establishment of order over chaos. It is a map of goodness as the correct order of time, space, and creatures. When things are not in the correct order, they are impure and dangerous.

This map of purity was reflected in the Temple cult and in many of the social rules governing everyday relationships.[9] The correct order of things spelled out in the sacred writings what *animals* could be offered, who could offer them, where such offerings could be made, when, and who could be present for them. Tradition also mapped *space* according to levels of holiness. The land of Israel was holy ground. Jerusalem was holier than other plots of land. The Temple was holier yet, and the Holy of Holies was the most holy of all. *People* too were mapped in terms of holiness. Priests were considered the most holy of persons. True Israelites were holier than converts. People with damaged bodies were the least holy people of the holy land.

Maps of time also designated holy *times* to be observed. They included the Sabbath, Passover, Day of Atonement, Feast of Tabernacles, Festival Days, Feast of New Years, Days of Fasting, Feast of Purim, and Mid-Festival Days.

To define what is holy is to map as well what is unholy, impure, and unclean. For Judaism, these included things associated with death, bodily fluids, and anomalous creatures that did not fit pure prototypes, such as "creeping things" that do not move with proper legs and feet, and, of course, people with disabilities.

8. It is widely accepted among Hebrew Bible (Old Testament) scholars that priestly scribes who returned from exile edited the sacred works of the Yahwist (J) and the Elohist (E), incorporated Deuteronomy, and added the Priestly Code to form the current Hexateuch, the first six books of the Old Testament.

9. See Neyrey (1988a).

There were two manifestations of mapped purity with which all Pharisees, regardless of interpretive school, were particularly obsessed: strict observance of the Sabbath and meticulous compliance with dietary cleanliness. A devout Jew demonstrated his entitlement to participation in the promise of God by obeying the Law of Moses as interpreted by the tradition, particularly with regard to meal etiquette and Sabbath observance. Of the more than six hundred rules with which Pharisees tried to comply in their daily lives, a great many were related to these subjects.[10] When Jesus healed the man with a withered hand on the Sabbath, he was violating the sacredness of the Sabbath by performing forbidden labor. When he broke bread with sinners and tax collectors, he was violating important purity restrictions by taking into his body food made unclean by the profane people at the meal.

Why were the Pharisees so obsessed with these particular laws? It is because these regulations publicly distinguished Jews from non-Jews more than any others, and their observance reinforced the perception of that difference.[11] The Pharisees understood that at the very heart of the difference that socially distinguished Jews from their neighbors were the purity rules about meals and Sabbath observance. As guardians of the holiness tradition, the Pharisees were passionate about diet and Sabbath regulations because they believed these observances were critical to the survival of the covenanted people.

The holiness perspective was the dominating view of reality for most Jews in the first century, including the nonobservant. Its roots were in the Temple sacrificial system, which required purity from the priests who made offerings to the Holy God. The Pharisees were engaged in a renewal movement intended to go beyond a representational holiness and to realize the vision of a nation of holy people, the priesthood of all Jews. By following the prescriptions of their teachers on diet and Sabbath observance, the Pharisees sought to demonstrate holiness as a possibility for the masses. Holiness was no longer confined to pilgrimage times and to those who could travel on those journeys and who could make, with the assistance of the Temple

10. See Boring (1995, p. 424) on Matt. 22:34-40, who states that the rabbis had counted 613 commands. Neusner (1973, p. 86) indicates that two-thirds, or some 229 of the 341 individual segments of material related to legal requirements for house or home, were associated with dietary and table matters.

11. Of course, circumcision was the physical marker of differentiation, but the Pharisees were concerned with establishing the understanding that circumcision meant little without obedience to the laws of purity.

priesthood, food offerings. Everyone, throughout the entire year and wherever they lived, could honor the sacred time of the Sabbath and participate in food rituals of purity.

A Clash of Paradigms

But there was another more ancient perspective in Jewish history and sacred literature that focused not on holiness and purity, but on loyalty to Yahweh and social responsibility. The prophets had declared God's judgment on the religious feasts, assemblies, and sacrifices of those who had failed in their obligations to God and other human beings.[12] They preached about justice, mercy, humility, and living in right relationship to God and neighbor. This tradition was not a complete rejection of all ritual, but a declaration that Yahweh despised rituals that failed to challenge injustice. Israel's God detested the implication that those rituals endorsed the positions of those who sanctimoniously carried them out while exploiting the needy. This was not, however, a complete rejection of concern for holiness. Rather, the prophetic message defined holiness in terms of a just and compassionate life.

It is not that all Pharisees were unaware of this other tradition. After all, some of them were able to answer correctly Jesus' question about the two commandments that encapsulated all of the Law and the Prophets. Most Pharisees believed themselves to be living in obedience to those commandments. The problem was that they understood love of God and love of neighbor through the eyes of those who perceived reality only in terms of purity and uncleanness. Love of God to them was keeping all the rules that ensured their holiness, and love of neighbor was a matter of practicing their piety so well that others would be converted to it. They sincerely believed this to be genuine spiritual devotion. They thought that when they did not associate with sinners, or touch or socialize with disabled or destitute persons, that they were in fact keeping the great commandments. It was that simple.

But Jesus understood that their preoccupation with purity was a preoccupation with self to the neglect of both God and neighbor. The Pharisees lived in a worldview that required them to separate and distinguish themselves in order to be pure and acceptable to God, a matter of survival for the

12. Amos 5:21-24; Mic. 6:6-8.

people of God. But for Jesus, it was clear that God was not interested in such a self-preserving mentality, since it was constructed out of a lack of trust in the care of *Abba*, self-will, and even cruelty, injustice, and discrimination toward the needy. Despite the sincerity of many of the devout, Jesus believed there were fundamental flaws in their way of looking at reality. Radical separatism carries within it the seeds of a mentality of superiority and the prideful shaming and shunning of other human beings that inflicts pain and suffering on those excluded. Among the excluded in Pharisaic separatism were the disabled, the destitute, and the despised.

The Pharisees criticized Jesus for eating with unclean persons. Jesus criticized the Pharisees for neglecting justice, mercy, and honesty.[13] It was a classic clash of differing paradigms. The Pharisees were focused on pure behavior, Jesus on purity of heart, manifested as a trusting relationship with the God of mercy and a compassionate relationship with neighbors in need.

The Anatomy of Purity

In addition to meal socializing with the outcasts and the despised, this conflict of worldviews realized itself in specific conflicts about washing hands before eating, fasting, healing, and gleaning grain on the Sabbath.

> The Pharisees and some of the teachers of the law who had come from Jerusalem gathered around Jesus and saw some of his disciples eating food with hands that were "unclean," that is unwashed. (The Pharisees and all Jews do not eat unless they give their hands a ceremonial washing, holding the tradition of the elders. When they come from the marketplace they do not eat unless they wash. And they observe many other traditions such as the washing of cups, pitchers and kettles.)
>
> So the Pharisees and teachers of the law asked Jesus, "Why don't your disciples live according to the tradition of the elders instead of eating their food with 'unclean' hands?"
>
> He replied, "Isaiah was right when he prophesied about you *actors,* as it is written:
>
> 'These people honor me with their lips,
>   but their hearts are far from me.

---

13. Q 43 (Matt. 23:23; Luke 11:39-40).

They worship me in vain;
> Their teachings are but rules taught by men.'

You have let go of the commands of God and are holding on to the traditions of men." (Mark 7:1-8; altered)[14]

Again, Jesus called the crowd to him and said, "Listen to me, everyone, and understand this. Nothing outside a man can make him 'unclean' by going into him. Rather it is what comes out of a man that makes him 'unclean.'" (Mark 7:14-16)

Minority cultures in danger of losing their identities through assimilation tend to be preoccupied with protecting bodily orifices from contamination.[15] This was especially true for ancient Israel. From the Pharisee perspective only kosher food should be eaten, and only with hands that had been ritually washed. This was not about modern hygiene, though there may have been some unintended side health benefits to the washing, provided the water was not polluted. This was centuries before the discovery of microorganisms and modern theories of sanitation. This was about protecting one's body and inner self from spiritual pollution. If the hands came into contact with people or things that were unclean, then that pollution could defile the whole inward person. The hands must first be ritually purified by washing prior to touching food that would be eaten.

The lips were an opening on the boundary of the body providing access to the inner body, and therefore dangerous to the inner person. Whatever passed the lips was potentially dangerous. The risk of eating something that would make one sick, or even something poisonous, was real. But just as real for the devout were the risks that the spiritual pollution associated with unclean people, and unholy food could cross the lips and corrupt the purity of the inner self. Such pollution not only endangered the devout individual, but endangered the blessings of Yahweh that were dependent on the descendants of Israel becoming a holy people.

---

14. I have translated *hupokritēs* as "actors" rather than "hypocrites" in order to better reflect the theater metaphor Jesus was using here and elsewhere in criticism of the Pharisees. "Actor" would have been an offensive attribution to the Pharisees, who desired to avoid all association with Greek and Roman culture and no doubt considered the theater to be an especially unclean place. Jesus used the metaphor to underscore the disconnect between the inner persons and the social presentations of those devoted to religious externalities.

15. See Douglas (1966).

Each person's body was symbolic of the covenanted social body. Just as the Jewish homeland needed to be protected from Gentile cultural intrusion and ethnic intermarriage, so the physical body was to be protected from profane contamination, lest Israel lose its soul.

In answering the challenge put to him by his adversaries, Jesus contrasted the traditions of men with the commandments of God, people's lips with their hearts, and what goes in with what comes out. The latter was intended as an earthy contrast. Eating food is not nasty; defecation of feces is. Honoring God by giving him lip service, either by dietary purity or with pious words, is unclean if the people's hearts are not in communion with him. The heart was considered the spiritual center, the true inner self that was the seat of all consciousness, emotions, and relationships. Lips may lie, but the secrets of the heart, the truth about the self in relationship, will be revealed.

> For out of the heart come evil thoughts, murder, adultery, sexual immorality, theft, false testimony, slander. These are what make a man "unclean"; but eating with unwashed hands does not make him "unclean." (Matt. 15:19-20)

> *Shame on you,* teachers of the Law and Pharisees, you *actors!* You give a tenth of your spices — mint, dill and cumin. But you have neglected the more important matters of the law — justice, mercy and faithfulness. (Matt. 23:23a; altered)

> *Shame on you,* teachers of the law and Pharisees, you *actors!* You clean the outside of the cup and dish, but inside they are full of greed and self-indulgence. Blind Pharisee! First clean the inside of the cup and dish, and then the outside also will be clean. (Matt. 23:25-26; altered)

> *How deserving of honor* are the pure in heart, for they will see God. (Matt. 5:8; altered)

It is not the digestive system that needs to be pure; it is the heart. It is not the externalities of people's lives that need to be cleansed; it is their attitudes and feelings toward others. It is not that people's bodies need to be made holy, but that their relationships with God and neighbors need to be made loving.

The Pharisee teachers of the Law developed extensive traditions, rules so specific that it was hoped they had anticipated every circumstance and every contingency in order that a devout person would know exactly how to achieve and maintain holiness in any situation. Among these rules were instructions for washing the outside of cups and plates. Jesus saw this as symbolic of the "yeast," the perspective of the Pharisees. They were preoccupied with externalities, with the ritual purity of the body, when they should have been concerned with the spiritual purity of the heart. Their extensive legalistic traditions dealt with surface purity.

Jesus tried to keep it simple. He focused largely on the Ten Commandments, for they were given by God and addressed the evil in human hearts. The commandments not to murder, commit adultery, steal, or slander all addressed crimes that begin in the heart, in passions of self-desire that inflict cruelty upon others. It is these passions that constituted for him the evil that is truly an abomination in the eyes of Yahweh.

Self-righteousness through ritual cleansing is an illusion. But, then, contrary to expectations, so is self-righteousness achieved through obedience to the Ten Commandments.

> You have heard that it was said to the people long ago, "Do not murder, and anyone who murders will be subject to judgment." But I tell you that anyone who is angry with his brother will be subject to judgment. (Matt. 5:21-22a)

> You have heard that it was said, "Do not commit adultery." But I tell you that anyone who looks at a woman lustfully has already committed adultery with her in his heart. (Matt. 5:27-28)

For Jesus, it is not enough to observe the commandments outwardly. To do so may result in avoiding human courts, but one must still face the divine court, which judges persons according to what is in their hearts, their real attitudes and relationships with others.

The "Yeast" of the Pharisees

When Jesus accused the Pharisees of having evil in their hearts while presenting themselves as exemplars of purity, he was not suggesting that their hearts were more evil than the hearts of others. The Pharisees' problem was not that they had evil hearts. That was everyone's human condition, a condition that could only be improved by forgiveness and the spiritually healing power of One greater than the self. The problem with the Pharisees, as Jesus viewed it, was their elaborate and stubborn persistence in the illusion that *their* hearts were *not* evil, because *they* were *good* people who obeyed the rules. That self-deception was a spiritual blindness that prevented them from recognizing the depth and persistence of sin in their own hearts and the repentance necessary to access the kingdom that Jesus announced.

Just as possessions were a stumbling block for the rich, devoutness was a hindrance for the Pharisees. Before one can truly repent of sin, one has to have an honest and accurate inventory of one's moral and spiritual failures, of wrongs done to others and the secret crimes of the heart. That is why the tax collector who prayed for mercy in Jesus' story went away justified and the Pharisee did not.[16] The tax collector had no trouble identifying the harm he had done or the corruption in his spiritual self. The Pharisee was blinded by his religious beliefs and his illusion of moral superiority.

Jesus' verbal attack on the Pharisees was not a condemnation of them as persons. Jesus broke bread with Pharisees as well as outcasts. His words of rebuke were challenges motivated by the desire to call them away from their wrong path to genuine repentance, and, at the same time, warnings to his followers not to be led astray by their ways.

"Be careful," Jesus *warned* them, "*Watch out for* the yeast of the Pharisees." (Matt. 16:6a; altered)

When Jesus warned his hearers to watch out for the "yeast" of the Pharisees, it was because he believed that it was very dangerous "yeast." The "yeast" of the kingdom of God was a sharply contrasting vision. "Yeast" was a powerful metaphor for the reality orientation and potent spiritual energy of each of these conflicting movements.

Meals as Social Currency

The radical difference in these energetic visions can be seen clearly in the contrasting significance of their approach to eating meals. Anthropologists have

---

16. See discussion of Luke 18:10-14 in chapter V.

long recognized that food and meals are social currency.[17] They are symbolic of social realities and objectives. Social eating functions across cultures as a means of healing conflicts and celebrating solidarity; of reinforcing models of status relationships; of celebrating life journey events of birth, marriage, and death; of incorporating changes in kinship and power, of redistributing material goods; and of communing with the gods. Every culture has rituals in the form of table etiquette. There are rules about what foods can be eaten, when and where they can be consumed, with whom, and in what pecking order.

Rituals and rules not only surround the social currency of shared meals, but eating is also symbolic of the relationship of humans to all of existence. To eat is to live off the death of other life, whether plant or animal. Appropriately sanctioned attitudes associated with consumption of food, such as humility, gratitude, and compassion, are common among most cultures, along with rules about the proper and respectful preparation of food. How humans eat provides a differentiation from the consumption of food in the animal kingdom. How various cultures eat provides distinctiveness that sets particular societies apart from their neighbors. When specific traditions associated with food and eating are challenged by an alternative model, it is not a trivial matter.

In the local Jewish culture, people ate two meals a day. Pharisees would only eat food on those occasions for which tithes had already been paid. This included tithes on every kind of food to be consumed, even the spices used for preparation such as mint, dill, and cumin. Such devotion meant that they sometimes went without food. Pharisees also required that all utensils and hands be washed, and they chose to eat only with those who strictly followed these rules.

Jesus and his disciples, on the other hand, ate with everyone, whether or not they were observant of purity rules.[18] They frequently ate whatever was placed before them, with unwashed hands, using unwashed plates and

---

17. A classic example is the Kwakiutl Native American potlatch first described by Franz Boas in 1897 and popularized by Mary Douglas in *Patterns of Culture* (1934). Potlatches were great feasts held for marriages, coming-of-age passages, and other important events. Other communities and tribes were invited and the feasts were marked by substantial exchanges of goods and indigenous currency. Social and economic obligations were created and reciprocity expected.

18. While Mark indicates that the disciples and not Jesus were the ones who failed to wash their hands, Luke records that Jesus himself ate without washing in the home of a Pharisee (Luke 11:38).

bowls, without regard to tithing. It is likely that Jesus himself followed his own commission to those he sent forth to assist with his work.

> When you enter a town and are welcomed, eat whatever is set before you. (Luke 10:8)

If, as a traveling wise man and healer, Jesus ate whatever food was placed before him, kosher or not, it is not surprising that he did not hesitate out of purity concerns to eat at the homes of tax collectors. It is unlikely that he received a kosher meal on those occasions. And Jesus would not have insulted a host by refusing to eat food that might not have been tithed, or out of dishes that might not have been purified.

On the other hand, Jesus seemed more than willing to offend a host who seemed to be obsessed with his mealtime purity. Jesus was constantly driven by his mission of healing the sick and disabled, and announcing the compassion of God, forgiveness of sins, and inclusiveness of the kingdom. It was that mission and purpose that prompted Jesus to use the opportunity of meals to challenge the conventional assumptions of hosts and others present with his radical vision and message. He was confrontational because he passionately cared about the Pharisees as children of *Abba*. Sometimes those confrontations appeared to be rude, but they were clearly intentional efforts to call the lives of his hosts into question in the hope of piercing their hardened defenses. His challenges to them were motivated by the desire to call them to abandon the preoccupation with their own personal devotion, righteous status, and social importance, and to enter *Abba's* kingdom of nobodies.

> One Sabbath, when Jesus went to eat in the house of a prominent Pharisee, he was being carefully watched. There in front of him was a man suffering from a *swollen mass of tissue*. Jesus asked the Pharisees and experts in the law, "Is it lawful to heal on the Sabbath or not?" But they remained silent. So taking hold of the man, he healed him and sent him away.
>
> Then he asked them, "If one of you has a son or an ox that falls into a well on the Sabbath day, will you not immediately pull him out?" And they had nothing to say. (Luke 14:1-6; altered)

Following the healing, Luke records that Jesus further used his mealtime opportunity to criticize those who were present for trying to sit in the seats with higher status. Even more outrageous was his chastising them for having a banquet and inviting only friends and relatives, while failing to ask the destitute, the crippled, the blind, and the lame.[19] His host and the friends of the host probably were deeply offended by Jesus' dinnertime meddling. From Jesus' perspective he focused the offense where he wanted it to be. The "yeast" of the Pharisees was exposed as exclusive, hierarchical, legalistic, and obsessive. The "yeast" of Jesus was revealed as inclusive, status-free, gracious, and spontaneous. Such orientations symbolized radically different views of the Messianic banquet.

The Intent of the Law

The healing of the man with the tumor-like illness in the home of a Pharisee revealed not only the difference in Messianic visions, but also the difference between the Pharisees and Jesus in relation to the Law of Moses. The fourth commandment stated:

> Remember the Sabbath day by keeping it holy. Six days you shall labor and do all your work, but the seventh day is a Sabbath to the Lord your God. On it you shall not do any work, neither you, nor your son or daughter, nor your manservant or maidservant, nor your animals, nor the alien within your gates. (Exod. 20:8-10)

The relationship between the Pharisees and this commandment was radically different from Jesus' relationship to it.

Not a Burden, But a Gift

The Pharisees had a very literal and concrete approach to the Sabbath. The problem was, "What constitutes work and what does not?" And how does one comply with the commandment when faced with situations in which obedience is particularly difficult? Are there legitimate exceptional cases? As in the case of meals, the Pharisaic teachers of the Law developed over time a very long and complicated list of rules and regulations providing answers to these questions. Observant Jews were supposed to know these regulations and try to follow them.

19. Luke 14:12-24.

And you experts in the law, *shame on you* because you load people down with burdens they can hardly carry, and you yourselves will not lift one finger to help them. (Luke 11:46; altered)

Jesus saw the Pharisaic tradition of legalese as laying a heavy burden on the people. On the other hand, his own "yeast" is described in sharp contrast.

Come to me, *every one of you who is exhausted and burdened down,* and I will give you rest. Take my yoke upon you and learn from me, for I am gentle and humble in heart and you will find rest for your souls. For my yoke is easy and my burden is light. (Matt. 11:28-30; altered)

Jesus' "yeast" not only does not exhaust and burden down, it is declared to be light and easy, and restful to the soul.

One Sabbath Jesus was going through the grainfields, and as his disciples walked along, they began to pick some heads of grain. The Pharisees said to him, "Look, why are they doing what is unlawful on the Sabbath?"

He answered, "Have you never read what David did when he and his companions were hungry and in need? In the days of Abiathar the high priest, he entered the house of God and ate the consecrated bread, which is lawful only for priests to eat. And he also gave some to his companions."

Then he said to them, "The Sabbath was made for man, not man for the Sabbath." (Mark 2:23-27)

Sabbath observance was a commandment, but its intent was to ensure the well-being of God's children. They should not work all the time. They need to rest on a regular basis from their labors. The commandment to keep the Sabbath was a gift of Yahweh's compassion. It was intended for the benefit of human beings, particularly those who were in servitude and at the mercy of the leisurely class who could pretty much rest any time they wanted.

Those who owned slaves and kept servants were inclined to get as much work from them as possible, since keeping them cost food, supplies, and other basic resources. The Sabbath assured those who served in Jewish households a time of respite. As the day consisted of a rhythm of activity and rest, so the week consisted of days of labor and a day of rest. To be sure, this weekly rhythm had benefits for productivity. People who rested a day a week were undoubtedly better workers the other six days. But the Sabbath was in its essence about the compassion of God and justice for those who were subservient.

In recalling the hunger of David and his companions, who ate the consecrated bread out of urgent need, Jesus underscored the point that the sacred rules existed to serve humankind. Jesus' revolutionary view was that such rules could be broken when human need required it. So also, when the disciples were hungry and began to gather grain from the fields, a gleaning that would have been perfectly legal for these now destitute followers of Jesus on any day but the Sabbath, they violated the Sabbath rule. They broke the commandment of God, but in satisfying their hunger they were obeying God by fulfilling the Law's compassionate intent.

The commandments were not intended to be a burden, but a gift from God. They were not substitutes for responsible decision-making; they were to be taken seriously within an understanding of God's compassion and responsibility for the well-being of the neighbor. Sometimes it was God's will that they be broken, if a higher good could be achieved. "Which is lawful on the Sabbath: to do good or to do evil, to save life or to kill?" Jesus asked. Deliberately and dramatically Jesus healed on the Sabbath in the presence of the Pharisees. Such "work" was a demonstration of the way in which Jesus understood the Law. The intent of the Ten Commandments, and of the legal requirements of the books of the Law, was the love of God and neighbor. These two great commandments summed up all the others for they revealed the intention behind the rest. A child of *Abba*, who lived in intimate relationship with him, was to discern God's will, in each human context, guided by the Law and true to its intent, without idolizing it.

Misuse of the Law

Jesus was focused on personal and social responsibility. People did not need more and more rules to clarify God's will. There was plenty of guidance already available in the Scriptures. That is why Jesus rejected the authority of the Pharisaic interpretive traditions. What was needed was for people to abandon a legalistic and moralistic understanding of the Scriptures for one that took seriously their intent, and to take responsibility for their own actions in relationship to the ultimate requirement to love God and neighbor.

The Pharisees were focused on certitude of behavior. By following the rules carefully, they could achieve their aim of becoming good and holy people, and, by implication, better than others. They believed the rules provided justification for their actions, and that their strict observance of the rules entitled them to judge those who did not observe them. Jesus, in contrast, trusted that the compassionate God alone could judge and justify the actions of people.

When the Pharisees condemned Jesus for breaking the Sabbath commandment, he enjoyed pointing out to them that their traditions were actually filled with exceptions to commandments; but their exceptions, unlike his, were not always motivated by a love for God and responsiveness to human need.

> And he said to them, "You have a fine way of setting aside the commands of God in order to observe your own traditions! For Moses said, 'Honor your father and your mother,' and, 'Anyone who curses his father or mother must be put to death.' But you say that if a man says to his father or mother: 'Whatever help you might have seen from me is Corban' (that is, a gift devoted to God), then you no longer let him do anything for his father or mother. Thus you nullify the word of God by your tradition that you have handed down. And you do many things like that." (Mark 7:9-13)

Once again, it is important to understand the intent of the Law. The commandment to honor father and mother was not simply intended to ensure the right relationships between parents and children while the children were growing up. It was also intended as the social welfare system of the day, which assured that the aging and elderly parents received compassionate care and support.

In religious zeal, some Pharisees were allowed to circumvent their responsibility to provide for their parents by declaring the resources that would have gone to that purpose as "dedicated to God."[20] By seeking their own personal holiness at the expense of the welfare of their parents through the declaration of Corban, they in fact made the commandment meaningless, for they had avoided its purpose. Social responsibility for those in need was the intent of the Law. Some Pharisees violated that intent by placing their own desires for personal righteousness above social responsibility.

Laws are not made to be broken; they are intended to serve humankind by ensuring justice, mercy, and responsibility. When laws burden people down and get in the way of justice, mercy, and responsibility, then obedience

---

20. The practice referred to in this passage is not found in later Jewish literature, but that is no reason to doubt that it was practiced at the time of Jesus by one or more schools of Pharisaism.

to the intent takes precedence over obedience to the literal meaning. This is not libertinism. This is radical obedience to the will of God involving personal accountability for social responsibility.

A Question of Divorce

Jesus was also concerned about the misuse of the Law to evade social responsibility, a kind of libertinism with legal justification.

> Some Pharisees came and tested him by asking, "Is it lawful for a man to divorce his wife?"
>
> "What did Moses command you?" he replied.
>
> They said, "Moses permitted a man to write a certificate of divorce and send her away."
>
> "It was because your hearts were hard that Moses wrote you this law," Jesus replied. "But at the beginning of creation God 'made male and female.' For this reason a man will leave his father and mother and be united to his wife, and the two will become one flesh. So they are no longer two, but one. Therefore what God has joined together, let man not separate." (Mark 10:2-9)

A group of Pharisees tried to trick Jesus with their question about divorce. The question was about the *lawfulness* of divorce. Jesus responded to their challenge by turning the question back on them. Their answer was that the Law *permitted* divorce. The reference was to Deuteronomy 24:1-4, in which a man who divorces his wife is commanded not to remarry her if she has subsequently married and been divorced by another. Some Pharisees interpreted this as legal permission to divorce. It was a kind of divine justification for those who had chosen to send their wives away in order to achieve a greater level of devotion.

Divorce was a one-way street in Jewish culture. Among the Romans, a woman might divorce a man, but among the Jews, only men could divorce women. They frequently did, creating a society with significant numbers of discarded and destitute women. Such divorce was a cruel practice of shaming women who no longer were pleasing to their husbands, and of turning them into outcasts without any honorable means of support.

In the debate, Jesus again focused on the intent of the Law. He pointed out that the Law was written because of the callousness of those men who discarded their wives with little or no concern for their welfare. The commandment was not permission to divorce, but recognition of the reality of such separations and the need to protect discarded wives from destitution, by assuring they had divorce papers that allowed them to remarry. It was, as Jesus said, necessitated by the hardheartedness of human beings.

Typical of the legalist worldview, the Pharisees lost the social responsibility intent of the Law and focused on its implied fine points. The Shammai and Hillel schools of Pharisees debated whether divorce could be for almost any reason, or only because of adultery. But Jesus refused to be drawn into choosing one side over the other.[21] Both were wrong, for they were trapped by their legalistic and moralistic presuppositions.

Jesus changed the issue from one of lawfulness to one of theological ethics. Jesus probably knew of many women who had been discarded by their husbands and who had become destitute in the process. The question of divorce was not a legal question. It was rather a question of what was the will of the compassionate God. For Yahweh, in his compassion, established marriage at the foundations of the world for the benefit of humankind. Marriage united two people into one, and established a family, an arrangement not only important to the two who became one, but to their children, their descendants, and society as well. And Yahweh, who befriended the victims of injustice, did not sanction the suffering created when a woman was discarded in divorce. A wife was not a piece of property to be thrown away. Such a holy union was not dissolved simply because a man grew dissatisfied with his mate and gave her a legal piece of paper. No such human act, no matter how legal, could so easily dissolve what God had united.

In revealing the fallacy of the Pharisees' position, Jesus was not, however, creating a new law prohibiting all divorce.[22] In establishing the premise

---

21. Matthew has Jesus take sides with those who limited divorce to an offense of adultery (Matt. 5:32). Most scholars believe that the version in Mark 10:11, which contains no such exception, is likely to reflect Jesus' words on the subject.

22. I am aware that many respected scholars have concluded that establishment of such a law is exactly what Jesus did when he declared that those who divorced and remarried committed adultery. It is important to remember that for Jesus those who remained married and had adulterous fantasies also violated the commandment against adultery. Of course, Matthew's portrait of Jesus as the new Moses, a second lawgiver, has influenced Christianity throughout its history. But when the issue of Jesus and the Law is looked at in its entirety, it seems to me that one is required to conclude that marriage, as the Sabbath that also is ad-

that divorce was an ethical rather than legal matter, Jesus was consistent with his position concerning Sabbath observance. While human beings could not dissolve what God had joined together, God could certainly dissolve what either human beings or God had joined together. Marriage was made for humankind, not humankind for marriage. Personal and social responsibility in the context of love of God and neighbor conceivably could require the breaking of marriage vows, just as the presence of a man needing healing might result in the breaking of the Sabbath commandment.[23] Marriage, for Jesus, was to be taken with utmost seriousness, for its intent was the well-being of humankind. But Jesus' conflicts with the Pharisees over the Sabbath made his position quite clear. The well-being of humankind can always best be served through the continuous exercise of compassionate personal and social responsibility, even in those relatively rare times when literal obedience to the Law gets in the way.

Responsibility and True Devotion

Scripture, for Jesus, was a wonderful gift of God's compassion. God's merciful and just intentions were clear to him behind every passage. This spiritual meaning beneath the words provided a framework for the choices he made in the privacy of his own heart about his own life and in relationship to the lives of others. Having so decided, he trusted the outcomes and the justification of those decisions to God alone.

> When you see a cloud rising in the west, immediately you say, "It's going to rain," and it does. And when the south wind blows, you say, "It's going to be hot," and it is.
> *Actors!* You know how to interpret the appearance of the earth and

---

dressed in the creation story, was made for humankind, not humankind for marriage. Jesus criticized the Pharisees for interpreting the Law as permission to divorce. He also criticized them for turning the Sabbath requirement into an absolute. Jesus' position consistently was focused on the compassionate intent of the Law.

23. To be sure, Jesus' position on the Law's intent leaves open the possibility for someone to rationalize and justify self-will and personal desire by reference to some higher good. But it is equally abhorrent and contrary to the intent of marriage that an absolutist approach would, for example, condemn a victim of violent spousal abuse to a life of living hell or violent death.

the sky. *So* how is it that you don't know how to interpret the present time?

And why can't you decide for yourselves what is right? (Luke 12:54-57; altered)

Jesus' contemporaries had no difficulty deciding what the weather was going to be when certain climatic conditions occurred. He chided them, telling them to apply those same powers of observation and wisdom to their present lives and situations, and to think and make decisions for themselves. They were responsible for their own lives and decisions. No authority of Scripture, law, or tradition could absolve them from that responsibility. To live in that kind of freedom with responsibility was revolutionary. In contrast, the complicated slavish legalism of the Pharisees was a giant stumbling block that prevented true devotion to *Abba*.

> *Shame on you,* teachers of the law and Pharisees, you *actors!* You shut the kingdom of heaven in men's faces. You yourselves do not enter, nor will you let those enter who are trying to.
>
> *Shame on you,* teachers of the law and Pharisees, you *actors!* You travel over land and sea to win a single convert, and when he becomes one, you make him twice as much a son of hell as you are. (Matt. 23:13-15; altered)

Jesus also criticized the Pharisees, or at least some of them, for their ostentatious displays of piety.

> And when you pray, do not be like the *actors,* for they love to pray standing in the synagogues and on the street corners to be seen by men. I tell you the truth, they have received their reward in full. But when you pray, go into your room, close the door and pray to your Father, who is unseen. Then your Father, who sees what is done in secret, will reward you. (Matt. 6:5-6; altered)

> *Shame on you,* Pharisees, because you love the most important seats in the synagogues and greetings in the marketplaces. (Luke 11:43; altered)

In contrast, Jesus instructed his disciples to turn to *Abba* in secret and to sit in the seats of the unimportant. True devotion is not about impressing other human beings. It is not about status in this world. It is about entering the status-free world of the Spirit. Genuine devotion is about entering into relationship with the unseen God who loves all his children extravagantly. It is about serving God, with humility, gratitude, and compassion.

Pharisee Enemies and Allies

Given their strong differences, relations between Jesus and many Pharisees were understandably tense. The Pharisees were insulted by Jesus' harsh remarks.[24] They considered Jesus' disregard for and disagreement with their theology as dangerous and blasphemous. His criticism caused the people who generally held the Pharisee sect in high regard to question its legitimacy. It interfered with their proselytizing and achievement of their vision of a nation made up of people who lived as they did. Because Jesus was a danger to that vision, their fears increased that he would contribute to the loss of Jewish identity and to the ever-present threat of cultural and racial assimilation, and ultimately the loss of God's favor.

The Gospel writers agree that the Pharisees tried to trap Jesus by challenging him with what they believed would be "no win" situations for the charismatic teacher. They accused him of being demonically possessed and in league with the "prince of demons."[25] All four Gospels agree that some of the Pharisees participated in the plot that led to his crucifixion.[26]

On the other hand, as we have seen, Jesus sometimes visited the homes of Pharisees and broke bread with them. Some evidently tried to assist him in avoiding arrest.

> At that time some Pharisees came to Jesus and said to him, "Leave this place and go somewhere else, Herod wants to kill you." (Luke 13:31)

John's Gospel tells us that Nicodemus, who approached Jesus at night (John 3:1-2), was a Pharisee, as probably was Joseph of Arimathea, the aristocrat who provided a burial cave for Jesus.[27] John reports that Nicodemus defended Jesus to members of the Sanhedrin.[28] While the Pharisees generally

---

24. Luke 11:45.
25. Mark 3:22.
26. Matt. 12:14; Mark 3:6; Luke 20:19; John 18:3.
27. Luke 23:50-53.
28. John 7:50-52.

were presented as stereotype adversaries, as villainous *dramatis personae,* in the Gospel dramas, in real life they consisted of individuals and subgroups who were distinct from one another in significant ways. And Jesus apparently agreed with the Pharisees against their rivals, the Sadducees, on such important matters as the existence of the spirit world and the resurrection of the dead.[29]

Nevertheless, Jesus found himself in profound conflict with many of the Pharisees. The eyes of Jesus pierced the souls of these religiously devout men and saw their preoccupation with superficialities, their self-righteous pretensions, their moral superiorities, and their positions of privilege as overwhelming obstacles to authentic relationships with *Abba* and their fellow human beings. This was a conflict that would contribute mightily to the decision of some Pharisee members of the Sanhedrin to call upon the ruling despots to put Jesus to death.

29. See Mark 12:18-25; Acts 23:8; and Josephus, *Jewish War* 2.164-66.

CHAPTER VII

Jesus and the Despots

A t the time of Jesus' birth, Herod the Great was "king of the Jews," a position he had held by the authority of Caesar and by decree of the Roman
Senate for almost forty years. During that time Herod had engaged in an
ambitious building program, including several military fortresses, royal palaces, and Roman-styled urban centers.

The most impressive architectural marvel undertaken during his reign
was the Temple in Jerusalem. Work began on the structure in 19 BCE and it
was not completed until sixty-six years after Herod's death, and only eight
years before its destruction. He doubled the size of the ancient Temple
Mount and enclosed it with massive hundred-foot-high retaining walls built
on a foundation of gigantic stones. The Temple's boundaries were approximately a fifth of a mile wide and a quarter of a mile long. Gold and silver
adorned the inner courts. By building the massive and ornate Temple, Herod
sought to win over support for his kingdom from a majority of the people
and to marginalize his enemies.[1] The success of this objective, however, was
undercut by his desire to please his Roman overlords. For example, when he
placed the image of a golden eagle, a symbol of Jupiter, the Roman god of
power, on the gate of the Temple, he enraged the teachers of the Law.[2]

1. Herod was an Idumaean. The Idumaeans were from the region immediately south of
Judea. They had been forced to convert to Judaism during the reign of John Hyrcanus (135-
104 BCE) and were not considered to be descended from one of the twelve tribes. Because of
this fact, Herod and his children were thought unworthy to rule or to appoint high priests by
traditional Jews.

2. Most of the information about Herod and Pilate discussed in this chapter is derived
from the works of the first-century Jewish historian Flavius Josephus.

Herod's Cruel Legacy

Herod the Great may have been a great builder but he was far from a great human being. He was by any reasonable standard a cruel and evil despot. His rule had been secured by the slaughter of Jerusalem's defenders on a Sabbath when devout Jews refused to fight, and by the execution at his command of forty-five Sadducee chief priests. His paranoia about the vulnerability of his position resulted over time in his ordering the murders of several family members, including his wife's seventeen-year-old brother, Herod's beloved wife herself, and her two remaining sons. While terminally ill and suffering in horrible pain with what was likely a kidney disease around 4 BCE, he also ordered the execution of a number of key Jewish leaders.[3]

At the death of Herod the Great, his son, Herod Antipas, was appointed by Augustus Caesar to rule over Galilee. This Herod followed in his father's footsteps by embarking on yet another ambitious building program. He rebuilt the city of Sepphoris, which had been destroyed in a rebellion following his father's death, and he constructed the capital city of Tiberius on the western shore of the Sea of Galilee in honor of his Caesar and as home to his own splendid palace.

Herod Antipas also perpetuated his father's legacy of paranoia and cruelty. Seditious threats were believed to be everywhere. It was this Herod who put John the Baptist in prison and ordered the outspoken prophet's beheading. When Jesus' activities in Galilee came to Herod's attention, he was, no doubt, profoundly distressed. He knew he had another troublemaker on his hands.

> At that time some Pharisees came to Jesus and said to him, "Leave this place and go somewhere else. Herod wants to kill you."
>
> He replied, "Go tell that fox, 'I will drive out demons and heal people today and tomorrow, and on the third day I will reach my goal.' In any case, I must keep going today and tomorrow and the next day — for surely no prophet can die outside Jerusalem." (Luke 13:31-33)

---

3. Dr. Jan Hirshmann, a University of Washington School of Medicine in Seattle physician, reported in January 2002 to the Historical Clinical Pathology Conference meeting at the University of Maryland that Herod probably died of chronic kidney disease, complicated by Fournier's gangrene. The execution of the remaining Jewish leadership was avoided in this instance when Herod's granddaughter, Salome, intervened.

When warned of Herod's intentions to kill him, Jesus sent a sharp message back to the Galilean tetrarch. It was a reply that challenged the ruler's honor. When Jesus called Herod a "fox," it was not a compliment about Herod's intelligence or even his cleverness. In rural Galilee, a fox was a pest. It was considered a nasty creature that lived in the ground and preyed upon the chickens and other fowl that were kept around the homes of peasants and villagers. This was the equivalent of the modern insult of calling someone a "rat," except that "fox" carried a more intense connotation of predator. It was a bold message that, if delivered, would have made Herod even more determined to do Jesus harm.

Jesus had no illusions about the character of his powerful adversary. But, for Jesus, Herod was not in charge. *Abba,* who guided and directed his work each day, was in charge. Jesus understood that he was likely to be killed because of his revolutionary ministry. Jesus identified himself with the prophets, and believed that he was destined to die, as they had died, in Jerusalem. But that would happen not according to Herod's plan, but according to God's plan.

Suffering under Pontius Pilate

Herod Antipas was not the only despot who perceived Jesus as a threat. Pontius Pilate was the fifth Roman governor of Judea since Archelaus, another son of Herod the Great, had been banished by the Romans for incompetence in 6 CE. Pilate ruled over the province from 26 to 36 CE, a period that included all of Jesus' active ministry. Pilate had the arrogance and brutality required of a provincial governor. He could be as merciless as Herod the Great and his progeny. For example, Pilate once angered the people by raiding the Temple treasury, entering the Temple itself, and confiscating funds by force, in order to pay for an aqueduct system for the region. He requested a meeting in Jerusalem with those who objected, ostensibly to hear their arguments. He then met with about three hundred protesters while seated on a tribunal, a raised wooden stage. Unknown to the crowd, he had his troops dispersed in plain clothing among them and when the people began to shout their protests, he signaled his troops, who then brutally beat and clubbed the unarmed people. A number of them, including Galilean protestors, died.[4]

4. This event may have been influenced in the tradition with regard to the "Galileans

Now there were some present at that time who told Jesus about the Galileans whose blood Pilate had mixed with their sacrifices. Jesus answered, "Do you think that these Galileans were worse sinners than all other Galileans because they suffered this way? I tell you no! But unless you *adopt a new orientation*, you too will all perish." (Luke 13:1-3; altered)

Jesus made two points when confronted with the information about the slaughtered Galileans. The first point was that their suffering was not because they were worse sinners than others. This point was aimed at the devout, those who believed their good fortune was evidence of their righteousness and the suffering of others was due to their sin. They had been slaughtered because of the viciousness of Pilate, not the punishment of God. The second point Jesus made on this occasion was that his listeners and their countrymen needed a whole new orientation, or such destruction would come upon them all. This point was primarily aimed at the violent, zealous patriots and the militants.

The Zealot Insurgency

The Zealots hated Pilate for his insults to the honor of their Temple. They despised Roman rule, and plotted the overthrow of the government.

Judas the Galilean appeared in the days of the census and led a band of people in revolt. He too was killed, and all his followers were scattered. (Acts 5:37)

Judas, who led a tax revolt near the time of Jesus' birth, was described by the Jewish historian Josephus as the founder of what he called the Fourth Philosophy.[5] In addition to the Pharisees, Sadducees, and Essenes, there was the "philosophy" of the Zealots. It was not so much a philosophy, however, as it was an insurgency. The followers of Judas had as their motto "No Lord but

---

whose blood Pilate mixed with their sacrifices" by another historical event. It is likely that the hot-blooded Galileans were among those massacred by Archaelus, son of Herod the Great, around a quarter of a century earlier. The Luke passage probably is referring to the clubbing to death of Jews in the Temple who protested Pilate's misuse of Temple funds described by Josephus (*Jewish War* 2.175-77; *Antiquities* 18.60-62), but there is no record by the historian of blood being mixed with sacrifices on that occasion.

5. Josephus, *Antiquities* 18.1.

God." Their beliefs were similar to those of the purity-obsessed Pharisees except that, in addition, they were ideological militants willing to fight, to risk the deaths of family members, and to die themselves before submitting to any ruler other than God. Their loyalty was to a kingdom of God, which they believed would be realized as God blessed their insurgency efforts. They organized small bands, virtually indistinguishable from bandits, which, off and on for decades, disrupted the peace and controlled parts of the countryside. Although Zealots were frequently defeated, captured, and executed, their movement continued to grow. Around 47 CE, Judas's sons, Jacob and Simon, were arrested and crucified by the governor Tiberius Alexander, presumably for sedition.

The Zealot movement is also credited with giving birth to the first-century version of terrorists in the years preceding the Temple's destruction. They were the *sicarii* who mingled with crowds and murdered with knives those who collaborated with the Romans.[6] It was ultimately this Zealot insurgency movement that led to the Roman destruction of the Temple and of Jerusalem in 70 CE.[7]

"The Temple of the Lord"

While the martyred Galileans did not suffer because they were greater sinners than others, their Zealot orientation had within itself the seeds of self-destruction. Their dangerous orientation was the conventional wisdom that was shared by many fellow Jews, in both Galilee and Judea. It was a combination of Jewish nationalism and the blurring of the lines between God and the Temple that created the delusion that because Yahweh was believed to dwell in the Holy of Holies, victory was guaranteed provided they militantly guard the Temple from sacrilege. If they kept the Temple pure, they reasoned, the Temple, as the dwelling place of God, would in turn protect them from and assure victory over their enemies.

Centuries before, the prophet Jeremiah had mocked those who believed that the Temple would protect them from conquest and destruction.

6. Some scholars have suggested that Judas Iscariot who betrayed Jesus was a *sicarri* or the son of a *sicarii*. This is based on a possible origin of "Iscariot" as derived from the Greek *sikarios*, which means "assassin." The *sicarii* as an organized resistance, however, probably did not appear until twenty years after Jesus was crucified.

7. See "Zealots" article by Kohler (2002b).

Do not trust in deceptive words and say, "This is the Temple of the Lord, the Temple of the Lord, the Temple of the Lord." (Jer. 7:4)

Jesus' revolutionary view, as that of Jeremiah, was that it was an illusion to believe the Temple would protect the people. Furthermore, the Temple itself, as it existed at the time, was an abomination to God, a corruption of the true faith. Rather than the dwelling place of Yahweh, it was an abandoned and vacant house.

Look, your house is *abandoned*. (Luke 13:35a; altered)

Not only was the Temple not occupied by Yahweh, it was useless as protection. It would itself be destroyed, despite its imposing and fortress-like structure.[8]

As he was leaving the temple, one of his disciples said to him, "Look Teacher! What massive stones! What magnificent buildings!"

"Do you see all these great buildings?" replied Jesus. "Not one stone here will be left on another; every one will be thrown down." (Mark 13:1-2)

The hope for avoiding the coming doom and destruction was not the presence of their mighty building, built by cruel despots. The only hope for the people was repentance, to change direction, to obtain an entirely new orientation before their misguided struggle against the despots on behalf of the corrupt Temple brought destruction upon them all. That was why Jesus "set his face" to go to Jerusalem. He set out on this road in order to call the people gathered from far and wide at festival time to repentance and to new life in God's kingdom.

---

8. While some scholars have concluded that statements foretelling the destruction of the Temple could only be redactions made after the fall of Jerusalem in 70 CE, it seems likely that Luke 13:35a and Mark 13:1-2 represent authentic words of Jesus in the spirit of the prophetic tradition. Jeremiah (Jer. 26:6) and Micah (Mic. 3:12) had made similar predictions about the first Temple. Such prophetic words were not about fortune telling. They were a call to repentance. The words in question here appear to belong to a very old passion narrative that predates the fall of Jerusalem and are consistent with Jesus' prophetic activities in Jerusalem and the response of the religious authorities to them (see Perkins, 1995, p. 685, notes on Mark 13:1-2). The prophecy certainly would have been recalled after the events of 70 CE as supporting the claims of the early church about Jesus.

Jesus' Jerusalem Mission

Jesus understood not only the risks associated with his journey to Jerusalem, but also the overwhelming probability of his own suffering and death at its conclusion. For three years or more he had carried out his ministry of teaching and healing, mostly in the rural villages of Galilee, avoiding the political hotbed cities of Sepphoris and Tiberius, where he would be seen quickly as a threat to Herod's rule. Nor did he go to Jerusalem, where he certainly would become a target of Pilate and the chief priests who would see him as one more dangerous radical.[9] But the time came when he arrived at the conviction that at this particular Passover he was being led by the Spirit to make the journey to the Holy City.

Jesus had demonstrated dramatically the inclusiveness of *Abba*. The disabled, the destitute, the despised, and even some of the devout had been beneficiaries of his teaching, of his healing, and of forgiveness and participation in the reality of a community of followers where human boundaries of wealth and status were irrelevant. Many were already experiencing this foretaste of the Messianic banquet and all its wonderful benefits. Now it was time to confront the despots, not as the Zealots had done and would continue to do, but as a prophet who believed himself not only sent to chastise, but also called upon to break the cycle of retribution, to demonstrate *Abba's* compassion even for and especially for the despots, and in doing so, for every human being, no matter how possessed by evil.

---

9. This is based on Mark's chronology as the earliest of the Gospels. Of course, if one adopts John's chronology rather than Mark's, Jesus visited Jerusalem several times. Many scholars prefer John's chronology because it seems more probable to them that Jesus was an observant Jew who would have attended many festivals, not just one. On the other hand, many of these same scholars reject just about everything else in John as not historical due to its late date. I believe there is a tendency on the part of some to overemphasize Jesus' orthodoxy (and John's chronology better supports that) and to underestimate his idiosyncratic style and innovator role. There is no way to know for certain which chronology is accurate. It is also possible, as a number of scholars have suggested, that Jesus went to Jerusalem that final year of his life during the fall Feast of Tabernacles and then was in and around Jerusalem teaching until Passover in the spring. Whether he made several trips, or was in the vicinity a week or six months, I am convinced he was there to preach the gospel of the kingdom of God, not to attend the festivals as an observant pilgrim.

A Cry for "Deliverance Now"

Passover was the annual spring festival that brought the largest crowds of the year to Jerusalem. Those unable to make the journey would celebrate the deliverance from Egyptian slavery with their families at home. But thousands would descend upon Jerusalem during the spring lunar month of Nisan each year to participate in the annual rites of Passover and the sacrifice of lambs. They would come in groups, many clustered together with their friends and neighbors, into the Holy City passing near the Mount of Olives. At both the fall festival of Tabernacles and this Passover pilgrimage they would sing psalms praising God and commemorating deliverance from oppression.

Passover was a volatile time and one that required vigilance on the part of the Roman governor. The symbols and images of the festival were ancient celebrations of the defiance of foreign rule. They spoke of the death and destruction of the ruling Egyptian households and armies and divine deliverance of the Israelites from foreign oppression. Such rituals could excite and motivate the people to follow seditious leaders, who continued to appear despite the gruesome crucifixions that frequently were used to discourage rebellion.

> As they approached Jerusalem and came to Bethphage and Bethany at the Mount of Olives, Jesus sent two of his disciples, saying to them, "Go to the village ahead of you, and just as you enter it, you will find a colt tied there, which no one has ever ridden. Untie it and bring it here. If anyone asks you, 'Why are you doing this?' Tell him, 'The Lord needs it and will send it back here shortly.'"
>
> They went and found a colt outside in the street, tied at a doorway. As they untied it, some people standing there asked, "What are you doing, untying that colt?" They answered as Jesus had told them to, and the people let them go. When they brought the colt to Jesus and threw their cloaks over it, he sat on it. Many people spread their cloaks on the road, while others spread branches they had cut in the fields. Those who went ahead and those who followed shouted, *"Deliverance now! Bless the one who comes in the name of the Lord! Bless the coming kingdom of our father David! Deliverance now!"* Jesus entered Jerusalem and went to the temple. He looked around at everything, but since it was already late, he went out to Bethany with the twelve. (Mark 11:1-11; altered)[10]

10. I have translated "Hosanna" as *"Deliverance now!"* which I take to be the meaning of the utterance in Ps. 118:25.

At or about the same time that Jesus entered the city from the east on a young donkey, Pontius Pilate and his troops entered the city from the west. The contrast was dramatic. Pilate came on a warrior steed, with imperial ceremony, all the might of Rome behind him, and trained cavalry and foot soldiers with deadly weapons around him. The presence of Pilate and his forces was designed effectively to intimidate and warn the crowds that no disturbance would be tolerated during the festival.

Jesus, on the other hand, was surrounded by unarmed festival pilgrims. Most were probably from Galilee and many were with him because their lives had been transformed through healing, forgiveness, and inclusive compassion. As was the custom, in preparation for the festival, they had palms and other branches from the countryside intended to be used in a later ritual that would take place in the Temple. As Jesus began his ride, they began to wave these branches and to sing traditional festival songs. They spontaneously removed clothes from the bags they were carrying and spread them in front of the colt.

This event instantly became much more than a group of pilgrims arriving in Jerusalem for Passover. The traditional symbolic palm branches and psalms suddenly took on a much greater significance. The palms had royal symbolism, dating from Hasmonean rule.[11] The Mount of Olives was the expected location of the coming of the Messiah.[12] The clothing served as a makeshift royal runner. Jesus was being hailed as a king. No such accolades accompanied Caesar's representative, Pontius Pilate, as he entered Jerusalem on the other side of town.

Singing the songs of "Hosanna," the cry for *"Deliverance now!"* his followers linked Jesus' ministry of liberating compassion to the deliverance of their ancestors from Egyptian slavery.[13] It must have been a strange sight, perhaps even laughable to the Temple authorities who observed this from their lofty watchtowers overseeing the road upon which the pilgrims came. Here was a man who probably looked like a beggar, riding a small donkey and receiving the honor due a king from a bunch of followers, most of whom looked like beggars themselves. This was a ragtag parade at best.

---

11. The palm branch became a symbol of the nation and royalty used in décor and coinage as an acceptable image that was neither man nor beast and therefore did not violate the second commandment.

12. Zech. 14:4.

13. The traditional psalms sung at both the fall festival of Tabernacles and Passover included Psalms 115–118.

The "No Messiah" Messiah

Jesus himself had carefully chosen his method of entry to be a public demonstration of his unique mission. He clearly wanted to show that he was not the Messiah that so many longed for. He did not come leading an army of armed combatants to wrest the Holy City from the Gentile oppressors. Nor did he come to force the hand of God and inaugurate a violent apocalypse. He came to Jerusalem to continue his ministry of calling human beings to repentance; to prepare them for the coming of God's kingdom in power whenever it might appear; and to invite them to a new relationship with *Abba* and to the realization now of the inclusive and caring relationship between *Abba's* children. He came as the prophetic messenger of compassion and peace. That is why Jesus chose an obscure passage from Zechariah to dramatize the meaning of his mission.

> Rejoice greatly, O Daughter of Zion! Shout, Daughter of Jerusalem! See, your king comes to you righteous and having salvation, gentle and riding on a donkey, on a colt, the foal of a donkey.
>
> I will take away the chariots from Ephraim and the war-horses from Jerusalem, and the battle bow will be broken. He will proclaim peace to the nations. His rule will extend from sea to sea and from the River to the ends of the earth. (Zech. 9:9-10)

This is a king who gently and humbly is riding on a young donkey. The king in Zechariah's vision does not come proclaiming war, but peace. His reign is a different kind of reign than most people predicted. Jesus engaged in a public demonstration at Passover in order to call attention to the very different nature of the kingdom of *Abba* from the kingdom of people's expectations. Jesus was not the Messiah they were looking for. Nor would there ever be such a one. Such hopes were illusions. They were the wish-dreams of those who wanted salvation on their own terms. The restoration of right relations with God and humankind could never be achieved by force. But that was only part of the meaning of the event.

Jesus' prophetic demonstration was intended to have a profound paradoxical meaning. Jesus, this "no Messiah," was in fact, "*the* Messiah," God's anointed.[14] He was the lowly servant of *Abba,* prophesied by Isaiah, sent to

14. One of the more hotly debated subjects in biblical studies for many decades has been the question of Messianic consciousness. Did Jesus understand himself to be the Mes-

save his people with his good news about God and the reign of compassionate healing and forgiveness. This "no Messiah," Jesus was dramatically stating, is all you get, but it is also all you need.

Prophetic Confrontation

Jesus' entrance was intended not only for the benefit of the crowd, but also as a statement to Pilate, Herod, their assistants, and their appointed priestly leaders. It was a prophetic demonstration revealing Jesus' relationship to the despots as that of prophet to king. As Nathan the prophet had confronted David the king about his despicable behavior in stealing Bathsheba from her husband Uriah and of causing the man's death, and as many other prophets had challenged their kings for their unjust ways, so Jesus came to Jerusalem to challenge the use of lordly might to inflict cruelty and suffering.[15] As many prophets had done before him, Jesus engaged in symbolic acts in order to convey his urgent message.[16] His prophetic journey into the city was a statement about the difference between godly government and the government of evil.

> You know that those who are regarded as rulers of the Gentiles lord it over them, and their high officials exercise authority over them. Not so with you. Instead, whoever wants to become great among you must be your servant, and whoever wants to be first must be slave of all. For even *this human being* did not come to be served, but to serve, and to give his life as a ransom for many. (Mark 10:42b-45; altered)[17]

---

siah? N. T. Wright (in Borg and Wright, 1999), for example, sees Messianic consciousness as a key to understanding Jesus' words and actions, while Borg (Borg and Wright, 1999) sees such consciousness as a retrojection of later theology. My own position is that Jesus had a particular and idiosyncratic type of Messianic consciousness. Key to understanding the words and deeds of Jesus is the notion of a Messiah that was "contrary to expectations," as discussed throughout this work. Such Messianic awareness did not include most of the extravagant metaphors and symbols of Messiahship later applied to him by the Christian community of faith. Those were the result of reflections on the meaning of the resurrection and the power of the Holy Spirit in the midst of the community.

15. See 2 Sam. 12. The prophetic literature of the Old Testament has numerous examples of the prophets, empowered only by the Spirit that possessed them, boldly criticizing and warning kings with the power of life and death over them.

16. See Hos. 1:4-9; Isa. 8:1-4; 20:1-6; and Jer. 19:1-15; 27:1–28:17.

17. Many scholars see "ransom" in this passage as an anachronism reflecting post-resurrection theology. But it is also reasonable to interpret this, as others have done, as an

The despots of the world are consumed with self-importance and with the advantages of their power. Caesar's objective was to bring the whole world into subjection and servitude to him. The despots came to be served, not to serve. But Jesus had a different vision for himself and his followers. The kingdom of God movement was not about self-importance and personal aggrandizement. Nor was it about the advantages of status and power for its leaders. It was not about being honored, but about demonstrating the honor due all of *Abba's* children. It was about radical service.

Jesus declared that his mission was to serve, and to expend his life on behalf of others. This cruciform life is what liberates others.[18] It is the "ransom," the price that is paid to free slaves and servants. When one lives radically on behalf of one's neighbors, defined inclusively rather than exclusively, the result is that neighbors are set free from their bondage. Those in slavery to their resentments, their personal guilt, their broken bodies, their hopelessness, their anxious fears, and their spiritual blindness are liberated by the ministries of those who selflessly and spiritually devote themselves to the compassionate service of others.

Compassionate Resistance

So Jesus came to Jerusalem, with knowledge of the risks, if not the inevitability of his death, to offer the cruel and blood-stained despots of this world, and their violently zealous enemies passionate for retribution, a different path, one of nonviolence, forgiveness, service, and self-sacrifice. The privileged supported the violent means by which Herod and Pilate, on behalf of Caesar, kept the peace. Many people of the land supported the violent way of the Zealots, seeing it as their best hope for deliverance from those despots. The eyes of Jesus saw that the despot's path was the violent oppression of the

---

authentic statement of a prophet who knew his ministry was an expenditure that would end in death as the necessary "price" for his ministry of liberation. Such a quote naturally would lend itself after the crucifixion to a developed atonement theology.

18. See chapter VIII for discussion of cruciform life. Every follower of Jesus at that time was familiar with the gruesome form of execution known as crucifixion. Most probably had witnessed this form of capital punishment at some point in their lives, as it was commonly and publicly practiced by the Romans whenever bandits and revolutionaries were captured and arrested. Jesus lived and called his disciples to a cruciform life — a life of suffering, expenditure, and death.

many by the few, and the Zealot's path was a violent violation of God's vision for his children that led to destruction.

The occupied Holy Land was up against a vastly superior military force. To challenge it with arms was to invite an even greater time of suffering and hardship upon the land. Jesus warned his hearers to abandon their violent insurgency before it brought complete disaster upon them and all the people.

But Jesus was not counseling his followers to give up in the face of cruel evil. It was not sufficient simply to abandon the Zealot's vision and mission. Jesus offered a new and innovative way of resistance to the cruelty of Caesar and his representatives. He called them to repent, to turn around, to change fundamentally their view of reality and their relationship to it. The reign of God was already occurring in their midst, not in their armed rebellion, but in the demonstration of God's compassion present in Jesus and his followers. The reign of God would not come through the destruction of one's enemies, but was already present in the lives of those who loved their enemies.

> But I tell you who hear me: Love your enemies, do good to those who hate you, bless those who curse you, pray for those who mistreat you. If someone strikes you on one cheek, turn to him the other also. If someone takes your cloak, do not stop him from taking your tunic. Give to everyone who asks you, and if anyone takes what belongs to you, do not demand it back. Do to others as you would have them do to you.
>
> If you love those who love you, what credit is that to you? Even "sinners" do that. And if you lend to those from whom you expect repayment, what credit is that to you? Even "sinners" lend to "sinners" expecting to be repaid in full. But love your enemies, do good to them, and lend to them without expecting to get anything back. Then your reward will be great, and you will be sons of the Most High, because he is kind to the ungrateful and wicked. Be *compassionate* as your Father is *compassionate*. (Luke 6:27-36; altered)

Just as *Abba* extravagantly distributes his compassion upon his children regardless of their righteousness, so those who have reoriented their lives in accordance with him will relate to all human beings, including their evil enemies, with compassion as well. If someone assaults you, do not assault him in return. If an oppressor, a Roman soldier or official, demands your coat, offer him your shirt as well. If he requires you to carry his load a mile, carry it two miles.

For Jesus, love was the weapon of choice in the fight against cruel oppression, and courageous creative endurance was the path of effective resistance to evil. It was not simply that the Zealots did not face reality in thinking they could defeat the militarily superior Romans; they also did not question their even more dangerous delusion that the ends they sought justified the means they had chosen. They failed to comprehend that the evil within their own hearts that desired to be unleashed in cruel revenge upon their fellow human beings was the greatest enemy of all. They failed to have insight into their own desire to drive out those in power so that they could then lord it over others. For Jesus, the evil that reigned in Caesar, Pilate, and Herod also dwelt in the hearts of every human being. That evil was the real enemy, not these human beings who were its chief representatives. Evil manifests itself as the infliction of cruel and unnecessary suffering. The victory of God occurs when the cycle of retribution finally is broken.

Jesus' way was not the way of passive submission, but of passive resistance. It was the only form of resistance to oppression that both protected its practitioners from becoming like their evil oppressors and, at the same time, provided them with a path of dignity and hope for ultimate liberation. In going the second mile the otherwise defenseless took the initiative, experienced the dignity and honor of free self-determination, and probably lived to serve God and humankind another day.

Jesus, then, was not a passive sufferer, but an activist prophet who accepted the likelihood of suffering as a necessary consequence of his mission. Jesus came to Jerusalem symbolically to confront, expose, and challenge Caesar, Pilate, and Herod and their cruel kingdoms. As with the prophets to the kings of old, Jesus' demonstration that first day of Passover week was designed to reveal the reality that kings sit on their thrones by permission of the God of history. Their function is to serve God by being servants of the people in their realm. He who governs with compassion and loves peace is a faithful servant of Yahweh.

Does this prophetic peace demonstration mean that Jesus would have opposed any use of arms, under any circumstance, by a government leader faithful to Yahweh? That is doubtful. Compassion would require such a ruling faithful servant to use force sparingly, and only when necessary, but to use it nevertheless, in order to protect the citizens under his charge from cruel suffering inflicted by violent predators. It is unlikely that Jesus would have opposed, for example, better police protection on the road from Jerusalem to Jericho where travelers, such as the one in the story of the man assisted by a Samaritan, were constantly being attacked by bandits.[19]

Jesus and his followers were not, however, in charge of the government. Neither were they fanatical Zealots. It is unlikely that Jesus, the leader of a nonviolent resistance movement, ever would have attacked anyone with swords or other weapons, as one of his disciples did the night he was betrayed, though one cannot rule out that Jesus allowed his disciples to carry the weapons for self-defense against robbers.[20] Be that as it may, Jesus and his followers were ordinary men and women of peace, engaged in a revolution of the spirit, demonstrating the inclusive and loving relationship between God and humankind, and between neighbor and neighbor.

The Temple Demonstration

Jesus was capable, nevertheless, of aggressive behavior. In a second prophetic demonstration in Jerusalem, Jesus physically disrupted the Temple market of sacrifice by tossing the tables of those exchanging currency and the market benches of those selling sacrificial doves to the poor. Mark narrates that Jesus went and looked around the Temple on that first day of the week of Passover, following the dramatic procession into the city. Then he and his inner circle of twelve went out of the city to stay the night at Bethany. The next morning he returned to the Temple.

> On reaching Jerusalem, Jesus entered the Temple area and began driving out those who were buying and selling there. He overturned the tables of the money-changers and the benches of those selling doves, and would not allow anyone to carry merchandise through the Temple court. And as he taught them, he said, "Is it not written: 'My house will be called a house of prayer for all nations. But you have made it a den of robbers.'"[21]
>
> The chief priests and the teachers of the law heard this and began

19. I am indebted for this example to George Webber's insight in *God's Colony in Man's World: Christian Love in Action* (1960).

20. See Mark 14:46-47. That some disciples had swords, or at least fisherman knives, with them for defense is almost certainly authentic. This fact is inconsistent with the tradition that Jesus told his followers not to carry a staff, which was considered a defensive weapon.

21. Jesus' words here may be a paraphrase of Isa. 56:7 and Jer. 7:11.

looking for a way to kill him, for they feared him, because the whole crowd was amazed at his teaching. When evening came, they went out of the city. (Mark 11:15-19)

Jesus had followed his initial civil demonstration in the form of a provocative parade by another less gentle prophetic act. In a deliberate act of civil disobedience and disturbance, Jesus interrupted the buying and selling of sacrifices and the exchange of currency necessary for those transactions. This was a direct challenge to the Temple cult.

At the head of the Temple cult was the high priest, Caiaphas, and, advising him, the ruling counsel of Temple operations, the chief priests.[22] Caiaphas was originally appointed as high priest in 18 CE by the then Roman governor Valerius Gratus. Caiaphas served during Jesus' entire ministry and until removed from office by the Roman governor who replaced Pilate in 36 CE.

Caiaphas and the other priests lived well as a result of their labors. They received abundant support from the tithes that flowed into the Temple from the people and ate large quantities of the sacrificial meat to which they were entitled under the Law. They and their families lived in luxury and participated in the benefits of their Roman benefactors. So, while there was tension between the high priest and the council of chief priests, they each had a common stake in keeping their Roman rulers happy.

The priests' roles were precarious. The people needed them for their priestly functions, to assure the forgiveness of their sins, to guarantee Yahweh's blessings upon his people, but they were not well thought of by the masses. The priests, and particularly Caiaphas and the chief priests, were seen by many of the people as corrupt representatives of the Gentile despots. New Messiah claimants arose fairly often, creating the possibility for revolution, and, should they be victorious, for the certain replacement, if not execution, of the high priest and the chief priests. There was a lot at stake for them in assuring peaceful operations.

Although there was serious tension between them, on this Caiaphas and the council of chief priests were in complete agreement. Also in agreement

22. In 1990 an elaborate stone burial ossuary was discovered in the Peace Forest near Jerusalem containing the bones of Caiaphas and his family. The chief priests usually are thought to be the Sanhedrin, the ruling body in matters of law, consisting of seventy learned scholars. The chief priests as referred to in the Gospel may have been, however, a smaller council of priests focused on Temple operations.

about crowd control were the cruel despots, Herod Antipas and Pontius Pilate. But all of these powerful men were bound by more than affluence and common enemies; they each shared an emotional deficit. Each had become desensitized to suffering because each had shed so much blood, animal blood in the case of the priests and human blood in the case of the rulers.

Caiaphas, sometime before that Passover marked by Jesus' crucifixion, had moved the marketplace where sacrificial animals could be purchased from the Mount of Olives to the courtyard of the Temple.[23] Pilgrims could now purchase unblemished animals according to their means inside the Temple, much closer to the sacrificial altar, where they would be offered by one of the myriad lower-level priests who kept the sacrificial machine going from day to day. Caiaphas also moved the moneychangers from the old market into the Temple. In order to pay the mandatory half-shekel Temple tax, silver coins were required. Pilgrims could exchange their currency at the tables of the moneychangers for a fee of 4 to 8 percent and receive the type of coinage required for proper ceremonial transactions. Cheating probably was commonplace.

The market within the Temple grounds was large and crowded. When Jesus entered the Temple that fateful morning, he headed straight to that marketplace that he had witnessed the evening before. There was no way he could disrupt all the activity before him. He chose to go to the benches where doves were sold for sacrifice. These were the offerings of the poor and the destitute who could not afford four-legged beasts. Jesus' civil demonstration was not about the sacrilege of moving sacrificial animal trade inside the Temple walls, a purity concern that belonged more to the Pharisees than to him. Jesus used the opportunity of the recently instituted market activity in the Temple to challenge the Temple authorities for their avaricious exploitation of the people, especially the poor and destitute. It was no accident that Jesus turned over the benches of those who sold doves to the poor and those of the moneychangers whose rates of exchange robbed those who lived in poverty.

So, on that morning in the Temple court, Jesus quickly and dramatically began turning over tables, scattering coins across the stone, manure-tracked floors. He obstructed the path to the "market" and turned back those who were there to do business. The whole thing lasted only a few minutes. Most

---

23. I am indebted to Chilton (2000) for this discussion, which is based on references in Josephus and rabbinic literature.

were not aware of the disturbance until word spread to them a little afterward.

To make sure the point of his demonstration was not missed, Jesus shouted to those present some words of the prophet Isaiah. He declared the purpose of the Temple to be that of bringing together the citizens of all nations in prayer.[24] Jesus then quoted another prophet, Jeremiah, as he accused Caiaphas and the chief priests of turning the Temple into a "cave of thieves."[25] Jeremiah had once spoken the Word of the Lord against all types of corrupt, oppressive, and unjust leaders, including the priesthood. As was true of those prophets before him, Jesus' criticism was not about an issue of purity; it was directed toward an issue of injustice. His prophetic attack upon the Temple leadership was because they had used their power to steal from the people. The priestly leaders were a bunch of thieves. That accusation went much further than the issue of the exercise of commerce in the Temple. It was intended to expose the Temple leaders as wealthy opportunists, living lavishly off of the tithes of widows and beggars and adding insult to injury by turning a nice profit off the animal trade and money changing that now could be fully controlled by them.

Jesus was not there to cleanse or purify the Temple. He was there to expose the inhumanity of its leadership, to prophesy its destruction, and urgently to offer an alternative. This building certainly was not pure. This magnificent building was tainted by the evil of its builder, Herod the Great, and by his progeny. This building was the focal point of the avenging Zealots. This building was about bloodshed and violence. The Temple was a brokerage firm, selling forgiveness and salvation to the gullible. One did not need to offer sacrifices any more than one needed to be a scrupulous keeper of the Law, to receive God's mercy and enter into a new relationship with *Abba* as his child. This Temple was not God's house, for if it were, it would be a gathering place for prayer for all peoples from all the different nations.

Jesus was not there to cleanse the Temple, but to replace it with his innovative new vision of a broker-less and inclusive kingdom. When Jesus saw the Temple in all its archeological magnificence that first night in Jerusalem, he was not impressed with its grandeur, but with the injustice and suffering it perpetuated. He did not see it as a dwelling place for Yahweh, for he knew from experience that *Abba* was present and available in the Jordan wilder-

---

24. Isa. 56:7.
25. Jer. 7:11.

ness, and in Galilee, Samaria, and the lands of the Gentiles. He did not view the Temple as divine protection from harm, but as a symbol of impending doom, unless people responded to his prophetic message.

Jesus might have been arrested that morning for disturbing the peace, but it was over quickly. No real harm was done, and everyone got back to business as usual. But when the high priest and chief priests learned of it, they wanted him dead.

The Tax Trap

That week, Jesus attempted to preach to as many of the pilgrims who had come to the Passover celebration as possible. He urgently shared with them his vision and invited them to follow his way. One day, while a crowd was listening to him teach, he was faced with the clever question about paying taxes to Caesar.

> Later they sent some of the Pharisees and Herodians to Jesus to catch him in his words. They came to him and said, "Teacher, we know you are a man of integrity. You aren't swayed by men, because you pay no attention to who they are; but you teach the way of God in accordance with the truth. Is it right to pay taxes to Caesar or not? Should we pay or shouldn't we?"
>
> But Jesus knew their hypocrisy. "Why are you trying to trap me?" he asked. "Bring me a denarius and let me look at it." They brought the coin, and he asked them, "Whose portrait is this? And whose inscription?"
>
> "Caesar's," they replied.
>
> Then Jesus said to them, "Give to Caesar what is Caesar's and to God what is God's."
>
> And they were amazed at him. (Mark 12:13-17)

According to Mark, it was both the Pharisees and the Herodians who tried to trap Jesus. The Herodians were supporters of Herod Antipas and probably were political appointees. They may have been advocates for Herod Antipas to become king of the Jews, to rule over all the territory his father had ruled, and thus to be rid of Pilate and direct Roman control. Be that as it may, the Pharisee leaders and members of Herod's party conspired together to discredit Jesus with those who were following him.

Popular and charismatic leaders, who talked about a kingdom of God and challenged conventional religious beliefs and political establishments, were dangerous. If the Pharisees and Herodians could succeed in causing Jesus to lose face with the crowds, they would stop following him and a potential crisis would be avoided. If not, perhaps they could expose him to the Romans as a teacher of sedition, in which case Pilate would not hesitate to destroy Jesus as a threat to the peace. The people who followed Jesus would then blame the hated Romans, and, in turn, this might even cause Jesus' supporters to shift their loyalties to the Pharisees and Herodians.

The trap was brilliant. They would approach the popular teacher in the Temple, when he was in the act of teaching a large crowd. They would first set Jesus up by flattering him as one who was fearless and would say what he believed without regard to the consequences. That way, he would be compelled to reveal his true position with all attending consequences. They would then ask him whether it was right to pay taxes to Caesar. If Jesus agreed that taxes should be paid, he would lose the support of large numbers of followers still harboring bitter resentment over the increased taxes imposed when Rome instituted direct rule over Judea and the subsequent violent suppression of the tax-related rebellion that followed. In addition, virtually every Jew had been profoundly unhappy about giving limited resources to the Romans to support their cruel oppression, and resented the opulent wealth of their rulers and their offensive, self-indulgent lifestyles. If Jesus said that taxes should be paid to Caesar, the crowd would dismiss him as a cowardly fraud, not a Jewish leader worth following. If, on the other hand, Jesus said that taxes to Caesar should be withheld, that word would quickly travel to Pilate, and Jesus would be arrested for sedition. Either way, Jesus' enemies would be rid of him.

If the trap was brilliant, Jesus' response to the challenge was even more so. Jesus, too, could play the trap game. He immediately recognized their insincerity and exposed their motive. Then he asked his challengers to give him a denarius, a Roman silver coin worth about a day's wages to a field laborer. On the coin was an image of Tiberius Caesar. When Jesus asked whose image was on the coin, the answer was obvious to all. The image was Caesar's. What was equally obvious to the crowd was that at least one of Jesus' challengers had brought a coin with the image of Caesar, who claimed to be a god, into the Temple. While such coins were now brought daily to the Temple to be exchanged, patriotic and courageous men were known to have given their lives to protest such idolatrous images in the Temple. Here were

Jesus' accusers not only carrying such sacrilegious symbols around, but also carrying them within the Temple walls.

Herod the Great had once had burned alive those who attempted to remove the golden eagle from the Temple gates. When Pilate first assumed his office, he had profaned the Temple by having his soldiers carry shields with Caesar's image when they entered the area to provide security during a feast.[26] On that occasion Pilate miscalculated. When an angry crowd came to the maritime city of Caesarea to protest, he threatened them with death. To Pilate's astonishment the Jews lay prostrate, exposing their necks and offering to become beheaded martyrs as objection to the blasphemous introduction of idolatrous symbols into the sacred Temple. Pilate was forced to back down, or to risk a massacre that would not serve him well with his Roman superiors. So when Jesus' challengers revealed themselves to possess, on the Temple grounds, coins with the image of Caesar, a pretender to the throne of God himself, it was no trivial matter. Jesus had exposed the hypocrisy of his challengers, but that was just for starters.

Jesus then told those listening to his preaching to give Caesar what belonged to Caesar and to give God what belonged to God. It was a brilliant response. No one could report accurately to the authorities that Jesus was teaching that the people should withhold their taxes. Go ahead and pay the taxes, they understood him to say, with those Roman coins. Give back to Caesar those idolatrous coins; God does not want them. Denarii belonged to Caesar; they were his currency. Let him have them back. It was no big deal.

On the other hand, it was difficult for traditional Jews to fault Jesus because he declared that people should give to God what belongs to God. As every Jew had learned in childhood, God was the Creator and everything in his world belonged to him. That could have been interpreted by the radicals to support their position of not paying taxes, an interpretation that would be misused against Jesus in trial before Pilate.[27] Jesus agreed with the Zealots that Caesar was not God, as the emperor and his appointees claimed. Caesar was just another tyrant who belonged to God, whether he recognized it or not.

---

26. This was a deliberate attempt of Pilate to demonstrate his authority and ingratiate himself with his superiors.

27. Luke 23:2.

A Question of Ultimate Allegiance

Was Jesus, then, just being a good politician on this occasion by not taking a decisive stand for one side or another? What was he really saying? The ambiguities in Jesus' answer were intentional, but they were not just a clever dodge. They were intended to put the responsibility where it belonged, on his hearers.

> And why can't you decide for yourselves what is right? (Luke 12:57)

Jesus was not creating a new law about taxes, which meant that judgment and prayerful decision were no longer required about such matters. On the contrary, as was true of the commandments, one must consider the godly intent of the requirement to pay taxes. Taxes are intended to provide good government, wise leadership, public works, and services that benefit the people. They are not intended to create poverty and misery by their excessive rates. They are not intended to be a form of legitimized stealing from the poor to benefit the wealthy. They are not intended to be used for the lavish and ostentatious lifestyles of the rulers. Taxes were made for humankind, not humankind for taxes.

Jesus did not create a new set of absolutes about this issue; he unveiled the context in which the question asked could be decided by responsible people. Each hearer was challenged to determine what belonged to Caesar and what belonged to God. Caesar was an evil despot, but did he not play a role in God's world?[28] Was his government not entitled to resources necessary to provide for the basic needs of the people? At what point was tax revolt justified, which would surely end in suffering and death, not only for the protestors, but for their families and neighbors as well? There were no easy answers.

Each hearer was confronted not only with the need to decide in the context of divine and social responsibility what was right for himself with regard to taxes, but was also confronted with a more fundamental question that went beyond the issue of government assessments. No matter what decision one makes about paying the taxes assessed, the question of ultimate loyalty and personal commitment was the important issue. In affirming the legitimacy of those who chose to pay their taxes, Jesus was not endorsing the

---

28. This appears to be the position of Paul in Rom. 13:1.

corrupt and cruel government of Caesar. On the contrary, he was asking of all his hearers, "Where does one's ultimate loyalty truly reside — with Caesar or with God?"

The kings and national leaders of this world have a way of demanding total allegiance. Anything less is considered a threat to the order and security of the state. But such allegiance belongs to God alone. Give to God what belongs to God. But what belongs to God? That which truly matters belongs only to God. Do not bend your knee to Caesar as your Lord and God. Do not give Caesar your worship, your ultimate loyalty, your hearts and souls. Do not live according to Caesar's will, but according to God's will. You can give Caesar back his money if you choose, but you and the commitments of your heart belong to God alone. God may require one to serve Caesar at times, but it is God alone who is being served. And such loyalty to God alone requires that if you decide it is God's guidance to engage in prophetic acts, then you do so in the spirit of *Abba*. Challenge evil, but resist in love, in nonviolence, and without resentment and revenge.

Death of the Servant King

Jesus believed that his own being belonged to *Abba*. As he continued to do the will of his Father and to teach and prophesy in the Temple, the alarmed chief priests were plotting against him. The story of his betrayal, arrest, legal hearings, beatings, and crucifixion are well known.[29] The Gospel writers vividly portray the brutality and unimaginable suffering he experienced. Caiaphas and the chief priests, Herod, and Pilate all took turns examining him and trying to discover the justification for killing him. The chief priests justified their desire to put him to death on the basis of blasphemy, presumably because he confessed himself to be the Messiah.[30] Pilate is portrayed as

29. Most scholars agree that the basic structure and content of the passion narrative emerged almost immediately after the events narrated. The earliest versions contained emotionally charged memories of participants and witnesses present or directly affected by these happenings.

30. Many scholars believe the details of the legal proceedings against Jesus are literary creations, as Jesus' followers would not have been present. On the other hand, Jesus is reported to have had some defenders among the chief priests and followers in Herod's household. That Simon could conceal himself among the guards and servants as reported in Luke and observe some of the events, while unlikely, is also possible.

reluctantly agreeing to crucify him, but as ultimately turning Jesus over to the executioners to be tortured and crucified for sedition.

On the cross, over his head were the words, "King of the Jews." This title, which had been worn so proudly by the evil despots, Herod the Great and his progeny, was intended both to mock Jesus and his followers and to send an unmistakable message to future rebels and Messianic prophets. Jesus, as so many before him, was crucified as a Messianic claimant, and thus as a rabble-rouser who was a threat to the peace and security of the despots. Luke alone records the words from the cross that characterize the relationship of this non-Messianic Messiah's relationship with the despots and those who carried out their orders.

Father, forgive them for they do not know what they are doing. (Luke 23:34)[31]

To Herod and Pilate, Jesus was one more revolutionary they did not need to worry about. To Caiaphas and the chief priests, Jesus was one more silenced, misguided prophet who no longer would trouble them. The eyes of Jesus saw these despots, and those who did their bidding, and exposed them as cruel exploiters and tormentors of the downtrodden. But he also recognized these same human beings as children of *Abba* who did not grasp their own degradation. Jesus practiced what he preached. As he was being tortured and killed by his powerful enemies, he forgave them. While he mockingly was being labeled a "king," Jesus demonstrated the compassionate, self-sacrificing nature, and the servant style of what he believed it meant to be called by God to a life of "kingship," of responsibility for humankind.

Jesus suffered and died in his mission to call humankind to repentance and to acceptance of *Abba's* compassion. He paid with his life for his efforts to deliver human beings from their sins and from the evil spiritual forces that did them harm. He died, as he had lived, so that human beings might experience their lives as *Abba* intended and might be free to love God and

31. Many scholars consider these words to be a Lukan literary creation (see Addendum to Part I for discussion of *Differing Dimensions of Truth*), as it is improbable that anyone was close enough to hear what Jesus said, if anything, from the cross. If that is the case, these words are certainly consistent with everything Jesus taught about one's enemies. Furthermore, if someone did hear his words, it is unlikely that that person would ever forget what Jesus said. I think it is even probable that someone, such as the centurion reported in Matt. 27:54, Mark 15:45, and Luke 23:47, was close enough to have heard these words.

neighbor. The cruel men who crucified him did not understand the significance of what they were doing. Jesus' disciples, those who had been mentored by him and participated in his ministry of healing, forgiveness, and inclusiveness, however, would be capable of doing so. They would soon put to use all that he had taught them. His revolutionary view of reality would not die the day he was crucified.

CHAPTER VIII

Jesus and the Disciples

It was not unusual for great teachers in the first-century Mediterranean world to have disciples. Many teachers of wisdom had such pupils and followers. Greek and Roman philosophers had disciples, or "learners," who sought to master their instructors' teachings. The Gospels refer to disciples of John the Baptist as well as disciples of the Pharisees.[1] In Judaism, disciples were generally those who studied under a particular teacher of the Law. The founders of the first-century major Pharisee sects, Shammai and Hillel, are believed to have had many disciples.[2]

The Inner Circle

No doubt the term *disciple* was used at times to refer only to those who lived and studied full-time with such a teacher, while at other times it referred to all of those who generally accepted and practiced the instructions of such a person. It would not have been surprising at all that a charismatic teacher and healer named Jesus would have a small, limited number of the first type of disciple, and many, perhaps thousands, of the second.

1. Luke 11:1 and John 1:35 refer to disciples of John the Baptist, while Mark 2:18 references disciples of the Pharisees.

2. According to the *Talmud* these disciples were referred to as "Beth Hillel" or "Beth Shammai," meaning "House of Hillel" or "House of Shammai."

"Fishers of Men"

Mark reports that the first persons selected by Jesus for his inner circle of full-time disciples were fishermen.

> As Jesus walked beside the Sea of Galilee, he saw Simon and his brother Andrew casting a net into the lake, for they were fishermen. "Come, follow me," Jesus said, "and I will make you fishers of men." At once they left their nets and followed him.
>
> When he had gone a little farther, he saw James son of Zebedee and his brother John in a boat, preparing their nets. Without delay he called them, and they left their father Zebedee in the boat with the hired men and followed him. (Mark 1:16-20)

While one may have the impression from the Gospel writer's account that these men were total strangers who responded to the authority of the voice of Jesus walking on the shore, immediately abandoning their trade and becoming his pupils for life, it is more probable that Jesus and these fishermen had a long and significant history prior to his invitation. Perhaps they knew Jesus from his days as a craftsman. He may have had the skill to make or repair boats or sculpt anchors out of stone. Or, as a young construction worker, he may have assisted in the building of homes in towns around the Sea of Galilee, perhaps even Simon Peter's wife's home in Capernaum. It is even possible that he had served as a day laborer for the local fishing families when his usual work was slow.

Of course, we have no way of knowing if any of these possibilities is true, but we do have considerable evidence that Jesus was quite familiar with the fishing trade. Most of his early ministry appears to have occurred in the towns of Bethsaida, Capernaum, Gennesaret, Magdala, Gerasa, Tyre, and Sidon, sea towns in which fishing was a major activity. Lessons to his disciples were taken from the world with which they were familiar.

> Once again, the Kingdom of heaven is like a net that was let down into the lake and caught all kinds of fish. When it was full, the fishermen pulled it up on the shore. Then they sat down and collected the good fish in baskets, but threw the bad away. This is how it will be at the end of the age. (Matt. 13:47-49a)

It is easier for a *big rope* to go through the eye of a needle than for a rich man to enter the kingdom of God. (Mark 10:25; altered)[3]

Salt is good, but if it loses its saltiness, how can you make it salty again? (Mark 9:50)[4]

Furthermore, the fishermen disciples, the Sea of Galilee, and passage by boat are prominent features of several Gospel narratives and narrative transitions.[5]

> One day as Jesus was standing by the Lake of Gennesaret, with the people crowding around him and listening to the word of God, he saw at the water's edge two boats, left there by the fishermen, who were washing their nets. He got into one of the boats, the one belonging to Simon, and asked him to put out a little from shore. Then he sat down and taught the people from the boat.
>
> When he had finished speaking, he said to Simon, "Put out into deep water, and let down the nets for a catch."
>
> Simon answered, "Master, we've worked hard all night and haven't caught anything. But because you say so, I will let down the nets."
>
> When they had done so, they caught such a large number of fish that their nets began to break. So they signaled their partners in the other boat to come and help them, and they came and filled both boats so full that they began to sink.
>
> When Simon Peter saw this, he fell at Jesus' knees and said, "Go away from me, Lord; I am a sinful man!" For he and all his companions were astonished at the catch of fish they had taken, and so were James and John, the sons of Zebedee, Simon's partners. (Luke 5:1-10a)[6]

3. One would not try to thread the thick rope used to tie a boat to a dock through the eye of a needle used to mend nets. See note 26, chapter IV.

4. Salt was commonly applied to the fish harvested as a preservative to prevent spoilage before marketing and consumption.

5. Narratives include calming of the storm (Mark 4:35-41); feeding of the multitude (Mark 6:35-44); and walking on the water (Mark 6:45-52). Transitions include Mark 3:9; 4:1; 5:2; 18:21; 6:32; 8:10; 8:13.

6. Most scholars agree that this passage is used by Luke in place of the story of the call of the disciples in Mark because it gives a context for why they would leave everything and follow Jesus. Some scholars have determined that this passage is not historical and is a miracle story based upon a saying such as that in Matt. 13:47, or perhaps is a resurrection miracle put back into the Galilean ministry period. While the story undoubtedly evolved in its meaning to provide lessons to the disciples about their dependence on Jesus in their mission

Anyone who has ever been fishing knows how discouraging it is not to catch anything. For someone whose livelihood depends on fishing, such failure not only is personally embarrassing, but a long period of empty nets can devastate the family finances. Simon Peter was an experienced fisherman. No doubt Simon believed that if anyone could locate fish, he could. But he and his companions had fished all night and caught nothing. To the skeptical, Jesus might have been lucky in knowing where the fish were. Perhaps later some other local fishermen would speculate that Jesus knew a secret about the fishing conditions of the lake that had escaped the experience of the professionals, such as a structural ledge or the hour that fish tended to swarm near the shore. Such knowledge would be known and protected as a valuable secret by a crafty fishing guide. But to Simon, who would later be called Peter, it was a miracle. It convinced Simon that Jesus was some kind of holy man, someone who was so close to God that he was able to perform great wonders. Simon felt so impure, so unworthy of being in the presence of this Spirit Man, that he begged Jesus to depart from him.

Many fishermen probably were among those citizens of the land who were considered "sinners" by the devout for their failure to observe the rules of purity. Simon may have been a particularly rowdy fisherman who frequently and flagrantly violated particular commandments. Or he simply may have been a man who went to work every day but felt estranged from the true meaning of his life. Whatever the case, Jesus could not have chosen a more apt mighty deed to convince a group of fishermen that God was with his ministry. Fishing was not only their livelihood; it was their way of life.

The economy of the Galilean region depended heavily on fishing.[7] Rights to use of the docks and the sea generally were held by families across generations. Simon and Andrew belonged to one such family. Zebedee and his sons James and John belonged to another. The men from these two families appear to have been partners in a kind of fishing guild.[8] Such a guild might have been composed of as many as a dozen members who benefited from the group's income. If there were not enough working members of such a group to do all the work, hired day laborers were used. Zebedee em-

---

as "fishers of men," I have concluded that the origin of the story probably is one of those emotionally charged memories that the fishermen disciples would have recalled vividly.

7. I am indebted to Hanson (1997) for this discussion.

8. Two Greek words (*metachos* and *koinōnos*) are used in the passage, both of which can be translated "partners." The latter term particularly may imply members of a partnering group or guild.

ployed such workers to help with the operation of his boat. The work required of such guild members and laborers not only included fishing and its accompanying labor-intensive tasks of cleaning and mending nets, repairing boats, and transport of catches, but also fish cleaning, processing, and trading. Each guild owned certain rights granted by the governing authorities that allowed them to pursue their living. Those rights were not without cost.

Guilds often were in debt for their operating expenses to the local government agents, who probably also served as tax collectors. In addition, the guilds had to bid against other groups for the rights to operate a fishing enterprise in a given location and to fish particular waters. Such a government agent and broker would have operated the toll office in Capernaum and would have been an important figure in the lives of Simon, Andrew, James, and John. A toll office operator named Levi is reported as the fifth disciple Jesus invited to his inner circle.

> Once again Jesus went out beside the lake. A large crowd came to him and he began to teach them. As he walked along, he saw Levi son of Alphaeus sitting at the tax collector's booth. "Follow me," Jesus told him, and Levi got up and followed him. (Mark 2:13-14)

Levi undoubtedly was a local man, identified as the son of Alphaeus, a father whose name probably would have been easily recognized in the fishing village of Capernaum.[9]

Capernaum was on the northwest shore of the Sea of Galilee. It was the location of the family home of Simon Peter's wife.[10] Simon and Andrew along with Simon's mother-in-law appear to have lived in a home there, perhaps with others as well. This house may be where Jesus stayed when in the region. Zebedee, his sons, and other members of that family probably lived in a home nearby.

James and John, the sons of Zebedee, were nicknamed "sons of thun-

---

9. The name "son of Levi" may imply that Alphaeus traced his lineage to the tribe by that name. Descendants of that tribe were considered eligible for the priestly role. Not everyone, however, who traced his lineage back to the tribe of Levi had pure lineage. Those with questionable ancestry might still receive civil favors and privileges from the ruling elite partially due to the family connections. Whatever the events that led to Levi operating a government toll station, it is likely that he was well known to Jesus as someone within the small circle of persons involved in the fishing economy of Capernaum.

10. John 1:44 indicates that Bethsaida was the hometown of Peter, Andrew, and also the disciple Phillip.

der" by Jesus.[11] The name may imply more than stormy personalities. It is possible that James and John, along with their father, had a reputation as militants and a history of participation in Zealot activities. Fishing was considered a lowly profession that was looked on with contempt by the aristocracy. These first disciples, including Simon and Andrew, were likely to have been physically strong, hardworking young fishermen who shared the typical resentful attitudes of similar men of low status toward Herod, his officials, the Roman overlords, and wealthy aristocrats. They no doubt also shared with other working poor the nationalistic hope for Messianic deliverance from oppression and scorn.

The fifth disciple, Levi, was a hated tax collector, an agent of the enemy, but he was also a local Galilean Jew, and it would have been natural for him to have shared deep resentment toward the foreigners who ran his life and pressured him to extort from his neighbors. Levi may have been recognized by the local fishing guild as a man whom they could deal with and who could provide some protection to them from the outside authorities. We do not know that this is so, but it would help explain the anomalous fact that Jesus brought together in his first disciples four fishermen and the tax collector who probably awarded guild fishing rights to them on behalf of the governing authorities.

Jesus called these members of the local fishing community away from their work to become fishers of human beings. Fishing was a metaphor for mission. Not only was it an image that could be grasped easily by those being called, it also carried with it a lesson about the nature of that mission. These men no longer worked for a fishing guild. They were now to be God's fishermen, casting their new nets in the form of healing and preaching in order to bring into *Abba's* realm of wholeness, compassion, and forgiveness those human beings in turmoil on the sea of life. As with their old fishing enterprise, some days they would catch nothing, other days they would gather a few, and still others they would have a great catch. And for every single one who entered the realm of God they were assured there was great rejoicing in heaven. But to engage in this calling they had to leave their old lives behind. Peter said to him, "We have left everything to follow you!" (Mark 10:28).

How did these first disciples come to have the desire to leave behind their livelihoods, their families, and the other significant relationships of their lives to follow Jesus? It is possible that they had been among the

11. Mark 3:17.

Galileans who had gone down to the Jordan River to be baptized by John and had witnessed there the Spirit transformation of Jesus from a young craftsman to a charismatic preacher. Be that as it may, these first disciples somehow came to understand that God's Spirit was upon Jesus, and when he called to them from the shore of the Sea of Galilee they felt themselves compelled to leave everything and follow him. That decision probably was motivated as well by their intense nationalism, militant leanings, and expectations that the Messianic age was near. These first disciples saw in Jesus a potential deliverer from oppression and bet their lives on a future with him.

The Twelve

While these earliest followers remained his innermost circle of disciples, Jesus appointed additional recruits, bringing the number to twelve and thereby creating a formally constituted inner circle, chosen to extend his ministry and to provide for future leadership in his movement.

> Jesus went up on a mountainside and called to him those he wanted, and they came to him. He appointed twelve[12] that they might be with him and that he might send them out to preach and to have authority to drive out demons. (Mark 3:13-14)

The choosing of the twelve was a symbolic and prophetic act. The number represented the original twelve tribes of Israel and was a deliberate sign that Jesus and his followers were destined to play a critical role in preparation for the Messianic age.[13] These disciples were not chosen from

12. Some manuscripts contain at this point the words "designating them apostles." I have omitted this phrase that was likely a late addition to the text.

13. That Jesus appointed twelve of his followers to be disciples in training for leadership is clearly historical, witnessed not only by the authors of the four Gospels, but by Paul as well. Many scholars have concluded that selection of the twelve is clear evidence of "Messianic consciousness" on the part of Jesus. I would agree to a point with that conclusion. There is little doubt that Jesus intentionally chose twelve rather than another number and that he had the twelve original tribes of Israel in mind when he did so. Given the Messianic expectations of his time, it is also likely that the twelve were chosen as a demonstration of the role of his followers and himself in preparation for the age to come. It sent a clear message that he and his followers were about nothing less than the renewal of Israel in preparation for the

the educated aristocracy as apprentices in preparation for ruling over their neighbors in the age to come. Nor were they chosen from religious scholars already shaped by traditional theologies. They were chosen from the working poor with limited education to be molded into preachers and healers and servants of humankind. Among them was a second disciple named Simon, who was a participant in the Zealot movement, and Judas Iscariot, who may have been a *sicarri,* a member of a militant subgroup of Zealots. It is probable that some, if not all, of the twelve had insurrectionist leanings.

Despite their humble beginnings and their militant ideologies, the disciples' human egos were not immune from manufacturing delusions of grandeur.

> Then James and John, the sons of Zebedee, came to him. "Teacher," they said, "we want you to do for us whatever we ask."
>
> "What do you want me to do for you?" he asked.
>
> They replied, "Let one of us sit at your right and the other at your left in your glory."
>
> "You don't know what you are asking," Jesus said. "Can you drink and be baptized with the baptism I am baptized with?" (Mark 10:35-38)

> They came to Capernaum. When he was in the house, he asked them, "What were you arguing about on the road?" But they kept quiet because on the way they had argued about who was the greatest.
>
> Sitting down, Jesus called the Twelve and said, "If anyone wants to be first, he must be the very last, and the servant of all." (Mark 9:33-35)

It is clear from the disciples' desire to have seats of grandeur in the kingdom to come and their arguments about which of them was the greatest, that these followers had fundamental misunderstandings about Jesus' mission. Their Messianic hopes were conventional ones and they expected to be

---

new age. But that presumption does not answer the question decisively concerning the nature of that mission or how he was determined to accomplish it. One must look at what he actually said and did and at all of his relationships to understand what it means to call that mission Messianic. While the choice of the twelve does demonstrate a kind of Messianic consciousness, I maintain that Jesus understood himself to have such a unique Messianic vision and personal calling, one that was contrary to current expectations, that in his case the common meaning of Messiah did not apply. One could therefore argue paradoxically, as I have done, that Jesus demonstrated a non-Messianic Messianic consciousness.

rewarded for their personal sacrifices in following Jesus when the new age arrived. But Jesus had a different perspective.

Jesus patiently and consistently instructed them in his unconventional vision and mission. The kingdom of God was about right relationships between God and humankind. The kingdom of God was not about pumped-up self-images of importance, or discipleship about promises of rewards to come. The kingdom was to be entered by becoming a child, an unimportant "nobody," who, in realizing the reality of being a beloved child of *Abba,* already had become all that was important. That was the pearl of great price, the treasure in heaven worth far more than all of the world's gold. Discipleship was not about worldly status, not even such status projected upon the age to come, but about service to all humankind, a pouring out of the self that could involve great suffering. Such servants, in pleasing *Abba,* already had all the status they would ever need.

Family and Discipleship

If the twelve who received intense instruction from their teacher had difficulty understanding, then it is likely that the larger circle of disciples were even slower to grasp the significance of Jesus and his mission. In reality, however, with the exception of additional private instruction, there appears to be little difference in Jesus' relationship to the twelve and to his disciples beyond the inner circle. Jesus looked upon all of these followers as his extended family.

Family Tensions

In his early ministry, and perhaps his entire ministry prior to his death and resurrection, the members of Jesus' natural family were not among his disciples. Evidently, the disciples frequently misunderstood Jesus, but that was nothing compared to his family's perceptions.

> Then Jesus entered a house, and again a crowd gathered, so that he and his disciples were not even able to eat. When his family heard about this, they went to take charge of him, for they said, "He is out of his mind." (Mark 3:20-21)

Then Jesus' mother and brothers arrived. Standing outside, they sent someone in to call him. A crowd was sitting around him, and they told him, "Your mother and brothers are outside looking for you."

"Who are my mother and my brothers?" he asked.

Then he looked at those seated in a circle around him and said, "Here are my mother and my brothers! Whoever does God's will is my brother and sister and mother." (Mark 3:31-35)

Shortly after Jesus began his ministry, his family came looking for him. His behavior had become so uncharacteristic of the young son and brother they had known that they believed he was out of his mind. Jesus not only had abandoned his role as a craftsman construction worker and contributor to the family's subsistence, he appeared to have suffered a dramatic change in his personality. This was not the Jesus they had always known. It was as if some alien spirit had replaced their loved one. They thought he was possessed. It was surely out of deep concern and profound love for their son and brother that Mary and Jesus' siblings came to take control of him. They probably were alarmed and embarrassed and wanted to remove him from the public eye, and to return him to the familiar surroundings of home in a desperate hope for his recovery, as any good and loving family might do under similar circumstances. Perhaps there he might rest and recover from this madness, or maybe they could seek the assistance of a folk healer nearby who might be able to exorcize the demon that now controlled his life.

As well-meaning as the family was, Jesus had no intention of being diverted from his mission by his loved ones. From Jesus' point of view, his mother and brothers not only did not understand what was really happening with him, but by coming to take him away, they were going against the will of God as he had come to know it for his life. At that moment Jesus was faced with a choice between his natural family's plans for him and *Abba's* plan for his life. He had come to know *Abba* as his spiritual Father and had caused many others to enter into a relationship as children of *Abba* as well. He looked around at those who were listening to his teaching, who believed in his mission, who followed him, and who were seeking to discover and carry out *Abba's* will for their own lives. "Here are my mother and my brothers!" he said. "Whoever does God's will is my brother and sister and mother."

Jesus thus declared his true family to be those who lived in relation to *Abba* and sought to do his will. Like many human beings then and now, Jesus experienced serious tensions within his own family. At this point, Joseph seems no longer to be in the picture, but Jesus' mother Mary and his brothers and sisters certainly are. Their rejection of his new lifestyle must have distressed him as much as his strange behavior did them. Much later, Mary, his brother James, and probably other siblings and relatives came to believe in him and his mission.[14] But during his Galilean ministry and probably until his crucifixion, Jesus found the human and supportive companionship one expects from family in his relationship with his disciples.

Jesus believed that every human being was a child of *Abba*, but most human beings did not yet consciously live in that relationship. The world was filled with children who lived in that proverbial foreign country eating the husks of the swine and who had not yet returned to their father's house to share in his joyous feast. Jesus passionately was preaching the "good news" of the invitation to return and participate in that banquet. One could say that for Jesus all members of humankind, including his natural family, belonged to "God's family." God continued to love his children no matter how far they continued to miss the mark. But his true family, the "family of God," consisted of all those who had returned home spiritually and were doing the will of their *Abba*. They were the ones who not only had found peace with *Abba*, but were also, at great personal sacrifice, extending Jesus' ministry to the rest of humankind.

Family Obligations

When Simon Peter declared that he and the other disciples had left everything to follow Jesus, that "everything" included family along with jobs, friends, and possessions. For Jesus, discipleship clearly was to take precedence over family obligations.

---

14. Despite both ancient and modern fiction concerning Jesus' family, we know little of their fates. At least some of Jesus' brothers are reported to have witnessed the resurrection and become believers afterward. James, one brother of Jesus, came to be the recognized and widely respected post-resurrection leader of the Jerusalem church (Gal. 2:9; Acts 15). The Jewish historian Josephus recorded James's martyrdom at the hands of the priestly authorities prior to the destruction of the Temple. James's leadership in the new church probably was handicapped by his failure to become a disciple during Jesus' ministry. His attitude toward the Law, for example, appears to have been more rigid and legalistic than is implied by Jesus' encounters with the Pharisees (see chapter VI).

Anyone who loves his father and mother more than me is not worthy of me; anyone who loves his son or daughter more than me is not worthy of me. (Matt. 10:37)

He said to another man, "Follow me."
　　But the man replied, "Lord, first let me go and bury my father."
　　Jesus said to him, "Let the dead bury their own dead, but you go and proclaim the kingdom of God." (Luke 9:59-60)

Certainly it was the experience of Jesus' followers that being disciples could involve very difficult decisions. Many found themselves both physically and relationally estranged from their natural families as a result of discipleship. One could not be a part of Jesus' inner circle without sacrificing the comforts of home, the affections of those left behind, and the pride of meeting one's many family obligations.

It was not that Jesus believed a family obligation, such as the burial of a father, to be unnecessary.[15] The eyes of Jesus saw that there were sufficient family members who were more concerned about the dead than the needs of the living to handle adequately the burial obligations. Of course, God's family, made up of all God's children, should take care of the obligations of their earthly families, but members of the family of God, Jesus' true family, were called into mission and to expend their energies on behalf of *all* humankind. The potential disciple, a child of *Abba*, was called to a much more important obligation than to tend the dead. There were people still breathing who were disabled and sick and in need of healing. There were people still living who were in need of hearing the message of *Abba's* compassion and forgiveness. As reasonable as the request seemed, *nothing* was to take priority over discipleship. In the scheme of life's priorities, compassionate service to the living trumped ritual obligation to the dead.

This is not to say that Jesus required every disciple to leave home and abandon family obligations. Despite estrangement from his own family during his ministry and his demand that disciples give priority to him and his mission over their families, Jesus was not anti-family.[16] As we have seen, he

15. Tradition and purity concerns required that a body be buried as soon as possible and usually within a day (Gen. 50:5; Tob. 1:17-18; 6:14-15).

16. Because of what appears at first blush to be an anti-family bias on the part of Jesus, it might be tempting to compare Jesus with a modern cult leader. Cult leaders frequently demand total loyalty from followers and complete avoidance of contact with families in order

strongly disapproved of divorce and reinforced the obligation to honor (and provide support for) parents as requirements rooted in God's compassion for women and the elderly.[17]

It is also important to remember that Jesus chose the natural family as a metaphor of the new loving and supportive community he founded. This community was what the natural family was created to be. The family was not intended by God to live in rebellion toward God, but to do God's will. The family was not intended to take the place of God in importance and to serve its own selfish interests, but to serve its Creator. The family was not intended to be a place of discord and hostility, but a place of peace. The family was not intended to be a fortress against neighbors in need, but a hub of service to humankind. As such parents were charged with the divine mission to raise and deliver to humankind children who were both socially responsible and compassionate. And children were responsible for assuring the compassionate care of their parents in old age.

Families in Mission

While Jesus' mission took precedence over traditional family obligations for all disciples, Jesus only called some to leave home in order to fulfill their calling. In fact, Jesus relied on certain followers who did not leave their families to provide support and respite for him and his traveling disciples. Apparently, many, if not most, disciples were to remain with their loved ones and to meet their family obligations as best they could, but to devote themselves to supporting his movement by providing shelter and resources to those traveling around preaching the gospel and healing the sick.

> As Jesus and his disciples were on their way, he came to a village where a woman named Martha opened her home to him. (Luke 10:38)

The home of Martha and Mary, which the Gospel of John indicates was in the town of Bethany, may have been used by Jesus on several occasions as a place to stay and from which to go out to the surrounding area to heal and to teach.[18]

---

to brainwash and control them. But upon examination, Jesus' relationship to families, as made clear in this discussion, does not fit that stereotype.

17. See discussion in chapter VI.

18. John 11:1.

When Jesus sent his disciples out to travel in twos and extend his ministry, he took for granted that they would need places to stay and to eat.

> When you enter a house, first say, "Peace to this house." If a man of peace is there, your peace will rest on him; if not, it will return to you. Stay in that house, eating and drinking whatever they give you, for the worker deserves his wages. (Luke 10:5-7)

Who were these people who opened their homes to the disciples? Some may have been old friends or extended families. More likely, they were people who had received healing for a sick or disabled loved one, or who already had heard Jesus teach and who believed in him and his message. To test whether or not this was a household of disciples, or at least those sympathetic to the movement, the traveling ministers, who dressed and looked like destitute beggars, were to use the traditional Hebrew *Shalom* greeting. It was a kind of password that would be answered appropriately by disciples or sympathizers who made their homes available. Those too afraid of being associated with this potentially Messianic movement, or those who outright rejected and resisted Jesus' message, or those who simply were too safety or purity conscious to open their homes to beggarly strangers would not return their greeting. Many probably slammed their doors in the faces of these unkempt people. The *Shalom* of the missionaries would go forth, and being unanswered, would come back to them like a boomerang. When that happened they were to move on until they found a home that "loves peace."

But, undoubtedly, there were many homes that did "love peace." A home that loved peace was a home that had come to know the peace that *Abba* bestowed upon his children when they entered into relationship to him as their Father. Such a home was living compassionately, rejecting human distinctions of status and discrimination, practicing nonviolence, and witnessing to the good news of God's being in charge. Such homes welcomed those who came to assist with the work of Jesus in their villages.

Women Disciples

While Martha and Mary hosted Jesus at home, there were many other women who are reported to have traveled with him, at least some of the time.

After this Jesus traveled about from one town and village to another, proclaiming the good news of the Kingdom of God. The Twelve were with him, and also some women who had been cured of evil spirits and diseases, Mary (called Magdalene) from whom seven demons had come out; Joanna the wife of Cuza, the manager of Herod's household; Susanna; and many others. These women were helping to support them out of their own means. (Luke 8:1-3)[19]

It is not clear whether these female disciples who had been cured of disease by Jesus always traveled with him or did so only periodically. Some of them played significant enough roles in the movement that they were remembered by name. Mary Magdalene, for example, was a woman from the Galilean fishing village of Magdala and was well known to the earliest Christians as someone who had been cured of a disease attributed to seven demons. She was one of the women who traveled with Jesus, witnessed his crucifixion, and, along with Mary the mother of James and Salome, was among the first disciples to discover that the tomb was empty.

The names of many other women disciples have been lost to the tradition. Some of these women may have been sent out paired with male disciples as "sister-wives" to carry out the work of the gospel.[20] It would have been dangerous for such women to travel alone or to be paired with other women, so they may have been assigned to act as if they were wives of male disciples so as not to attract unwanted attention and to lessen the threat of assault. Or, they simply may have traveled by day with Jesus in a group large enough to afford safety. Whatever the case, it is clear that some women disciples provided food and shelter, some provided financial support, and some were a vital part of the traveling ministry.

That women disciples were prominent in Jesus' band of followers would have been contrary to expectations. Women had far fewer rights than men in the traditional patriarchal culture of the Middle East and were assumed to be inferior beings to men. There is no evidence that other teachers of that time and culture had women disciples. But Jesus sought to embody within

---

19. Also see Mark 15:40-41.

20. This has been suggested by Crossan (1991, p. 335), who bases this possibility on the term *adelphēn gunaika* (sister-wife) in 1 Cor. 9:5. Gen. 12:10-20 tells of a different kind of "sister-wife." In that story, Abram's wife Sarai pretended to be Abram's sister and was taken into Pharaoh's harem, a successful hoax, for a while, that won Pharaoh's protection and favor for Abram while in Egypt.

his community of followers the reality of the age to come, in which all kinds of distinctions of privilege and superiority over subservience and inferiority would not exist. As such, it can be inferred that Jesus practiced during his ministry the reality that in the realm of God already present there is no distinction between male and female.[21] It is not that male and female are not different from one another. That point is obvious. It is rather that showing up male is in no way superior to showing up female, or vice versa. Both male and female human beings are *Abba's* children, and as *Abba* treats his loved ones, members of both genders are to treat each other with compassion and mutual respect.

Mentoring for Mission

Being one of the many disciples of Jesus meant far more than living in and providing support for a community of peace in which human barriers have been broken down in imitation and expectation of the coming age. It was also about mission to the world.

> After this the Lord appointed seventy-two others and sent them two by two ahead of him to every town and place where he was to go. (Luke 10:1)

> The seventy-two returned with joy and said, "Lord, even the demons submit to us in your name."
> He replied, "I saw Satan fall like lightning from heaven. I have given you authority to trample on snakes and scorpions and to overcome the power of the enemy, nothing will harm you. However, do not rejoice that the spirits submit to you, but rejoice that your names are written in heaven." (Luke 10:17-20)

The number seventy-two probably is not a literal but a symbolic number. It represents the list of all the nations in Genesis 10, and therefore implies that Jesus sent out many disciples not only to the villages he planned eventually to visit, but also to all the nations of the world to carry out his ministry.[22] That world mission is certainly what eventually took place. But

21. Gal. 3:28.

22. The Hebrew Bible lists seventy nations in Gen. 10, while the Greek Septuagint account lists seventy-two. Some New Testament manuscripts read seventy for this passage

initially Jesus gathered together a large number of his followers, paired them up, and assigned them to go to various villages in his homeland to heal the sick and spread the word. They went forth and returned with great excitement. They were awestruck that their efforts had produced such miraculous results. They had witnessed previously Jesus healing the sick, casting out the demons, and pronouncing forgiveness of sins. Now they had experienced their own amazing abilities to perform such wonders acting under Jesus' authority. The ministry of compassion that they had watched Jesus carry out, they now were able to do themselves.

Jesus had sown the seed of the word, and it had found good soil in the disciples' hearts. Now the harvest was multiplying rapidly and miraculously through their own good work. This was an important aspect of the genius of Jesus. He was able to recruit and empower disciples who could continue and multiply the effectiveness of his work. They were essentially able to do themselves what he had been able to do.

There may have been an additional reason, beyond immediately extending his ministry, as to why Jesus sent out these pairs of disciples. Just as a teacher or physician learns not just from listening but from doing, so the disciples internalized Jesus' message and mission at a much more profound level once these pupils became practitioners. But while their understanding was increased, it was not yet perfected.

When they returned enthusiastically recounting their successful adventures, it would have been natural for Jesus to be a teacher proud of his disciples and his own accomplishments in preparing them for their work. But Jesus saw a danger in their enthusiasm. The disciples were a little too preoccupied with their own newly found abilities. There was a risk that they would come to believe the wonderful healings were their own doing, rather than extensions of the miraculous power of the Spirit in Jesus. There were great temptations to pride and exploitation of others inherent in their enthusiasm. They clearly were not fully ready for their destiny as missionaries to all the nations.

Jesus warned them not to rejoice that they had accomplished great

---

while others read seventy-two. At any rate, the number is intended to underscore in Luke that Jesus appointed a large number of disciples to go into all the world and gave them power to cast out demons. While it is possible that Jesus appointed this precise number intentionally as he did the twelve, it more likely that Jesus sent forth a large number in pairs to continue his work in Galilee, and the use of the number seventy-two (or seventy) was a later development supporting the mission to the Gentiles.

things and had exercised power over the evil forces that brought cruel suffering to fellow human beings. They needed to rejoice concerning only one thing: "their names were written in Heaven." In other words, the only cause for rejoicing was that these disciples had entered into personal and intimate relationships with *Abba*. They had received healing and forgiveness themselves. They were to rejoice in the amazing reality of *Abba's* love.

The Cost of Discipleship

The disciples had begun to imitate Jesus and in doing so they had grasped the meaning of his message more deeply. But Jesus knew that they still did not truly understand the nature of his role in history and that they remained naïve about the cost of discipleship. Once again, he instructed them in the realities of his role in history.

> He then began to teach them that *this human being* must suffer many things and be rejected by the elders, chief priests, and teachers of the law, and that he must be killed and after three days rise again. He spoke plainly about this, and Peter took him aside and began to rebuke him.
>
> But when Jesus turned and looked at his disciples, he rebuked Peter. "Get behind me, Satan!" he said. "You do not have in mind the things of God, but the things of men."
>
> Then he called the crowd to him along with his disciples and said: "If anyone would come after me, he must deny himself and take up his cross and follow me. For whoever wants to save his life will lose it, but whoever loses his life for me and for the gospel will save it." (Mark 8:31-35; altered)

When Jesus predicted that he would be rejected, suffer, and die, Simon Peter was deeply troubled and angry with his Teacher. Peter had come to believe that Jesus was the Messiah. The disciple had witnessed Jesus' Spirit-filled ministry and believed it was replete with signs that Jesus was God's Anointed. But Peter still did not get it. This talk about suffering and dying must have felt to the impetuous disciple like a complete rejection of that role. The Messiah was supposed to destroy evil and overthrow the cruel despots. The Messiah was supposed to restore Israel to its rightful place among nations. The Messiah was supposed to usher in a new age, one in which the disciples themselves would enjoy places of honor. This talk about suffering and dying probably sounded to Peter like a rejection of Messianic destiny and, along with it, the destiny of the disciples as well.

Simon Peter took Jesus aside so as not to embarrass him before others, and reprimanded him. The outspoken and impulsive disciple must have been stunned by Jesus' sharp retort. Jesus called Peter "Satan" because Jesus saw Simon's challenge as a temptation to abandon the path of suffering he believed to be God's will for his life. Jesus already knew that temptation all too well. He accused Peter of thinking only in human terms about the Messiah and the Messianic age, not in the terms that God had called Jesus to fulfill. Jesus' way was the way of suffering, service, and ultimate sacrifice. Jesus told all his disciples and would-be disciples that they too were called to suffer and to sacrifice their lives in his work and mission. God had shown Jesus the path that was necessary to overcome the spiritual enemies of humankind. Unless Jesus and his followers were willing to be obedient to God and to journey even through the dark valley of death, the world could not enjoy the blessings that God had prepared for it.

Jesus used "tough love" with Peter and the other disciples. He understood that their romantic and fanciful illusions about the future and their trumped-up notions of status and importance associated with these illusions were great obstacles to the lives that God intended for his followers. Jesus did not try to ease the shock. He knew it was necessary to intervene sharply in order to break through the assumptions that were standing in the way of their real destinies. Peter likely was deeply hurt when Jesus called him "Satan." Jesus was willing to let Peter and the others experience some emotional pain in the present in order to prepare them spiritually for the realities they surely would deal with in the future. Jesus was not afraid to "discipline" his disciples, his new family, when they needed it. Jesus chose actively and intentionally to love the disciples by calling their present lives, based on false assumptions, into radical question.

Peter and the other disciples were called upon to die that they might live. They first had to die to their illusions about life in order to be truly free to live as *Abba* intended. They had to die to their desires to be important, powerful, and better than others. They had to die to their desires for revenge upon their enemies and the enemies of their people. They had to die to their desire for an easy and painless path to the full realization of God's reign. They had to die to their ideas about who they thought Jesus ought to be and to accept him as he really was. They had to shatter the lenses through which they looked at their own reality and to see the world and their lives as Jesus saw them.

But death was more than a powerful metaphor for letting go of their old orientation to reality and embracing Jesus' view of things. Physical death was not only their ultimate destiny, as it is for every human being; it was their calling to go where they did not choose to go, and to suffer what any human being would try to avoid. It was their calling to pour out their lives each day in Jesus' work and to risk their deaths daily. They were not called to die in bed of old age, but to embrace a life that was likely to end in martyrdom. Every follower of Jesus at that time was familiar with the gruesome form of execution known as crucifixion. Most probably had witnessed this form of capital punishment at some point in their lives, as it was commonly and publicly practiced by the Romans whenever bandits and revolutionaries were captured and arrested. Jesus called his disciples to a cruciform life — a life of suffering, expenditure, and death.

But just as disciples were called to "die" to illusions and old self-understandings and to live in the new reality Jesus had introduced to them, so those who were to die physically in their lives of service to humankind would have new resurrected lives in the world to come. For Jesus, "to die is to live" was both a truth about human existence and a truth about the termination of human life, as we know it.

The Meaning of the Meal

When he observed the Passover meal with his disciples on the night before he was crucified, Jesus had a strong premonition of what lay ahead. He is even reported to have known that one of his disciples would sell him out to his enemies. His focus during that meal was not upon himself, but upon the needs of his inner circle. He knew that without his leadership they would feel abandoned and hopeless. Jesus used the bread and the wine that evening to transform the traditional symbolism of the Passover into the new symbolism of what would later be called the Last Supper.

> While they were eating, Jesus took bread, gave thanks and broke it, and gave it to his disciples saying, "Take it; this is my body."
>
> Then he took the cup, gave thanks and offered it to them and they all drank from it.
>
> "This is my blood of the new covenant, which is poured out for many," he said to them. "I tell you the truth, I will not drink again of the

fruit of the vine until that day when I drink it anew in the kingdom of God."

When they had sung a hymn, they went out to the Mount of Olives. (Mark 14:22-26)

Jesus saw in the bread of that meal that night a symbol of his own physical body and his own human life. In giving thanks for the bread, Jesus offered thanksgiving to God for the wonderful gift of his life as a human being. In breaking the bread, he embraced the brokenness of life itself and the brokenness of his own life — the destructive manifestations of existence and relationships that were about to culminate in his own most personal death. He invited the disciples to partake of that bread and embrace that brokenness and the brokenness of their own lives as well.

Then he took the cup into which dark red wine had been poured and saw in it his own life-blood, blood that he dreadfully anticipated would soon be drained out of his body, either from the wounds of being stoned or from flogging and crucifixion. At this meal, he probably was reminded of the sacrifice of the paschal lamb that had occurred that day in the Temple in anticipation of the Passover meal and which had been prepared for the meal, at his instructions, by the disciples that afternoon. The lamb's throat had been pierced and its blood drained upon the altar of the Temple in that traditional sacrifice.

Jesus had celebrated such a Passover feast many times back in Nazareth as a child with his family. Now he celebrated it with very close members of his new family. His own blood would soon be poured out like that of the lamb and that of the fruit of the vine and he tried to share in that moment the significance of that symbolism with his disciples. This wine, representing blood to be poured out from his own body, symbolized a new beginning, a new community covenanted together with God and one another in a new way. This community was the beneficiary of God's compassion and the forgiveness of sins that was not dependent on the animal sacrifices of priestly brokers of mercy, or the obsession with purity, holiness, and personal righteousness as brokered by the interpreters of the Law. This community shared an experience of the amazing grace of God in their own wretched lives and the lives of those around them. And this community was covenanted together to be God's family in mission to the world, expending their lives on behalf of others. Jesus shared the cup with the disciples, inviting them also to embrace the pouring out of their own lives on behalf of all humankind.

As Jesus drank the wine, he conveyed to his inner circle the realization that it would be his last time to share a drink with them. On many occasions he and the disciples were present for a meal in someone's home or out on a hillside. There, in happier times, they had given thanks, broken bread, and drunk wine together. They had done so as a community of acceptance and mutual respect. Status did not belong at these gatherings, for they were celebrations of the Messianic meal to come, where all God's children would be honored. Now Jesus realized that the next time he drank wine he would do so at that Messianic meal. He would do so as one raised to new life in the fullness of God's kingdom. It must have been a bittersweet moment, remembering the past, experiencing the present, anticipating the suffering and death before him, and having the great expectation of a joyful celebration in the kingdom of God.

Death and Resurrection

The disciples would long remember that meal and the events of the night to follow. They each might remember the details somewhat differently. But these were emotionally charged events branded on their memories until death. They would recall many times their anger and fear when Jesus was arrested. They would remember their own brief feeble attempts to defend Jesus and their escapes to safety. Peter always would remember with shame his denials, as he tried to avoid the same fate that awaited Jesus. They also would remember their own despair and sense of complete defeat. The dream had died when Jesus died. And the fishermen among them sadly would return to their nets. But soon they would have a new emotionally charged experience to remember and pass on to others that changed everything.

> For what I received I passed on to you as of first importance: that Christ died for our sins according to the Scriptures, that he was buried, that he was raised on the third day according to the Scriptures, and that he appeared to Peter, and then to the twelve. After that, he appeared to more than five hundred of the brothers at the same time, most of whom are still living, though some have fallen asleep. Then he appeared to James, then to all the apostles, and last of all he appeared to me also as to one abnormally born. (1 Cor. 15:3-8)

Paul, the writer of this passage, had received from his teachers in the faith the testimony of a series of resurrection appearances to the disciples.[23] According to the apostle there were many still alive at the time he wrote his letter to the Corinthians who were able to testify to the reality of these experiences, including Paul himself. These experiences were mysterious visions. With two probable exceptions, they occurred to those who already were disciples and who had spent considerable time with Jesus during his life and ministry. James the brother of Jesus was one of the exceptions. He probably was not a disciple prior to Jesus' death, but, of course, knew him well as a sibling.[24] The other exception, Paul, was a Pharisee during Jesus' ministry and one of the first persecutors of the early Christian community. Paul had had no direct experience with Jesus' ministry.

In writing about the resurrection, Paul implies that his own late experience was comparable to that of those others who had seen Jesus in the early days following the crucifixion. In writing elsewhere about the resurrection hope of all Christians, Paul described a resurrected body that no longer had the limitations of the flesh, a kind of spiritual body.[25] This view was no doubt a reflection of Paul's perception of Jesus' resurrection appearance to him. To all the disciples, these phenomena were understood as "appearances" of Jesus who interacted with them after his death, if only briefly. They were spiritual encounters that only took place for a limited period of time and involved a particular set of people. They were trans-

23. This is the earliest reference to the resurrection of Jesus in the New Testament. Paul wrote around 55 CE. There is a broad consensus among scholars that these appearance traditions were being shared among Christians, substantially in the form Paul uses, between 30 and 33 CE. The Greek verb *optanomai*, translated as "appeared," connotes visionary experiences.

24. While it is possible that James became a disciple prior to Jesus' death and resurrection, there is no evidence that he did, and Mark 3:21 makes clear that Jesus' family were not among his followers. James likely became a leader of the Jerusalem church based on his resurrection experience, kinship to Jesus, and devout personality. While James grew up knowing Jesus, he may not have benefited much at all from Jesus' days of teaching and preaching. James's theology appears to have been more like traditional Jewish piety than like the innovative faith Jesus taught. But James did come to believe that Jesus was the Messiah. He became a recognized leader of the church who was known for his insistence on Jewish Christians continuing to observe the purity laws (Gal. 2:12). On the other hand, James supported the mission to the Gentiles and some latitude for Christian Gentiles with regard to the Law (Acts 15:19). James was a martyr for the faith, put to death, according to the Jewish historian Josephus, by the chief priests several years before the destruction of the Temple in 70 CE.

25. 1 Cor. 15:35-44.

forming spiritual experiences that were overwhelmingly significant in the lives of the disciples.

The disciples returned to their nets after the crucifixion because they had not fully understood the prediction of death and the promise of the resurrected life. That all changed when they experienced Jesus as their risen Lord. That experience finally brought about an epiphany of the meaning of Jesus' message that whoever loses his life will save it.[26] That message, "to die is to live," was now their own experience with regard to the way they viewed reality. They had died to their lives as disciples. They had died to their misperceptions and self-centered motivations. They had died to their old Messianic expectations. They had died to their hopelessness and despair. And they had been raised to lives as apostles, missionaries of faith and hope, living new lives of radical expenditure on behalf of all humankind. They also had found the firm conviction that when physical death came, and it often came sooner than later for the disciples, they could pass through death to be raised as Jesus had been raised. His resurrection was the promise of a transformed existence in the life to come.

As Jesus nurtured and prepared his disciples during his lifetime for their calling to be fishers of men, so the disciples experienced themselves continuing to be cared for by their Master after his death. They gathered with one another, and with new converts who had not known Jesus during his life in the flesh, and celebrated that sacred meal again and again. They did so, as they had done with Jesus during his ministry, in affirmation of the truth about life that "to die is to live," and in anticipation of the Messianic banquet to come in which God in his marvelous compassion would end all cruelty and suffering, and his children would live in perfect peace with one another.

---

26. Of course, even after the epiphanies that occurred with experiences of Jesus' resurrection, the disciples continued to understand imperfectly, as demonstrated by the substantial differences in beliefs that challenged the early church. But despite their theological differences, they seemed to have shared their commitment to the cruciform life and the Messianic significance of the one who died on a cross.

PART II

Seeing Jesus through the Eyes of Faith

CHAPTER IX

The Revolutionary Hero

The disciples had struggled with the question of Jesus' identity through-out his remarkable ministry. Here was a man who spoke with the au-thority of a great prophet, and a man with spiritual wisdom far beyond his years. Here was one who could leave his opponents speechless when he re-sponded to their challenges, a Spirit-possessed man who cast out demons, healed the sick, and did many other wondrous things. Here was a human be-ing who, as is true for all human beings, needed sleep and who once fell into such a slumber while in a boat that even a fierce storm failed to awake him. But here also was one who, when he finally was aroused from that sleep, shouted to the storm to calm down, and, amazingly, it immediately did just that. "Who is this, that even the wind and the waves obey him?" they asked in awe.[1]

---

1. Many scholars have considered the calming of the storm (Mark 4:35-41) to be a meta-phorical narrative creation (see Addendum to Part I for discussion of *Differing Dimensions of Truth*) of the post-resurrection community's faith in Jesus as the incarnate Yahweh having power over the natural forces, and a metaphor of the risen Christ's power to calm the spiri-tual storms of life, and the promise of an end to the times of political turbulence and perse-cution. As such, it is a confession of Jesus' transcendent significance rather than a literal his-torical event. It is worth noting, however, that the story carries with it two important events: (1) Jesus commands the storm to be still, and (2) the storm immediately dies down. It is cer-tainly conceivable, even to modern skeptics, that these two events could have happened in the sequence in which they are reported. The skeptic would, of course, see coincidence where faith would see the gracious activity of God. Such an event would have been inter-preted later according to the theological questions and pastoral needs of the Jesus move-ment as it faced trying times.

The Messianic Question

Throughout Jesus' ministry, the question of "Who is this?" appears to have been the subject of significant speculation on the part of many who came in contact with him or heard about his activities.

> Jesus and his disciples went on to the villages around Caesarea Philippi. On the way he asked them, "Who do people say I am?"
>
> They replied, "Some say John the Baptist, others say Elijah, and still others, one of the prophets."
>
> "But what about you?" he asked. "Who do you say I am?"
>
> Peter answered, "You are the Christ."
>
> Jesus warned them not to tell anyone about him. (Mark 8:27-30)

Caesarea Philippi was an important urban Gentile community in the upper Jordan valley region northeast of Galilee that was ruled during Jesus' ministry by Philip, a son of Herod the Great. Philip had built the city into a splendid place and had named it in honor of both Tiberius Caesar and himself. Nearby was a cave from which poured fresh water that helped to make possible the lush vegetation of this oasis community. In Old Testament times the cave had been a sacred center for the worship of Baal, and during the Greek period it was the location of a pagan shrine devoted to the god Pan and was decorated with statues of the nymphs. Nearby Herod the Great had constructed a temple made out of white marble dedicated to Caesar Augustus. And it was while visiting the villages in this region, rich in pagan religious and imperial symbolism, that Jesus asked the disciples to say who they believed him to be.

Evidently there were several popular theories at the time about the possible transcendent significance of Jesus. Some people, according to the disciples, thought he was John the Baptist. One of these was reported to be Herod Antipas, who had ordered the beheading of John and who was greatly disturbed by reports of Jesus' activities, fearing that Jesus was John raised from the dead.[2] Presumably there were others who also thought Jesus was a reappearance of John the Baptist, or that Jesus was possessed by John's spirit and with the help of that spirit performed his mighty deeds.[3] Still others thought

---

2. Mark 6:16.

3. Mark 6:14b. Whether people literally believed that a prophet such as John would have been physically resurrected, or that John's spirit would possess another, as it was believed

Jesus was Elijah, the heroic ancient prophet with extraordinary powers, who popular legend thought would one day return to prepare the way for the Messiah.[4]

When Peter, a Galilean fisherman with militant tendencies, was asked who he believed Jesus to be, the title of significance that was on the disciple's lips was not that of Elijah or John. Peter did not think Jesus was a great prophet whose role was to be a forerunner of the Messiah. Peter believed Jesus was none other than the Messiah himself.[5]

The word *Messiah* is a transliteration of the Hebrew expression meaning the "Anointed One." In Old Testament times, when someone was believed to be set apart by God for a sacred role, that person was ritually anointed with oil. Those who were to serve as priests were inducted into their holy office by anointing.[6] Elijah anointed Elisha as a prophet to succeed him.[7] Likewise, the kings of Israel were ceremonially anointed as they assumed their thrones. David, who would later become king himself, refused to harm King Saul because Saul was Yahweh's anointed.[8] After the end of the monarchies, during times of exile and occupation, the "Anointed One" became a title for a hoped-for and expected hero, a person descended from King David, who would end the reign of the foreign overlords and restore the kingdom of Israel.[9] In the more popular versions of this dream, this Messiah, this "King of the Jews," would also usher in a new and glorious age and rule under

---

Elijah's spirit had possessed the prophet Elisha, is not clear. Both types of thinking may have been present among the people at the time.

4. See discussion in chapter II above for background on John and Elijah.

5. This chapter is focused primarily on the Messianic hope of Israel as an expression of the transcendent significance of Jesus within the traditional monotheism of Judaism. Some might term this an exploration of "low Christology." In the following chapter we will look primarily at the preexistent Word, or *Logos,* as a way of understanding Jesus' divine significance in a Hellenistic context. Some might term this an exploration of "high Christology." But, in these chapters, we also speak to the ways in which Hellenism influenced Jewish Messianic ideas, and how Jewish beliefs reshaped Hellenistic concepts. And within every "low Christology" there are some elements of "high Christology," and vice versa. Subsequent chapters will explore the meaning of Jesus as representative of both God and humankind in the roles of redeemer, reconciler, ruler, and resurrected life amidst a coming together of Jews and Gentiles in the emerging Christian community of faith.

6. Exod. 29:7.

7. 1 Kings 19:16.

8. 1 Sam. 24:6.

9. This view is dramatically stated in *Psalms of Solomon* 17 written in the first century BCE.

215

Yahweh's authority over all the nations.[10] The Greek translation of "anointed one," or "Messiah," was *Christos.*

The Universal Hero

The Jewish vision of a Messiah was a particular cultural manifestation of a universal human longing. Throughout the world and over the centuries, particularly in times of great difficulties, people have longed for a hero who will rescue them from their troubles.[11] They have surveyed the coming generation with eyes of expectation, looking for signs of charismatic abilities and noble courage. And they have attempted to prepare themselves for miraculous external intervention through rituals of preparation. Whatever their difficulties, whether from natural events or political ones, the sense of overwhelming powerlessness has given birth to the hope for deliverance.

Such hopes are not without foundation in human and historical experience. Many societies trace their origins and survival to heroic figures who led their ancestors in overcoming great difficulties. Through time, these heroes have tended to take on larger-than-life roles in the collective memory of a people, helping to shape their values, character, and future hopes. One needs only to think of Sidhartha Gautama the Buddha, or King Arthur of Britain to understand the point.[12] The courageous deeds and exemplary behaviors of

10. Isa. 11:1-9 describes the Messianic utopia with extravagant poetry about a peace that extends to all of nature. Isa. 14:2 prophesied that Israel would rule over all its oppressors. Some Messianic expectations looked for an earthly or heavenly warrior, others a sage who would rightly interpret the Law of Moses, and still others a high priest. As discussed in chapter II, the Essenes evidently looked for two Messiahs, one a warrior and the other a high priest. The common thread of the diversity of Messianic hopes was the restoration of Israel among the nations and the vision of world peace accomplished through Yahweh's just might. The purification (and after 70 CE the rebuilding) of the Temple was also a major theme.

11. Joseph Campbell's *The Hero with a Thousand Faces* (1972) and a number of studies based on his work have illustrated the universality of heroic narratives. One does not have to accept Campbell's Jungian and Freudian assumptions in order to understand the power of such stories in the human psyche and in cultural belief systems. Such narratives speak to the universal existential questions that are formulated in culturally specific ways by diverse peoples. The extraordinary popularity of the *Star Wars* series and the *Lord of the Rings* trilogy are examples of the appeal of such narratives in our time.

12. Though scholars disagree on whether the Arthurian legend was based on an actual historical person, and, if so, whether that person was a king, it is probable that a warrior around the fifth century CE inspired the legend.

these heroes were passed down from generation to generation in the folklore, the festivals, the arts, and the rituals of a society. And when a new crisis occurred, they were recalled with great passion. At such times, some people hoped for the return of the ancient heroes while others hoped for one to be raised up in their midst who was made of the same "right stuff."

The heroic narratives that cultures preserve and continuously repeat, whether about historical persons, fictional superheroes, or half-god half-human demigods, reveal the universal desire for heroic deliverance from troubles. And they also reflect various modes of understanding and dealing with the problems of suffering and evil in the world. A worldview that sees existence as a life-and-death struggle between good and evil often emphasizes narratives about warrior heroes and great kings. Societies that view life as tragically trapped in endless suffering, on the other hand, tend to be preoccupied with heroic spiritual journeys.[13]

The universal hope for external rescue also can be profoundly personal. The sense of powerlessness that comes from disease and disability cries out for healing. Overwhelming fear in the midst of great personal danger generates prayers for deliverance. A feeling of being possessed by uncontrollable compulsions brings about desperate cries for some form of exorcism. Human beings are constantly bumping up against the reality that life is radically insecure and that they are not in control of their own destinies. Sometimes hope's desire is for a return to a sense of safety and normalcy in life. And sometimes it is for a far more radical kind of deliverance. Sometimes it is a longing to be rescued from insecurity itself, from "the way life is."

The Messiah of Expectations

And so there is a universal longing that comes to the fore at times of great difficulty, when persons and societies are feeling desperate and powerless.[14]

---

13. The ancient Babylonian culture with its drama of creation as a great battle is an example of the first, while the culture of the Indian subcontinent with its Hindu and Buddhist heroic figures is an example of the second. See Ricoeur (1967) for an instructive look at the existential differences between key symbolic systems of the ancient Near East and Mediterranean world. Of course, several views and heroic types can exist alongside one another competing with and influencing each other, particularly in times of conquest and cultural intrusion.

14. See the discussion in chapter II of millennialism.

Jesus lived in such a time and place and among such persons. While there were alternative heroic prototypes available in their tradition, many people in Jesus' oppressed homeland during the first century were preoccupied with the collective yearning for a warrior hero who would drive out their enemies, the foreign conquerors they believed responsible for their miseries, and who would in victory become Yahweh's anointed king and usher in a new age.[15]

Stories of the warrior heroes of the Maccabean period were passed down from generation to generation and celebrated in household rituals. And the sacred Scriptures reminded the people of the great warriors who had been victorious, who had won the battles that made possible the occupation of the land of promise and the establishment of the throne of David. One such warrior was named Joshua, or Yoshua, a name that means "Yahweh is the deliverer." When the name was later transliterated it became Jesus. And one of the many first-century Jews who were given this popular heroic name was Jesus of Nazareth.

Because Jesus was not engaged in leading a revolutionary militia, but was a traveling preacher and healer, Peter's expression of faith that Jesus was the Messiah, the Christ, was remarkable. Others had seen Jesus as more like a wonder-working prophet than a potential liberator. Prophets could prepare the way, but surely, most people must have thought, when the Messiah comes, whether as a mighty spirit being descending from heaven or as heroic human revolutionary, he will be a great warrior, not this nonviolent wandering healer and teacher.[16]

According to Mark's Gospel, Jesus told Peter not to tell anyone else that he was the Messiah. While Jesus' failure to rebuke Peter for calling him the Anointed One indicates approval of this sacred title, it would not have been wise for the disciples to broadcast that claim. That was especially true while

---

15. The appearance of several Messianic claimants in the first century who gathered considerable followings should be adequate evidence of this preoccupation. See, for examples, Acts 5:36-37 and Josephus, *Antiquities* 20.8.5, but also see notes 10 above and 17 below.

16. It is important to remember that the coming of a human Messiah was not conceived so much as the coming of a military genius but as the arrival of a warrior of Yahweh whose deeds would be accomplished by miraculous divine intervention, as had been true of Moses and the exodus from Egypt, and of Joshua and the conquest of Canaan. The alternate apocalyptic view was similar, but instead of a human Messiah, God's victory would be carried out by a supernatural being. In Daniel's vision (Dan. 7:13), this was one like the Son of Man who would come on the clouds of heaven.

visiting a region with such powerful pagan and imperial significance. In the Roman-occupied territories, potential Messiahs were seen as insurgent revolutionaries and were subject to immediate arrest and execution.

But it is also probable that Jesus was well aware that the disciples' understanding of the Messiah as heroic revolutionary warrior, which was consistent with the popular beliefs of their countrymen, was very different from the way he had come to understand his own mission.[17] While Peter's words were correct, Jesus knew that Peter and the other disciples were not yet able to understand their true meaning.[18]

With the crucifixion of Jesus, the hope that Jesus would be the Anointed One, the great liberator, the revolutionary hero, must have appeared to his followers to be a cruel joke. Instead of defeating the enemies, he was destroyed by them. Instead of becoming an exalted king and receiving the highest honor, he had died the shameful death of a common criminal. Their hopes were dashed. The band of militant-leaning fishermen who had followed Jesus returned to their nets. "How could we have been so wrong?" they must have thought. Jesus had been crucified. He had become just one more in a long line of prophets and Messianic hopefuls destroyed by the enemies of God's people. At that moment, they must have wondered if all Messianic hope was an illusion.

But the resurrection appearances changed all of that. For the resurrec-

17. Levine (2006) has argued that Jewish Messianic expectations were very diverse in the first century, and that the belief that most Jews expected a warrior Messiah is not well supported. The point concerning diversity is well taken, as is her criticism of the attempt to portray Jewish hopes as violent and Christian ones as peaceful. One only needs to consider the apocalyptic violence of the New Testament book of Revelation in order to see the oversimplification. Nevertheless, while conceding the existence of diversity (see note 10 above) and the unfair comparison argument, I believe historical evidence and insights from anthropology support the idea that most Jews were hoping for a successful Jewish uprising led by a warrior hero. The Anointed One was associated with warrior kings in the psalms and in some prophetic literature, while apocalyptic writings spoke of heavenly warriors. Those who were not aristocrats or from the priestly class, but were members of the peasant class and were living under heavy foreign taxation, daily humiliation, and the physical dangers of an occupied people naturally would have hoped for deliverance from oppression. It is likely that these ordinary people shared a fairly common understanding of deliverance. The region was an agonistic one in which tribes and nations had long been in conflict and where ancient resentments cried out for retribution. As have other peoples in other times and places, most first-century Jews almost certainly longed for a divinely appointed hero who would drive out their enemies.

18. The reader should recall here the discussion in chapter VIII of Jesus' rebuking Peter for objecting to Messianic suffering.

tion was experienced as an overwhelming reaffirmation of Jesus' ultimate transcendent significance for them, for Israel, and for humankind. They now believed with confidence that Jesus was in fact the long-expected Messiah. And with that realization, they were immediately faced with new questions. "What does it mean that the Messiah is the crucified and resurrected one? What kind of revolutionary hero and king of the Jews can this be?" The question of "Who is this Jesus?" had taken on an entirely new dimension. In the decades immediately following the death and resurrection of Jesus his followers devoted themselves to reexamining the Scriptures in an effort to come to terms with this question.

Of the biblical texts that the Jesus movement was drawn to, none were more intriguing than the poems of Isaiah of the exile, which spoke of a "suffering servant."[19] In the context of the sixth century BCE, these passages probably referred to faithful Israelites called to be in mission to all nations, or, alternatively, some contemporary servant of God, perhaps even the prophet himself, whose faithfulness and suffering served as a guilt offering for the people. But the post-resurrection community read these passages with new eyes. It was Jesus who was God's chosen servant.[20] It was Jesus who was despised and rejected by men, a man of sorrows and familiar with suffering.[21] It was Jesus who was pierced for the people's transgressions and healed the people with his wounds.[22] It was Jesus who was led like a lamb to the slaughter and was stricken for the transgression of the people.[23] With new eyes of faith, these passages were now seen as ancient witnesses to the coming of a crucified Messiah.

The Crucified Messiah

Around 35 CE a Pharisee named Saul was journeying to Damascus in Syria, where he intended to persecute those in the Jewish synagogues who had become members of the Jesus movement, a movement that he and others perceived to be heretical and guilty of blasphemy.[24] While on the road he expe-

19. The poems are usually identified as Isa. 42:1-4, 49:1-6, 50:4-9, and 52:13–53:12.
20. Isa. 42:1.
21. Isa. 53:3.
22. Isa. 53:5.
23. Isa. 53:7.
24. The accusation was, no doubt, related to the claim that Jesus had divine signifi-

rienced the risen Jesus and was transformed from fanatical opponent to the one who would, in a few years, become the movement's chief missionary to the Gentiles.[25] Saul became Paul who preached far and wide the message that the crucified one was the long-awaited Messiah.

It is Paul who recorded in his letters the clearest statements of how the early Jesus movement reinterpreted the symbolic title Messiah or Christ in light of the crucifixion.

> For the message of the cross is foolishness to those who are perishing, but to us who are being saved it is the power of God. For it is written
>
> "I will destroy the wisdom of the wise;
>   the intelligence of the intelligent I will frustrate."
>
> Where is the wise man? Where is the scholar? Where is the philosopher of this age? Has not God made foolish the wisdom of the world? For since in the wisdom of God the world through its wisdom did not know him, God was pleased through the foolishness of what was preached to save those who believe. Jews demand miraculous signs and Greeks look for wisdom, but we preach Christ crucified: a stumbling block to Jews and foolishness to Gentiles, but to those whom God has called, both Jews and Greeks, Christ the power of God and the wisdom of God. For the foolishness of God is wiser than man's wisdom, and the weakness of God is stronger than man's strength. (1 Cor. 1:18-25)

A Messiah who was crucified was a stumbling block to Jews and foolishness to Gentiles. For the vast majority of Jews the cross was an insurmountable barrier. "How could the long-expected Messiah be executed, and executed shamefully by those he was supposed to drive out and defeat?" And, "How could the Messiah already have come in a man whose own death demonstrated that the world was still filled with suffering and evil?" they wanted to know.

If God had intervened to drive out and destroy the enemy that last week when Jesus was in Jerusalem for the Passover, or if God had somehow, even at the last moment, miraculously rescued him from the cross, or even if God

---

cance. Lev. 24:16 called for a blasphemer to be put to death. Throughout the centuries, religiously orthodox persons in most religions, including devout Christians in the Middle Ages, have, on occasion, executed people accused of heresy, and blasphemy in particular.

25. Acts 7:54–8:1.

had performed some other unmistakable marvelous sign that made it clear to everyone that Jesus was the Messiah, then they might have believed. But nothing like that happened. They probably thought, "These Jesus freaks are deluded."

For most Jews, then, the Messiah was still to come, and his coming would not be in weakness, but in power. Whether as a warrior hero descended from David leading an army into the final battle to overthrow the overlords, or the warring angel of apocalyptic dreams destroying Satan and the demons in the final struggle between good and evil, the coming of the Messiah was going to be cataclysmic and unmistakable. For them, the Messianic hope could never be associated with, much less fulfilled by, one who did not eradicate suffering and evil, and who died in shame and defeat. It just did not fit the vision.

For many Greeks, on the other hand, the very idea of a Jewish Messiah must have seemed strange and foreign. And a crucified Messiah was just plain foolishness. They had not been reared in a culture that spoke often and emotionally about God's Anointed. They certainly had great traditions of warrior heroes, but for many the important heroes were the intellectual giants of philosophy: Socrates, Plato, Aristotle, and the respected teachers and leaders of the various philosophical schools. Many Greeks longed for a new age as much as the Jews, but their vision was that of a utopia in which reason would prevail and people would live in luxury without labor and in peace with nature and each other.[26] And, they believed, the path to that new world was not through a crucified Jewish peasant, but through philosophical discourse. The idea of a Jewish crucified Messiah as the agent of the utopian age must have seemed terribly illogical and even superstitious to most educated members of the Greek-speaking world.

But for members of the Jesus movement, in both the Jewish lands and the Greek cities where Paul organized and nourished churches, the crucified Messiah was experienced as the power of God and the wisdom of God. They had come to believe and understand that the crucified Christ was God's revelation that the depth of the human condition plaguing humankind could not be addressed and overcome by external miraculous rescue, by rearranging the seats of human power, or through scholarly wisdom.[27] That human condition could only be addressed and overcome by a radical spiritual trans-

---

26. *Eclogues* 4, by the Roman poet Virgil in the first century BCE, paints such a utopian vision of the golden age.

27. 1 Cor. 2:6.

formation.[28] To see Jesus the crucified as the Messiah is to have one's spiritual eyes opened, one's delusions about life and of human power, wisdom, and spiritual pride shattered. It is for the reality of one's life to become the realization of God's power in weakness, and God's wisdom in what appears to be intellectual foolishness.

> When I came to you, brothers, I did not come with eloquence or superior wisdom as I proclaimed to you the testimony about God. For I resolved to know nothing while I was with you except Jesus Christ and him crucified. I came to you in weakness and fear, and with much trembling. My message and my preaching were not with wise and persuasive words, but with a demonstration of the Spirit's power, so that your faith might not rest on men's wisdom, but on God's power. (1 Cor. 2:1-5)

It was Paul's understanding that faith in Jesus as the Christ was not a product of human words or convincing rhetoric. Nor was it a matter of achieving a mental belief in an intellectual proposition, a form of works righteousness that would allow one to boast of one's faith. Faith in Jesus as God's Anointed was synonymous with living in the Reality of Jesus as one's Ultimate Reality. It was to live one's own weakness, fear, and trembling, guided by and empowered by God's Spirit while expending one's life in God's service, as Jesus himself had done. Jesus was the crucified Christ, the Messiah contrary to human expectations, and to understand that truth was to experience the self-understanding of one's own life in the world as transformed. The externals of life had not been changed, but such things as honor and shame, power and weakness, wisdom and foolishness, and blessings and troubles had been redefined radically.

So, within the first few years of the Jesus movement, those who were seeking to understand Jesus' transcendent significance indelibly had linked the Jewish version of the universal hero, the Messiah, translated as Christ, to Jesus. And with the assistance of the Scriptures, the meaning of that title was reexamined and reinterpreted consistent with the humble servant life and shameful death of Jesus. In the process, members of the Jesus movement appropriated many other metaphorical expressions and titles in order to clarify for themselves and others what it meant to confess Jesus to be "God's Anointed."[29]

---

28. 1 Cor. 2:6-16.

29. While many scholars tend to approach Christology these days historically and developmentally, moving from earlier concepts to later ones, I have chosen an approach that

The Son of God

One such titular expression in Jewish tradition was "Son of God." King David had been declared in an oracle of the prophet Nathan to be God's son.[30] Psalm 2 also had associated the "Anointed One" with the words, "You are my Son."[31] "Son of David" had become a messianic title because the expectation was that the Messiah would be a descendant of David. The messianic "Son of David," as was true of David himself, would be "God's Anointed" and by implication Son of God.

But the transcendent metaphor "Son of God" in Jewish culture was merged very early on with another powerful symbolic tradition. This "son of god" title was associated with the Greco-Roman version of the universal hero, with the heroic Hellenistic conqueror, Alexander the Great, and with Caesar Augustus the Roman victor, considered ruler of the world and establisher of the Pax Romana, the Peace of Rome. Because of their remarkable military accomplishments, both Alexander and Caesar Augustus had been declared gods, and were made objects of worship. And their cults proclaimed each of them to be the offspring of the union of a male god and a female human being.[32] From the time of Caesar Augustus forward, the Roman emperors were called "son of god," a title that was carved on monuments and inscribed on coins throughout the occupied territories. And from time to time, in order to assure the obedience of the conquered lands, there were efforts to force the populace to express allegiance and confess their belief in the divinity of these emperors. Refusal to do so could end in being fed to wild beasts or to other terrible deaths.

Mark's Gospel begins with the words "The Gospel of Jesus Christ, the Son of God." The writer links the title "Christ" with the title "Son of God." Except

---

looks dynamically at key Christological metaphors and transcendent roles as topics for examination. I have chosen this method because I believe it better serves my purpose of uncovering the existential and spiritual meaning of these metaphors and transcendent roles for faith, as opposed to providing a chronological history of early Christian thought. The idea of Messiah, for example, is both early and late, as is the idea of preexistence, and my intention is to look behind these expressions by reference to diverse authors to find the underlying, unifying meaning for faith then and now.

30. 2 Sam. 7:14.

31. Ps. 2:1-7.

32. Plutarch in his *Life of Alexander* records the "virgin birth" of Alexander. Suetonius in *The Lives of the Caesars* describes how Augustus was conceived with a human mother, Atia, and a divine father, Apollo.

for the introductory sentence, the acknowledgment that Jesus is the Son of God is not made in Mark's narrative by a Jewish follower, but only by terrified demons during the early days of his ministry and by a Gentile, a Roman soldier, at the end, following Jesus' crucifixion.[33] The confession by Peter that Jesus is the Messiah, the Christ, occupies the dramatic centerpiece and turning point of Mark's Gospel narrative. Mark thus linked the heroic Jewish hope for a revolutionary freedom fighter, destined to become king of the Jews, with the Gentile image of divine emperor, the conquering victor and world ruler.

Unquestionably, the recollection of Jesus' intimate relationship with the God of his understanding, whom he called *Abba,* or Father, contributed to the use of "Son of God" as a title pointing to Jesus' significance among the post-resurrection Jesus movement. And the early usage of that term among Jewish Christians probably was associated with the hope and longing of a conquered and oppressed people for a Jewish Messiah, the Anointed One from the lineage of David, the heroic. But by the time Mark's Gospel was written, "Son of God" was widely used by many Christians as a title for Jesus that was intentionally symbolic of the ultimate power and authority in the Gentile world.

"Son of God," then, when applied to Jesus, was a subversive transcendent metaphor, at once suggesting the exalted honor associated with the heroic virtues and successes of the conquering Caesars, and, at the same time, a renunciation of the emperor cult and virtually everything it stood for. It was a statement of faith that the one who in fact rules the universe was crucified by Caesar's agents, raised from the dead, and exalted by God the Most High. And that one was Jesus, the true Son of God.

In Mark's narrative, Peter's confession in the vicinity of a center of pagan worship and imperial authority declared Jesus to be the Jewish Messiah and true Son of God whose victory over pagan might and spiritual powers is sure. Mark wrote his Gospel during a time of great crisis for the churches.[34] Nero, emperor of Rome from 54 to 68 CE, in order to divert rumors that he was responsible for the great Roman fire of 64 CE that burned a large section of the city, placed the blame on Christians. Nero had large numbers of believers arrested and martyred. Their deaths were horrific. Some were

---

33. Mark 3:11 and 15:39.

34. Most scholars date Mark either just prior to the fall of Jerusalem in 70 CE, when its end was near, or shortly afterward. It also is possible that there was an earlier version of Mark, written around the time of the persecution of Nero, that was subsequently revised and edited after the fall of Jerusalem.

wrapped in animal skins so that dogs would attack and kill them. Others were nailed to crosses and set afire, and the light from those fires provided lamplight for chariot games in Nero's gardens.[35]

These were not the first to die for their faith in Jesus. Stephen's death by stoning, the first recorded instance of a Christian being martyred, is detailed in the book of Acts.[36] At his death, looking on with approval, was a Pharisee named Saul, who would later himself become the greatest of Christian missionaries. There also are accounts in historical sources of the times, that James the Just, brother of Jesus and leader of the Jerusalem church, was put to death by the religious authorities in that city, probably in 62 CE.[37] Undoubtedly, there were many others, whose names are lost to history, who died similar deaths. Paul was beaten and imprisoned on several occasions.[38] Tradition records that all but two of the disciples were martyred and that Paul and Peter were put to death in Rome after being imprisoned there, probably between 62 and 64 CE.[39] Tradition also has it that Mark's Gospel was written not long after their deaths.

Mark's Gospel also was written near the time of a cataclysmic crisis in Jerusalem. Jewish freedom fighters had become increasingly confrontational with the Roman authorities. War broke out in 67 CE and Jerusalem fell under siege. Some Christians left the city and sought sanctuary in other regions. In 70 CE Jerusalem fell. The Temple was destroyed and the Jewish nation with it. Both Jews who had joined the Jesus movement and those who had not, who survived the slaughter of what was estimated at more than six hundred thousand persons, scattered far and wide.[40] Because most Christians were Jewish, they remained for many years doubly in danger of persecution throughout the empire, sometimes brutalized because they were Jews, and sometimes because they were Christians.

35. Tacitus, a contemporary critic of Nero who considered Christianity to be a destructive superstition, is the source of the information about the persecution (Tacitus, *Annals* 15.44).

36. Mark 7:54–8:1.

37. James's death is not reported in the New Testament but was recorded by Josephus (*Antiquities* 20.9.1) as a stoning and by Hegesippus, as quoted by the third-century church historian Eusebius (*History of the Church* 2.23.4-18) as being thrown from the Temple tower.

38. 2 Cor. 11:23-25.

39. The deaths are described in 1 Clement, chapter 5.

40. Josephus (*Jewish War* 5.7) gives this figure as the number of dead bodies thrown out of the gates. While Josephus tended to exaggerate numbers, some modern scholars have placed the figure even higher.

The first half of Mark's Gospel narrates the active life and ministry of Jesus. The book reaches its climax with Peter's confession of Jesus as the Christ. The second half of the book is about Jesus' preparation for dying and his death, the passion story. The book concludes with a brief epilogue reporting the empty tomb. This then, is a Gospel about living and dying and dying and living. Mark's universal hero, the Messiah and Son of God, is not a military warrior, but a spirit warrior demonstrating for those who have eyes to see what it means to live authentically. He is the spirit revolutionary who lives in the intimate presence of God, battles the temptations and conflicts of life, pours out his energies, and uses his abilities in alleviating human suffering and in restoring human dignity. He assists persons from all walks of life in finding forgiveness, finds peace in the storms of life, and walks safely on the troubled waters of life.

And, for Mark, Jesus is the ultimate model for authentic dying. He is the spirit warrior who models what it means to be faithful unto death; to endure false accusations, taunts, suffering, and barbaric cruelty; and to die with courage, trust, and hope. For Mark, Jesus is more than a son of man, a child of Adam, he is *the* new measure of what it means to be a human being.[41] To have faith in Jesus as the Messiah, the Son of God, is to model one's life of faith on his life of faith and to embrace one's suffering and death as he embraced them. And when that happens, Mark strongly implies, there are others who will come to understand, as did the Roman soldier at Jesus' crucifixion, that Jesus truly is the Son of God. Later it would be said that the blood of the martyrs would be the seed of the church, but, in his own way, Mark already dramatically had made the point.[42]

Despite the frightening times, when many turned fervently to their hope for Jesus' swift return, Mark appears far more concerned with challenging Christians with serious discipleship than with stirring up apocalyptic fervor. Even the warnings not to tell anyone the secret that Jesus is the Messiah, so evident in Mark's Gospel, serve the purpose of providing guidance to the faithful in times of persecution. There are times when it is not only acceptable, but it is preferable, not to talk publicly about one's faith. Mark's Jesus also provided a model for how persecuted believers were to deal with accusations before the courts.[43] Those facing martyrdom were not to worry about

---

41. See the discussion of Son of Man in the Introduction to this book.
42. Tertullian, *Apologeticum* 1, is the source of the expression.
43. Mark 15:1-5.

what to say when they were arrested and brought to trial, but, as did Jesus, to say only what the Spirit moved them to say.[44]

Because of the cataclysmic times, many Christians who escaped and survived the persecutions and wars between the Jews and Romans had believed that the destruction of the Temple was God's judgment on the Jews for their sins and for participating in the death of the Messiah. And they expected, along with those events, that Jesus, the Son of Man, would come again on the clouds of heaven. But in his Gospel, Mark, while still affirming the nearness of the Christ's return, cautioned that the terrible events of the time were only the beginning of the end, not the end itself, and reminded his readers that they must always be vigilant, for no one knows the hour or the day, not even the Son, but only the Father.[45]

For Mark, Jesus was the preeminent martyr and the prototype of human courage and faith. He was also the one who ultimately will set all things right. The Gospel paints a picture of Jesus who is at once the example of how to live and die amid persecution and violent executions, and simultaneously a vision of hope and assurance that the ultimate victory belongs not to the persecutors, but to those faithful unto death.[46] Jesus is the model human being in the face of suffering and death, and the divine promise of God's ultimate and just victory over evil, even though that deliverance may not come as soon as some hope or expect.[47]

The New Moses

The Gospel of Matthew, which used Mark as a primary source, also speaks of Jesus as Messiah and Son of God. But Matthew, who probably belonged to a Jesus movement group in upper Galilee, or possibly in Syria, and wrote approximately a generation after Mark, was focused on a different heroic image of Jesus' significance. For Matthew, the transcendent significance of Jesus could best be expressed as the "new Moses."

In order to appreciate adequately the heroic metaphor of "Moses" for Jesus' significance, it is important to remember that Jesus and the earliest

---

44. Mark 13:11.
45. Mark 13:32.
46. The "little apocalypse" of Mark 13 is the dramatic expression of that hope.
47. Chapter XIII will explore more fully Jesus as the ultimate victory of God.

leadership of the Jesus movement were Jews who had no intention of separating from Judaism. After Jesus' death and resurrection, these Jewish believers dedicated themselves to convincing all other Jews that Jesus was the Messiah.[48] Their vision was to renew Israel as a means of bringing light to the Gentiles. Moreover, in Judea and Galilee, there were few Gentile converts, and the leadership tended to interpret Jesus' message and significance within Jewish cultural parameters.

Around the time of the cataclysmic fall of Jerusalem in 70 CE, many Judean Pharisees and a number of Jerusalem members of the Jesus movement are believed to have migrated to Galilee and Syria.[49] These rival sects engaged in a war of words for the souls of the Jewish faithful and for the Gentile God-fearers who had adopted Jewish beliefs and who had provided support and political protection for the synagogues.[50] Most of the Jewish religious leadership, including the Pharisees, persistently had rejected the preaching that Jesus was the Messiah, and had viewed the Jesus movement as a dangerous sect that needed to be stamped out. Despite this opposition, the Jesus groups grew and began to transition from a loose movement to an organized body. Matthew, writing sometime during the last two decades of the first century, when the strain between these two Jewish groups was nearing the breaking point, wrote to strengthen the faithful and to answer the burning questions raised by the virulent conflict.

In such a time, among the Jews who believed Jesus to be the Messiah, the question of "Who is this Jesus?" took the form of "What does it mean to call Jesus the Messiah, the hope of Israel, when most of the people of the covenant are rejecting him and many Gentiles are embracing him?" Matthew's solution to this question was to reframe the meaning of Jesus the Messiah,

---

48. The circumcision controversy recorded in Acts 15:1-12 points to the conservative Jewish thinking particularly present among believers centered in Jerusalem. In Matt. 10:6 the disciples are sent out only to the house of Israel, but Matthew concludes his Gospel with the Great Commission in Matt. 28:19-20.

49. The third-century church historian Eusebius (*The History of the Church*, 12.2-3) states that the Jerusalem church fled to Perea, southeast of Galilee, prior to the destruction of Jerusalem. In addition to the Galilean community initiated by Jesus, it is probable that Jerusalem believers also settled in Galilee around this time. Many scholars see Luke's narrative, which mentions synagogues throughout Galilee, as indicative of their strong activity there following 70 CE. It is incorrect, however, to suggest that the Pharisees were absent from Galilee prior to that time. See chapter VI of this book.

50. Crossan and Reed (2004) have argued persuasively that many of the Gentile converts to Christianity were from the God-fearers.

the Son of God, as Jesus the new Moses, the spiritual liberator and mediator of the new covenant between the one true God on the one hand, and the church, the new Israel, on the other.[51]

Mark's Gospel already had told the story of the transfiguration of Jesus.[52] In that account, both Moses and Elijah were seen by the disciples speaking with Jesus. In the narrative, Moses symbolized the Law and Elijah the prophets. The transfiguration dramatically illustrated that Jesus, the Son of God, had authority greater than Moses and Elijah, and was the preeminent interpreter of the meaning of the Law and the Prophets. While Mark's Gospel tended to emphasize Jesus' role in comparison to the prophets, Matthew was preoccupied with Jesus' transcendent significance in relation to Moses.

Moses was the revolutionary hero who, more than a millennium earlier, had challenged the Egyptian Pharaoh, the mightiest ruler in the world at the time. A man of marvelous deeds, Moses had been Yahweh's agent in leading the former slaves out of Egypt, through the parting of the waters, and into the Sinai desert. It was this larger-than-life spirit warrior who delivered the Hebrew people from slavery without fighting a single military battle. It was also Moses, the spiritual mediator, with whom God established the covenant between himself and the tribes of Israel, promising that they would be led to a homeland of plenty where they would be showered with God's continuing blessings. And it was this heroic figure who was the recipient of God's Law as the reciprocal requirement of that covenant.

Moses was the liberator of the nation-to-be, but he did not establish the royal line from which the Messiah was prophesied to come. Nor was Moses the founding father. The honor of founding father belonged to the patriarch Abraham, the legendary nomadic Semite, who had fathered through his son Isaac the people who eventually found themselves slaves in Egypt. Long before Moses, as told in the book of Genesis, God had initiated a covenant with Abraham, and Abraham had lived his life in the reality of that covenant. And long after Moses, Yahweh had anointed David as king, blessed his kingdom, and promised a Messiah from his offspring. Matthew's Gospel begins by introducing Jesus as "the son of David, the son of Abraham." But it is the heroic figure of Moses, whose great deeds were the critical temporal hinge between Abraham and David, who is the paramount interpretive device Matthew employs to illuminate the transcendent significance of Jesus.

---

51. I discuss in later chapters the responses of Luke and John to this conflict.
52. Mark 9:2-12.

Matthew's parallels between Jesus and Moses are inescapable. When Moses had authenticated himself to the slaves in Egypt, he had done so by reference to Abraham and Abraham's God.[53] The Gospel begins by tracing Jesus' genealogy back to Abraham.[54] As all the children of Egypt were to be destroyed by Pharaoh's decree, but only Moses miraculously survived the edict, so Matthew's Jesus alone survived the slaughter of the Bethlehem innocents by Herod the Great.[55] As Moses had escaped out of Egypt, Jesus' family had escaped Herod by traveling down to Egypt, then coming out of Egypt when it was safe. As Moses went up on the mountain to receive the Law of the covenant, so Jesus went up on a mountain, in Matthew's Gospel, to teach the "Sermon on the Mount," the law that was to be written on people's hearts.[56] As Moses fasted for forty days and forty nights on the mountain recording the Law of God, so Jesus fasted for forty days and forty nights in the desert.[57] As there were five books in the "Law of Moses," Jesus delivered five discourses in Matthew's Gospel.[58] And while "Moses" was not a title for Jesus the Messiah in Matthew, there are many other clues in the Gospel's narrative that suggest that Matthew understood the significance of Jesus as the new Moses.[59]

For the first of the five discourses, Matthew's Jesus went up on a mountain in order to give the "new Law" to his followers, the "new Israel." In the second, he organized his movement and appointed the twelve disciples, just as Moses had organized his followers and established the twelve tribes of Israel. In the third discourse, Jesus addressed the crowds, along with the disciples, with the message of the kingdom of heaven, the reign of God. In the fourth, he instructed the Jesus movement in matters of community discipline and in becoming a community of forgiveness. In the fifth discourse, Jesus, as the new Moses, redefined the hope that God will make all things right. He reinterpreted this hope regarding when it would happen, what should be done in the meantime, and what the nature of final accountability would be like.

At the heart of Matthew's Gospel, at the pinnacle of his work, is the

53. Exod. 3:15.
54. Matt. 1:1-17.
55. Matt. 2:13-23.
56. Matt. 5:1–7:29.
57. Matt. 4:2.
58. Discourse (1) Matt. 5–7; (2) Matt. 10; (3) Matt. 13; (4) Matt. 18; and (5) Matt. 23–25.
59. See Allison (1993).

third discourse on the kingdom of heaven. For Matthew, the parables and sayings about the kingdom are Jesus' message to Israel about the new covenant community, and a critical word from Jesus to the emerging community concerning its external challenges and internal problems. For Matthew, the Jesus movement, the new covenant community, is the kingdom of God now. But to be in the Jesus movement is not to be in a community with no problems or difficulties. The community in this age is made up of many different people with differing motives and points of view. And some, Matthew's Jesus suggests, may even be in league with the enemy, Satan. But, despite the serious risks to the community of such diversity and deceit, Matthew's Jesus counsels forgiveness and acceptance, rather than judging and excommunication. The separation of those who authentically belong to the kingdom of heaven from those who do not is a matter for God's final judgment.

Thus Matthew's Jesus, modeled on Moses, is a spiritual revolutionary movement establisher, organizer, and instructor. As Moses affirmed and made use of the heritage of Abraham and the patriarchs in the establishment of a community under the covenant of Sinai, so Matthew's Jesus reaffirmed those earlier covenants while establishing the new covenant community. Yet Matthew makes clear that while Jesus is the fulfillment and completion of those earlier covenants, he also is now the ultimate interpreter of the Law and the prophets, as well as the final authority on matters of the spiritual life.

Jesus, the Son of David, the Messiah, was a Son of Abraham, a Jew whose revolutionary mission, according to Matthew, was to complete the old covenants of Abraham and Moses and to transcend them. Through Abraham and the miracle of a child's birth, God had promised a nation of descendants. Through Moses God had delivered Abraham's descendants from slavery, and promised them a land, a society based upon sacred law, and a mission of their own. Through Jesus, the Son of God had dwelled among humankind, and had issued an invitation, first to the household of Israel, and then to all the inhabitants of the world, to receive the promise of the kingdom of heaven, both now and in the world to come. And he had established that kingdom in the form of the Jesus movement, the new covenant community, the emerging church. And it is the mission of this church to go into the world, to all the Gentile nations, and to preach the good news that the Messiah, Jesus, has come, and to bring those who believe into his reality and community of faith through baptism.

The task of evangelizing the world was not to be an easy one. Those early believers knew the cross was a stumbling block to the Jews and foolishness to the Gentiles. "If the Messiah has come," listeners asked, "then why is the world still a place of oppression and human misery?" For Jesus to be the Messiah was contrary to expectations, and many would not or could not abandon those expectations. Jesus was an unexpected revolutionary hero. He had come not as a military warrior, but as a spirit warrior demonstrating the possibilities of authentic, faithful living and dying. He had not come in validation of the self-importance of the rich, the powerful, or the devout, but rather calling into question the political and religious authorities of this world, and challenging humankind with a new set of priorities, a radical ethic of love, a new style of leadership, a new basis for community, and a new vision of the future.

Faith in Jesus as the Christ

"Who, then, was this Jesus?" "And what did it mean to confess him to be the Messiah?" Paul, who spoke of the foolishness of God being wiser than human wisdom, wrote in his letter to the Romans, "If God be for us, who can be against us?"[60] Matthew, who saw Jesus as liberator, lawgiver, and movement initiator, understood the advent of Jesus to be "Immanuel," God with us.[61] And Mark, who saw Jesus as the model of what it means to be human, encouraged the faithful facing persecution and death with the promise that God will never forsake us.[62]

Each of these New Testament writers expressed within the symbolic framework of their time and place in history the idea that the human longing for heroic intervention and the liberation from life's difficulties and dangers had encountered in Jesus as the Messiah both the judgment of God and the mercy of God. The crucified Christ, as the judgment of God, had shattered the popular illusion of a superhero who would come and rescue humankind from the dangers, stresses, sufferings, and tragedies of existence.

---

60. Rom. 8:31.

61. Matt. 1:23. Matthew not only introduces his Gospel with reference to the prophecy of Immanuel as God with us, but concludes it with the promise, in Matt. 28:20b, "I am with you always, to the very end of the age."

62. Mark 13:26-27; 16:7. This understanding of God never abandoning us will be addressed more completely in chapters XIII and XIV.

No matter how much human beings longed for it, they could not have life on their own terms. The universal hero, the Messiah, God's anointed, had come in the weakness of a human life, and had endured a human death. The lives human beings were given were the lives they must live.

But Jesus as the Messiah also had revealed the mercy of God. Human beings were not alone in their struggles. God had revealed in Jesus how to live an authentic human life in the midst of all difficulties. Through the humiliation and crucifixion of the Christ, God had come in the power of God's weakness and the wisdom of God's foolishness among humanity and shown the way to authentic existence in the world as it is. Those in the Jesus movement had come to grasp that they were no longer hapless victims before the circumstances of life that confronted them, for God's presence was with them, God's power emboldened them, and God's wisdom guided them in the midst of their own journeys through the dark valleys of life.

Paul, Mark, and Matthew each expressed in different ways the understanding that to have faith in Jesus as the Messiah, the Christ, is to live in the reality that he did not come to deliver humankind from "the way life is," but to transform and deliver us in the midst of "the way life is." It is their witness that the Jesus Christ event has shattered the human illusion that God is our enemy and our life in the world unbearable, and has replaced it with the reality of God for us, God with us, and God never abandoning us.

CHAPTER X

The Revealing Word

In most cultures, it is deemed important to know the origin of strangers in order to determine the best way to relate to them. When we know where others come from, we generally assume we know something about their relevant cultural experiences and attitudes, and we can evaluate the potential dangers and benefits of social interactions with them. That is why "Where are you from?" is a commonly asked question when two people first meet. It is one of the more important ways we seek to answer for ourselves the questions, "Who is this?" "How should I relate to this person?" It is not surprising, then, that in seeking to understand "Who is this Jesus?" those confronted by him, whether in person or through witnesses, also asked, "Where did he come from?"

Origin and Honor

In ancient Mediterranean and Middle Eastern cultures, with their intense preoccupation with honor and shame, there were two fundamental ways to determine the appropriate degree of honor to bestow upon another.[1] The first was to acknowledge honor and status in society due to circumstances of birth related to social class, ethnicity, and genealogy over which the individual had no control. The second way was to recognize acquired honor. One could enhance the honor of one's station in life through achievement. Con-

1. I am indebted to Malina (2001) for this discussion of how one comes to have honor and shame.

versely, one could lose honor through failure and shameful behavior. The way of acquired honor was confirmed by social reputation while the way of ascribed honor was closely associated with the question of origins.

Thus, determining both the respect that was related to the natural station of strangers and the accolades to which they were entitled because of their accomplishments was important for deciding the degree of honor to bestow upon them. And this was no small matter, for it was important for one's own status, if not survival, to honor those who had the power and authority to help or harm one's own being. So the question, "Where are you from?" was loaded with social meaning during New Testament times.

The post-resurrection Jesus movement, having experienced life-changing transcendence in and through Jesus' life, death, and resurrection, addressed the question of origin with extravagant language. The titles of ultimate honor they employed were to them the only appropriate language with which to speak of his significance considering what had been revealed to them through him. It proclaimed that Jesus' beginnings were not earthly, but heavenly. His genesis was not in time but in eternity. Jesus was the particular manifestation of the universal Word of God, through whom all things were made. He was the Revealing Word who disclosed in the flesh of his humanity the truth about life and the reality of God's gracious relationship to humankind. Consequently, the faith community he founded believed that Jesus was deserving of the highest honor imaginable.

Geography and Genealogy

When John's Gospel says Nathaniel asked, "Can anything good come out of Nazareth?" it is clear that behind the question was a presumption that Jesus was from a disrespected place, and could not possibly be deserving of honor.[2] Likewise, when the villagers in Mark asked, "Isn't this Mary's son and the brother of James, Joseph, Judas and Simon?"[3] it was clearly implied, because of his birth family, that the people did not think Jesus was entitled to respect. These critics also must have concluded that it would be ridiculous to think that Jesus could be the Messiah, as some seemed to believe, because the Messiah could not possibly come from such undistinguished beginnings.

2. John 1:46.
3. Mark 6:3b.

Both Matthew and Luke addressed the problem of origins by narrating birth stories indicating that Jesus was not born in Nazareth but in Bethlehem, the city of David. Both also provided genealogies intended to show that Jesus was descended through David's royal line.[4] Matthew, emphasizing Jewish credentials, traced Jesus' ancestors back to Abraham, while Luke, emphasizing Jesus' universal significance, traced his genealogy back through Adam to God. Both of these Gospels also contained narratives dramatizing that Jesus' birth was due to the direct and miraculous activity of God.[5] These stories of origin underscored the point for members of the Jesus movement, who were faced with constant challenges to their faith, that Jesus alone deserved the title "Son of God," and that it is Jesus, not Caesar, who is truly divine and deserving of the highest possible honor.[6]

The Heavenly Hero

There were yet other traditions concerning Jesus' transcendent significance that went even further with regard to origin and honor.

4. Matt. 1:1–2:1; Luke 2:4; 3:23-38. Most mainstream scholars consider the "origin" narratives, including the genealogies in Matthew and Luke, to be reverent creations (see Addendum to Part I and discussion of *Differing Dimensions of Truth*) of the Jesus movement that functioned to identify the place of Jesus in the history of Israel, and of humankind, and to reinforce faith in Jesus as the Messiah, the Son of God. The differences between the two Gospel genealogies notwithstanding, it may not have been unusual for ordinary families in a culture with lively oral and written traditions to possess and even to be able to recite genealogical lines back to some heroic forefather. Such traditions, whether accurate or imaginative, would have served to remind the emerging generations of the family heritage of honor and the potential that bad behavior could turn that honor into shame.

5. Matt. 1:18-24; Luke 1:26-28; 2:4-7.

6. These origin narratives are read by many scholars and theologians as expressions of theological rather than literal truth, as transcendent metaphorical narratives rather than as historical accounts. Theologically they affirm the understanding that God was fully present in the humanity of Jesus, that Jesus was God incarnate. Bonhoeffer (1960, pp. 104-5) questioned the notion of a literal virgin birth as failing not because of its miraculous nature, but theologically at the decisive point of the incarnation, because in a literal virgin birth "Jesus has not become man just like us." Bonhoeffer further saw the problem with much theological reflection on the meaning of the virgin birth as a focus on the "How?" of the incarnation rather than the "Who?" The question confronting humankind in Jesus is not "How can he be the Son of God?" but "Who is this Jesus?" and "What does it mean for us to confess him to be the Son of God?"

Who, being in very nature God, did not consider equality with God something to be grasped, but made himself nothing, taking the very nature of a servant, being made in human likeness.

And being found in appearance as a man, he humbled himself and became obedient to death — even death on a cross!

Therefore God exalted him to the highest place and gave him the name that is above every name, that at the name of Jesus every knee should bow, in heaven and on earth and under the earth, and every tongue confess that Jesus Christ is Lord, to the glory of God the Father. (Phil. 2:6-11)

Writing to the church in Philippi during one of his imprisonments, Paul was quoting words of what was probably a hymn. These verses, which may have been used in worship as early as the reign of Caligula (37-41 CE), appear, in many respects, to be a concise version of the universal hero story.[7] In the prototypical narrative, the hero, in the midst of his normal surroundings, received a call, which he could either refuse or accept. If he chose to accept the call, he would take a journey to another realm and undergo a series of trials that usually ended in death. This heroic sacrifice bestowed a boon or set of blessings on others. The hero subsequently was miraculously restored and, upon returning to his place of origin, honored for his mighty accomplishments.

In most versions, the starting point of a hero narrative was the world of normal earthly life, and the journey was to a distant mysterious, extraordinary, and magical other world where the trials usually ended in a terrible final ordeal, followed by the return of the hero to the everyday world.[8] In the hymn that Paul quotes, however, the hero appears to start out in heaven, what is for humankind "the other world." Heaven is, of course, the divine hero's natural abode, and his trials take place in the earthly world where he is killed before he returns "home" and is exalted to the highest place of honor. Many citizens of the Greek and Roman world readily would have grasped the possibility of such a heroic journey that began in the heavenly realm and passed through the earthly one. In the mystery religions that gave rise to later Gnostic thought, preexisting souls descended to earth, tak-

---

7. See Seeley (1994) for Caligula dating. See Campbell (1972) and discussions in chapter IX concerning the prototypical hero story.

8. This is also the prototypical journey of a shaman, a holy man or woman in a traditional society, who journeys to the spirit world in order to undergo initiation.

ing on human form, and underwent ordeals before returning to the heavenly realm.[9]

As probably sung in the house churches of Greek and Roman cities, the hymn answered the question of "Who is Jesus?" by reference to a heavenly being from the heavenly realm, with a divine nature. In Jewish folk belief, Enoch, Abraham, Elijah, and other just souls were thought to dwell in heaven along with the angels.[10] In popular Greek thought, all souls had existed in heaven before taking on human form at birth.[11] While those singing the verses may have had somewhat differing metaphysical presuppositions, in the Philippian hymn, a heavenly being, with a divine nature, received and answered the call to "empty himself" of all the glory and privilege that his heavenly status could offer in order to undertake a mission of service to humankind that involved experiencing a horrible and humiliating death. But then this being, this Jesus, was exalted to a place of honor so high, that "every knee should bow, . . . and every tongue confess that Jesus Christ is Lord."

The Firstborn of Creation

The theme of the preexistence and sovereign supremacy of Jesus the Christ was developed even more clearly in Colossians.

---

9. I am speaking here of the mystery cults and esoteric beliefs present in the Hellenistic world and in Egypt during the first century CE that influenced Christian theology and were later developed into the full-blown Gnosticism of the second century. For example, one of the main tenets of the cult of Mithra was that the soul of man descended from heaven through the realms of the seven planets, taking on vices at each level so that salvation involved participation in secret rites of liberation of the soul from these vices in order to ascend to one's "heavenly home." Scholars do not agree on the dating of the origins of Gnosticism proper. Some have seen strong Gnostic influences in the New Testament, while most today see Gnosticism as a much later second-century development. While the Gnostic texts currently available probably date from the second century, it is not at all implausible that Gnostic-style hero myths were already present in the Hellenistic world of Paul and John.

10. For Enoch, see Gen. 5: 24 and the apocalyptic 1 Enoch and 2 Enoch. For Abraham, see 1 Enoch 22; 4 Macc. 13:17; 2 Esd. 7:36, 38, 88-99. For Elijah, see 1 Kings 19:19-21; 2 Kings 2:1-18; Mal. 4:5.

11. While the "immortality of the soul" is alien to traditional Judaism, this Greek idea appears to have influenced the Wisdom of Solomon (3:1-3; 9:15).

He is the image of the invisible God, the firstborn over all creation. For by him all things were created: things in heaven and on earth, visible and invisible, whether thrones or powers or rulers or authorities; all things were created by him and for him. He is before all things, and in him all things hold together. (Col. 1:15-17)

In both this and the Philippians passage, the question of the transcendent significance of Jesus has been answered by reference to cosmic origin. These texts declare that Jesus' significance cannot be understood in human social terms, but only in theological ones. Thus he is described as "being in very nature God," and as "the image of the invisible God." While these words hark back to Genesis 1:27, where human beings were declared to be made in the "image of God," the significance of the reference is clear: in order to truly know God, and to understand one's own true human nature, one must see Jesus through the eyes of faith as the revelation of God.

In the Colossians text, Jesus is declared to be God's "firstborn." This metaphor would have been understood clearly by members of the Jesus movement because of the tradition of privilege, honor, blessing, and inheritance, along with the accompanying family responsibilities, to which firstborn male children were entitled in the ancient Middle East.[12] In the Jewish tradition this metaphor was also associated with the collective memory of the saving of the Israelite firstborn males amidst the death of the Egyptian firstborn, the belief that the firstborn son in any marriage belonged to God, and the requirement to sacrifice to God the firstborn male offspring of all clean livestock.[13] The way this metaphor was employed in Colossians also alluded to a comparison between Adam, who was made in the image of God, but disobeyed God and ate the fruit that promised to elevate him to the status of divinity, and Jesus the Christ. For Christ, as the Philippian hymn had celebrated, went the other way. He chose not to seek divinity, but obedience as a servant, even obedience unto death, and, as such, was the true firstborn of God, upon whom God restored and heightened the blessing of divinity.

The Colossians text, then, identified the significance of Jesus with God's act of cosmic creation. The claim was an extravagant one that was intended to make clear that the nature of the cosmos and the meaning of human existence cannot be grasped from the point of view of Adam and sinful human-

12. Gen. 27:1-40; Deut. 21:15-17; Isa. 61:7; 2 Kings 2:9.
13. Exod. 11; 13:12-15; Num. 18:15-16.

kind, but only as revealed in Jesus the Christ. Jesus the Christ is God's agent in the creation of all things, visible and invisible. And he is the purpose for which all things have been created. He precedes the beginning of all things, and holds the cosmos together. This is extraordinary language indeed. And it is sacred poetry that is echoed and even expanded upon in the Gospel of John.

The Logos of God

One does not have to be a biblical scholar to recognize the substantial difference between John's picture of Jesus and that of the Synoptic Gospels.[14] All four of the Gospels were written in order to proclaim the transcendent significance of Jesus and to strengthen the faith of those who believed. But in those earlier Gospels, the authors relied heavily on a very early collective memory of the words and deeds of Jesus' ministry. In those works, Jesus' style was that of a Jewish rabbi, healer, and prophet, who spoke in parables and had sharp but brief interchanges with some of his contemporaries. Jesus' message was not focused on himself but on the kingdom of God. And miraculous deeds notwithstanding, the Synoptic Gospels frequently disclosed Jesus' human limitations and the conflicts that underscored the ambiguity of his identity.[15]

In the Fourth Gospel, on the other hand, John portrayed Jesus consistently, from beginning to end, as transparently and radiantly divine, as all-knowing and all-powerful. Of course, John also had indications of Jesus' hu-

---

14. Most scholars agree it is highly improbable that the Fourth Gospel was written by the disciple, John, son of Zebedee, as tradition holds. In fact, it is impossible to determine with any degree of probability the identity of the author. But for convenience, I have chosen to follow tradition by referring to the Gospel and its author by the name John, in what follows.

15. In addition to portraying Jesus as one who engages in such ordinary human activities as eating, sleeping, and getting away from it all, the Synoptic Gospels share traditions that underscore that Jesus experienced life the same way as other human beings. In these Gospels, Jesus denies that he is "good" (Mark 10:18). Jesus is portrayed as agonizing over his impending death, as would any human being (Mark 14:32-36); and, on the cross, he is quoted as expressing the emotional pain of abandonment by God (Mark 15:34). In addition, Mark's Gospel presents the true identity of Jesus as a "secret," while in all of the Synoptic Gospels the significance of Jesus' identity became clear to the disciples only toward the end of his ministry and then only imperfectly until after the resurrection. In other words, in the Synoptic Gospels, the divinity of Jesus was not nearly as transparent as is presented in John's Gospel.

manity. Jesus is portrayed as having a life in the flesh that gets thirsty, tired, angry, and sad.[16] John's Jesus was flesh and blood and had a real body, but that body was clearly presented as the human body of the incarnate God. In John, Jesus did not speak in parables about the kingdom, but in long discourses about his own divine significance. And unlike Mark's Jesus who cried out on the cross those words that any human being who has ever known profound suffering can understand, "My God, My God why have you forsaken me," in John's Gospel, Jesus the incarnate one concluded his divine work, as the "Lamb of God who takes away the sins of the world," with the noble words, "It is finished."[17]

All of this is to say that, while all four Gospels are theological constructions, John's Gospel is not so much about the transcendent significance of Jesus the human being as about what the transcendent God of all creation has revealed and done in and through Jesus.[18] As such, the Fourth Gospel was never intended to be mistaken for a literal rendering of Jesus' life, but was to be experienced as theological drama. "Truth," for John, as we see in the story of Nicodemus, is not *literal* truth, the truth of concrete, this-worldly historical existence, but the deeper and more profoundly personal reality of theological, existential, and spiritual truth.[19] Therefore, John's Gospel should always be read as a transcendent interpretation of the meaning of the Jesus Christ event in history. For John's Jesus is the Revealing Word who confronts the audience member/reader with a decision about the nature of reality and the meaning of his or her own life.[20]

16. See John 4:6-8; 2:13-16; 11:35.

17. Jesus' words in Mark 15:34 of being forsaken were quoted from Psalm 22. Jesus evidently found in those words an expression of his state of being as he was suffering and dying. Some scholars reject the historicity of this quote because they find it highly unlikely that anyone could get close enough to hear Jesus' words. And some suggest that if the quote is seen in the context of the entire psalm it speaks not to abandonment but to ultimate vindication. But the use of an Aramaic quote with the explanation that some near the cross thought Jesus was calling Elijah argues for authenticity. It is the type of Aramaic expression that would have been reverently preserved in the oral tradition. And the assumption that these words expressed a sense of abandonment is supported by the reasonable assumption that had Jesus wished to quote words that expressed vindication there were many verses available to him. In addition, these words, within the framework of the Gospels, are fundamentally dissimilar to the overall Christological aims of the authors.

18. See Addendum to Part I for discussion of literary construction.

19. See the discussion of Nicodemus and literalism in the Introduction to this book.

20. The Gospel of John should be approached very cautiously with regard to historical

In the beginning was the Word, and the Word was with God, and the Word was God. He was with God in the beginning.

Through him all things were made; without him nothing was made that has been made. In him was life, and that life was the light of men. The light shines in the darkness, and the darkness has not understood it.

. . . He was in the world, and though the world was made through him, the world did not recognize him. He came to that which was his own, but his own did not receive him. Yet to all who received him, to those who believed in his name, he gave the right to become children of God — children born not of natural descent, nor of human decision or a husband's will, but born of God.

The Word became flesh and made his dwelling among us. We have seen his glory, the glory of the One and Only, who came from the Father, full of grace and truth. (John 1:1-5, 10-14)

These words also appear to have been a hymn. Whether created by the Gospel author or quoted by him, they served a dramatic purpose in what well could be described as a Gospel play composed after the model of a Greco-Roman theatrical tragedy.[21] This prologue to the Gospel, as was true for the opening choruses of classical plays, set the cosmic stage for a tragedy of immense proportions. The tragic element was stated pointedly in the hymn as the irony that those the Word had brought into existence did not recognize him, and that those who were his own did not receive him.[22] Yet the audience was not, in this case, to be left solely with a sense of pathos, as in most classical tragedies, but was to be confronted instead with the possibility of spiritual rebirth.

John's answer to the question of "Who is this Jesus?" is that he is the *Logos*, the Word. *Logos* was a familiar term in Greek culture. It could be as mundane in meaning as a simple thought expressed in a sentence. But beginning with the Greek philosopher Heraclitus (535-475 BCE), this term referred in scholarly circles to the rational principle underlying all reality.[23] When the Jewish Scriptures were translated into the Greek text referred to as

---

information concerning Jesus the human being, although, as we have suggested, some of the author's narratives and editorial comments may contain core stories and remnants of much earlier traditions.

21. See Brant (2004).
22. John 1:10-11.
23. Heraclitus, *Fragment* 1; *Fragment* 50.

the Septuagint around 275 BCE, the Hebrew word *dabar*, which is now translated into English as "word," was then translated into Greek as *logos*. Thus the Greek idea that reality is rational, preexistent, and universal, and the Hebrew belief that God speaks, and that God's Word creates, sustains, and judges all that is, were conjoined in Hellenistic Judaism. As God in the first chapter of Genesis created the cosmos through the power of his spoken word, so the reality of creation was thought to be founded upon, sustained by, and permeated with the *Logos*, which underlies reality, meaning, and purpose.

The *Logos* of God also was associated with the concept of wisdom, which had emerged after the Hebrew word for wisdom, *chokmah*, was translated into the Greek *sophia*. The classical Greeks were known throughout their sphere of influence as "philosophers," literally as "lovers of *sophia*." Hebrew "wisdom" had focused on practically prudent and spiritually sound behavior, while, from the time of Plato forward, Greek "wisdom" pursued cognitive insight and rational truth. By the time of Jesus, "Wisdom" had become poetically personified in the female gender in several sacred works.[24] "She" was described in the literature as God's first creation, and as the fashioner of all things. While the "Word" of God was a masculine word, and the "Wisdom" of God a feminine word, their philosophical meanings were closely related. Underlying most of these theological speculations about the "Word" of God and the "Wisdom" of God was an affirmation of the underlying goodness and meaningful purpose of all of creation.[25]

When the author of John wrote his Gospel drama, probably in the Greek city of Ephesus sometime during the last decade of the first century CE, he began, then, with the *Logos*, the Word, the underlying Reality that in

---

24. Proverbs (1:3; 9); The Wisdom of Jesus the Son of Sirach; and Wisdom of Solomon.

25. But there were also Greek philosophical influences on Jewish thinkers that differentiated between the ideal world and the real world of matter, and which, rather than affirming the goodness of the cosmos, viewed it as seriously flawed. The Hellenistic Jewish philosopher Philo (25 BCE–40s CE), for example, had used Platonic thought as a way of interpreting the stories of beginnings in Genesis. In his schema, Philo saw the creation of all things in the first chapter of Genesis as the calling into being of Platonic ideal forms, while he considered the potter-style shaping of Adam from the earth in the second chapter of Genesis an inferior copy of the original pattern. Philo called the ideal human form "logos," or "Word." The "Word," for Philo, was the first Adam, the "Humanity" that preceded all human beings. While there are some similarities, the Fourth Gospel used the *Logos* of God quite differently, not as the ideal form for human substance, but as a mode of speaking of an aspect of God and God's acts of grace and revelation.

the beginning was with God and was God, and through whom all things were made.[26] As the Gospel prologue set the cosmic context and invited the audience/reader to experience the presentation, the opening chorus asserted that Jesus' origin was not some date within history, but that he preceded creation itself.

It was in this manner that the author of John, speaking as a person of faith, addressed the question of Jesus' origin and honor. The honor due Jesus is the "glory" that accompanies the coming of the "One and Only" Word into human history.[27] That honor, that "glory," was not based upon human criteria and expectations. It was not derived from genealogical credentials or established by circumstances of birth. Neither could it be proved by the use of human logic or appeal to a collection of evidence. For in Jesus, the world has been confronted by the *Logos,* the logic of God, that divine Word which calls into question all human efforts to establish truth apart from God. Jesus' transcendent significance, however, has been revealed only to the eyes of faith. And what has been revealed is nothing less than the underlying reality of creation, of all that is, including human existence.

The Revelation of Reality

In the postmodern world the classical idea that the universe is rational and reality knowable has been called into question in a radical way.[28] In the current philosophical view, reality is a human construction, arising from and bound by a particular historical setting and language, and consequently there are many constructed realities. Accordingly, no human being can so transcend particular historical and linguistic "blinders" as to stand above the limitations of human existence in order to verify any claimed universal reality or to assert absolute knowledge of what is real versus what is not real. In the language of postmodern thought, we do not have the option of seeing reality through "God's eyes." We can see, comprehend, and communicate only as our historically and linguistically limited human eyes permit. And so, it is widely and popularly held that one person's reality is as good as an-

26. Scholars also have suggested that the Fourth Gospel may have been written in Alexandria or in Antioch.

27. The Greek noun *doxa* can be translated either as "honor" or "glory."

28. Kuhn (1970) has been particularly influential with regard to this postmodern concept.

other's, and no one has the right to impose his or her own construct of reality on anyone else.

Contemporary psychiatry, which is quite familiar with constructed realities in the form of idiosyncratic delusions, has a somewhat different view. Psychiatry takes for granted the idea of delusions and consequently holds that not all "versions of reality" are of equal value. Some constructed realities are delusions that are potentially harmful, or at a minimum not practical, for living in society and the world.[29] If persons attempt to live in a presumed reality, for example, in which gravity does not exist, they will be in store for a serious if not deadly correction should they step out the window of a tall building. Likewise, if persons have the delusion that the laws of society do not apply to themselves, they may well experience an equally abrupt reorientation to reality.

Psychiatry takes for granted that being oriented to person, place, and time as culturally defined by the larger society is important for successful survival and social interactions in the world.[30] Diverse cultural beliefs are certainly important for understanding illness and health, and social normality takes widely differing forms amidst the worldviews of various peoples. But cross-cultural psychiatry also has clarified that there are some basic commonalities among societies concerning what is normal and what is abnormal, and what is healthy and what is pathological. Orientation to reality is linked to these commonalities.

The Fourth Gospel approaches the question of reality from another perspective entirely. On the one hand it affirms the fact that human beings may choose to live in reality, as John and the community of faith understand it, or not to live in that reality. Reality does not force itself on anyone. In that sense, John's understanding is compatible with the postmodern rejection of the imperialistic efforts of authoritarian groups to force ideologies and theologies on others. But just because the Word as reality does not force itself on the world does not mean that the choice one makes in relation to this reality is without consequence. In that sense John's view is not unlike the psychiatric understanding of reality, for orientation to the reality revealed in Jesus is a matter of ultimate concern. John declares that Jesus, as the revelation

29. *DSM-IV-TR* (American Psychiatric Association, 2000) identifies delusions as indicators of schizophrenia and several subtypes of "Delusional Disorder."

30. "Reality Orientation" also is currently the name of a particular psychological therapy for persons suffering from dementia (Spector et al., 2001) that is intended to reduce confusion and inappropriate behavior in patients.

of reality, is not one reality among others, but Reality Itself.[31] To miss living in this Reality is to miss life itself.

By beginning with Reality as revealed in Jesus in the flesh, John's Gospel employs a theological framework intended to show that the ultimate significance of Jesus the Word for all humankind is both *universal* and *particular*.

The Universal Word

The Word of God is universal because it precedes the cosmos and is the creative aspect of God, and that Word is the underlying reality that "holds all things together." It follows that to be alive is to experience the Word, and to have human consciousness is to know the Word. It also follows that this same Word is universally present everywhere and in every culture, and in every dimension of social and human experience. As God spoke to the prophets of Israel many times and in various ways, so also have there been spokespersons of the Word among all the peoples of humankind.[32] And the Word of God has been encountered by human beings not only in the religious sphere but also as an ever-present reality in the human experiences of family, play, work, and commercial and civil interactions.

> The wrath of God is being revealed from heaven against all the godlessness and wickedness of men who suppress the truth by their wickedness, since what may be known about God is plain to them, because God has made it plain to them. For since the creation of the world God's invisible qualities — his eternal power and divine nature — have been clearly seen, being understood from what has been made, so that men are without excuse. (Rom. 1:18-20)

31. The Greek noun *alētheia,* translated as "truth" in John 1:14; 8:32; 14:6; 17:17; 18:37-38, refers to "reality" that underlies appearance. Likewise, the adjective *alēthinos,* which speaks of Jesus as the "true" light (John 1:9), true vine (John 15:1), and the like means that he is the "real" light, as opposed to counterfeit lights or illusions, and the real vine, as opposed to the pagan god Bacchus, also known as Dionysus, or some other illusion of connection with the divine.

32. Heb. 1:1. To affirm that God revealed God's Self in the history of Israel does not mean that God was without spokespersons among all the nations of creation. The Word of God is not the private possession of Israel or the Christian faith, but a gracious gift that clarifies and affirms that which is true, noble, holy, excellent, and praiseworthy (as in Phil. 4:8) wherever it is found.

Paul, author of the letter to the Romans, like the author of John, expressed the belief that God had revealed God's "Self" in creation. In order to appreciate today the significance of this New Testament belief in the universality of the Word, the revelation of God in creation, it is important to consider the profound implications of this view for a contemporary understanding of the nature and consciousness of humankind.

To take seriously the universality of the Word is to grasp that one encounters that Word in one's own human existence every day. To have life and to live in the world is to know, at some level of awareness, the reality of that mysterious power that has made life the way it is and has made each of us the way we are, and the truth that we are bound inescapably to live in relationship to that same mysterious power and to one another. To have human consciousness is to experience the universe as a sacred place and to understand that if we fail to appreciate and respect it, we do so at our own peril. To show up in life as a human being is to know in one's heart the sacred worth of every creature and therefore to know also the obligation to treat every other human being with dignity and honor. And to be a human being is also to experience, whether ever acknowledged, moments of grace in which the goodness of creation and the blessedness of one's own particular life have become transparent.

Despite great diversity in belief and practice, and the frequency of socially reinforced behaviors to the contrary, the universality of these understandings is well attested among diverse peoples and the religions of humankind across time and cultures.[33] Many noteworthy people of good will in diverse societies and across history have listened to their inner spirits, consulted their consciences in the midst of difficult choices, exercised great courage in the face of evil, and all too often paid the supreme sacrifice for their integrity. The great spiritual heroes of every culture, while not glossing over their diversity of thought, have been true in their lives to some very basic principles that appear to disclose a common grounding in a universal Re-

33. Certainly this should be obvious for those familiar, for example, with Native American spirituality and the spiritual consciousness of the religions of the Asian subcontinent. There are elements in all religions consistent with at least some of these understandings. Sometimes the commonalities are hidden because different religions tend to exhibit a diversity of transcendent preoccupations. The wiser Christian missionaries always have trusted that the Christ Word preceded them, have recognized important manifestations of that Word already present in the indigenous religion and culture, and have allowed that already present Word to inform their own understanding of the gospel and of faith as well as to provide the basis for criticizing indigenous culture and religion.

ality. And there have been many ordinary people as well, throughout the world and all of history, who quietly have lived noble lives in the midst of life's difficulties, intuitively knowing and responding to an understanding of existence that appears to be a response to a common grasp of a universal Word about life.

In addition, Paul and John also articulated forcefully that the universal Word conveys both grace toward, and judgment upon, all humankind.[34] And this understanding of the universal Word also has immense implications for a contemporary understanding of the human condition and consciousness. To take seriously the universality of the Word is to recognize that to be human is to be accountable. It is to realize the reality that human beings, while bound to that mysterious power that has brought everything and everyone into being, nevertheless, largely have failed to recognize, acknowledge, honor, or accept the reality of that relationship. They have disrespected the universe, exploiting and damaging it with little or no remorse. They have dehumanized, hated, and inflicted suffering and atrocious deaths upon their fellow sojourners on the earth. And they have ignored and turned away from those moments of grace in their lives that could have brought about a spiritual transformation, and have chosen instead to suppress the truth of their own experience, along with the authentic spiritual wisdom of their own times and cultures, and to live selfish, superficial, uncaring, and perverse lives.

To grasp the universality of the Word is also to understand the human desire to hide from personal accountability in the garden of one's own personal journey. It is to have the consciousness of profound guilt and shame. It is to suspect that we human beings are somehow responsible and ultimately without excuse for our lives of escape from and rebellion against what we know in our hearts is reality. Yet, despite this awareness, most of us have refused to change our ways. We have continued to do so, even though most of us also suspect that such persistent rebellion hardens hearts, causes spiritual blindness, and destroys the ability to experience guilt and remorse. And, as history attests, such hardness of heart can manifest itself tragically in unspeakable crimes against humanity.

And even when human beings of good will and persons of integrity have lived the truth of the universal Word, whether consciously or unacknowledged, their visions and lives, as they themselves have attested, have been less than perfect. The spirit giants in our midst always and especially have been

34. Rom. 1:18 and John 3:36.

aware of their own personal demons, their failures to be true to their own beliefs, their character defects, their weaknesses and tendencies toward arrogance and pride. And while these lives nevertheless have shone like lights in dark places, their contemporaries frequently have preferred to remain in the darkness altogether. It is in the midst of a pervasive estrangement from the universal Word and the seductive presence of competing words, according to the New Testament writers, that the particular Word appeared.

The Particular Word

The Word is particular because it has been embodied and actualized in a flesh and blood person in history. The author of John makes clear that it is none other than the *universal* Word that has become a *particular* Word in the human being named Jesus. The Word of God was the primordial light of God that overcame the primordial darkness. And the Word of God made flesh was that same light that had entered the darkness of the human condition. Humankind had succumbed to the great lie about human existence and the consequent failure to understand the true nature of ultimate reality.[35] The underlying logic of the world's wisdom assumed that God is not real; or if God should be real, that God is not relevant or that the world's suffering demonstrates that God could not possibly be good. And when those who saw themselves as the defenders of God against the world's unbelief attempted to use the logic of the world to demonstrate the superiority of their religious position, the great lie also manifested itself as a claim to possess knowledge of God and truth without genuine spiritual transformation. John's theology asserts that humankind is trapped in these delusions that manifest themselves at a personal level as spiritual blindness. To overcome that darkness is why, John says, the universal Word became flesh.

The transcendent metaphors of light and darkness were quite well known in the world of Hellenistic Judaism. The Scriptures contained powerful allusions to these concepts.[36] In the midst of the primordial darkness, God's first creation through the Word was light. Familiar Scriptures portrayed God as covered with brilliant illumination. And God was understood to be the provider of the lamplight for human pathways of living. The

---

35. John 1:5; 3:19-20; 8:42-47.
36. Gen. 1:3; Pss. 104:2; 4:6; 43:3; 119:105; Zech. 14:7.

prophet Isaiah spoke of the coming of the hope of Israel as the coming of a great light. And the desert Qumran community of Essenes believed that the world was the locus of a fierce struggle between the spiritual forces of light and those of darkness.[37] There was also something primordial and universal, perhaps rooted in the emergence from the darkness of the womb at birth and reinforced by the emergence of the sun each day from the darkness of the night, that appears to have given rise to the transcendent symbolism of the light in most, if not all, of the world's traditional cultures.[38]

There is, then, a universal human desire for the light, a desire for spiritual enlightenment that is present in all religious belief and practice.[39] There is a longing for the light, for spiritual wholeness, in the souls of human beings that lies beneath every spiritual quest. It is not surprising, then, that it was John's assertion that the light of all human longing was to be found in Jesus, and that the light of Jesus was the true light of God that had penetrated the darkness of the human condition, shattering the dangerous illusions of humankind, and revealing the ultimate truth about reality.

But what is that reality that can now be understood in the light of Jesus? How are we to understand today the meaning of the claim that Jesus is the revealing Word? In the first place, as we have seen in John's work, the particular Word in Jesus is none other than the universal Reality that underlies and holds together all that is. And we also have seen that the human problem is that the universal Word has been obscured and has become hidden from humanity by the darkness of the human condition. It is the testimony of those who saw Jesus through the eyes of faith that into this world of darkness Jesus the Revealer has now come and has made brilliantly clear the unmistakable meaning of this universal Word, the true nature of Ultimate Reality.[40]

Once again, the implications for contemporary understanding are pro-

37. Vermes (1998).

38. The sun was an important religious symbol in Egyptian and Mesopotamian religions, and in Mithraism, Roman and Greek religion, Hinduism, Buddhism, the Druid religion of England, and the Mesoamerican, Inca, and Native American religions. Dark and light were particularly central to Zoroastrian mythology and were primary concepts associated with the *yin* and *yang* in Chinese thought.

39. The New Testament writers also speak frequently of those who live in darkness and choose darkness rather than life. See Matt. 4:16; John 1:5; 8:12; 12:35, 46; 1Cor. 6:14; 1 John 1:5; 2:8-9, 11, for examples.

40. Although I do not use the term *Ultimate Reality* in precisely the same manner as did Paul Tillich, I am indebted to him for this expression. See particularly Tillich (1963).

found. In Jesus, the Word made flesh reveals and appeals to the authentic self, the image of God that lies within every human being, to fulfill the promise of that marvelous creation. The Word made flesh destroys the delusion that life as it is, as God has created it, is good only when it feels good or serves some selfish purpose. It declares with new clarity the Word of creation, "And God said, 'It is good.'" In Jesus, the Word made flesh, the light in the midst of darkness, God has disclosed in dramatic power that God is good, not just some of the time, or when we humans judge God's activity in their lives as good. Rather, God is good *all the time.*

The Revelation of God as Loving Self

According to John, Jesus the Revealer has made known reality because he has disclosed not just the nature of God's creation but the true nature of God as "Loving Self." To know Jesus as the Word made flesh is to know God as "Self," as "Person." In Jesus, God is revealed in all of God's mysterious otherness to be the ultimate "Thou" in relation to each "I." John's Jesus spoke of the divine nature in terms that every student of the Old Testament could understand when he used the words, "I AM."[41] In identifying himself with the "I AM," the God of Moses and the exodus, Jesus has again revealed God as the One who speaks and acts. God is not an impersonal principle, a remote first cause, or merely a unifying, sustaining, and directing force, and certainly not just a mystical speculation. God is revealed in Jesus as Divine Self in relation to creaturely selves.

In the earliest remembered traditions of Jesus' ministry is the recollection that Jesus' relationship with God was as *Abba,* the Father, a title that suggested parental love, intimacy, and reliability. And Jesus called his disciples also to live in relationship to the Father as intimate and loving parent. In John's Gospel, this relationship to God as Father is central to understanding Jesus' transcendent significance and, at the same time, to the disclosure of the truth of God's relationship with humankind. Jesus, the Son, is one with the Father. In him the honor, the glory, of the Father shines through. To know Jesus is to know the Father. The significance of these theological statements for John is that God, who is invisible and mysterious, is revealed in Jesus as the Thou who intimately loves, as a parent loves, the children of the world.

41. Exod. 3:14.

The Meaning of Faith in Jesus

In John's Gospel, the love of the Father has been demonstrated in the work of the Son. It has been the mission of the Son, as the divine emissary of the Father, to expend himself in order to restore humanity to its right relationship as members of the family of God.[42]

> For God so loved the world that he gave his one and only Son, that whoever believes in him shall not perish but have eternal life. (John 3:16)

This verse sums up what the Fourth Gospel declares to be reality. And to live in the light, rather than the darkness, in reality rather than illusion, is to live in the world as loved by God. To believe in the Son is synonymous with living in that reality, the reality of God's love. That is what it signified when people of faith said, as did the early Jesus movement, that Jesus' name is exalted above every name, that there is no other name and no other way.[43] For there is no other reality than *Reality Itself,* and that reality which faith perceives is none other than the *Reality of Jesus.*

A thoughtful reading of John's Gospel today discloses some important insights concerning this Reality. For example, believing in the Son is not a matter of asserting a doctrine that provides eternal security. To look to right beliefs as a means of securing the blessings of life and eternity has always been the way of religious illusion. The issue, in Jesus' day, should not have been upon which mountain one was supposed to worship, or whether one was descended from Abraham.[44] Such beliefs and practices could even be spiritually dangerous. For they could clothe the religious practitioners in false security about their ultimate status with God, giving the illusion that genuine spiritual transformation was unnecessary.

That is why, when today one encounters John's words about "the Jews" and their spiritual blindness, one should not think specifically of Judaism, for to do so would be to miss the point and to participate in the very religious attitude that John's Gospel calls into question.[45] Rather, one should

---

42. I speak of this mission much more extensively in subsequent chapters.

43. Phil. 2:10; Acts 4:12.

44. John 4:20; 8:33.

45. See especially John 5:16-17; 7:45-52. The Gospel of John was written at a time of great tension between the Jesus movement, which was still predominantly a movement within Judaism, and the Pharisaical rabbinical Judaism that became prominent following the de-

think about all forms of religious beliefs and practices, and for Christians, especially those of contemporary Christianity. For as the universal Word is present in all faiths, so is the universal lie. The great lie of religion, and this applies to all religions, is that its adherents come to think that their beliefs and practices place them in a privileged position, a position that allows them to possess a corner on supposed truths, to boast of their moral superiority, and to pass judgment upon others, and ultimately upon God. As such, religion itself, rather than being a vessel for the universal Word, often becomes a defense against that Word, a great ideological umbrella preventing the blazing light of God's love from penetrating the human spirit. And thus the Word continues to come to God's own, and many of his own continue not to receive him.

To believe in the Son, then, according to John, is not to assent to an intellectual idea, or to possess some secret knowledge that makes one superior to those who do not have it. For to believe in the Son is to become reoriented to reality, to live in relationship to God as the Father and to the world as loved by God. This is a transformation so radical that it could only be described as being "born again."[46] And to live in that Word is to enter into and participate in eternal life, in life as it was intended to be in all its fullness and spiritual richness, and to do so without end.[47]

A second example produced by a thoughtful reading of John's Gospel today is that the *particular* Word now makes it possible to detect and affirm the *universal* Word wherever it is met. For those who are transformed by the Word in Jesus, it is Jesus, and only Jesus, who defines the Word of God.[48] The Scriptures become the Word of God only when they are read through the eyes of Jesus, through the revelation of God in Jesus. And when the Bible is

---

struction of the Second Temple. The Jesus movement undoubtedly had experienced periodic persecution from established Jewish authorities and may already have been expelled from synagogue participation by the time the Gospel was composed. John's reference to the Jews would not have been understood by John or his original readers as an anti-Semitic statement. After all, most of the believers in his community were ethnically Jewish. Nor should the references be understood as literal history. "The Jews" in John are a literary device, *dramatis personae,* a collective symbolic character in his tragic drama, symbolizing the rejection of Jesus by established religion. Thus, one must look today to all established religions, including Christianity, in an effort to understand the implications of the harsh portrayal aimed at the religiously devoted who remained "spiritually blind."

46. John 3:3.
47. John 10:28.
48. John 5:39.

not read through the Word in Jesus, but with the eyes of human wisdom, whether secular wisdom or religious wisdom, the Scriptures no longer speak God's Word.

For those who have chosen to live in the reality of Jesus, it is Jesus as the Word who makes possible their encounter with and understanding of the Word of God wherever they find it. Their eyes have been opened to see that God's work and Word is everywhere and among all God's children throughout the world. So other traditions, as well as Judeo-Christian ones, also can be affirmed when read through the eyes of Jesus, through God's revelation in Jesus.

Those who see through the eyes of faith also understand that in Jesus God has revealed God's true nature, the true nature of humankind, and the true nature of God's relationship with humankind. The Word comes to humankind as both grace and judgment. As John says, God does not condemn anyone, and therefore neither should we.[49] But it is also important to take note of John's warning, that to live in some other construct of reality, other than the reality of God's love for the world as revealed in Jesus, is to be condemned already. It is to miss life as it has always been intended to be lived. God incarnate in Jesus makes clear the distorted and false nature of this-worldly understandings of the self, and of others, and clarifies the reality of the image of God in which all human beings are made.

Jesus, according to John, has revealed the universal Word in clarity so that all human beings are confronted with a crisis. "Is the Jesus reality, my reality?" Much of the Gospel of John speaks to the spiritual concerns of his own community of faith. John begins his drama with the opening words affirming the truth of the incarnation, that in Jesus God is with us. John continues with the narratives that speak of living water, new birth, and symbolic healings, and the discourses that speak of the bread of life, vine and branches, and the Father's love for the world, all of which tell us that God is for us. And John's Gospel speaks of a counselor, advocate, and spiritual guide and promises that God will never abandon us. Consequently, while the picture of Jesus in John's Gospel is very different from the portraits of the New Testament authors discussed in the previous chapter, we can see that there is great congruity among all of these Gospels as to the underlying message. Each used extraordinary language to convey the transcendent significance of Jesus and to convey with urgency that each human being must de-

---

49. John 3:17.

cide whether to believe or not to believe that in Jesus God and God's Reality have been revealed.

To the question of "Where did Jesus come from?" John answers that Jesus comes from God and is filled with the honor and glory that belong to the Creator of all that is. But the meaning of that answer is what is truly significant. To know Jesus as the Word made flesh is to know oneself in relationship to God and others as God in creation intended one to be. To live in the Reality of Jesus is to live in the world as truly loved by God, and not to miss the destiny for which human beings were created and to which God has called them through his Word, Jesus.

CHAPTER XI

The Redeeming Sacrifice

Those early members of the Jesus movement who believed that their crucified and resurrected leader was more than a mere man, and that he was to be honored above all men and spiritual beings, did not do so because they thought his divinity was a self-evident fact for all to see. For obviously, many contemporaries did not grasp the divinity of Jesus or understand why anyone else did. His followers came to believe he was more than a mere man because of what Jesus had done for them, and what they had come to understand Jesus had accomplished for the whole world.

What Jesus had done for them was far more than healing and feeding their bodies, or providing them moral instruction. For in Jesus they had experienced a radical, spiritual transformation that they understood to be of ultimate and eternal significance. In seeking to comprehend the transcendent meaning of what Jesus had accomplished in their lives and for all of humanity, they quite naturally turned to the symbolic heritage of Judaism. And there were no more powerful symbols in first-century Judaism than those dramatized in the cultic activity of Temple sacrifice.

> For all have sinned and fall short of the glory of God, and are justified freely by his grace through the redemption that came by Christ Jesus. God presented him as a sacrifice of atonement, through faith in his blood. (Rom. 3:23-25a)

Here Paul spoke of redemption, sacrifice, atonement, and blood. These were powerful images taken from the sacrificial dramas that were quite familiar to his readers. To modern sensitivities, however, the notion of blood sacrifice seems alien, offensively violent, barbaric, cruel, irrational, and superstitious. Many may wonder what such expressions possibly could mean in a world that has long forgotten the awe surrounding the frequent and recurring sights, sounds, and smells of animal sacrifice.

For spiritual seekers today, the use of the language of sacrifice with regard to Jesus frequently presents a stumbling block rather than an avenue to faith. For many, the rationale for sacrifice appears to be at once incomprehensible and, at the same time, morally and theologically repugnant. What kind of deity, the contemporary mind wonders, needs or demands the ceremonial killing of innocent animals? Yet, despite this contemporary bewilderment and revulsion, the near universality of blood sacrifice in most traditional cultures points to primordial aspects of the human spirit and psyche that may be eclipsed from consciousness today, but that still influence human thought and behavior in profound ways.[1]

In order to understand the exceptional usage by Paul and other New Testament writers of these remarkable metaphors taken from the world of cultic sacrifice, it will be helpful if we first explore the meanings of sacrifice among the world's traditional cultures. In doing so we will see how sacrifice ritually portrayed for many ancient and traditional societies the ambivalence and ambiguity of the reality that life is dependent on killing and death, particularly symbolized in the reenactment of a primal death from which life generated. Furthermore, especially in the more organized ancient societies, sacrifice was an acknowledgment that life is a gift and a means of giving honor and thanksgiving to divine benefactors, and, when the gods became offended, a way to win back their favor.

Following that discussion we will look at the meaning of sacrifice in ancient Israel as a means of affirming and renewing the covenant with Yahweh, and the significance for the early Jesus movement of key metaphors from

---

1. Freud, in *Totem and Taboo* (1950), linked sacrifice to the Oedipus complex. This has lost favor in recent decades and anthropologists have rejected Freud's notion of a primordial parricide (see Kroeber, 1979) as the origin of ritual sacrifice. Carl Jung saw sacrifice, which for him was one of the universal themes in dreams, as a symbol of the victory of man's spiritual nature over his animal nature (Jung, 1956, pp. 394-440; 1964, pp. 143-46). While the interpretive significance of sacrifice is debatable, it would be difficult to deny the power of such symbolism in the shared human unconscious. See the discussion that follows for my own interpretive approach, although I also maintain that the symbolism of sacrifice is multifaceted and cannot be reduced to a single line of interpretation.

this cultic world of sacrifice. Specifically we will explore the meaning of the symbols of high priest, sacrificial lamb, and redemption.[2] Finally, we will look at ways to express in terms that are comprehensible today the meaning of these powerful symbols.

The Meaning of Sacrifice in World Cultures

Our ancient human ancestors were far more intensely connected to the mystery of life and the reality of death than most of us who live today in affluent Western societies. Life spans were much shorter, food far scarcer, injury and illness exceedingly more lethal, dangers from wild animals and rival tribes more immediate. Only exceptional families were untouched by the death of a child, the killing of a warrior, or the early loss of a parent. And by the time of adulthood, most knew the experience of hunger and disease that can weaken and kill in time of famine and plagues, and the awesome destructive community tragedies associated with storms, floods, volcanic eruptions, drought, earthquakes, and tribal wars. In pre-modern societies, life instinctively was understood to be a fragile gift and death an ever-present danger and future certainty.

Ritualizing Life's Dependence on Death

The mystery of life and the reality of death also were linked clearly and consciously in the consciousness of those who lived in primitive and ancient times. In hunter and herding societies the food of life was immediately dependent on the killed and the slaughtered. And where agriculture flourished, the living plants, which were invested with spiritual significance in the worldviews of those cultures, also died in order to become food for life.[3] Un-

---

2. It is not suggested here that these symbols in any way exhaust the meaning of Jesus' death for the early church, only that they are three key metaphors that are taken from the cult of sacrifice. We will look at additional metaphors taken from other social contexts in chapter XII.

3. In various cultures the spiritual significance of plants may be a manifestation of various underlying concepts: *animism,* the belief that all things are possessed by spirits or are spiritual beings; *animatism,* the mystical personification of natural things and forces; *totemism,* belief in ancestry from particular animals and plants that guides food practices,

like the modern sanitized consciousness associated with shopping in a supermarket, for earlier generations it was an inescapable and personal reality that the miracle of life was dependent upon killing and death, again and again and again. And with the awareness that living things must die in order that human beings might live came a sense of profound ambiguity about "the way life is." The sense of awe, of fear and fascination about this reality, was expressed clearly in the mythology, folklore, and rituals of most traditional peoples.[4] A major manifestation of this in a number of separate and diverse cultures has been the reenactment of what indigenous peoples believed was a primal death.

Anthropologists long have noted a fascinating commonality among the root-crop cultures of the world, particularly India, eastern Indonesia, New Guinea, and the Americas, with regard to ritual killings.[5] Their sacrificial ceremonies appear to be reenactments of a primal event that was believed to have occurred in a previous era, in which Dema rather than humans inhabited the earth.[6] The Dema were thought to be immortal beings who were sometimes in the form of human beings and sometimes in the form of animals. The Dema, at some point, killed their Dema deity, with the outcome being the Dema became mortal human beings, living, propagating, and dying. The sacred crop plants so essential for the sustaining nourishment of the mortals were formed from the slain body of the dead god.

Another cultural version of this theme of primal death making human life possible is seen in cosmic origin narratives that tell of self-sacrificing deities. In the Aztec culture of fifteenth-century Mesoamerica, the legend of the sun described the self-sacrifice of the gods so that the sun would move on its course and humanity could live.[7] This "creation" narrative was a kind of "charter" for the Aztec belief that sacrifice was essential for the existence of

---

marriage, and kin systems as well as religious ceremonies; or combinations of these. In more developed agricultural societies, the primary crops upon which indigenous peoples are dependent will often be represented by particular divinities and will be the subject of important myths. The god Demeter, who was said to have given wheat to the Greeks, Dionysus, the god of grapes and wine in Greek culture, and the Corn Woman myth in Mesoamerica are examples.

4. See Jensen (1951).

5. Jensen (1951, p. 167).

6. A remnant of such thinking may be reflected in the narrative tradition behind the Nephilim in Gen. 6:4.

7. Bierhorst (1990, p. 184).

life and the universe, and the reenactment of such sacrifices became a sacred obligation reflecting a preoccupation with the consciousness that death is required in order that life can be sustained.[8]

Ritual sacrifice was a regularly repeated drama among many cultures that addressed the profound ambiguities surrounding the fact that living things must die in order that humankind might live. This symbolism did more than address the psychological issues surrounding killing for food. Many rituals of sacrifice were followed by a communal eating of the sacrificed creature.[9] The act of eating the sacrificial victim usually was understood as a participation in a communal meal with the deity who, as we saw above, had given his life that the participants might have life. As such, the ritual became a symbolic means for affirming all of life's ambiguities and negativities.

Life is inexplicable, insecure, and messy. Human beings may desire a world in which the lion sleeps with the lamb, but they live in a world where, when the lion gets hungry, he will kill and eat the lamb. They may desire a world in which everything that happens makes good sense, but they actually live in a world where mysteries, contradictions, and chaos abound. One of the more profound but often unconscious meanings of ritual sacrifice is that the realities of life can be affirmed. Suffering and death can be embraced as necessary to human survival and social well-being, and the limitations of human logic can be transcended.[10]

Giving Honor and Thanksgiving to Divine Benefactors

At a conscious level, however, the meaning of most religious ceremonies in most cultures has been to give honor and thanksgiving to divine benefactors. Human beings long have been concerned that the mysterious powers that created the life forms that were killed and consumed would be offended by those deaths and could cause the food source to disappear. Such possibili-

---

8. Malinowski (1954) suggested the interpretation of myths as "charters" for various social realities and rituals.

9. Because of this fact, some anthropologists have sought material explanations for the meaning of sacrifice in terms of protein consumption. See Harner (1977) and Harris (1977).

10. Some anthropologists, most notably Levi-Strauss, have looked to myth as a means of overcoming logical contradictions at the level of the collective unconscious. See particularly Levi-Strauss (1963).

ties appeared to be confirmed in times when hunters returned empty-handed or when crops failed. Rituals intended to assure that such killing and consumption properly honored the ultimate source of the life-giving food were common among the diverse peoples of the world. Spirit beings, such as "the master of the animals" and the primal ancestors of the various species, were the intended recipients sometimes of trickery to defer blame for the kill, and sometimes of thanksgiving for the gift itself.[11]

This motif of giving honor and thanksgiving through blood sacrifice was a particularly important one in highly stratified civilizations. The sky gods of the sun, of thunder and storm, and of stars were worshiped in the more complex ancient civilizations with ritual killings, blood sacrifice, and vegetable and grain offerings. These cultic acts honored and served the gods by giving back to those who were believed to be the origin of living things the gift of representational life through the spilling of blood, an offering enhanced by pleasant aromas for the senses, and in flesh and plant food transformed into smoke by fire for spirit-world feasting.

Throughout the pre-modern high civilizations of China, the Indian subcontinent, the Mediterranean, the Middle East, and Mesoamerica, the relationship of human beings with believed-in divine spirit beings perhaps can be better understood if we also consider the normal social relationship of clients and patron benefactors in those stratified civilizations.[12] In the first-century Roman Empire, as in other highly organized cultures, the relationships between imperial families as patron benefactors and their loyal client aristocratic followers were governed by clearly defined social rules. The aristocrats were in turn the patron benefactors of their own clients. The Jewish historian Josephus, for example, understood himself as a loyal client of the emperor.[13] At the same time, Josephus was a patron benefactor in relation to his soldiers and many local persons of influence in Galilee. The relationship between wealthier families and their household servants and slaves also was one of patron and benefactor, while those at the bottom of the social structure seldom were able to become patrons themselves.

The social rules that governed the relationship between patron benefactor and client often involved gifts of protection, position, provision, and ma-

11. See Jensen (1951) with regard to this as well as the discussion in the following paragraph.

12. I am indebted to Neyrey (2005) for this discussion of patron and benefactor in antiquity.

13. Neyrey (1994).

terial reward in the form of land, shelter, and monetary income. In return, clients were above all to be loyal, manifesting that faithfulness in serving the will and the interests of the patron, and by enhancing and preserving the patron's honor. And while reciprocity was clearly at work, it was never the reciprocity of an exchange between equals. Although clients were usually dependent upon patrons, the patrons were generally powerful enough easily to replace one client with another, or to do without certain clients altogether. In such situations of inequality, the client was dependent upon the goodwill and generosity of the patron benefactor and easily could become the victim of his wrath. In some situations, that could lead to deadly outcomes. Consequently, the client was obliged to behave at all times toward the patron in such a manner as to ensure the patron's good pleasure and a continuation of benefits.

Very early in the history of religions, this unequal relationship of benefactor and client became a means to understand the relationship between human beings and the gods. As servant clients lived in the houses of aristocrats serving and feeding their masters, so priests dwelled in the sacred temples and served sacrifices to the gods. For the gods were understood to be the source of life, the givers and withholders of all good things. They were patrons of the highest order. They were to be honored with praise, thanked again and again for their benevolences, and loyally served.

Life was the greatest gift of all, and the blood of life was sacred, for it belonged only to the gods. Sacrifices were a means reverently and respectfully to acknowledge the source of life, to give thanks, and to celebrate the kindness of the gods. While certainly there were those who understood the sacrifices as crass bribes, as a magical purchase of blessings, as a means to obtaining from the gods the desires of the people, reflective persons in all cultures appear to have understood that the gods could not be bribed, for they did not need anything that human beings could offer.[14] Nevertheless, both the common folk and many of those philosophically inclined understood that the gods could become unhappy and withhold blessings at any time. Even though the divinities might not need what humans offered, it was feared that calamities would result should those who had been blessed with the gift of

---

14. Jensen (1951) argued that rituals suffer from "semantic depletion" in which the original profundity degenerates into a kind of magic in which the act is believed to change outcomes for those performing them. The idea that the gods are dependent on sacrifices could be seen as a product of such semantic depletion. Tradition holds that Buddha, Confucius, Quetzalcoatl, and several prophets of Israel taught against blood sacrifice.

life withhold or improperly carry out the sacrifices that symbolized the relationship of proper respect, esteem, and gratitude toward the gods.

Gaining Back the Favor of Offended Deities

This leads us to yet one more related meaning of sacrifice in world cultures. Ritual killings were considered a means to gain back the favor of offended gods. In most, if not all, pre-modern cultures there has been little difference between the established rules of society and the cultural perception of the requirements of the gods, whether ritual precepts or ethical ones.[15] Universally, human beings have feared offending the gods, although offense may have been understood very differently across cultures. Indeed, people in traditional societies tend to believe they have offended the spirits again and again. Even where the gods have given way to impersonal forces, as in the Hindu concept of *karma*, existential concern about the consequence of violating taboos and ethical norms remains, and such fears actually may be increased.

Some cultures place greater emphasis on guilt feelings, others on shame, and still others on a more objective collective alienation from the gods or from eternal truth. But it is a virtually universal reality that human beings experience themselves as having created through their actions and personal failures a rift between themselves and that which they consider to be the source of their lives and cultures.[16] The prevalence of sacrifice among traditional cultures throughout the globe bears witnesses to the profound need of the human psyche and of social communities to address this rift. While all of the motifs discussed above can be discerned in the cultic sacrifice system of ancient Israel, what was paramount in that culture was the need to address the rift between Yahweh and the people of the covenant.

---

15. That religion and society were one reality was the well-known thesis of Emile Durkheim's *The Elementary Forms of the Religious Life* (1915).

16. There also was a tendency, particularly in times of famine and other distresses, to increase the numbers of sacrifices, so that there was a natural tendency to conclude that if sacrifices influenced the gods to look kindly on human beings, the more sacrifices the better. Evidently, this is what occurred in Mexico among Aztecs, with regard to human sacrifices, during the times leading up to the conquistadors. During the final decades of the Second Temple in Jerusalem, the fact that animal sacrifices were held strictly according to the priestly law probably mitigated this tendency to think that more was better. Nevertheless, the numbers undoubtedly were substantial.

Jesus and Sacrifice in the Context of Ancient Israel

The use of blood sacrifice as a transcendent metaphor for the significance of Jesus and his accomplishments was a very natural and clear expression in the first century. Animal sacrifice was the central act of worship in the Temple of Jerusalem.[17] Each day, two lambs were sacrificed on the altar, one in the morning and one in the evening, accompanied by cereal and drink offerings.[18] On the Sabbath, on the first day of each lunar month, and on other special days and festival times, additional sacrifices were required.[19] As substantial in number as these were, there were many more Temple sacrifices offered than those ritually required by calendar. The Temple was a place of bustling activity and virtually continuous sacrifices of cattle, sheep, goats, doves, and pigeons brought or purchased on site by the people as sacrificial first fruits, tithes, and offerings.[20]

Sacrifice was widely practiced among all peoples of the region. But there was a unique character to sacrifice in Israel. In the faith of Israel, sacrifice was a means of affirming and renewing the covenant between Yahweh and his people. Others might sacrifice to many gods, but Israelites were to sacrifice to Yahweh alone. And it was spelled out clearly in the Law of the covenant that sacrifices were to be offered at particular times following specific rules, by a legitimate priesthood.[21] And the great ceremonies that remembered God's gracious deliverance from Egypt and the establishment of the covenant in the desert were to be commemorated with sacrifices.

Jewish members of the Jesus movement, while seeking to understand the transcendent significance of Jesus and his divine accomplishments as the bearer of a new covenant, appear to have been particularly drawn to three symbolic aspects of this sacrificial system as interpretive devices: (1) the high priest, (2) the sacrificial lamb, and (3) the redeemer from sin.

---

17. Members of the Jesus movement who lived far from Jerusalem in other parts of the Greek and Roman world also were quite familiar with blood rituals. For sacrifice was also the frequent and common central act of worship of the pagan deities in Greek and Roman cultures, as the early Christian controversy over eating food offered to idols makes clear. See 1 Cor. 8:4-6; 10:18-20.

18. Exod. 29:38-42.

19. Num. 28:9–29:40.

20. Lev. 23:9-14; 27:30-33; Num. 18:24.

21. Lev. 21–23.

A High Priest in the Order of Melchizedek

While first-century members of the Jesus movement undoubtedly were vividly aware of the sacrifices associated with the Temple of Jerusalem, the author of Hebrews chose to exhort his audience not with reference to the high priest of the Temple cult, but with regard to the legendary figure of Melchizedek, who was said to have given the patriarch Abraham bread and wine and blessed him in the name of "God Most High."

> We have this hope as an anchor for the soul, firm and secure. It enters the inner sanctuary behind the curtain, where Jesus, who went before us, has entered on our behalf. He has become a high priest forever, in the order of Melchizedek. (Heb. 6:19-20)

> When Christ came as high priest of the good things that are already here, he went through the greater and more perfect tabernacle that is not manmade, that is to say, not a part of this creation. He did not enter by means of the blood of goats and calves; but he entered the Most Holy Place once for all by his own blood, having obtained eternal redemption. The blood of goats and bulls and the ashes of a heifer sprinkled on those who are ceremonially unclean sanctify them so that they are outwardly clean. How much more, then, will the blood of Christ, who through the eternal Spirit offered himself unblemished to God, cleanse our consciences from acts that lead to death, so that we may serve the living God! (Heb. 9:11-14)

The mysterious figure of Melchizedek appears only very briefly in the book of Genesis, where this priest of God was identified as the king of Salem, an ancient city probably located at the later site of the city of Jerusalem.[22] To him, Abraham gave tithes taken from the spoils of battle. Around this figure, as was true for several characters who suddenly appeared and disappeared in biblical narratives, there grew over time religiously significant speculation.[23] In Psalm 110, which the author of Hebrews relies upon for his argument, the "Lord" is described as a priest forever, in the order of Melchizedek. In New Testament times this psalm was believed to be a Messianic prophecy.[24] In the

22. Gen. 14:17-20.

23. As we have seen, Elijah and Enoch also generated considerable speculative veneration.

24. Most scholars agree that the original historical meaning of the psalm involved God's address to the king, but in Mark 12:35-37 Jesus appears to have interpreted the psalm as David speaking to the Messiah.

popular imagination, then, the Messiah, the Anointed One, was associated with Melchizedek, and was to be spiritually set apart for the priestly functions in the coming age just as God had ordained the mysterious ancient priest of Abraham. In the desert ascetic community known as the Essenes, founded when a group of priests retreated into the desert in the second century BCE in religious dispute over the legitimacy of the Temple priesthood, particularly over the legitimacy of the appointed high priest, there was a slightly different understanding.[25] The Essenes thought of Melchizedek as an exalted heavenly being and an instrument of God's judgment in the final year of grace and on the day of salvation.[26]

In using Melchizedek to clarify the transcendent significance of Jesus, the author of Hebrews made the dramatic point that, like the priest of Abraham, Jesus is a Great High Priest, superior to all the high priests of Israel who have ever entered the Holy of Holies and offered purification sacrifices there. In the rhetorical logic of Hebrews, Jesus was far more deserving of honor than those who offered the daily and yearly sacrifices. They entered the curtain of the Holy of Holies of a tabernacle made by human hands. Jesus entered the heavenly tabernacle made by God where he dwells in God's presence. They were descended from Levi, but Jesus was God's firstborn. They made many sacrifices and died. Jesus offered himself as one sacrifice and lives eternally. They made sacrificial atonement for the ritually impure. Jesus' sacrificial death redeemed humankind from the slavery of sin and death.

Though he belonged with Melchizedek in a higher spiritual order, Jesus was an even greater heavenly being than the priest of Abraham, or than any other spiritual being, for he was the Son of God. On that basis, the author of Hebrews argued, the new covenant between God and humankind that came into being with Jesus went far beyond the covenant between God and Abraham. The hope of Abraham, secured by the promise of God, was that his descendants would be as numerous as the stars in the heavens. The Jewish people were the living evidence of God's faithfulness to that covenant. The hope of Jesus fulfills the promise of God through the prophet Jeremiah in which the Law of God is written on the people's hearts, sin is remem-

25. See discussion of the Essenes in chapter II.

26. See 11 QMelch of the Dead Sea Scrolls. Melchizedek, as the anointed one of the spirit, may have been associated in the Essene imagination with the "priestly" Messiah who would preside as high priest in the Messianic age, after the warrior Messiah had defeated the forces of darkness. See also discussion and notes on the Essenes in chapter II.

bered no more, and God's people live in the fellowship of God's eternal presence and peace.[27]

This new covenant supplants not only the covenant made with Abraham, but the sacred agreement made with Moses at Sinai as well. Instead of referring to the Jerusalem Temple and the sacrifices there, the author of Hebrews wrote of the sacred tabernacle that was believed to have been the place of sacrifice during the wanderings of Moses and the ancestors in the desert wilderness. Tradition holds that it was there, on *Yom Kippur,* the annual Day of Atonement, that the person anointed high priest of Israel would sacrifice on the altar a bull for himself and a goat for Israel.[28] He would then proceed through the sacred curtains that concealed the inner sanctuary of the tabernacle while creating a smokescreen from incense. As an unholy mortal human being, the high priest was able to enter the Holy of Holies without being struck dead only because he performed his task of purification according to the strictest of rules.[29] There in the Holy of Holies, he would sprinkle the life-blood of the bull and the goat on the sacred cover of Yahweh's throne, the ark of the covenant, as a means of purifying that most sacred place from any contamination that might have been caused by impurities during the preceding year.

The Hebrew word for "atonement" literally means to "cover over."[30] As the priest sprinkled blood on the cover of the ark, the blood symbolically hid the people's transgressions from the eyes of God and washed them away. Through the proper offering of sacrifice, forgiveness of sins was believed to be assured.[31] And these particular transgressions would not again defile the people and create estrangement between them and their God. For on the Day of Atonement there was one more important ritual. The high priest symbolically would place the sins of the people on a second goat that was then driven into the wilderness, taking their sins away.[32]

The author of Hebrews speaks of these things in order at once to show in what way Jesus' work was consistent with that of the high priest, to contrast the work of Jesus with the traditional holders of that office, and to demon-

---

27. Jer. 31:31-34.

28. Lev. 16:1-34 provides the ceremonial instructions for the Day of Atonement discussed below.

29. Lev. 10:1-2.

30. *Kaphar.* See Strong (1984) and Vine (2007).

31. Lev. 4:26.

32. Lev. 16:20-23.

strate that Jesus had supplanted the work not only of the high priest but of all the priests. The descendants of Aaron, the brother of Moses, were priests under the old covenant of Sinai. They offered repeated sacrifices of animals to purify ritually the people under that covenant. But, the writer points out, Jesus offered his own blood once and for all in order to mediate the new covenant between God and humankind, a covenant based on God's initiative, graciousness, and righteousness. The sacrifice of Jesus overcame the rift between God and humankind once and for all, so that those with faith might live eternally in God's presence and partake of God's benevolence.

The Sacrificial Lamb

Not only was Jesus spoken of in the Jesus movement as the Great High Priest making the offering, but Jesus also was understood to be the one who was sacrificed. This leads us to the second profound metaphor of the significance of Jesus' accomplishment through his death on the cross — the sacrificial lamb.

> The next day John saw Jesus coming toward him and said, "Look, the Lamb of God, who takes away the sin of the world!" (John 1:29)

The early church no doubt was drawn to the symbol of the Lamb of God by the words of Isaiah, who spoke of the servant of God as led like a lamb to the slaughter.[33] And while the Gospel of John mentions the title only once, as an announcement by John the Baptist concerning Jesus' divine role, the drama of that work clearly presents Jesus in the symbolic framework of the paschal lambs that were sacrificed on the eve of the Passover. In Mark's Gospel, as well as in the Gospels of Matthew and Luke, Jesus' trial and crucifixion both occur on the day of the Passover celebration; but in John these take place on the preceding day. The significance of this for the Fourth Gospel is that Jesus' trial and crucifixion are identified with the preparations for Passover on the traditional fourteenth day of Nisan of the Jewish calendar and with the sacrifice of the paschal lambs. That Jesus is himself to be understood as the Paschal Lamb is underscored by John's testimony that Jesus' legs were unbroken during the crucifixion, though the legs of those crucified

---

33. Isa. 53:7; Acts 8:32.

with him had been broken. For, as everyone who celebrated Passover knew, the bones of a paschal lamb were not to be broken during the ceremony.[34]

Paul also had identified Jesus' death with the sacrifice of the Passover lamb, and it is therefore likely that the symbolism of the Lamb of God was a common way for members of the Jesus movement from very early on to understand the significance of Jesus' divine work.[35] For those who could make the pilgrimage to Jerusalem, the Passover lambs were sacrificed on the altar of the Temple by the priests on the eve of Passover. The lambs were consumed by families at the symbolic Passover meal that evening. At that meal the people recalled the first Passover in Egypt in which the blood of the lambs slain by each of the Hebrew slave families was obediently smeared on the doorposts and lintels of their houses, providing protection from the plague that destroyed the firstborn children of their slave masters. In the later priestly traditions, which were probably in effect in the time of Jesus, during the Temple sacrifices of thousands of Passover lambs, the blood was sprinkled by the priests about the altar for the symbolic purification of God's people.[36]

Consequently, the lambs slain at Passover were symbols of God's protection and deliverance. Jesus, then, and his blood, identified with the Passover lamb, were understood in terms of divine protection and deliverance. But Jesus was not one more lamb from the human flock. Jesus was understood by the community of faith as *the* Lamb *of God*. The meaning of this distinction is highly significant. For this lamb belongs to God and it is God who does the offering. God does so out of God's immense love for the world, in order to remove the sin of the world. As God dramatically acted in the history of Israel to free the chosen people from slavery and oppression at the hands of the Egyptians, so God once again dramatically has intervened, this time to free all humankind from the slavery and oppression of sin, the law, and death.

Jesus the Redeemer

The Passover lamb was, as required by priestly law, a lamb without defect. Its blood provided the protection needed so that freedom could result. In New

34. John 19:33-37; Exod. 12:46; Num. 9:12; Ps. 34:20.

35. See 1 Cor. 5:7. The "Lamb" is also a major image in the book of Revelation, in which the slain lamb is the victorious figure of the apocalypse.

36. 2 Chron. 35:11.

Testament thought, it was the blood of Christ, the Lamb of God, that redeemed humankind from sin.

> For you know that it was not with perishable things such as silver or gold that you were redeemed from the empty way of life handed down to you from your forefathers, but with the precious blood of Christ, a lamb without blemish or defect. He was chosen from the creation of the world, but was revealed in these last times for your sake. (1 Pet. 1:18-20)

> Christ redeemed us from the curse of the law by becoming a curse for us, for it is written: "Cursed is everyone who is hung on a tree." He redeemed us in order that the blessing given to Abraham might come to the Gentiles through Christ Jesus, so that by faith we might receive the promise of the Spirit. (Gal. 3:13-14)

In these texts both the author of 1 Peter and Paul, in his letter to the Galatians, employed a third major metaphor pointing to the significance of the death of Jesus on the cross related to sacrifice — Jesus the redeemer. The Jesus movement understood that what Jesus had accomplished through his death on the cross was none other than the redemption of humankind.

The idea of redemption in the ancient Middle East, where people frequently ended up in servitude and slavery due to debt and misfortune in war, was an important one. Slaves serving the central governing kings and priests usually were captives whose lives had been spared. The slaves of private citizens were likely to have been debtors who entered into service in order to pay off a debt. The majority of slaves were household workers and field laborers.[37]

In Israel, a slave could receive freedom in several ways. After six years of service Jewish Law required that slaves be set free.[38] The Law also mandated the release of those owned by another in the year of Jubilee, which occurred every fifty years.[39] While Gentile masters did not honor Jewish Law, they sometimes granted freedom as a gift, and they occasionally adopted slaves and granted them the benefits of family membership and citizenship. In addition, slaves sometimes could purchase their own freedom, or more com-

---

37. See Bartchy (2003), Bradley (1994), and Wiedemann (1989) for background on slavery in the Roman Empire.

38. Exod. 21:2.

39. Lev. 25:10.

monly, could have their freedom purchased by a kinsman, usually a brother. In fact, such relatives were obligated to attempt to accumulate the resources necessary to effect such purchase or redemption.[40]

The idea of redemption also had a significant historical association with the sacrificial system and the priesthood.[41] The firstborn children were believed to belong to God, and in very ancient times probably were offered as human sacrifices.[42] The story of God providing a ram to redeem Isaac, Abraham's firstborn, from the sacrificial altar, may well have represented a transition from human to animal sacrifice.[43] As the ram miraculously provided by God in the Abraham story "redeemed" Isaac, so ritually acceptable animals were understood to be God's living gifts that could be substituted for human thank offerings and could die for the sins of Isaac's descendants.

Apparently, the firstborn of Israel continued to belong to Yahweh and for a time were set aside for service to God.[44] This sacred calling was associated for Israel with the Passover that celebrated God's saving of Israel's firstborn, an event marked by the sacrifice of lambs whose blood provided protection. The priestly tradition held that God, through Moses, allowed the firstborn members of Israel's tribes to be redeemed, relieving them of their sacred obligations through the substitution of the Levites, who were henceforth set aside as sacred priests. And because there were fewer Levites than firstborn, the payment of money *redeemed* the remainder.

It is within the social context of the metaphor of a kinsman redeeming a slave in service to an outsider, the ancestor redeemed by the blood of an animal, and the priesthood as substitutes for the firstborn that God's redemp-

40. Lev. 25:47-49. Redemption of property by kinsmen was also common practice (Lev. 27:15-20; Ruth 4:1-6; Jer. 32:1-15).

41. See particularly Exod. 13:15.

42. The near sacrifice of Isaac (Gen. 22) certainly indicates this to have been a possibility. Despite interpreter attempts to suggest otherwise, the narrative of Judg. 11:29-40 makes it clear that Jephthah sacrificed his virgin daughter to make good on a promise to Yahweh due to military victory. And pagan child sacrifice in the region is referred to in 2 Kings 17:31. In Israel, firstborn offspring of every womb, both man and animal, were to be offered to Yahweh (Num. 18:15), but there was provision in the Law requiring that they be redeemed for five shekels of silver each. Presumably the redemption was in place of sacrifice.

43. The story of Abraham's offering of Isaac in which God substituted a ram at the last moment (Gen. 22) is a "charter" for the practice of animal sacrifice. As the people would not have come into existence had Isaac been allowed to be sacrificed, so the ongoing sacrifices were believed to be necessary for the existence and well-being of the Israelites.

44. Num. 3:40-51.

tion of humankind was understood by the followers of Jesus. Isaiah of the exile had spoken in the sixth century BCE of God as a "Redeemer" of Israel who would bring about their freedom and restore them to the land of promise.[45] The Jesus movement believed that God had through Jesus paid the ultimate price, not with material wealth but with Jesus' own life's blood, for the spiritual redemption of his spiritual kinsmen. That blood, like the blood of Abraham's animal sacrifice and that of the Passover lambs, provided protection and deliverance, but it also had a connotation of payment.

The redemption metaphor, as used by the New Testament writers, presupposes that humanity has "sold" itself into the slavery of sin. God is the Redeemer, the purchaser, and the life-blood of Jesus is the payment that requires the owner to let go of those in slavery. That owner, in this symbolic usage, is none other than the power of sin in the lives of human beings made even more oppressive by the Law and its demands, and the stranglehold of death that is the consequence of that servitude.[46] It is not that the power of sin chooses to release its slaves. For unlike some benevolent slave-masters, it is not in the nature of sin to do so. But now sin has no choice but to release its slaves, just as a human slaveholder in the ancient world had no choice once the necessary redemptive price had been paid. The slave, however, does have a choice. For it remains a possibility, even after the ransom price has been paid, that the slave will choose to remain a slave. Freedom is available, but it would not be freedom if it were compelled.

The author of Hebrews spoke of Jesus as the Great High Priest, the Son of God through whom all things were made, who offered himself as a blood sacrifice in order to bring grace to humankind and to initiate the new covenant. The Gospel of John spoke of the Word that was God who became the Lamb of God who takes away the sin of the world. When Paul used the language of sacrifice, blood, atonement, and redemption to speak of the significance of Jesus' death, he also expressed the theological point that would have been contrary to the expectations of those who participated regularly in Temple sacrifices. Paul, the former Pharisee, made it clear that the sacrifice of Messiah Jesus was not an offering *to God* performed by a human priest as a work of righteousness. It is not *God* who is the recipient of the sacrifice. And it is not a human member of the Jerusalem priestly class that offered the

---

45. "Redeemer" is a key metaphor for Yahweh in Isa. 41–66.

46. This power of sin was often personalized by the Jesus movement as Satan or the spiritual powers of darkness.

sacrifice, but, taking on the role of the priest, *God offered Christ Jesus* as a blood sacrifice in a redeeming act of grace and righteousness.[47] And both Paul and the author of 1 Peter spoke of Jesus' death as a redemptive event in which God set humankind free from sin and death.

The unified witness of the early church was that Jesus' death was the gracious sacrificial offering of God's "firstborn" son for the sins of humankind. The fully human Jesus, who was, according to Hebrews, like us in every way, though without sin, and was, at the same time, the divine Son of God, the Word of God through whom all things were made, sacrificed himself for the world.

Understanding Jesus' Sacrifice Today

As I have said, it is difficult for those who live in a world so far removed from the truth that life lives off the death of other living things, and a world so distantly alienated from the ancient pervasive experience of civilizations in the cults of blood sacrifice, fully to grasp the symbolism of sacrificial images with regard to the meaning of Jesus' death. To the early Jewish members of the Jesus movement the symbols of sacrifice, particularly those associated with the major fall New Year feast, *Yom Kippur,* the Day of Atonement, and the major springtime feast of Passover, were familiar, sacred realities that required little or no explanation, other than to interpret their relevance for faith in Jesus.

For someone who stands in one culture to understand a profound ritual that has transcendent meaning in another culture, it is necessary both to attempt to translate the beliefs underlying the ritual into concepts meaningful to the one seeking understanding, and to identify somewhat analogous ritual experiences in one's own culture that evoke similar feelings, while at the same time acknowledging the natural limitations of such endeavors. Such translation is made possible, despite remarkable human diversity, by the fact that, genetically and physiologically, and in recognizable commonalities in social behavior and consciousness, human beings are pretty much the same wherever and whenever they show up in history. So, while understanding the symbolism of blood sacrifice is difficult for us today, we are quite capable of grasping the truly important underlying assumptions.

47. Rom. 8:3.

A good starting place for persons today, who would seek to understand the meaning of Jesus' death on the cross as a sacrifice for humankind, would be to see Jesus' death as the fulfillment of all the human longing expressed in all cultures and all faiths wherever rituals of sacrifice have been practiced, and particularly as manifested in the faith of Israel. At the same time, they should seek to make as comprehensible as possible the underlying theological assumptions of Jesus' "sacrifice" prevalent in New Testament reflection.

Embracing the Ambiguities and Sufferings of Life

As we have seen, blood sacrifice can be understood as an expression of the universal longing for the spiritual freedom to embrace life as it is in all its ambiguity and mysteriousness. To be alive as a creature of God is to experience existential insecurity and difficult choices. Faith in Jesus as the Christ perceives that God in Jesus has entered into this human situation, rejecting the path of escape from life's negations, and choosing the cross, suffering, abandonment, and death. In the cross, life in all its terrors has been experienced and affirmed by God, not only "as it is," but as the way life "is supposed to be."

In the faith of the Jesus community, it is not just the human being Jesus, but God Incarnate, who has submitted to everything that human beings fear and endure. God did not come to humankind in Jesus in order to answer the questions of why life is the way it is, or why bad things happen to good people.[48] God came to humankind to participate fully in the struggles of finite existence and to demonstrate what it means to be fully human in the midst of them. To understand Jesus both as the one who sacrifices and as the sacrifice itself is, for faith, the assurance that God is always with us in our own most personal pain. God suffers when we suffer, and God mysteriously will transform our suffering for God's good purposes if only we will allow God to do so.[49]

Moreover, as people of faith have come to understand the representational nature of Jesus' death, they also have experienced themselves freed to live in humility and gratitude in the reality that their lives are dependent on the deaths of others. Not only do human beings have divine permission to live off the death of other living things in terms of the food they eat, but they

---

48. To believe this would be a form of Gnosticism.
49. Rom. 8:28.

also have permission to partake of the benefits bestowed by those who have risked their lives and sometimes died for the benefit of others and the good of society. Human beings are free to embrace the gifts of those sacrificed lives and to honor them. And those who understand and embrace the sacrifice of Jesus also become willing to be lucid about life and to see the suffering of humanity, to feel its pain, and to respond to it. And to live in such faith is to be free to live one's own life sacrificially, willing to expend one's self, and to suffer, if need be, on behalf of others, as Jesus suffered.

Accepting the Greatest Gift of God's Love

Blood sacrifice, as we have seen, symbolizes across many cultures the recognition that all the gifts of life that humankind experiences are blessings bestowed by a higher power. In Israel, sacrifice symbolized loyalty to Yahweh. It was a way to give thanks and to honor the God of the covenant. When today persons reflect seriously upon their lives, they are likely to understand that life is a sacred gift that is sustained at each moment by a power greater than themselves. Many speak of that power as God, the Creator and Sustainer of their lives, and know in their hearts that God is deserving of thanksgiving, honor, and service.

In seeking to understand the meaning of Jesus' death, the early church believed that Jesus was God's sacrifice, not a human offering. Jesus was the heavenly Son of God who was sacrificed on the altar of the cross, given as God's greatest gift to humankind. In Jesus, God held nothing back. As such, Jesus' death on the cross also was God's affirmation that all human blessings were indeed gifts of a gracious and loving God. And the cross was also the revelation that the way genuinely to honor and give thanks to God is to accept God's greatest gift and to live in the reality of God's transforming grace. This leads us immediately to a related meaning of sacrifice.

God's Love Has Overcome Sin

In ancient Israel the blood of animals, particularly those slaughtered on the Day of Atonement and at Passover, "covered" the sins of the people. For the Jesus movement, Jesus' death on the cross was God's affirmation that God shared the human desire for humankind to be free from the burden of sin.

The question the modern mind often asks is, "What kind of God would require the blood of Jesus as a payment for our sins?" But, from the standpoint of New Testament thinking, the question is faulty. For the question assumes Jesus was offered by human beings to God as a sacrifice. That is not the New Testament claim. As we have seen, the New Testament faith held that it was God, or Jesus as God's representative, who made the offering. Consequently, a better question might be, "What kind of creatures are we that our lives have needed God to offer such a sacrifice for us in order that we become willing and able to receive God's love and dwell in it?"

Blood sacrifice is an embodiment of a widespread human hunger to be free from the burden of one's transgressions against life and its ultimate source. There are few who would deny that all human beings have failed in their everyday obligation to live lives of gratitude for that which has benefited them, and for which they cannot take credit. And few, who acknowledge the reality of God, will deny that they have fallen short of honoring God with their lives, and have failed again and again to do God's will. This failure, this missing of the intended meaning and purpose of existence, is what the New Testament community of faith considered to be sin. They understood that sin alienates human beings from the God who creates and sustains their lives. And though some human beings have tried much harder than others, all who have attempted to overcome that alienation, if they are honest with themselves, know from experience that human beings are unable to do so through their own efforts, whether those labors are in the form of good deeds or of various types of self-inflicted suffering.

It was the experience and the preaching of those who knew Jesus and witnessed his horrifying death and resurrection, that in Jesus, God revealed that God's love had overcome the sin that alienates. This understanding always has been an incomprehensible mystery that can be glimpsed only through inadequate symbols. But the experience of God's grace in the lives of those who have faith has continued through the ages to bear witness to the faith that Christ died for the sins of the world.

The cross continues to symbolize, for faith, the reality that God did not abandon humankind to perish in sin. For through the suffering and death of Jesus the Messiah, the Son of God, the Word made flesh, God has demonstrated that God's grace is not cheap grace, but costly grace. God's love is not sentimental feeling, but the tough love of suffering expenditure that confronts humankind with the cost to God of human disobedience and estrangement. Through Jesus' death, sin has been condemned and its power broken and banished from the human spirit. And through it God's judgment has been pronounced as absolution, as forgiveness for all sin and all sinners. In the sacrifice of God on the cross, the Word of God has spoken, overcoming the rift that separates humankind from its Source and freeing those who have faith to live in continuous gratitude, glorifying God and doing God's will.[50]

Reenacting the Sacrifice of Jesus

This discussion is not to suggest that the meaning of the blood sacrifice of Jesus on the cross can be reduced to a set of rational statements. Sacrificial rituals never have been fully rationalized in the minds of those who participated in them. Rituals speak in nonverbal ways to the depths of human emotion and experience, and point to the incomprehensible mysteries of existence in ways that mere words and rational constructs can never achieve. The experience of meaning occurs during sacred rituals in every society precisely because such rites go beyond cognitive understanding, and it is impossible to reduce their meaning to a set of rational statements. It is yet one more truth about human existence that in order genuinely to understand a ritual one must participate in it.

Jesus' own interpretation of his death on the cross was reenacted by the Jesus movement each time they participated in the Eucharist. Jesus had spoken of the bread that was broken as his own body and the wine that was shared as his blood for the establishment of the new covenant between God and humankind. As families for generations had eaten the lambs that were sacrificed on Jewish holy days, so the disciples were to eat the symbolic body of their sacrificed Lord frequently as a remembrance and thanksgiving for what he had done for them, and as a participation in that new covenant. As the bread was eaten, the participants reaffirmed that the death of Jesus was for their sins, celebrated anew the gift of God's grace, and participated in the new covenant and the great banquet feast of the life to come in a way too profound to express in language alone.

In the sacrifice of animals, the blood was sacred and belonged to God alone. It was not to be consumed by human beings.[51] But in the sacrifice of

---

50. We will explore this meaning more fully in the following chapter.
51. Lev. 17:10.

God in Jesus Christ the blood that belonged to God was shared symbolically by God with the community of faith who were charged with drinking the blood, while remembering how Jesus poured out his life for all. The drinking of the sacred blood of life, which belonged to God, symbolized God's inclusion of human beings in God's eternal fellowship. By drinking the symbolic sacred blood of the sacrifice, the people experienced all over again the presence of God's Spirit in their midst, their spiritual unity with God and the community of faith, and the promise that they would continue in that unity in the world to come.

By interpreting the death of Jesus on the cross as a blood sacrifice, the New Testament writers expressed both the way in which sacrifice illumined the transcendent significance of that event and how that transcendent meaning had supplanted that very same cultic ritual. Ironically, in Jesus' sacrifice, the cult that inspired these dramatic metaphors had been supplanted. Temple sacrifice formally ended for Judaism when Jerusalem and the Temple were destroyed in 70 CE. But the theology of Paul made it clear years earlier that for the Jesus movement animal sacrifices were no longer needed, a point that was strongly reaffirmed later by the author of Hebrews. The "once and for all" nature of Jesus' sacrifice made forever unnecessary the practice of repetitive blood sacrifice. The Jesus movement stood in the tradition of the prophets who had denounced the reliance of the people on the sacrificial system to save them from God's judgment, and went beyond it. For they spoke of God sacrificing God's own firstborn son as the ultimate final sacrifice, in order that Jesus' followers be empowered by the forgiveness of sins to act justly, to love mercy, and to walk humbly with their God.

While the sacrifice of Jesus was "once and for all," it was to be remembered and experienced anew again and again by those who saw Jesus through the eyes of faith. For the new covenant people of Jesus, modern distaste for the imagery notwithstanding, the Eucharist in which bread was broken and wine poured out would, nevertheless, forever be spoken of as a sacrifice. These were no empty words, for in this central ritual the brokenness of being human and the poured-out nature of life expended were celebrated as constantly renewed by the redeeming accomplishment of Jesus as the Christ.

CHAPTER XII

The Reconciling Savior

The societies of the Mediterranean and Middle East are considered by anthropologists to be *agonistic* cultures, demonstrating a pattern of prevailing combativeness in human interactions.[1] From ancient times the region has been characterized by peril and refuge, with the "in-group" of family and kin most often defining refuge. All outsiders, those who were not members of one's own family or kin, or in larger conflicts, one's ethnic and geopolitical groupings, generally were regarded with suspicion. And everyday interactions with others were experienced as contests in which the limited goods of prosperity and honor might be enhanced or diminished. Frequently, when material well-being and honor were endangered, violence would break out and homicidal blood feuds and wars would erupt that sometimes lasted for generations.

It is not startling that in the midst of such conflict-oriented cultures the relationship between disobedient and sinful human beings and their God would be understood in terms of enmity. And in seeking to understand the transformation that Jesus had accomplished in their lives and his significance for all of history it is not surprising that the Jesus movement spoke of reconciliation, of peace with God, and of Jesus as their savior from the terrible consequence of being enemies of God.

---

1. See Malina (2001) for background of this paragraph and also the discussion of peril and refuge in chapter II of this book.

Therefore, since we have been justified through faith, we have peace with God through our Lord Jesus Christ, through whom we have gained access by faith into this grace in which we now stand. (Rom. 5:1-2a)

Since we have now been justified by his blood, how much more shall we be saved from God's wrath through him. For if, when we were God's enemies, we were reconciled to him through the death of his Son, how much more, having been reconciled, shall we be saved through his life. Not only is this so, but we also rejoice in God through our Lord Jesus Christ, through whom we have now received reconciliation. (Rom. 5:9-11)

In Paul's thought, the idea of reconciliation clearly was linked to the demonstration of God's love in the death of Christ. As such, reconciliation is the universal and final resolution of the longing, expressed in cults of sacrifice in all times and places, for things to be made right between human beings and transcendent divinity. Reconciliation is an overcoming of the rift between God and human beings through Jesus' death, not as a human work of salvation, but as the miraculous generosity of God. But the meaning of the "reconciliation" metaphor, as used by Paul, is derived not so much from the symbolism of sacrifice, as discussed in the previous chapter, as from the symbolism of human relationships in the face of conflict. And its implications are to be further found in the "salvation" metaphor, of rescue from danger, and in the idea of life transformed in its relationships to others.

Enmity and Reconciliation in Society

People everywhere and in all times have had problems in relationships. Conflict and estrangement between parents and children, between husbands and wives, and between and among neighbors, tribes, and nations is a commonality of existence, though the intensity of such difficulties varies from circumstance to circumstance. Whenever and wherever relationships are seriously broken, there can be tragic consequences, unless reconciliation can be achieved. In order better to understand the meaning of reconciliation, it is helpful to recall some of the ways in which the problem of enmity between human beings has been addressed by traditional peoples.

While cultures differ in how they manage conflict, there are some common ways in which tensions between parties and tribes historically have been resolved. Peace between social organizations competing for the same resources is usually fragile. Almost any type of incident can lead to bloodshed unless there are more peaceful avenues available. Sometimes potential tensions are handled through *seasonally scheduled rituals* in which goods are exchanged and feasts are shared.[2] Or a special ceremony is organized because of a particular incident in order to reduce animosity and improve trust.[3] Such events can be highly successful in maintaining peaceful relations between differing tribes and communities. Nevertheless, it often takes only one event of violence to destroy the peace.[4] And particularly in societies that are agonistic, the dangers of unleashing cycles of retribution are always great.

When a life has been violated or taken, peace between the perpetrator's group and the victim's group usually becomes exceedingly difficult. In order to control the disastrous consequences of unrestrained retribution, *customs and laws* often dictate that when an injury has been inflicted or a murder has taken place, retaliation be carefully measured. For example, in some societies if a woman of one kin group has been killed by a member of another kin group, then a female from the murderer's kin, who is of similar age and marriage status, is expected to be killed.[5] Because these limitations on payback are respected by all parties, peace, albeit an uneasy one, may be restored by the revenge killing. In ancient Israel the law of retribution required an "eye for an eye, tooth for tooth, hand for hand, foot for foot, burn for burn, wound for wound, bruise for bruise."[6] It was against this law of retribution that Jesus dared to take a stand, advocating nonviolence and forgiveness.[7] But it is important to remember that the law of retribution originally set legal limits on violent revenge and no doubt helped to reduce the incidence of recurring blood feuds.

Many societies also rely on *intermediaries* to bring about reconciliation in difficult situations.[8] Independent parties may play an important role in

2. An excellent example is to be found in Malinowski (1922) and Uberoi (1962), who describe the *kula*, a ceremonial exchange system of the Trobriand Islanders that serves to cement friendships across several hundred miles of island tribal groups.

3. Native American peace pipe ceremonies are a familiar example.

4. An example would be the rape of Dinah in Gen. 34.

5. An example would be the Berbers of North Africa (Beattie, 1964, p. 175).

6. Exod. 21:24-25.

7. Matt. 5:38-42.

8. An example is found among the Ifugao of the Philippines where respected aristocrats help settle political disputes (Barnouw, 1978, p. 196).

checking the potential cycle of revenge that can occur when a blood feud is in the offing. Anthropologist Evans-Pritchard, for example, reported on the role of the "leopard skin chief," or holy man, in mediating between kin groups among the Nuer of the Sudan after a murder.[9] In that culture the murderer was permitted to take refuge with the "leopard skin chief" while that respected holy man sought to work out an arrangement of payment between the murderer's kin and the victim's relatives that would end the matter. Through compensatory payment, usually with livestock, peace could be reestablished.

Similarly, *official messengers*, or ambassadors, sometimes representing a third group friendly to both parties, may serve as intermediaries between nations that are facing potential conflict. In the Old Testament, Abraham took on the role of an intermediary, pleading the case with Yahweh for sparing the city of Sodom from destruction, much as an official messenger might plead for mercy for a weaker army on the eve of an attack by a stronger one.[10]

Making peace with an enemy in which there is a history of violations of honor and vengeful retribution is never an easy matter. And when there is enmity between two parties that are unequal in status, the difficulty is multiplied many times over. The party with status and power possesses the greater perceived honor requiring defense, and usually the overwhelming ability to destroy enemies, while the party with less status often will have few if any resources to bring to the negotiating table or with which effectively to strike back.

In the ancient world the terms of peace between warring peoples usually were determined by the will of the victorious army following military success. Because of the conflict-oriented cultures of the region, the Pax Romana, the Peace of Rome, was considered by many to be a remarkable achievement. Beginning with Caesar's conquests and maintained by military victories over periodic uprisings, the Roman peace lasted for three hundred years. During this time piracy was reduced on the high seas and banditry on the roads. While remaining a major problem for individual travelers, such attacks were less common than in previous times.[11] Under the Pax Romana,

9. Evans-Prichard (1940).

10. Gen. 18:16-33.

11. See Shaw (1984) and De Souza (1999). The extent of banditry in the empire remains controversial partially due to the designation of the term *bandit* in ancient literature being applied to armed insurgent bands as well as groups of robbers. De Souza, while acknowledging that the campaign of Pompey the Great against the pirates was impressive in a number of

private and family feuds were largely forced either to play out in sublimated ways or to use the courts. To do otherwise was to come up against the mighty arm and brute force of the Roman overlords. But for the conquered peoples, the harshness of Roman occupation and rule also reinforced the belief that foreigners and outsiders were enemies to be despised. And the Roman Peace served to increase the conflicts among indigenous peoples, especially between those who embraced Roman culture and those who resisted, and between the wealthier classes and the poor.[12]

The first-century political backdrop of an empire's overwhelming might, at odds with largely impotent rebellious subjects, is an important context for understanding Paul's metaphor of reconciliation. But instead of peace and reconciliation being initiated by an oppressive and evil regime, Paul pointed in his use of the concept to the holy and gracious God of all creation.

Enemies of God

Reconciliation, as used by Paul in the earlier quoted passages, presupposes that all of humanity throughout all of human history has been at enmity with God. We were, as he says, "enemies of God." Paul did not concern himself so much with the "how" of this state of being, as with the reality of it.[13] That all have sinned and fallen short of the glory of God was, for Paul, a fact of existence. But it was a fact of existence that could not be blamed on God. This situation came to exist not because of anything God had done, but because of what human beings had done.

In order to understand what Paul meant by "enemies of God," it is helpful to see the implications of that phrase for those who take seriously the reality of God. Enmity is the state of relationship between human beings and God that exists because human beings show up in, and willfully participate in, a world of estrangement and disobedience. Human beings are enemies of

---

ways, indicates that its benefits probably were temporary. But the ancient literature clearly indicates that Roman might made dangerous travel and trade routes less perilous than those not under the protection of Rome, though they were in no way safe by modern standards.

12. This is clearly supported by the works of the first-century historian Josephus.

13. It is true that Paul speaks in Rom. 5:12 of sin entering the world through Adam, yet it is important not to read into that statement later theories of "original sin." Paul's point is about death's origin in sin, and the reality of sin for those who did not have the Law.

God because God is dishonored when they attempt to live life on their own terms, by living lives of arrogance, ingratitude, selfishness, and maliciousness. Estrangement exists because people pursue their own wills rather than the will of God, deal with their neighbors as enemies rather than as God's loved beings, and treat God's creation as a bunch of things to be exploited and consumed for their own selfish pleasure rather than a gift entrusted to humankind for coming generations.[14] Consequently, this world is one in which people who believe in God sense God to be their enemy, because they know in their hearts that their lives are in conflict with God's purposes.

The Desire for Peace with God in Ancient Israel

The idea that Yahweh would exercise retribution for the wickedness of human beings who had grievously offended the honor of God was largely taken for granted in the theology of the Jewish people. The prophets particularly understood that there were dire consequences for violating the covenant, for rebellion against God. And despite the words of God's mercy and compassion in Jeremiah, Second Isaiah, and Hosea, God was still seen as that ultimate power and authority with the overwhelming ability to destroy those who offended God's honor. If the consequence of offending the honor of an earthly ruler meant destruction by the wrath of that authority, how much more, they reasoned, would God's wrath be visited upon those who had offended the honor of God. Plagues and famines generally were believed in Old Testament times to have been sent as retribution for offenses against God.[15] It was quite common for kings and rulers to be blamed for some breach of sacred law or custom that resulted in God's punishment.[16] Prophets and seers would challenge the rulers in such times, and restitution and sacrifices were made in the hope of ending the time of suffering.

As we have seen, the ceremonies of sacrifice at the Temple were expressions of the human desire to overcome the enmity between the people and their God. And the priests functioned as intermediaries, representing ordinary citizens before God during those ceremonies. The Law also functioned

---

14. Paul's discussion of sin in Rom. 1–8 speaks to the problem of self-will out of control. The view that the creation has been damaged because of sin lies behind Rom. 8:19-21.

15. Exod. 32:35; Lev. 26:21; Num. 11:33; 14:37; Ezek. 14:21.

16. See Hanson (1996) and 1 Sam. 5–6; 2 Sam. 21, 24.

as a kind of intermediary, particularly in the thought of the Pharisees. For it was their understanding that meticulous observance of the Law would bring about peace between God and those made pure by obedience.[17]

The Persistent Power of Sin

It was Paul's conviction, however, that these efforts at bringing about reconciliation had failed. They had failed because the rift was too wide, the enmity too great, the damage too irreparable, the self-deception too rampant. It failed because no amount of human effort was capable of saving humankind from the consequences of being enemies of God.

The fundamental human problem Paul addressed was that the sinfulness of humankind is deeply and stubbornly entrenched in people's lives, relationships, and societies. It cannot be overcome simply by willing to cease to live in sin and getting on with doing what is right. For the fundamental human problem is that even when human beings desire to do that, something holds them back. Persons may arise on many days intending to do so, but before the day is over they realize they have failed miserably in their efforts. The human inability consistently and fully to embrace and live what is the true meaning of human existence is precisely the problem. As Paul says, "For what I do is not the good I want to do; no, the evil I do not want to do — this I keep on doing."[18] Without God's assistance, according to Paul, humankind is unable to change, to truly change.

Of course, Paul, the former Pharisee, understood that people can change some things on the outside. They have the power to clean up their acts, much as we today see violent criminals cut their hair, shave their beards, and wear nice suits when they go to court.[19] But it was Paul's experience that only with God's help can human hearts be changed. That people need God's help to change was not a matter of doctrine for him. It was not something people ought to believe, along with all those other things they ought to do. It was a realization of human wisdom that came from his life experience.

This understanding of sin readily can be grasped by many today who

---

17. See discussion in chapter V of this book.
18. Rom. 7:19.
19. Such cleaning of the outside was Jesus' criticism of the Pharisees.

also have had the life experience to discover that sin is cunning, baffling, and powerful. They have come to understand that sin is the universal addiction, not to a substance, but to living life on one's own terms, to a pattern of existence supported by delusions that feed the pride of self. And as is often the case with substance addiction, addiction to a life of sin, of living a life lacking in spirituality and pursuing self-will, also often requires someone to "hit bottom" in order to be willing for change to occur.

Paul believed that sin had consequences, and that "a man reaps what he sows."[20] Almost everyone can grasp Paul's point. It is easily observable that people's actions set in motion consequences that cannot be undone, much as a rock thrown at a neighbor cannot be called back in mid-air. Yet it also seems to be the case that people often appear in this world to "get away with" all sorts of evil behavior with no apparent consequence. For Paul, however, whether or not people experienced misfortune in this life because of their sinful behaviors, sin sets in motion spiritual and eternal consequences that, humanly speaking, are inevitable.[21] The consequence of sin is death. For to live in sin is to live apart from God, the source of life. It is spiritual death in the present and eternal death for those who refuse to believe in and remain unwilling to live in the reality that God has reconciled the world unto himself.

A Savior from Spiritual and Eternal Death

But, in Paul's thought, what is humanly impossible has become fully possible through God's gracious work in Jesus. Or, as the author of Luke-Acts expressed it, God has sent Jesus into the world to be the Savior.

> Today in the town of David a Savior has been born to you; he is Christ the Lord. (Luke 2:11)

> The God of our fathers raised Jesus from the dead — whom you had killed by hanging him on a tree. God exalted him to his own right hand as Prince and Savior that he might give repentance and forgiveness of sins to Israel. (Acts 5:31)

20. Gal. 6:7.
21. Rom. 6:8.

The author of Luke-Acts traditionally has been identified with Luke the physician, a companion on Paul's missionary journeys.[22] Whether it was this companion or another, it is likely that the author was a learned person who was strongly influenced by Paul's theology. One could even argue that the overarching theme of the two-volume work of Luke-Acts is the reconciliation of the world through the saving work of Jesus, the Christ.

While it is not possible to date precisely the writing of the Gospel of Luke and the Acts of the Apostles, the author probably wrote in the mid-80s. Although the memory of earlier times of persecution is clearly reflected in Acts, the tone of Luke's work reflects a quieter time for the church, probably sometime before the persecutions of Jews and Christians associated with the later years of the emperor Domitian's reign.[23] Luke's purpose primarily appears to be that of guidance and nurturing for new Christians.

Prior to becoming a Christian, Luke probably was a Gentile God-fearer, also known as a God-worshiper.[24] Such persons were Gentiles who admired the Jewish religion, attended synagogue services on the Sabbath, and often were known to provide financial support and a political buffer for Judaism with the Gentile authorities. But these God-fearers did not fully convert to Judaism. They did not become circumcised and they did not necessarily observe Jewish dietary laws or even abandon the pagan religions. The two-volume work of the author Luke probably was written primarily for new Christians who, like himself, were converted God-fearers.[25]

While, as we have seen, Mark portrayed Jesus as a martyr and Messiah contrary to expectations, and Matthew's Jesus was the new Moses of the new covenant, the transcendent significance of Luke's Jesus was primarily as the

22. I agree with those scholars who find no good reason to question the tradition that Luke the companion of Paul wrote the two-volume work. That the author was also the physician referred to in Col. 4:14 is somewhat less certain.

23. The extent of Christian persecution under Domitian is controversial due to limited source evidence, but it is likely that Christians and Jews refused to worship the cruel emperor when, in the later years of his reign, (around 95 CE) they were ordered to do so.

24. I find the arguments of Crossan and Reed (2004) and others that Luke was a God-fearer or God-worshiper convincing.

25. In addition to a number of contextual clues indicating this audience, Luke addresses his work to Theophilus (Luke 1:3; Acts 1:1). While we do not know whether Theophilus was a patron of Luke's or a literary device symbolized by a name meaning "friend of God," in either case it is suggestive of a work written for Christian Gentiles who were God-fearers.

Savior, the Spirit-filled servant of God, carrying out the ministry of reconciliation with his life, death, and resurrection, a ministry that was continued through the amazing work of the apostles.

Although the metaphor of "Savior" is used sparingly in Luke-Acts, "salvation," "save," and "saved" occur frequently. Zechariah and Simeon testify to the salvation that has appeared in the birth of Jesus.[26] Jesus said to those he healed or forgave that they had been saved by their faith.[27] He announced to Zacchaeus that salvation had come to his house.[28] And Luke's Jesus also described his own ministry, both directly and in the implied meaning of parables, as being sent to seek and to save the lost. On the cross, Jesus was mocked because he saved others but could not save himself.[29] Luke's Peter addressed the eleven, the remaining living disciples on the Day of Pentecost, by quoting the prophet Joel's words that everyone who calls on the name of the Lord will be saved.[30] And when the jailer asked Paul and Silas what he must do to be saved, they told him to have faith in Jesus and that he and his whole household would be saved.[31]

The Meaning of "Salvation"

In Old Testament times, the idea of salvation was not conceived as salvation from sin, but was synonymous with deliverance from difficulties, from defeat in battle, from enslavement, pestilence, or the dangers posed by one's personal enemies.[32] Yahweh was the Savior, who delivered the people from their troubles. And salvation generally was conceived as the reestablishment of peace and prosperity. Persons such as Moses in the exodus and Joshua in the conquest of Canaan were seen as instruments of God's deliverance, of God's salvation. And in that regard, it is relevant to note that the name Jesus is a transliteration of the Hebrew Joshua. Joshua is derived from a root word

26. Luke 1:69, 71, 77; 2:30; 3:6.
27. Luke 7:50; 8:48; 17:19; 18:42.
28. Luke 19:9-10.
29. Luke 23:35, 37, 39.
30. Acts 2:21.
31. Acts 16:30-31.
32. *Yasha'* is sometimes translated "save," sometimes "deliver," or "rescue" or "help." See Josh. 10:6; Judg. 12:2; Deut 22:27; 28:29; 2 Sam. 14:4; 2 Kings 6:26; 1 Sam. 10:27; Hos. 13:10; Pss. 3:7; 20:9; 72:4.

meaning "deliver" or "save" and means "Yahweh is salvation," or "Yahweh is the Savior."[33]

It is only in the New Testament that the idea of the salvation brought by this latter Joshua, or Jesus, becomes clearly associated with salvation from sin. Jesus was understood as Messiah, as deliverer and savior, but not in the commonly expected sense of traditional Jewish expectations. Rather, he came to be understood as the cosmic savior from the power of sin and death, as the reconciler of the world to God. And it was the seeds of this reinterpretation of God's salvation that found fertile soil among the Gentiles, particularly those God-fearers who had been attracted to Judaism because of its ethical qualities.

In Roman times the Greek word *sōzō* ("to save") had the everyday meaning of "rescue" from material or temporal danger or suffering.[34] The rescue of sailors tossed overboard in a storm comes to mind. But by the time of Luke's writing, Gentile Christians may have been aware as well of pagan religious cults that spoke of heroic saviors who rescued the souls of men from the prison of this world.[35] Be that as it may, the question raised by Paul and Luke and the other New Testament writers who spoke of a savior and salvation is the question of the nature of the danger and of the rescue implied in the transcendent metaphor. From what does Jesus save, and what is the outcome for the believer?

Jesus as Savior from the "Wrath of God"

For Paul it is clear that human beings are saved from the "wrath" of God.[36] This is understood as the rescue of people of faith from spiritual and eternal

---

33. See Matt. 1:21.

34. The verb *sōzō*, "to save," and the noun *sōtēria*, "salvation," are used in the New Testament in the sense of deliverance from temporal danger as well. See, for examples, Matt. 8:25; Mark 13:20; Luke 23:35; John 12:27.

35. I am not speaking, as did Bultmann (1951), of a full-blown Gnosticism present in the late first century. The origins of Gnosticism remain unclear due to the lack of unambiguous evidence of pre-Christian Gnostic cults (Yamaouchi, 1983). But I am speaking of the likelihood of pre-Gnostic religious ideas derived from Platonic dualism, the mystery religions, and Egyptian and Babylonian religious traditions present in the Greek world during New Testament times.

36. Rom. 5:9. The discussion in this paragraph is based upon Rom. 5–9.

death, the terrible outcomes of human rebellious behavior. Through God's intervention, his gracious activity in Jesus, God has taken away that which is perceived and experienced from a human point of view as God's wrath, the agony of spiritual death and the dark despair of eternal death that is the consequence of sin. And God through Jesus has "saved" human beings while they were still sinners from the consequences of the coming day of accountability, from being declared guilty at the final judgment, and from being sentenced to eternal death for their lives of sin. God has done what no human effort could accomplish. God has declared, in his great generosity, peace with humankind. That peace is the gift of God's amazing love. But this salvation is not forced on humankind and thus there is a caveat. God's marvelous love can only become real in the lives of those who believe in it and choose to live in its reality.

Jesus as Rescuer of the "Lost"

While the idea of salvation from "wrath" as the consequence of sin is also present in the Gospel of Luke, the Gentile God-fearer appears to have had much less interest in the symbolism of sacrifice for understanding the significance of Jesus than the other Gospel writers and Paul. In the place of sacrificial imagery, the metaphor of "lost" appears to have been particularly meaningful for Luke's understanding. Of the Gospel evangelists, both Matthew and Luke record the parable of the lost sheep, but Luke alone records Jesus' parables of the lost coin and the lost son, underscoring the saying that Jesus had come to save that which was lost.[37]

The "lost" metaphor must have been particularly meaningful for Luke's readers. Life is perilous under ordinary circumstances. But to be lost in the wilderness or at sea, perils that threatened all who traveled far from home in ancient times, was to be in great danger.[38] As in cases today in which someone is lost amidst winter weather in a mountain wilderness or during a storm at sea, without external rescue death is likely to come swiftly. Whether one had wandered like a lost sheep in ignorance away from the care of God, or

37. Luke 15 and 19:10.

38. Acts 27 tells of Paul's experience while under arrest of a storm at sea and shipwreck. Verse 20b states, "we finally gave up all hope of being saved." Scholars long have wondered if the "we" indicated that Luke was on the boat himself, an interesting possibility given the importance of the metaphor of salvation in his work.

through carelessness had become lost like a coin, or deliberately had left the care of God like a rebellious son, Luke's Gospel message proclaimed that a Savior had come and rescue was available. The Savior was seeking the lost in order to restore them to their rightful owner, guardian, and accepting Father.

Jesus as God's Emissary

The prophets in Old Testament times had functioned as *intermediaries,* amidst the enmity between the people of the covenant and their God. They were *special messengers* and *emissaries* from God, who brought the message of God's warnings and called the people to repentance. Jesus' prophetic work falls within this type of mediation. But Jesus' role as a messenger, intermediary, and emissary of God goes beyond prophetic proclamation. Luke's Jesus is like the emissary son of a powerful landowner who has been killed by the tenants to whom he was sent.[39] But in the shared theology of Paul and Luke, God has been vindicated through the resurrection and exaltation of the emissary son, and, at the same time, the forgiveness expressed by the Savior on the cross toward those who put him to death has been validated.

In Jesus, God has wept over the sin of God's people and has become one with the suffering of humankind. God's compassionate work in Jesus has broken the power of sin for all humankind. And it is the acceptance of this divine sacrifice, this saving work in the lives of those who have faith that, mysteriously and amazingly, has brought about reconciliation and peace with God, commuting the sentence of spiritual and eternal death for sin, and re-creating the image of God where it had been distorted and lost.

The Social Meaning of Spiritual Salvation

It would be a mistake, however, to interpret this understanding of the transcendent metaphor of Jesus as Savior of the lost, of those doomed by the consequences of their sin, in highly individualistic terms. The Greek idea of preexisting souls that were lost and imprisoned in earthly bodies may have tempted some early Christians in that direction, as our individualistic culture does today. But the movement in New Testament times from "lost" to

39. Luke 20:9-19.

"found," from "enmity" to "peace," was marked by the transition from social participation in pagan or Jewish families and communities to the fellowship of the church, the community of the risen Jesus. It was a transformation that was more sociological than psychological in the modern sense. To participate in the reconciliation of the world was to become a new creation that had concrete significance for all social relationships.

> So from now on we regard no one from a worldly point of view. Though we once regarded Christ in this way, we do so no longer. Therefore, if anyone is in Christ, he is a new creation; the old has gone, the new has come! (2 Cor. 5:16-17)

> There is neither Jew nor Greek, slave nor free, male nor female, for you are all one in Christ Jesus. (Gal. 3:28)

In order better to understand the transition from regarding people "from a worldly point of view" to seeing them through a transformed perspective, it is helpful to understand what it meant to be a "self" in the New Testament world. In the societies of the ancient Mediterranean and Middle East, a self was far more group-oriented than is typical of Americans or Europeans today.[40] In the New Testament world, identity was derived from the group and group understanding. People valued conformity more than independence, authority more than consensus, group reliance more than self-reliance, and group loyalty more than personal autonomy. Given this worldview, the transformation the members of the early church experienced was not, as we might imagine, from a group orientation to a more individualistic perspective. Rather, the remarkable change brought about in the lives of those who saw Jesus through the eyes of faith was from their former group perspective to a radically new understanding of group identity.

Reconciliation in Luke-Acts

Luke more than any of the Gospel writers reveals Jesus as not only reconciling the world to God, but in doing so, as also reconciling human beings to one another. This theme runs throughout Luke's two-volume work. To enter the community of faith meant that no one was excluded from table fellowship;

---

40. I am indebted to Malina (2001) for this discussion of first-century consciousness.

that women were regarded with dignity; that the destitute were deserving of honor; and that everyone, including the disabled, strangers, and foreigners, were neighbors.[41] The picture of fellowship, while perhaps a bit idealized in Acts, is also one that exemplifies a community that has let love overcome the differences of the world, particularly in the sharing of resources.[42]

It is Luke, as well, who records the story we know as "the good Samaritan." In it a man challenged Jesus by asking him, "Who is my neighbor?"[43] a question in the narrative that was a test designed to force Jesus into saying which human beings were neighbors and which were non-neighbors. By implication, the question was about which human beings God requires us to love and which ones God gives us permission not to love. Jesus' response changed the question, as he told the story of the man who fell among thieves, to "Who was a good neighbor?" This was Jesus' response and challenge to the premise of the original question. The story clarified that a good neighbor does not make a distinction between neighbors and non-neighbors.

Distinguishing between Neighbors and Non-Neighbors

The view of reality expressed by Paul and Luke, which no doubt was based upon the words and example of Jesus, made it clear that salvation involved a transition away from dividing the world between neighbors and non-neighbors, friends and enemies, and from relating to others based on ethnic boundaries. And salvation was a transition toward a new creation of an inclusiveness that took with utmost seriousness human equality in the light of the reconciling love of God.

In order to appreciate the radical nature of this inclusiveness it is helpful to reflect upon the way in which most people throughout history and across cultures have understood social boundaries. Virtually all peoples have considered their inner circle of parents, spouses, and children as human beings of worth and value to be loved and protected. While various cultures have

41. We have seen in Part I that this status-free view dates back to Jesus, but it no doubt had particular significance for the Gentile Luke, as it had for Paul the apostle to the Gentiles, who struggled with the discrimination against Gentiles on the part of some Jewish Christians.

42. Acts 4:32.

43. Luke 10:27.

had differing kinship rules, it is virtually a universal obligation to prevent and alleviate the suffering of one's kin, to provide them assistance with the problems of living, and even to confront and correct them when they appear to need it. Most people experience this obligation even when they dislike and disapprove of a family member. That is the human truth behind the saying that "blood is thicker than water."

There are exceptions, of course, but few people have difficulty understanding that they have an obligation to love their immediate family members. And there can be no doubt that this responsibility to loved ones is a constructive one that is of great benefit to humankind. In virtually all cultures, the family is where children are nurtured and acculturated so that they may become responsible citizens and contributors to the larger society. When parents fail in that responsibility, it can have disastrous results for their fellow citizens. When they succeed, the society is strengthened and enriched.

Most people also understand that their inner circles of extended family, friends, fellow workers, social acquaintances, and those who live nearby are also within the sphere of their neighborly responsibility. Such persons are to be treated with respect and kindness and are at times to be beneficiaries of generosity. If for no other reason, this is an obligation that most people feel they should not ignore because there is a reciprocity involved in fulfilling one's obligations to these neighbors that may be important to one's own well-being. Such concern for one's family and inner circles usually is beneficial to everyone.

For most people, family and personal acquaintances are the neighbors with whom they interact most often, and whose needs seem most real. Those who believe in God, for example, may find it rather easy, most of the time, to see these particular neighbors as God's beloved children and to understand that they are to love these neighbors as God has loved them. Such affection and responsibility for one's family and friends is quite common but is not necessarily a sign of religious devotion. Even pagans and cruel despots tend to love their own families and inner circles.[44] It also is common among human beings everywhere to interpret the responsibility for those near and dear to themselves as implied permission to exclude any responsibility for those outside their inner circles.[45]

---

44. Matt. 5:46-47; Luke 6:32.

45. It is possible that Jesus' inclusiveness is behind the strain between Jesus and his birth family recorded in Mark 3:31-34.

Furthermore, the distinction between neighbors and non-neighbors is often reinforced by conventional social and religious beliefs. Non-neighbors may include foreigners, enemies, and unbelievers along with those who are social or religious outcasts. And, as we have seen, in agonistic societies these non-neighbors have been regarded with great suspicion. In virtually all societies, people agree that one is certainly to love one's neighbor, but they also believe it is perfectly acceptable not to love, or even to hate, one's non-neighbors. Jesus, and those serious about following him, had a different view.

Living in the New Reality

In the faith of Luke, to be saved, to be reconciled to God through Jesus, is to live in a new reality. It is to see oneself "saved" not only *from* the consequences of sin, but *to* a new relationship with both God and neighbors. It is to see that every human being is one's neighbor. The implications of that perspective are revolutionary. For it means one is obligated to love *every* human being, no matter what their social status, their geographical proximity, or how much one may dislike or fear them. Those who disgust us and offend our sensibilities are to be loved. Those who have done terrible and cruel things to us or to others are to be loved. Even those who threaten our very existence are to be loved. There are no exceptions.

This does not mean, however, that everyone is to be treated the same. For the question naturally arises, amidst the ethical ambiguities of human society, as to what it means to love at once the man who fell among thieves and the thieves themselves. How is one to live in the reality of God's love for all, and remain faithful to that understanding, when some of one's neighbors are causing harm to other neighbors? Jesus is portrayed in the Gospels as interacting with those who accused him and wanted to do him or others harm very differently than he did with those who were among his inner circle. And he sent his followers out like sheep among wolves to be as cunning as serpents while remaining as innocent as doves.[46] By implication, the disciples' behaviors toward those who wanted to do them or others harm was not necessarily to be identical with their behaviors toward those who posed no threat. That being said, Jesus' followers were, nevertheless, always required to

---

46. Matt. 10:16.

love and not to despise their enemies. And it was the awareness of what others truly needed, rather than fear and prejudice, which was to guide their behaviors. Yet, as any thoughtful person will recognize, this was never a simple matter. That is why, for many people of faith throughout church history, the ministry of reconciliation has involved a fundamental commitment of the faithful to work for justice wherever injustice is found, to defend the defenseless, and to call to account those who prey on others.

Furthermore, the New Testament writers believed that the Jesus movement, the church, was called upon to embody the new reality of reconciliation. There were to be no more distinctions between Jew and Greek, male and female, kin and non-kin. The community was, as Jesus had indicated to his followers during his ministry, his new family and friends. This was the new "in-group," a society in which the pride of superiority was not allowed. But it was also an "in-group" with a whole new attitude and relationship to outsiders. In place of suspicion and enmity, or even a sense of superiority in relation to those "not saved," there was to be humility, compassion, and forgiveness. And rather than focusing on their own salvation, believers were to devote themselves to the ministry of reconciliation.

The Ministry of Reconciliation

As we have seen, Paul and the early church understood that the fundamental human problem, behind all other problems, was estrangement from God. The self could not know genuine peace, or find the blessedness of life for which it was created, until it was restored to its intended station as a beloved child of God. And reconciliation with God was also the key to reconciliation among human beings.

> All this is from God, who reconciled us to himself through Christ and gave us the ministry of reconciliation: that God was reconciling the world to himself in Christ, not counting men's sins against them. And he has committed to us the message of reconciliation. We are therefore Christ's ambassadors, as though God were making his appeal through us. We implore you on Christ's behalf: Be reconciled to God. (2 Cor. 5:18-20)

> Therefore as we have opportunity, let us do good to all people, especially to those who belong to the family of believers. (Gal. 6:10)

To live in the reality of a world reconciled to God is, at the same time, to be called to the ministry of reconciliation. It is to "do good to all people," not just those to whom one is naturally drawn. It is to live among others with compassion, not counting their sins against them. And it is to share with others the message of reconciliation in the most effective ways possible. It is especially to participate in the community of faith with such empathy and caring for one another that God's love for the world in Christ is transparent to all.

To be sure, the idea of a community of faith that lives in peace and love with one another is an ideal picture. As anyone who has read his letters knows, Paul's "on the ground" experience was that things were far from the ideal in the New Testament congregations. There was much room for spiritual growth. The old ways of being selves in the world, the ways of enmity, unfortunately had been brought into the fellowship of believers and had contaminated that fellowship. It was as true then as now that a community of faith is a work in progress. And so Paul exhorted the people of the community of faith to be reconciled to God and to live as the new creations they were in Christ.

And while outsiders certainly were a threat, even unto death, the relationship with those who were not in the community of faith was to be just as loving and honoring as to members of the faith. To live in the reality of reconciliation is to know that in Christ, even the walls between those who believe and those who do not are transparent walls. For the world, and every human being in it, is loved by God. Christ died for everyone, and the community of faith is to demonstrate in all relationships the reality of the peace of God. This is the ministry of reconciliation in which refuge from danger does not lie within the protective shield of the community but with the gracious care of its Lord.

For those who see Jesus through the eyes of faith, he is their Savior, the Reconciler of the world. To accept Jesus as Savior is to be saved from the power and consequences of sin and to be reconciled to God. And to live in the reality of reconciliation is to celebrate life as a sacred gift that is sustained at each moment by God. It is continually to praise God, the Creator and Sustainer of all lives, as deserving of thanksgiving, honor, and service. It is to participate in the community of faith as a status-free fellowship of loving care and mutual respect. And to live in the reality of reconciliation is also to realize that one never meets another human being who is not already radically loved by God.

CHAPTER XIII

The Reigning Lord

Despite the fact that his life and death were contrary to conventional Messianic expectations, the resurrection confirmed for Jesus' early followers that he was the long-expected Messiah. Yet those resurrection appearances occurred only in the lives of a select group of followers and continued for only a very short time. As a consequence, the post-resurrection community was challenged to understand the significance for faith that Jesus was God's anointed, was crucified and raised from the dead, but was no longer appearing to anyone. The reality of his transcendent significance had been disclosed to them by his words, deeds, and appearances, and was confirmed by the coming and indwelling of the Holy Spirit, but seemed hidden from the world around them. In seeking to understand and to express the implications of these events for their lives and for history, those early followers turned to the Scriptures. There they found narratives that foreshadowed their experiences and poetic language that helped them to see in Jesus both the fulfillment of long ago promises and a fresh understanding of what it means to trust God amidst life's trials and difficulties.

In biblical times, people took for granted a three-story universe, consisting of an underworld below, the heavens above, and the earth in-between. The heavens were the dwelling place of God and other spiritual beings, and the underworld was the abode of the dead. The followers of Jesus were familiar with the Old Testament stories of Enoch and Elijah being taken from earth to heaven. Jesus' final resurrection appearance was also perceived by them as an ascending of Jesus to the highest heaven, to the very throne of God. As they continued to remember his words and deeds and to search the

Scriptures, they began to reconceptualize the traditions they inherited from Judaism in light of the central and transcendent role of Jesus. In the process, they came to understand that Jesus was now sitting at God's right hand where he reigns over the cosmos. Jesus had not abandoned them. As confirmed by their experience, he had sent them the Holy Spirit to strengthen, comfort, and guide them.[1] And, they believed, Jesus would come again soon. This time he would come in power as the judge of humankind, and as the one who would make all things right and new.

As we live today in a very different era and take for granted an entirely different worldview, it is necessary for us again to engage in the task of reconceptualizing, for our time, what it means to confess the central and defining transcendent role of Jesus for faith. That task requires us to examine carefully the symbolic language of the exalted and coming Lord. And, as we have done with other transcendent metaphors and images in previous chapters, it is important to identify the universal human longings to which these images speak, to place them in their cultural context, to dialogue with their theological assumptions, and to open our own lives to be addressed by the existential realities and the faith to which they point.

The Exalted Lord

Relying on Psalm 110:1 and other similar passages, the post-resurrection community of faith understood Jesus to have ascended to the Father and now to be the reigning "Lord" at God's right hand.

> God has raised this Jesus to life, and we are all witnesses of the fact. Exalted to the right hand of God, he has received from the Father the promised Holy Spirit and has poured out what you now see and hear. For David did not ascend to heaven, and yet he said,
>
> > "The Lord said to my Lord:
> > 'Sit at my right hand
> > until I make your enemies
> > a footstool for your feet.'"

---

1. In the following chapter, I discuss the gifts and indwelling of the Spirit as the continuing presence of the "Lord" and as an ongoing sign of the transcendent significance of Jesus in the life of the transformed community of faith.

> Therefore let all Israel be assured of this: God has made this Jesus, whom you crucified, both Lord and Christ. (Acts 2:32-36)

Jesus is "Lord"

"Lord" was used as a title for Jesus in the New Testament more than any other transcendent metaphor.[2] Sometimes, of course, it was a simple term of respect used by persons addressing Jesus during his ministry, a title of honor that would have been appropriate for any rabbi or social superior at the time.[3] It was the equivalent of calling him "sir" in English or *"señor"* in Spanish. In these cases it implied authority but not divinity.

The title "Lord," however, also was used widely in Greek and Roman culture as an indicator of divinity. The pagan gods commonly were referred to as "lords." Paul reminded the church at Corinth that there were many "lords," but only one God the Father, and one Lord, Jesus Christ.[4] And "lord" was a particularly important title in the imperial cult that referred to Caesar with that term as an acknowledgment of his divine authority.[5] Consequently, when members of the Jesus movement called Jesus "Lord," that designation of honor had implications not only for their relationship to Jesus but for their relationship to Caesar and the empire as well.

Pagan worshipers might be able to call many divinities "lord," but the Jesus movement, grounded as it was in the monotheistic faith of Judaism, could acknowledge only one Lord, the one whom the one God and Father had made to be both Christ and Lord. And it was the reality that one can serve only one Lord that led to confrontation with the Roman authorities, who interpreted the unwillingness to submit to the "lordship" of the emperor as dangerously subversive.

Despite Christian efforts to persuade the guardians of Rome that they

2. "Lord" appears 688 times in the New Testament.

3. In Mark 7:28, for example, a Gentile woman was reported to have addressed Jesus in this way. The fact that "Lord" could be both a human and a divine title of respect created an ambiguity of reference that may have helped to delay for a time the eventual split within Judaism between those who called Jesus "Lord" and those who did not.

4. 1 Cor. 8:6.

5. In Acts 25:26 Festus refers to the emperor in the Greek language as "my lord." Horsley (1997) makes a strong case for the cult of Caesar having become the dominant one in the regions where Paul preached.

had nothing to fear, the Roman authorities, from the standpoint of their self-interest, had good reason for concern about this. The Pax Romana, the Peace of Rome, depended upon the absolute loyalty of its people. Any social movement that subordinated the authority of the empire to a higher authority struck at the very foundation of a way of life that had been built on the fiction of divine destiny, on the one hand, and on the people's fear of suffering, as a means to maintaining order, on the other hand. For in declaring Jesus to be the one true "Lord," the Jesus movement necessarily diminished and relativized the claims of Rome on their lives. And this was manifest not only in the refusal to participate in emperor worship, but also in the way in which the faithful conducted their daily affairs. In everyday social relations, while generally following the conventions of a stratified society in order not to alarm the authorities, they did so as those who had no earthly superiors.[6] For to live under the "Lordship" of Jesus was to see others as Jesus saw them and to make no status distinctions among them.

That word *Lord* had rich connotations for Judaism as well. The Greek word *kyrios,* which is translated "Lord" in English, was also the word used in place of the sacred name of Yahweh, the God of Israel, when the ancient Greek translation of the Old Testament known as the Septuagint was read by Greek-speaking Jews in New Testament times. The early church understood the dual use of "Lord" in Psalm 110:1, contained in the quote from Acts above, as the declaration of the *Lord Yahweh* that the *Lord Messiah* was now sitting at the right hand of the divine throne. To call Jesus "Lord" was to declare that Jesus was not only the Messiah, but also the "Lord," the chosen means of God's reign over the world, the church, and the life of faith.

In the life of the church, the use of "Lord" would at times merge the ordinary title of rabbinic respect with that of the recognition of Jesus as divine ruler. Paul, for example, would refer to the "word of the Lord." By this he meant the teachings that he no doubt received from those who had preserved the sayings of the earthly Jesus, which were deemed to have ultimate authority in the life of faith.[7] And when in the Gospel narratives Jesus was called "Lord," the authors often implied a double meaning. Jesus was the Lord in the sense of a rabbi or teacher, and, at the same time, was

6. Gal. 3:26-27 speaks to radical equality in Christ. Rom. 13:1-7 speaks to conformity to the conventions of Roman society.

7. 1 Cor. 7:10; 9:14; 11:23.

the one made transparent to the reader as the divine Lord of the post-resurrection faith.[8]

In one narrative, however, it is unambiguously clear that to call Jesus Lord is to confess the full divinity of Jesus. In John's resurrection story of Jesus' appearance to Thomas, the disciple said to him, "My Lord and my God!"[9] This confession underscores the high Christology encountered throughout the Gospel of John.[10] God, in the form of the creative Word made flesh in Jesus, is life and light, the revelation of the "I AM." Here Jesus unambiguously is identified as truly the eternal one, without beginning or end. Jesus is understood by John to be God, but not all there is to God. Jesus, as the Son, is not identical with the Father, but is one with the Father. He shares in the Father's honor, and exercises the Father's judgment and resurrecting power. Jesus is the personification of God's grace and truth. These are the very same aspects of God that had been at work in the history of Israel. And these are the same aspects of God that are now at work during Christ's reign as Lord of heaven and earth.

The Right Hand of God

That reign of God's grace and truth was powerfully expressed by the early Christian assertion that the "Lord" sits at the right hand of God. To say that Jesus sits at the right hand of God was to affirm Jesus' place of honor, his divine status. But, at the same time, it was also a statement about God's relationship with humankind.

Many ancient and traditional peoples have considered the right hand to be a symbol of righteousness, power, and authority.[11] These associations probably are derived from the predominance of right-dominant hands among human beings, and the consequent belief that right, as opposed to left, was synonymous with might. While the right hand often has been held in esteem, the left frequently has been stigmatized. Most of us are familiar, for ex-

8. This double meaning is reflected especially in the Gospel of Luke in 6:46; and in those passages where Jesus is spoken of as "*the* Lord." For examples, see Luke 7:13; 7:31; 10:1; 11:39; 17:15; 18:6; etc.

9. John 20:28.

10. See the discussion of John in chapter X.

11. In some traditional societies the left hand is considered profane, while the right hand is associated with the sacred. In Islamic cultures today, the left hand is considered "unclean" and only the right hand is to be used for public interactions.

ample, with the expression "left-handed compliment." Some cultures have even gone to considerable lengths to suppress left-handedness because of their negative beliefs about persons with left-dominant hands.[12] Of course, the left has not had sinister associations in every society. But in most cultures, even when to be on the left hand of someone important was to have a place of honor, the place to the right of the dignitary carried with it greater status.[13]

In ancient Israel the right hand was used to impart a blessing and to offer assistance.[14] As the hand of power, it also could be the hand that committed murder, offered bribes, or otherwise became the instrument of evil deeds.[15] That probably is why Jesus referred specifically to the right hand in his saying about cutting off the right hand if it causes one to sin.[16] But even these negative images support the notion that the right hand was supposed to be the hand of righteousness. It was the hand that swore to tell the truth, and the hand that was offered in friendship.[17] And, above all, it was the right hand that was mentioned in sacred poetry referring to God's victorious power, righteousness, and blessings.[18]

When the Egyptians were destroyed in the sea during the exodus it was the right hand of God that was said to have accomplished that mighty and victorious deed. God's right hand was the bearer of justice and salvation to his people. And it was the hand that protected God's people, blessed them, and comforted them in time of trouble.

Embedded in the meaning of this transcendent metaphor was the idea that Jesus is not simply at the right hand of God, but that Jesus *is* the right hand of God. Jesus is the justice and righteousness of God. Jesus is the saving work of God. Jesus is the healing, life giving, and comforting activity of God in the lives of God's people. As people often offered the right hand in friendship to others, so the Father had offered Jesus, God's own right hand, as an

12. The pre-colonial Maori of New Zealand, for example, were reported to have physically repressed the development of the left hand.

13. In ancient China, for example, the right hand of the emperor traditionally was considered the place of highest honor, but at some point it appears that the place of highest honor was changed to that of the left hand, presumably because the emperor faced south and the East was on his left hand.

14. Gen. 48:14; 2 Kings 10:15; Pss. 16:11; 77:10; Isa. 41:13.

15. Gen. 4:11; Ps. 26:10.

16. Matt. 5:30.

17. Ps. 144:8, 11; Rev. 10:5-6; Gal. 2:9.

18. For examples of these qualities and those in the paragraph below, see Exod. 15:6; Pss. 17:7; 18:35; 20:6; 48:10; 98:1.

act of reconciliation and friendship, and in order to draw all of his children into his loving care.

The Coming Lord

The transcendent significance of Jesus was symbolized by the post-resurrection community not only as the exalted Lord at the right hand of God, but also as the coming Lord who would usher in the final victory over evil, raise the dead, judge humankind, and bring forth the new creation, the new heaven and earth. Probably one of the earliest prayers of that community was the Aramaic expression *Marana tha,* which means: "Come, O Lord!"[19] And the expectation of that coming was hoped for and held onto throughout the difficulties and persecutions of the decades in which the New Testament writings were created, even after it was clear that the cataclysmic event had not come as soon as expected.

> But do not forget this one thing, dear friends: With the Lord a day is like a thousand years, and a thousand years are like a day. The Lord is not slow in keeping his promise, as some understand slowness. He is patient with you, not wanting anyone to perish, but everyone to come to repentance.
>
> But the day of the Lord will come like a thief. The heavens will disappear with a roar; the elements will be destroyed by fire, and the earth and everything in it will be laid bare.
>
> Since everything will be destroyed in this way, what kind of people ought you to be? You ought to live holy and godly lives as you look forward to the day of God and speed its coming. That day will bring about the destruction of the heavens by fire, and the elements will melt in the heat. But in keeping with his promise we are looking forward to a new heaven and a new earth, the home of righteousness. (2 Pet. 3:8-13)[20]

This vision of the coming again of Jesus was rooted in Jewish apocalyptic traditions that spoke of the "Day of the Lord" and the coming of one like

19. In 1 Cor. 16:22 the Aramaic is used followed by the translation. The expression also appears in Greek translation in Rev. 22:20.

20. Most scholars believe that 2 Peter was written by an unknown author whose work was attributed to Peter, and was composed following the deaths of the first-generation disciples. The letter addressed the crisis in faith created by the "delay" of the second coming. A probable date would be sometime after 80, but more likely in the 90s.

a "Son of Man" on the clouds of heaven.[21] And this expected coming came to be associated with powerful images of trumpets sounding, the descending of God's Anointed, a time of great tribulation, the dead being raised, the faithful being gathered and rescued, the court of divine judgment, punishment and eternal death for the wicked, and a joyous welcome and eternal life for the faithful. And it also was associated with the promise of the coming of a fresh creation, a new heaven and earth where all things would at last be "as they ought to be." Unlike the present creation, this new existence would be without disease and suffering, without wars and human conflicts, without sorrow and death, without division and enmity. And these extravagant visions of the end of all things old and the beginning of all things new were sometimes accompanied by a multitude of other vivid symbolic images.[22]

That which set the Jesus movement apart from these traditional Jewish visions was not the types of images employed, but the way the symbols were transformed in the consciousness of faith by Jesus' life, death, and resurrection. In light of their experiences with Jesus, they now understood the primary question confronting the Jewish hope for the Messianic age was not "Where?" "When?" or How?" the Day of the Lord would come. That question was, "*Who* is the coming one?"

To believe the coming one is Jesus was to understand the meaning of hope very differently from would have been the case if they had been looking for another. The one who is coming, the one who judges the living and the dead, the one who brings to an end the old order and creates all things new, is the same one who already has come revealing God's merciful love for all humankind.

The Final Accountability

When one lives on the margins of society and is at risk of being hauled into court at the whim of those in power, the image of a trial before a judge generally is a very familiar one. While all the subjects of Rome were no doubt fa-

21. See for examples Isa. 13:6; 34:8; Jer. 46:10; Lam. 2:22; Ezek. 30:3; Joel 1:15; Amos 5:18; Obadiah 1:15; Zeph. 1:7 for "Day of the Lord" and Dan. 7:13 for "Son of Man."

22. The book of Daniel in the Old Testament contains a number of such images. Many more are to be found in the Apocryphal books of 1 and 2 Enoch, 4 Ezra, 2 and 3 Baruch, Jubilees, and the Apocalypse of Abraham. In the New Testament the book of Revelation is rich in such symbolism.

miliar with the courts, the Jesus movement, living as it did in tension with the Roman government and refusing to worship Caesar as Lord, was, no doubt, painfully aware of Rome's power to deprive one of freedom, to punish harshly, and to condemn to death. This certainly was true of the apostle Paul, who was brought before the courts on many occasions.[23] If it is also remembered that Paul was a Pharisee with extensive training in the Jewish Law, it is little wonder that the apostle to the Gentiles used the legal terminology of trials and verdicts, of justification and righteousness, in explaining the meaning of Jesus as the Christ to his congregations.[24] And it is not surprising that Paul built much of his thought with an eye to "the day when God will judge men's secrets through Jesus Christ."[25]

> For this very reason, Christ died and returned to life so that he might be the Lord of both the dead and the living. You, then, why do you judge your brother? Or why do you look down on your brother? For we will all stand before God's judgment seat. It is written:
>
> "'As surely as I live,' says the Lord,
> 'every knee will bow before me;
> every tongue will confess to God.'"
>
> So then, each of us will give an account of himself to God. (Rom. 14:9-12)

The idea that human beings ultimately are accountable for their lives before a transcendent standard is virtually universal. In the Asian subcontinent of India that consciousness of accountability was powerfully expressed in terms of *karma*.[26] Among the peoples of Asia proper ultimate accountability often has been visualized in terms of shame or saving face before the

---

23. Acts 16:20; 18:12; 24:1-27; 25:1-12; 25:23–26:32. In 2 Cor. 11:23-25 Paul describes floggings, beatings, and imprisonment, some of which, no doubt, were the results of legal proceedings.

24. While the Pharisees' understanding of the Law largely was substantive rather than procedural, procedural knowledge of Sanhedrin and other Jewish legal proceedings was, no doubt, included as well, as the Pharisee Nicodemus's knowledge illustrates in John's Gospel (John 7:51).

25. Rom. 2:16.

26. *Karma* is a central concept in Hinduism in which the deeds in the present life determine a future reincarnation, be it human, animal, or some torturous existence based on past behaviors.

spirits of the ancestors.[27] Among Native Americans, accountability generally was believed to take place during one's journey to the spirit world, for the way one lived and died in this world shaped one's experiences on the way to and in the other world.[28] And the traditions of many societies speak of punishment and rewards by the gods in the afterlife.

In the ancient Middle East, the idea of accountability was shaped by the monarchical city-states in which systems of stern written laws were enforced by kings and their judicial representatives who had the absolute power to decide life or death for subjects.[29] During the settling of Canaan, Israel had a social structure based on tribal leaders who functioned as judges, settling disputes and enforcing the punishments required when the Law of Moses was violated.[30] During the Roman occupation, the formal legal system of the conquerors resolved most criminal and civil matters important to the empire, while the Jewish courts addressed violations of religious importance. As the trial of Jesus demonstrates, the sorting out of which legal authority is responsible for which matters was not always clear.[31]

Accountability in human courts ideally strives for justice. But most people realize, especially the oppressed, that human courts are incapable of achieving that ideal. Judges may be corrupt, and the courts may be used by those in power for unjust ends. Evidence may be lacking to convict, and innocent people may be convicted on false testimony. In a larger sense, it is evident that those who are unjust often appear to escape justice. Good things happen to bad people, and bad things happen to good people. In this world, the suffering of human beings is not meted out according to behavior. Everyone knows that the words parents often tell children are true: "Life is not always fair."

Those who have experienced the unfairness of existence, and particu-

---

27. In the religious and cultural traditions of Japan and China the ancestors are spirits whose honor one inherits, but through shameful deeds shame can be brought on the ancestors. When the ancestors are shamed unfortunate things can be expected.

28. See Hultkrantz (1988).

29. See Snell (1997).

30. Exod. 18:21-22; Deut. 16:18-20.

31. The Gospel accounts indicate that the charge before Pilate, the Roman governor, was sedition, while the concern of the Jewish Sanhedrin was blasphemy. We cannot be certain that the Sanhedrin, which appears to have had the power to sentence adulterers to death by stoning, was forbidden from carrying out a sentence of death in this case, but the "trials" of Jesus seem to suggest that to be the case.

larly those who have been innocent sufferers at the hands of others who have not been made accountable for their evil deeds in this life, understandably long for a day of final reckoning when genuine justice will prevail. If real justice exists, they reason, then good people will be rewarded in the life to come and evil people will be punished.

The problem for human beings, however, is that when we honestly look at our own lives, and inventory all our past deeds, and realize that our own decisions have brought harm to others, we become painfully aware of our own failures. And even as people attempting to do the right thing and to live according to God's will, we are not so sure we want to face that ultimate accountability ourselves. For God, as Paul reminds us, will judge all the secrets of our hearts.[32] In such consciousness it may feel like good news that people who deserve to be held accountable for their actions in this world are going to finally get justice. But it may also feel like bad news that we might be among them.

The early Christian community of faith had been taught by its Lord that there would be a day of reckoning. Not only had the resurrection convinced them that God had the final Word about people's lives; it also persuaded them that Jesus Christ was that final Word. This was a shift in meaning from typical Jewish understanding with profound implications. In seeing Jesus as God's Messiah and appointed Judge over all the earth, the day of reckoning was transformed in the consciousness of the community of faith. The criterion upon which humanity was to be judged was now to be Jesus Christ.[33] The person, words, and deeds of Jesus, the reality of his being, became the standard against which all human life would be measured. Each one must come before God and be judged according to how Christ-like their lives have been.

And that judgment, that accountability with Jesus Christ as the standard, means that "all have sinned and fallen short of the glory of God."[34] Yet, for the final Word of God about a human life to be Jesus Christ, is for that fi-

---

32. Rom. 2:16.

33. This is one of the important meanings of the New Testament belief that Jesus was "without sin." That belief was not based upon the idea that Jesus was not fully human. Nor is "sinlessness" asserted as a result of taking a moral inventory of Jesus and determining that he never did anything wrong. For by what criteria would one make such a determination? "Sinlessness" is an expression of the faith of the church that Jesus is the standard by which all human beings are made accountable. Of course, the other relevant meaning of being "without sin" is that of the "unblemished" nature of the lamb of sacrifice discussed in chapter XI.

34. Rom. 3:23.

nal Word not to be condemnation but the reality of God's grace, of God's forgiveness and acceptance of human beings as children of God. God's righteousness has been exercised in Jesus as mercy.

The tension in which the early church found itself was between, on the one hand, the truth that God's justice required every human being to be judged according to his or her lived existence, and, on the other hand, the truth that God so loved the world that the Son of God had died for the sins of every human being in the world. In this faith was the hope for the salvation of everyone, and, at the same time, the conviction that only through the *received* mercy of Christ could that salvation occur.[35]

Belief that God would judge the secrets of humankind through Jesus Christ had another more immediate implication as well. In the light of the coming judgment, the faithful were warned against passing judgment on others and looking down on them.[36] Judgment belonged to God alone.

And so, the post-resurrection faith shared the belief that all are held accountable before God for their lives. And that same faith maintained that it is God alone who will judge through Christ, the merciful Savior, and that no human being was to judge another before the Lord comes again.[37]

The New Creation

The prayer, "Come, O Lord!" was a prayer for the final victory of God over all evil and for eternal salvation. In the cross, God was in Christ reconciling the world unto himself, overcoming the enmity between human beings and their Creator. For the community of faith, that victory over evil and all the powers of evil had already occurred, although those who believed remained subject to the sufferings and tribulations of this age. The world continued, however, to be a place of injustice and tragedy. Consequently, the victory of God was hidden from those who did not yet believe and over whom the

35. The author of John handles this by indicating that Jesus did not come to judge the world, but to save it. Judgment and condemnation are what human beings bring upon themselves by rejecting the Word (John 12:47-48), though John also says that the Father judges no one but entrusts judgment to the Son (John 5:22).

36. This prohibition is no doubt based on the "word from the Lord" in Matt. 7:1-2 and Luke 6:37. See Rom. 14:10; 1 Cor. 4:5; James 4:11.

37. Evidently Paul believed that the saints would in fact participate in judging the world at the last judgment (1 Cor. 6:2). But judging others was not to be exercised in this life.

powers of darkness continued to have power in this age. And unless they did come to believe, that victory would only become clear to them on the day of his coming again. For on that day, for which the faithful prayed, evil was destined finally to be destroyed and this troubled creation replaced by one in which things will be as they are supposed to be.

> Then I saw a new heaven and a new earth, for the first heaven and the first earth had passed away, and there was no longer any sea. I saw the holy city, the new Jerusalem, coming down out of heaven from God, prepared as a bride beautifully dressed for her husband. And I heard a loud voice from the throne saying, "Now the dwelling of God is with men, and he will live with them. They will be his people, and God himself will be with them and be their God. He will wipe every tear from their eyes. There will be no more death or mourning or crying or pain, for the old order of things has passed away." (Rev. 21:1-4)

People throughout the centuries have longed for a world in which things actually would be as human hearts longed for them to be. Confucius dreamed of a society in which the king and his subjects embodied the principles of the *Tao*.[38] Plato wrote of a republic that perfectly embodied the ideal principles of reason. Isaiah dreamed of a time of peace in which wolves and lambs would live in peace together.[39]

Isaiah's vision for Israel was, in New Testament times, a broadly shared one of a future in which God's people would be restored and established as rulers over the nations of the world. This hope, as ethnocentric and nationalistic as it might seem to outsiders, was based upon faith in Yahweh as the one true Lord of heaven and earth, and in the persistent belief that God would keep God's promises.

As Isaiah and the other prophets often reminded them, the people of Israel understood themselves to be called to be "a light for the Gentiles," God's agents of salvation for all.[40] The vision of hope was not simply a vision of privilege, similar to that held by Rome in the time of Jesus, but one of responsibility to humankind as God's people. It would be a time in which all people would come under the "Law of God" and a world of genuine justice

---

38. The *Tao* in Confucian thought was thought to be the eternal order of the cosmos, and social forms were derived from the principles inherent in that order.

39. Isa. 11:6.

40. Isa. 42:6.

would result. It would be a time when the world would obey God and people would live in peace and prosperity. It would be a time when all things would be made right.

Originally, this vision was an entirely "this-worldly" one. But by the time of the Roman occupation, there were strong theological undercurrents present no longer maintaining that the Messianic age could or would occur in this world. From the time of the Babylonian captivity forward, the longing and the belief in the promises of God for God's people increasingly had been expressed in dramatic apocalyptic visions. The new creation where all things would finally be made right, it was now believed by many, would come into being only after this world had passed away.[41]

This was, more or less, the common vision of many of Jesus' contemporaries. But the apocalyptic vision of the post-resurrection community, while similar, was also unique. For the New Testament community's vision was defined by Jesus. As such, the new creation was not just one more version of a general utopian dream, but the transformation of all human longing into the vision of Christ where his justice and compassion would establish and sustain God's peace among humankind in eternity. Hope was now hope "in Christ."

Hope "in Christ"

The resurrection of Jesus Christ was understood by the New Testament community as the promise of God that the final day of resurrection and the making of all things right were surely coming. Believing in that promise transformed the relationship to life, to existence in this world, for all those who received the good news in faith.

> If only for this life we have hope in Christ, we are to be pitied more than all men. (1 Cor. 15:19)

While some have interpreted the words of Paul to mean that people of faith have no hope in Christ for this life, and, therefore, should withdraw from the world in order to prepare for his coming, that is not what Paul was saying. For what Paul actually said was that such hope for earthly futures is

---

41. Isa. 65:17; 4 Ezra (2 Esdras) 7:43; Rev. 21:1.

not the *only* hope people of faith have. In other words, people of faith do indeed have hope *in Christ* in this life. After all, the hopes that were born of the promises of God to Abraham and to Moses were hopes for this world. God's covenant with Abraham promised descendants that would number like the stars in the heavens.[42] The covenant with Moses promised that those who had been "no people" would become "a people" and inherit a land flowing with milk and honey.[43] And Paul himself expressed his temporal hopes for the people of the churches he had founded and served.[44]

It also would be a mistake to interpret Paul as saying that those who hope "in Christ" have substantially different hopes from most others. For people of faith also hope for their families to be safe and their children to prosper. They hope to live long and healthy lives and to have enough resources to support them in the process. They hope for the healing of disease and the restoration of broken relationships. And they hope for a future in which the world will not suffer plagues and famines, or otherwise run out of resources. And they hope for an end to social instability, lawlessness, and violence, and a world of justice and peace.

But, as Paul reminds us, for people of faith the visions of the future are also guided and shaped by their understanding that Jesus is Lord. We should understand that to mean, among other things, that they hope their families and children will experience the joy and grace of the Christ. They hope God will be with them and see them through all their trials and difficulties. They hope God will heal the sick and will comfort the bereaving. They hope for their neighbors and for perfect strangers to find peace with God, and for the leaders of the societies and nations of the world to be guided increasingly by the spirit of Christ. And, because of their hope that is in Christ, they devote themselves to the realization of these hopes in this life and this world.

Nevertheless, while Paul no doubt understood the legitimacy of hope in this world, he also clearly realized that if persons *only* have hope in this life and this world, their existence remains tragic. Sooner or later most people come to see that natural hopes in this world are notoriously disappointing. Such lucidity may be greater at times of severe difficulty, particularly when faith is being tested by persecution. But it is also self-evident to all thought-

---

42. Gen. 15:5.

43. Exod. 3:8.

44. Paul, for example, expressed the desire that the churches be free from division (Rom. 1:17-18; 1 Cor. 1:10) and the desire to visit and spend time with the churches (Rom. 1:11; 1 Cor. 16:7; 2 Cor. 13:10).

ful persons who face a personal loss for which there is no hope in this life for restoration. Everyone who has ever lost a dear loved one in death, and who has felt the profound separation that death brings to a relationship, can understand this truth. And everyone who has ever experienced despair over any significant disappointment or tragedy can be clear about the limits of hope in this world.

Through the eyes of faith, Jesus' early followers grasped a hope, an anchor for the soul that would not disappoint.[45] God in the resurrection of Jesus had made a promise. As important as worldly hopes in Christ might be, they are nothing compared to that which is to be revealed with his coming again, and it is this hope that is born of faith, the hope in the final victory of God and eternal life with the Father that is expressed in the prayer, "Come, O Lord!"

Confessing "Jesus is Lord" Today

Because we live today with a very different understanding of the physical cosmos, and we take for granted, in our world of airplanes and space travel, that one will never be able to journey to God's dwelling place by literally ascending into the sky, many people find it difficult to understand and grasp the relevance of the dramatic symbolic images of Jesus' Lordship so important to the New Testament communities of faith. And alienation from these symbols is not simply a problem of worldview. Contemporary understanding is made even more difficult in our time because the early church evidently believed that Jesus' coming again in power was going to take place while some of the original disciples were still living. After more than two thousand years and many generations, that coming has not yet happened. "What then," people ask today, "is the relevance and meaning for faith of the transcendent symbols of the exalted Lord, and of his coming again on the clouds of heaven?"[46]

---

45. Heb. 6:18-19.

46. It is still tempting for some today, as it often has been across the centuries of Christian history, to seek relevance by attempting to construct a cohesive and literal blueprint of things to come from the many apocalyptic images in the Bible. But to do so always has been a futile exercise in unfaith. These symbols speak of that which cannot be spoken about adequately with human language. They are poetic visual metaphors that are capable of imparting important nourishment for the human spirit. But they can do so only if their meaning is

Living "in the Lord" in the "Now"

Let us first look at what it can mean for people of faith in our time to speak of Jesus as exalted to the right hand of God. Paul used the expression "in the Lord" to point to a life lived authentically, faithfully, and ethically, as defined by Jesus, in the present age. To be a person of faith in the "now," between the past and the future, is to allow oneself to be ruled *now* in all one's thoughts, deeds, and relationships by the Lord Jesus Christ. It is to submit *now* to that reign as reality, the way life really is.

To live in the reality of Jesus' Lordship is also to participate *now* in the fellowship and shared ministries of his bodily presence in the world, his church. This moment of our lives, in the midst of time, yet consciously belonging to eternity, is the time of the church, the new people of God, who pour out their lives on behalf of all humankind. It is the time for witnessing to the reality of Jesus Christ among all peoples and all cultures by the most effective means possible. It is therefore a time to embody and work for the vision of justice and compassion that has been revealed in Jesus Christ. And it is the time of sacrificial service to humankind and of demonstrating through acts of extravagant kindness the amazing love of God for all of God's created children.

To live in the reality of Jesus' Lordship in the "now" is to submit to that reign in one's personal living and to participate in the fellowship of other people of faith and to be engaged in the church's mission to the world. Further, it is to live today *in the world itself,* as it is, in all its sinfulness, in the reality of the Lordship of Jesus Christ over the world. To live in faith in this world is not to attempt to separate oneself from the world in search of personal purity, safety, and rescue from the problems of life. It is, on the contrary, to get one's hands dirty, to risk exposure to the impurities of this world, as Christ did, in order be his presence in the world today. It is to give oneself as a living sacrifice to the difficulties of this world, and to be willing to participate in life's obligations, ambiguities, struggles, successes, and failures. To live in faith in this world is to allow Christ to reign over one's life,

---

explored in the hope that is grounded in faith and driven by the desire to live in the reality of Jesus Christ, rather than the wishful thinking that is grounded in curiosity and pride, and driven by the desire for certitude and privileged knowledge. Their meaning genuinely can be grasped only by one willing to make the effort to discover the deeper reality toward which these symbols are pointing.

over every secular corner and profane aspect of one's existence with others, understanding that Christ rules there as well.

Thus, to live under the Lordship of Christ is to give oneself completely to living in this world, yet it is to do so as one whose true citizenship belongs only to heaven, to eternity, to the reign of God in Jesus Christ. It is to live vigorously at once in two worlds, the world of human experience and relationships and the world of spiritual experience and one's relationship with God. It is to live between the world that already is and the world that is not yet, while always remaining loyal to one's true citizenship in the "world to come."

Consequently, calling Jesus "Lord" is not a matter of intellectual doctrine. It is a matter of ultimate significance about what it means to live in the "now." It is about living in *the reality* of his "Lordship," a reality anchored in hope.

Living "in Hope" in the "Now"

The first-century Jewish worldview naturally led to the assumption that the day of accountability and the final victory of God over evil would happen to everyone at once, on the last day of history. Within this cosmology when people died it was assumed by most that they either remained dead and eventually only their bones were left, or, in addition, they dwelled as shadowy spirits in the gloomy underworld beneath the earth until the day of resurrection. That resurrection was to be followed by the final judgment, the end of the current creation and the beginnings of the new one. For the Jewish members of the Jesus movement, the resurrection of Jesus was quite naturally interpreted as a sign that the last day was coming soon.

After all these many generations, and in a time when we take for granted a very different cosmology, this hope may be more meaningfully expressed for our time in terms that remain faithful at once to the imminence of Christ's coming and, at the same time, acknowledge the possibility that many more generations may live before the victory of God has been revealed to all.

While for faith the final victory of God over evil in the universe is sure, the *imminence* of that cosmic final day is by no means certain. It is now more than two thousand years and counting. But faith also understands that the imminence of Christ's coming is, nevertheless, a reality for each person living today. Life is uncertain and death is sure for each of us. Even a life lived to the fullness of old age is but a short journey from the cradle to the grave. We are, as the writer of James reminded us, "a mist that appears for a little time and then vanishes."[47] To live in this world is for death to be imminent. For the person of faith, that means that Christ's coming is also imminent. And that means that the time of accountability before God for our lives and the fulfillment of our hope for the life to come are imminent as well.

Death comes to each of us as a certainty of our existence in this world. It is the end time for us as persons. But it is also a time of transition. It is not a transition in time and in space, but a transition from this world to the other world, the world of the spirit, and from time to eternity. Moreover, for persons of faith, it is a transition from eternal life already experienced in this world through Jesus Christ, to the eternal life of the Spirit.

And for persons of faith, this eternal life is the hope that will not disappoint, for God has promised it through Jesus Christ and his resurrection from the dead, and faith knows that God always keeps God's promises. That is truly all that is important for faith. To desire more is natural, and to seek greater knowledge is to be human. We would like to have a blueprint of the afterlife. But all we have are metaphors taken from our earthly experience that point to a transcendent reality revealed in Jesus Christ, a reality that only can be seen if we see spiritual reality as he saw it. The promise of God is all we get at this point, and, as was true for the pioneers in faith before us, it is all that people of faith need today.

This is not to say, however, that this creation will not also at some point pass away. Nor is it to take for granted that such a cataclysm could not happen in our own generation, though most of us suspect this world is more likely to be around for quite a while. We can be certain, however, that one day this world and all that is in it will indeed pass away. From a human perspective we encounter in this truth a tragedy of profound significance calling into question whether life in a finite universe can have meaning at all. And that nihilistic perspective has tried to impress itself upon us for well over a century in which reality has been reduced in modern consciousness to the material universe.

But the promise of God in the resurrection of Jesus Christ provides another perspective. It is God who has the final word, and that word is not nihilism but Christ as the hope of humankind. The promise of God in Jesus

47. James 4:14.

Christ is the hope that remains when all other human hopes are dashed. It is the hope that is left when all the dreams for which we have labored and planned for many years have come to naught. It is the hope we hold on to when the relationships that we thought would last an eternity are irreparably torn apart. And it is the hope that comforts us when we face the reality of mortality. To pray "Come, O Lord!" today is to pray to be comforted in the "now" by that ultimate hope.

It is also important to mention one other meaning of the prayer, "Come, O Lord!" for people of faith today. When beginning a conscious life of faith, persons seeking to experience the salvation of Jesus Christ call upon the "Lord" to come into their lives bringing forgiveness and healing. And they invite the "Lord" to provide care and guidance for their journeys through life. For many, as each day begins, they once again pray, "Come, O Lord!" renewing that invitation so that the life of faith may be lived in the moments before them in the presence and power of Christ Jesus. As such, it is an opening of themselves to the in-breaking of the eternal, the living Word of God, the Word of grace, the power of the Spirit, and life eternal in the "now."

The crucified but resurrected Jesus, the Son of God and Son of Man, the Lord of lords, has transformed the hope of humankind. Ultimate accountability is now defined by the compassionate servant king, Jesus, as the Judge of the living and the dead. And the vision of eternity, of the life and world to come, is to be the final realization not of our wish dreams, but of the hope Christ has planted in our hearts. To live in the reality of Jesus' reign is to live in this world in the "now" as a citizen of heaven, to love and serve this world, as he did, and to hold fast to the hope in the final victory of God as that which will be fully realized in God's time.

CHAPTER XIV

The Resurrected Life

The metaphors of faith employed in an effort to understand and declare the transcendent significance of Jesus were drawn, as we have seen, from the symbolic heritage and cultural environment of that time and place in history. One cannot account for the Jesus movement's reformulation of those symbols, however, simply by reference to their original context illumined by rational exploration of their new meaning. For the transformed appropriation of those expressions arose out of, and was dependent upon, three intimately related, shared spiritual experiences. The first was a personal and spiritually challenging involvement with the unique and innovative life of Jesus the human being. The second consisted of the startling resurrection appearances of Jesus experienced as the personally transforming divine revelation of him as the Christ, the Son of God. And the third was the shared experience of the Holy Spirit's presence and care in their community and personal lives, manifested as radical spirituality and free responsibility.

Consequently, one cannot adequately appreciate or understand the extravagant transcendent metaphors used by the New Testament writers unless one is willing to see them not simply as theological titles and beliefs, but as expressions of the spiritual transformations that had occurred and were continuing in the lives of believers. In this chapter, we first will take a brief look at spiritual transformations as cross-cultural phenomena. Next we will examine the transformation journeys of the disciples, exploring in the process the metaphors they employed to speak of their shared experiences of "new life" and "new consciousness." Finally, we will discuss those remarkable, recurring, and continuing spiritual experiences and journeys that were understood by the faithful to be the presence and helping activity of the Holy Spirit.

Spiritual Transformations in Cross-Cultural Perspective

Anthropologists and social scientists long have studied the religions of various cultures by examining their beliefs and rituals.[1] In recent decades there has been a growing awareness that an in-depth understanding of particular religions never can be based solely upon the knowledge and interpretation of the group's beliefs and rituals, even when competently explored within their cultural and historical contexts. What people assert they believe, how they carry out their ritual activities, and the contextual background of those symbols certainly are important to that understanding. But many contemporary scholars also understand that it is necessary, if one is to grasp in depth the meaning of an indigenous perspective, to seek to understand the spiritual experiences of its adherents.[2] Such experiences generally are understood by those who live their faith to be formative, sustaining, and decisively important for self-understanding.

Spiritual transformations are phenomena that are well known among the diverse religions of humankind. These life-changing experiences have been categorized according to type, and have been charted in terms of stages, by a number of scholars, though no broadly accepted consensus has emerged with regard to specific taxonomies and progressions.[3] However, a general agreement appears to be emerging that there are significant universal commonalities amidst the individual and cross-cultural diversity of spiritual transformations.[4] These include the non-lineal spiral nature of an ever-deepening awareness, the consciousness and spiritual connectedness that

1. For example, "beliefs" and "rituals" formed the two-part structure of Durkheim's *Elementary Forms of the Religious Life* (1915).

2. For example, see Stark (1991). Anthropological contemporary interest in religious experience is evidenced by a subfield of the anthropology of religion devoted to mental states and altered consciousness in religious experience and practice, course descriptions that specify spiritual experience as a topic of study, and "life history" studies in which ethnographic informants describe spiritual experiences and transformations.

3. For a review of the literature on spiritual transformation, see Schwartz (2001).

4. I am indebted to Vieten et al. (2006) for a number of points in the discussion that follows.

takes place in the transformation process, and the similarity in types of changes and outcomes that observably emerge from such transformation experiences.

There is no single prototypical spiritual transformation. But there appear to be a limited number of prototypes representing the diversity of transformation experiences. Some changes are sudden, unexpected, and immediately life altering due to spiritual visions. The conversion of Paul historically has been seen as that type of experience. Closely related are the transformations that take place through overwhelming emotional upheaval associated with repentance and new beginnings. These conversions have been considered prototypical by much of American evangelical Protestantism.

Another type of transformation that is quite common, however, includes a change process that evolves over extensive time, with steps forward, backward, and sideways along the way. The apostle Peter's journey likely was of this type and it probably is typical of many who began their spiritual journeys at a very early age. It is also likely to be typical of many who change faiths and enter an extensive period of instruction and study at a later age.

Some transformations also occur through intuitive insights, usually arrived at during a spirit journey, trance state, or extended period of meditation, resulting in the radical reconstruction of worldviews and spiritual perspectives. Traditional shaman spirit journeys and the "awakening" of Gautama the Buddha fit this paradigm.

Others appear to be transformed by what largely is an intellectual process in which reason demolishes old assumptions and the intellectual defenses to a new faith. This seems to have been the journey of C. S. Lewis, who self-reported a transition from atheism to faith.[5] It is likely that this type of transition also has been the path of a number of contemporary scientists who have gone through a rational process from agnosticism to belief in God.[6] And there are no doubt many other pathways to spiritual transformation.

If the pathways are diverse, the metaphors used by those experiencing spiritual transformations to describe them, and the outcomes of those phenomena, are remarkably similar.[7] Informants speak of rebirth, dismemberment, and reconstitution, of death and resurrection, of realization, of seeing

5. Lewis (2001).
6. See, for example, Collins (2006).
7. Collins (2006).

the light, of awakening, and of arrival at a destination they always knew was there, a kind of coming home. And they often describe remarkably similar resulting changes in character and behavior.

Transformed persons often are understood, by self and others, as no longer ego-driven, narcissistic, or deceptive, but as childlike, truthful, serene, transparent, loving, wise, compassionate, patient, tolerant, and forgiving. These socially desirable qualities generally are not experienced as personal achievements, but as the by-products of a direct spiritual connectedness. This sense of connection may be with a divinity or with a particular transcendent consciousness such as the *Tao* of Chinese thought. Such direct experiences of transcendence are seen as revelations, illuminations, and the emergence of a spiritual understanding that reorients a person's relationship to life and to others. And, in the tradition of the universal hero story, these transformations bring blessings to the world and initiate the transformation process in other persons and communities.

The Disciples' Journey of Spiritual Transformation

The disciples of Jesus appear to have undergone a transformation process that appears to have been similar to the type experienced by many who convert to a different religious community than the faith of their upbringing.[8] Jesus was the leader of a reform movement within Judaism that was unique and distinctive. Jesus' teachings challenged conventional religious thinking. The twelve and many other disciples were enlisted in a spiritual movement that uprooted them from their homes, their families, and their traditional religious upbringing. They underwent an intense period of instruction intended to reorient their thinking, followed by supervised opportunities to practice their new faith.

It is common for such converts, at some point in their journeys, to undergo a crisis of faith, in which they are torn between the old and the new after trying on the new religious orientation.[9] At such times, some fall away.

8. See Peace (2000) and Pitulac and Nastuta (2007). Schwartz's (2001) summary of Poston (1992) indicates that only three of seventy-two converts to Islam reported a sudden emotional Pauline-type conversion. Zinnbaurer and Pargament (1998) found that changes were dramatic for both sudden and gradual Christian converts.

9. Rambo (1993) proposed a seven-stage model of spiritual transformation with crisis being one of the stages. A crisis often is assumed to precipitate a sudden conversion, but cri-

And some disciples of Jesus appear to have abandoned his movement during his lifetime. While many remained loyal disciples until his arrest, the death of Jesus created a spiritual crisis of disillusionment and despair of immense proportions for each of them. It was a crisis, however, that was subsequently resolved by overwhelming spiritual events. Jesus' resurrection appearances and the advent of the Holy Spirit in their individual and collective experiences changed everything. Afterward, the consciousness, worldview, attitudes about life, moral character, behavior toward others, and life mission of the disciples all were radically altered, and their lives were forever changed.

Devotion to Jesus

One of the remarkable changes that occurred was the shift in emphasis in their worship and personal devotion from an exclusive focus on the God of Israel, to one that included the person of Jesus.[10] The Jesus movement held strong monotheistic convictions. Rooted in the faith of Israel, it rejected any form of pagan worship as idolatry and promoted the worship of the one true God of the Jewish Scriptures.[11] Yet, as we have seen in previous chapters, Jesus' divinely exalted status was expressed early on and affirmed, in the face of much opposition, throughout the New Testament period.

A Roman ambassador to Pontus and Bithynia in northwestern Asia Minor, named Pliny the Younger, wrote the emperor Trajan around 112 CE to report his handling of matters involving Christians in the area. In that letter, in which Pliny indicated that some Christians had been arrested, interrogated, threatened, tortured, and executed under his authority, he also related that Christians confessed "they were accustomed to meet on a fixed day before dawn and sing responsively a hymn to Christ as to a god."[12]

While this pagan report describes a practice approximately eight decades after Jesus' crucifixion, there is substantial evidence within the New Testament that similar, if not identical, praise and worship practices devoted to Jesus began very early, probably within the first decade. Philippians 2:5-11, discussed in chapter II, is thought by many scholars to be an example of a

---

ses also occur during gradual conversions, particularly when the social cost of the conversion becomes painful (Pitulac and Nastuta, 2007).

10. I am indebted to Hurtado (2005) for much of the discussion in this section.

11. 1 Thess. 1:9-10.

12. *Letters* 10.96-97.

hymn used in very early worship. The prologue to the Gospel of John, as discussed in that same chapter, may have been a hymn as well. And it is possible that Psalm 110 also was sung in very early times as a "Christ hymn."[13]

Another indicator of early devotion to Jesus was the invocation of Jesus' name in healings, in prayer, and in corporate worship.

> To the church of God in Corinth, to those sanctified in Christ Jesus and called to be holy, together with all those everywhere who call on the name of our Lord Jesus Christ — their Lord and ours: Grace and peace to you from God our Father and the Lord Jesus Christ. (1 Cor. 1:2)

In this passage, from one of Paul's earliest letters, written around twenty years after Jesus' death, the Jesus movement is identified, unified, and set apart by the practice of *calling on the name of the Lord.* And the blessings of grace and of peace are invoked from both God the Father *and* the Lord Jesus Christ. In addition to invoking Jesus' name in prayers to the Father, there is evidence that the early Jesus movement also prayed directly to Jesus. As discussed in chapter XIII, *Marana tha,* translated "Come, O Lord!" reveals an Aramaic prayer that probably was a part of the devotional life of the earliest groups. In addition, the shared symbolic meal, in which Jesus' final supper with the disciples was reenacted, was understood by the community as a communion with Jesus, a participation in his being, and an experience of his being in their midst.

Devotion to Jesus, then, was manifested in the Jesus movement within a very short time after his death, as confession of Jesus' exalted role in bringing salvation and the divine presence of his Spirit among the community of faith. It is unlikely that such devotion originated among disciples immersed in Jewish culture simply from theological discussion and speculation. It is far more likely that the theology of Jesus' divine significance was the natural outgrowth of the shared spiritual experiences of the Jesus movement and their subsequent reflections upon those happenings. While the language of worship, praise, and devotional experience required theological reflection, it did not, in the beginning, require a logical thinking through of all the theo-

---

13. Many scholars believe that the early churches sang psalms, as Jesus and the disciples were likely to have done at the conclusion of the Last Supper (Mark 14:26). Given the importance of Psalm 110 in Messianic thought, that psalm is likely to have been among those sung. Other possible hymns in the New Testament include Col. 1:15-20, and portions of Romans 6 and 1 Peter may have had similar usage. See the article on "Hymn" in Achtemeier (1996).

logical implications. That would come soon, however, amidst internal strife and challenges from without.

Serious tensions between traditional Judaism and the Jesus movement arose at a very early time, primarily because of the differences between the groups concerning the exaltation of Jesus by the latter. The hostility of traditional Judaism toward the idea that Jesus was the Messiah turned what was intended as a reform movement into a sect. But it was the practice of religious devotion to the person of Jesus that no doubt ultimately drove an irreparable wedge between Judaism and that sect.[14] That devotion came out of profound and transforming spiritual experiences that convinced believers that *God had exalted Jesus and willed their devotion to him.*

The resurrection appearances of Jesus affirmed for those who experienced them that Jesus was the Christ, the Son of God. The experience of the coming and indwelling of the Holy Spirit provided profound assurances for the validity of that faith. These phenomena were far more than the medium through which divine authoritative information about Jesus was transmitted. These were spiritual experiences that were renewed and sustained through shared devotion to Jesus. And these spiritual experiences transformed lives and reconstructed personalities.

Metaphors of New Life

As the Jesus movement attempted to understand the significance of Jesus, they simultaneously were seeking to comprehend the radical spirituality that had come upon them and that had dramatically changed their lives.

> We are therefore buried with him through baptism into death in order that, just as Christ was raised from the dead through the glory of the Father, we too may live a new life. (Rom. 6:4)

> In the same way, count yourselves dead to sin but alive to God in Christ Jesus. (Rom. 6:11)

> Jesus said to her, "I am the resurrection and the life. He who believes in me will live, even though he dies; and whoever lives and believes in me will never die." (John 11:25-26a)

14. John's Gospel clearly reflects a time when the conflict had grown so great that Christians were excluded from the synagogues, presumably because of "blasphemy."

The resurrection of Jesus came to those who experienced it as promise and hope for their own resurrection to come. But "resurrection" also became a powerful metaphor for the spiritual transformation that had happened already. Baptism was likened to the death and resurrection of Jesus, and existence in faith was described as new life, a new creation.[15]

Nowhere in the New Testament is the radical spirituality of existence in the Jesus faith more dramatically stated than in the metaphors employed in the Gospel of John to symbolize the relationship of Jesus with those who believed. When Jesus was quoted by the author of John as saying, "I am the resurrection and the life," "the resurrection and the life" meant far more than past historical event and the future hope of salvation. It symbolized a radical spiritual reality in the present.

In John's Gospel, Jesus is seen as "the way, the truth and the life."[16] Jesus is the *pathway* one must travel in order to experience life as it is supposed to be and to reach its intended goal. Jesus is the *truth* that births a life of integrity, free from the delusions of this world and immersed in the reality of God's love for humankind. Jesus is *life,* as it was always intended to be, destined for eternity and blessed with abundance and the fullness of possibilities. Within the revelation of the transcendent significance of Jesus is the realization of authentic human existence as radical spirituality.

In the Gospel of John, "water" was an important symbol of spiritual existence. As we have seen, throughout the desert and oasis environment of the ancient Middle East, "water" symbolized "life." But Jesus was not described by John's Gospel simply as "life," conventionally understood as existence in the world. Jesus was described as "living water," a term used for fresh, moving water, the kind of water that flows from mountain streams in the spring. John was saying that Jesus is life that is fresh and flowing. The life that Jesus is and bestows is not stagnant life, but exuberant life that is effervescent and, according to the Gospel, life that quenches spiritual thirst forever.

Another important symbol of life in John's Gospel is that of "bread."[17] Jesus is contrasted, however, with the bread that sustains existence in this world. And those who come to him simply to have their stomachs filled miss the point entirely. Jesus is the "bread *of life.*" He is not only living water but living bread as well. This is bread that feeds the human spirit. It fills the spir-

15. 2 Cor. 5:17.
16. John 14:6.
17. John 6:51.

itual "hole in the soul" of all who partake of it in faith. And those who partake of this "living bread" never hunger in spirit again. As living water and living bread, Jesus is the awesome, life-giving spiritual force in the universe.

Metaphors of New Consciousness

Jesus was more than the initiator of the gift of transformed spiritual existence in faith. Jesus defined the new consciousness of the transformed life. The apostle Paul often used the expression "in Christ" to refer to those who believed and responded to the gospel.

Therefore, if anyone is in Christ, he is a new creation. (2 Cor. 5:17)

So, in Christ, we who are many form one body, and each member belongs to all the others. (Rom. 12: 5)

When Paul, in his letters, spoke collectively of those who belonged to the churches, he referred to them as "in Christ." Likewise, when he remembered and greeted particular members of the faith, it was his practice to refer to them and address them as "in Christ."[18] This was more than a means of distinguishing believers from nonbelievers in Jesus as the Christ. It was an intentional way of describing and reminding the faithful of the reality in which they lived.

To be "in Christ" was to live in the reality of grace, in freedom from the law of sin and death, and to possess a hope that would not disappoint.[19] It was to live in the world as reconciled by God to himself and to live in the love of God and the trust that no power can separate one from it.[20] And it was to live in the truth of the gospel and to speak it honestly.[21] It also was to live in unity without status distinction with others who were in Christ.[22] To be "in Christ," then, was to live in the reality of his character and his saving work.

To live in the reality of Christ, was also to experience the transforming presence and power of Christ *within* as persons and as a community.

---

18. For examples, see Rom. 16:3; 16:7; 16:9.
19. Rom. 3:24; 8:1-2; 1 Cor. 15:19.
20. 2 Cor. 15:19; Rom. 8:39.
21. 2 Cor. 2:17; Rom. 9:1.
22. Gal. 3:28.

I pray that out of his glorious riches he may strengthen you with power through his Spirit in your inner being, so that *Christ may dwell in your hearts* through faith. (Eph. 3:16-17a; altered)

To them God has chosen to make known among the Gentiles the glorious riches of this mystery, which is *Christ in you,* the hope of Glory. (Col. 1:27; altered)

I have made you known to them, and will continue to make you known in order that the love you have for me may be in them and that *I myself may be in them.* (John 17:26; altered)

The expression "Christ in you" is both a descriptive statement of transformed lives, and, at the same time, a way of speaking about a sense of Christ's spiritual presence and power in those lives. This dual meaning is captured unmistakably in the metaphor of the vine and the branches found in John's Gospel.

I am the vine; you are the branches. If a man remains in me and I in him, he will bear much fruit; apart from me you can do nothing. (John 15:5)

The metaphor of the vine and the branches identifies Jesus, the Word made flesh, as the vine and the disciples as the branches. In an earlier story in John's Gospel, Jesus' transforming power was demonstrated when he miraculously changed purification water into exceptionally good wine.[23] In subsequent stories and commentary, spiritual transformation metaphorically was described as being born anew of the Spirit, as the quenching of spiritual thirst, as the healing of spiritual paralysis, as the spiritually blind given sight, and as the dead raised to new life. But the metaphors of the vine and wine seem to have played an especially important role in John's narrative.

The symbolism of wine and vine was common among most of the religious traditions of Mediterranean societies where wine was the favored cultural drink, and where wine production played a major role in the economy.[24] In the courtyards and nearby gardens, household grape vines climbing a tree or trellis and whole vineyards were commonplace. Wine, because

23. John 2:1-11.

24. I am indebted to the article on "Vine" in Achtemeier (1996) for several points in this discussion of the vine.

of its color, was associated with blood, and thereby with life itself.[25] And the transformation of the fruit of the vine into an effervescent drink that could be ecstasy-producing quite naturally led to the symbolization of spiritual experience and transformation.

The intended audience of John's Gospel was likely to have been familiar with the cultic festivals of Dionysus and Bacchus, the Greek and Roman names respectively for the god of wine. They may have known, as well, of pagan festival rituals in which empty kettles were sealed in temples devoted to the god of wine only to be miraculously filled with wine the following day when the seals were broken.[26] And they may have been aware of the belief that the presence of the grape vine was believed in pagan worship to mean that the god was near and in the midst of the cultic worshipers.[27]

There were, however, other associations with the cults of the god of wine. Dionysus was believed to be a god of agricultural and human fertility, and festivals devoted to him were often accompanied, with the assistance of the wine, with the loss of sexual inhibition and with what would be considered as wild partying in any culture. Such debauchery also had been seen in Israel's history in the fertility-oriented religious traditions of Canaanite culture. Prophetic denouncement testifies to how tempting such celebrations of the flesh were to the Israelites.

Despite the association with pagan festivals, the vines and vineyards became powerful, positive symbols of Israel's relationship to Yahweh. And much of the audience of John's Gospel surely would have been familiar with this symbolism of the vine and the vineyard in Israel's history, for the metaphors of vine and vineyard were expressions of Yahweh's planting and nurturing of his people. Isaiah declared, "The vineyard of the Lord Almighty is the house of Israel."[28] When Jeremiah delivered God's Word to the nation, he said, "I had planted you like a choice vine."[29] Ezekiel's prophecy likened "mother" Israel to a vine planted by water that had been fruitful and full of branches, but which had been uprooted in judgment and consumed in fire.[30] Hosea also spoke of Israel as a vine as a metaphor of prosperity and judgment.[31]

25. Wine was spoken of as the "blood of grapes" in Gen. 49:11 and Deut. 32:14.
26. Pausanias, *Guide to Greece* 6.26.1-2.
27. Kerenyi (2003).
28. Isa. 5:7.
29. Jer. 2:21.
30. Ezek. 15; 19:10-12.
31. Hos. 10:1-2.

The vine actually became the visual symbol of Israel in the time of the Maccabees, being cast on their coins. And a golden vine with grapes adorned the front of the Temple in Jerusalem in the first century. So, when John's audience heard Jesus speak of vine and branches, there were already rich associations. They would have understood clearly that it was Jesus, and not Dionysus or Bacchus, who was being proclaimed as the authentic divinity of spiritual transformation and abundant life. And they would have recognized immediately that the Jesus movement was the new Israel, the vineyard tended by the Father, in which the Son is the vine and the people are the branches.

Moreover, the metaphor of the vine and the branches, as found in John's Gospel, disclosed an important truth about spiritual transformation. Grape vines must be tended, nourished, and pruned in order to produce good fruit. Those who have undergone spiritual transformation remain dependent on the miraculous agent of that remarkable change.[32] Transformation is neither permanent nor complete unless it continues to be nurtured by direct connection and ongoing participation in its source. Jesus, as the vine, draws his life from the Father, and the disciples, as the branches, draw their life from the Father through Jesus. And because they continue to receive life from the Father through the Son, they are able to produce abundant fruit.[33] But if a branch is cut off, if a disciple no longer remains in Jesus and Jesus in the disciple, then that disciple can do nothing. Such a disciple, cut off from the source of spiritual transformation, is, like a pruned branch, useless and destined to wither and die.[34]

In John's Gospel, to be "in Christ" and to experience "Christ within" is to dwell in the love of Christ and to be filled with his joy.[35] Joy is promised to those who, as they weep and mourn in the midst of life's tribulations, remain connected to him. To live in Christ and Christ within is to know him as a friend, and it is to love those he loves with his same kind of self-sacrificing love. For love is the enduring outcome of a spiritually transformed life.[36]

32. John 15:4.
33. John 15:5.
34. John 15:6.
35. John 15:9-11.
36. John 15:12-15.

Life in the Spirit

The spiritual transformation that had occurred and was continuing to mature in the lives of members of the New Testament community was understood by them not only to be a participation in the new creation, the resurrected life, and a direct and intimate devotional experience with the living Lord, but also as a *life in the Spirit*. "Life in Christ" and "life in the Spirit" were not distinct realities but differing ways of describing the transforming and ongoing transcendent significance of Jesus in their lives.

> You, however, are controlled not by the sinful nature but by the Spirit, if the Spirit of God lives in you. And if anyone does not have the Spirit of Christ, he does not belong to Christ. But if Christ is in you, your body is dead because of sin, yet your spirit is alive because of righteousness. And if the Spirit of him who raised Jesus from the dead is living in you, he who raised Christ from the dead will also give life to your mortal bodies through the Spirit, who lives in you. (Rom. 8:9-11)

In this remarkable passage, Paul identified the indwelling of God's Spirit with the Spirit of Jesus the Messiah, as the source of the spiritually transformed life, and as a sign of the resurrection to come.[37]

The Presence of the Spirit

As we saw in chapter III, many traditional cultures have believed in spirit intrusion and possession. In those societies, spirits, such as those that cause illness, have been considered malevolent. But there also have been benevolent spirits, usually divine beings, legendary heroes, ancestors, and spirits of animals that have been thought at times to possess people, particularly during certain ceremonies and rituals.[38] In folk healing ceremonies, for example, a

---

37. See also Phil. 1:19 for "Spirit of Jesus Christ" and Gal. 4:6 for "the Spirit of his Son," and 2 Cor. 3:17-18 for "Spirit of the Lord."

38. Spirits may be seen as benevolent or malevolent, depending on the circumstances. As discussed in chapter III, malevolent spirits may be blamed for illness and disabilities. As we saw in chapter II, the benevolent spirit of Elijah was thought to possess his immediate successor Elisha, and much later to possess John the Baptist. For cross-cultural examples and comparative discussion of spirit possession, see Bourguignon (1968). For a fairly recent cross-disciplinary discussion of spirit possession, see Klass (2004).

particular spirit is often believed to come upon the healer in order to be his "spirit guide" and helper to bring about wholeness.

It is also quite common, among widely diverse societies, for a group of persons who are dancing and rhythmically chanting to experience a kind of communal spirit possession. The "spirit-possessed" often describe themselves, on these occasions, as no longer being in control of themselves, but as being physically moved in dance, or being cast about and thrown down. And they may have uttered sounds and cried out words that were attributed to the spirits.

These "possessions" have been experienced most often as wild, though usually culturally predictable, ecstatic events. In such ceremonies, it has been quite common for the people undergoing "possession" eventually to become tired and to fall into a deep sleep, and, afterward, for those participating to believe that the spirits have returned to their spirit world. Upon arising they usually have reported feeling refreshed and renewed, though return to a full "normal consciousness" may have taken some time.

There certainly are some similarities between these cross-cultural spirit possessions and the New Testament experiences of the Holy Spirit. For some members of the Jesus movement, the coming of the Holy Spirit was accompanied by ecstatic behavior, particularly "speaking in tongues" and the channeling of vivid symbolic "prophecies." Of course, such emotionally overwhelming experiences only occurred at certain times. People did not, for example, speak in the language of the spirit world continuously. And others appeared not to have those types of experiences at all. These others, apparently, were believed to have experienced different, quieter, and more practical gifts of the Spirit.

Unlike many of the spirit possessions of traditional cultures, but similar to the spirit possession of most shamans and other "holy" men and women, the Holy Spirit was understood by the New Testament faithful to have remained within and in their midst at all times.[39] Whatever the type of Spirit experience of various members of the New Testament community, life in the Spirit was, for them, a continuous, ongoing, intimate, personal, shared experience of divine presence. No doubt there were times when the early churches felt the presence of the Spirit more dramatically than at others. At such times they may have felt their consciousness taken over by the Spirit,

39. See Eliade (1964) for discussion of the way in which shamanism differs in its experience of the spirit world from other "possession" phenomena.

but they also believed the Spirit to be within them even when they were fully in control of their faculties and in the midst of their everyday lives. Life in the Spirit, in the early church communities, was a constant rather than sporadic phenomenon.

The New Testament experience, while similar to other possessions, was uniquely defined for believers by the identity of Jesus as the Christ.[40] It was not just any spirit that came upon the apostolic community. It was the Holy Spirit, as the Spirit of Christ. The charismatic community understood its spiritual experience to be structured and defined by Jesus, the Messiah, the Son of God and Lord.

In other words, experience of the Spirit was, for them, an ongoing and direct experience of the same Jesus they had known in life, death, and resurrection. It was his words and deeds that were confirmed by the experience of the Spirit. It was his saving grace and the joy of his salvation that possessed them. It was his love that made possible the love they had for each other. And it was he, as Spiritual Presence, who was in their midst whenever two or three of them were gathered together.[41] Jesus as Christ and Lord did far more than shape and define the theology of the early community of faith; he defined and facilitated the spiritual transformation and the devotional life of the community as well. Life in the Spirit was life in Christ and Christ within. And, as such, it was the inner presence of a "helping Spirit," a "Spirit guide."[42]

The Helping Spirit

It is difficult for modern Christians in the West to grasp what it must have been like to be associated with Judaism during the political turmoil sur-

---

40. The universality and particularity of spiritual transformation is complementary to the universality and particularity of the Word discussed in chapter X. The cross-cultural quest for spiritual transformation can be understood both as illustrating the universal longing for communion with the transcendent, and as the reality of the transforming power of the universal Word wherever and whenever the "fruits" of spiritual transformation are one with the fruits of the particular Word and the Spirit of Christ discussed below.

41. Matt. 18:20.

42. The idea of "spirit helpers" is quite widespread, particularly among folk healers. In shamanism spirit helpers or guides often are animal spirits, but various folk healers across cultures also consider themselves aided by ancestor spirits, cultural heroes, and divinities. See Eliade (1964) for discussion of "helping spirits" in shamanism.

rounding the fall of Jerusalem, or to confess allegiance to Jesus as the Christ during periodic times of horrifying persecution. To be an ordinary human being in the first century was to know hardship and suffering. To be a Jew was to know the sorrow of being a conquered people, and to grieve over the bloody fall of Jerusalem. To be early members of the Jesus movement was to know these troubles, and to have added to them the hostility and rejection of their neighbors, the loss of their heroes and friends to martyrdom, and to face sufferings and deaths themselves because of their loyalty to Jesus.

In the midst of these difficulties, it was their shared experiential understanding that their faith and fellowship was being sustained by the indwelling of the Spirit.

> All this I have spoken while still with you. But the Counselor, the Holy Spirit, whom the Father will send in my name, will teach you all things and will remind you of everything I have said to you. Peace I leave with you, my peace I give you. I do not give to you as the world gives. Do not let your hearts be troubled and do not be afraid. (John 14:25-27)

The root of the word translated in this passage as "Counselor" referred in the Greek language to one who was "summoned to the side" of another to provide assistance.[43] That help was usually in the form of encouragement, consolation, and comfort. In the writings of Isaiah of the exile, the Messianic vision had been one that spoke of comfort to the people of God.[44] The New Testament writers before John's Gospel had spoken of the *encouragement* of Jesus Christ, of the Father, and of the Holy Spirit, sometimes through the Scriptures and through prophecies.[45] John's Gospel employed the Greek term *parakletos* for an encouraging, helping, consoling, comforting, advocating "Counselor" as a descriptive synonym of the Holy Spirit.[46]

Moreover, the indwelling of the Holy Spirit was more than a mere feeling of spirituality; it was the conscious presence of an inner "spirit guide." Such spiritual guidance was an essential part of the ongoing spiritual transformation process encouraging spiritual growth for believers. As the Spirit

43. Vine (2007).

44. Isa. 40:1.

45. See 2 Thess. 2:16; Luke 2:25; Acts 9:31; Rom. 15:4-5; 1 Cor. 14:3.

46. *Paraklesis*, which is often translated as "encouragement" (see note above), literally means "a calling to one's side." John used *parakletos* as a title for Holy Spirit that literally meant "one who is called to one's side," or "one who gives aid." It was a term that also had usage as a legal advocate in a court setting and is used of Jesus in that sense in 1 John 2:1.

had "led" their Lord, during the days of his ministry, the apostolic community also experienced itself as "led by the Spirit."[47] The Spirit of Jesus as the Christ was within and among them, providing direction for what they were to say and do, as they shared the gospel with others, as they debated their opposition, and as they faced persecution.

The Holy Spirit as "Counselor" also continued to instruct, and to keep the memory of Jesus, his words and his deeds, alive in the believer.[48] When Jesus was reported to have pronounced his *Shalom,* his peace, upon the disciples, this promise of spiritual tranquility in the midst of life's turmoil is one of those statements of Jesus that the "Spirit Helper," at a later time, assisted the disciples in remembering. For one of the functions of the Spirit that was promised was that the faithful would be reminded in such times that they live in the reality of Christ's peace. It is not the peace of this world, but the spiritual *Shalom* that transcends this world and all its difficulties. At the center of the transformed life of the Spirit, according to the testimony of John's Gospel, is the tranquility and serenity that cannot be disturbed by anything this world has to offer.

The Holy Spirit not only brought spiritual peace in the face of great difficulties; it brought courage, spiritual confidence, strength, and the power to accomplish marvelous deeds.

> When they saw the courage of Peter and John and realized that they were unschooled, ordinary men, they were astonished and they took note that these men had been with Jesus. (Acts 4:13)

> I can do everything through him who gives me strength. (Phil. 4:13)

> I pray that out of his glorious riches he may strengthen you with power through his Spirit in your inner being. (Eph. 3:16)

> I will not venture to speak of anything except what Christ has accomplished through me in leading the Gentiles to obey God by what I have said and done — by the power of the Spirit. (Rom. 15:18)

When courage and confidence were needed to face trials and tribulations, the Holy Spirit gave them what they needed. When the right words

---

47. Rom. 8:14.
48. John 14:26.

were desired in order to be faithful witnesses, the Holy Spirit provided them. When compassionate healing was needed, they experienced the Holy Spirit empowering them to heal, as Jesus himself had been empowered.

It was the experience of those who had been spiritually transformed that they did not need to rely on their own inadequate human strength in order to carry out their mission to the world. As spiritually transformed persons, they could rely on the Holy Spirit, that transcendent power that dwelled within them, flowed through them, and blessed those around them. On their own strength they could do nothing, but they could do all things through Christ who strengthened them through his Spirit.

The Gifts and Fruits of the Spirit

As I have suggested, some members of the New Testament community of faith experienced the Spirit as ecstatic possession and some as a quiet inner voice or presence. The Spirit also bestowed diverse gifts on different persons, allowing them to contribute to the fellowship and mission of the community in a variety of ways.

> There are different kinds of gifts, but the same Spirit. There are different kinds of service, but the same Lord. There are different kinds of working, but the same God works all of them in all men.
> Now to each one the manifestation of the Spirit is given for the common good. (1 Cor. 12:4-7)

While spiritual gifts were not the same as natural gifts, those abilities that are frequently referred to as "talents," the Spirit appears to have manifested itself in the New Testament community in differing ways, most likely depending on tendencies within various personalities.[49] Paul's descriptions of the variety of gifts of the Spirit manifested among those in Christ probably were intended to be illustrative rather than comprehensive.[50] But his lists appear to have illustrated two broad types of spiritual gifts.

---

49. Studies in recent years of religious experiences seem to support the idea that particular spiritual gifts and religious styles tend to be associated with particular personality types. A number of researchers have used the Myers-Briggs personality inventory to explore these associations.

50. Rom. 12:6-8; 1 Cor. 12:8-10; 12:28; 12:29-30.

The first type of spiritual gift might be termed a gift of *transcendent consciousness*. In Paul's first letter to the church at Corinth, among the gifts of the Spirit listed, "speaking in tongues" and "prophecies" belonged to this type. These and other gifts of transcendent consciousness were understood to be visible and experiential signs of the sacred and awesome presence of God's Spirit in the midst of the congregation. They also were considered as signs for unbelievers and as evidence of God's direction in the life of the church.[51]

It is clear from Paul's discussion, along with descriptions in the book of Acts, that "speaking in tongues" were utterances in what today's social and psychological scientists would call altered states of consciousness. It appears that the faithful believed the utterances spoken during at least some of these trances were the language of spirit beings referred to by Paul as the "tongues of angels," and that God understood such "tongues."[52] These utterances were unintelligible to most of those who experienced and witnessed them, though some appear to have had the ability to "translate" and interpret for the community of faith the meaning of the utterances.

In 1 Corinthians, it is quite evident that the practice of "speaking in tongues" had given rise to problems in the congregation. There evidently were those in Corinth who saw such a gift as evidence of spiritual superiority. While declaring all gifts to be gifts of the one Spirit and intended for the common good, Paul specifically warned of the dangers of overvaluing such practices, and he encouraged the cultivation of "prophecy" over unintelligible "language." Paul gave specific instructions about the practice of "tongues" to ensure order in worship, and he evidently ranked this gift as the least desirable one.[53]

"Prophecy" was preferable to "speaking in tongues" because it was intelligible and, therefore, met the criterion that acts of worship "must be done for the strengthening of the church." "Prophecy" evidently occurred during an altered state of consciousness in which it was believed that the Father or the Son, or perhaps some other Spirit being, "channeled" a revelation. Many of these, no doubt, were filled with rich symbolic imagery, similar to that found in the book of Revelation and other apocalyptic literature. At times,

---

51. See 1 Cor. 14:22. In Acts 10:46 Gentiles began to speak in tongues, demonstrating God's approval of the Gentile mission.

52. 1 Cor. 13:1 speaks of "tongues of angels." For other textual support for the discussion in this section the reader is referred to 1 Cor. 12–14.

53. See 1 Cor. 12:28; 14:26-33.

however, they may have taken the form of claims to instructions from heaven that were of a more practical nature, providing guidance to the church during conflicts and difficult challenges. The problem, of course, was that not every claim to "prophecy" was a revelation from God. And so the young church very early on found itself seeking to clarify how its members could determine which prophets were false prophets and which were genuine ones.

The second broad type of spiritual gift was that of *practical service.* To this category belonged gifts of service to others, particularly to those within the household of faith. It included such things as the ability to heal and perform other miraculous deeds, to teach, to interpret prophecy, to care for the needy, to help others, and to perform acts of administration.

Closely related to these "gifts of the spirit" were the "fruits of the spirit."

> But the fruit of the Spirit is love, joy, peace, patience, kindness, goodness, faithfulness, gentleness and self-control. (Gal. 5:22)

These were the qualities that characterized a life in the Spirit, and, by implication, these are the fruits by which the faithful were to discern the difference between true and false prophets, between those under the influence of evil spirits and those in whom the Holy Spirit dwells.

> Watch out for false prophets. They come to you in sheep's clothing, but inwardly they are ferocious wolves. By their fruit you will recognize them. Do people pick grapes from thornbushes, or figs from thistles? Likewise every good tree bears good fruit, but a bad tree bears bad fruit. A good tree cannot bear bad fruit, and a bad tree cannot bear good fruit. (Matt. 7:15-18)

If a person prophesied, or taught, or otherwise claimed to be inspired by the Holy Spirit, then, before his or her words were to be honored, the spiritually discerning believer was to look behind the claim for evidence of love, joy, peace, patience, kindness, goodness, faithfulness, and self-control. Only when such qualities were present was the "message" to be regarded as authentic. In other words, these attitudes should have been evident in the lives of all who had undergone genuine spiritual transformation. And, likewise, these attitudes would be absent, or replaced by their opposites, if one was under the influence of demonic spirits.

Just as the qualities of spiritual transformation were evident in those who had been so transformed, so it was that such persons also experienced and demonstrated a state of grace that manifested itself in free responsibility.

> It is for freedom that Christ has set us free. Stand firm, then, and do not let yourselves be burdened again by a yoke of slavery. (Gal. 5:1)

> Therefore, there is now no condemnation for those who are in Christ Jesus, because through Christ Jesus the law of the Spirit of life set me free from the law of sin and death. (Rom. 8:1)

Life in the Spirit manifested itself as freedom from the desires of one's sinful nature, and from the personal and social consequences of self-will run riot. It was no longer sin that controlled one's will, but the Spirit. And being led by the Spirit meant that one was no longer bound by the Law, and was free from the legalistic, moralistic, and self-righteous lifestyle of one who was obsessed with self-justification. For it was no longer spiritual pride that motivated, but gratitude for God's gracious salvation.

To live the resurrected life, then, was to be raised to a life in Christ and Christ within, a life in the Spirit. It was to experience spiritual transformation and an ongoing radical spirituality. And it was to know the freedom of those who dwell continuously in this world in the reality of God's grace.[54] Freedom in Christ was a spiritual relationship to the obligations of existence as viewed through the reality of God's love for creation and for humankind. It was the willingness to accept responsibility and, with the help of the Holy Spirit, to seek to know and do the will of God on behalf of the well-being of the world and neighbor. It was a willingness to be led by the Spirit in that mission and to trust in the grace of God to make one's efforts efficacious. It was to be free from the need to "boast," to be proud of one's good works. Instead, it was to be free to allow the *Shalom* of Christ and the fruits of the Spirit to flourish in one's life and relationships.[55] And it was to live in that free responsibility as one who relied not on one's deeds, but on the grace of God in Jesus Christ for one's hope in this world and in the world to come.

54. See especially Gal. 5. See also Bonhoeffer (1955, pp. 248-62) for a profound discussion of freedom and responsibility.
55. See particularly Eph. 2 and John 14–16.

CHAPTER XV

Jesus, Reality, and the Life of Faith

The first disciples experienced the humanity of Jesus very personally. Some of them may have known him before his ministry when he was working his trade, perhaps building houses in the region or repairing boats for the fishermen on the Sea of Galilee. And all of the disciples heard him speak with authority and saw him perform amazing deeds. They journeyed with him up and down the dusty roads of Galilee, Judea, and Samaria, where they witnessed his interactions with the crowds of people who came to him to be taught and healed, and they observed his amazing skill at responding to the verbal challenges of his opponents.

But the disciples also had moments with him when the crowds were not present. At such times he no doubt relaxed with them, and interacted with them as a down-to-earth human being, the craftsman from Nazareth whose background was so very similar to their own. We can be confident that they knew him as they knew members of their families, and as a person who did not always wear his public face. He was their rabbi and charismatic leader, but he was also a man who had bodily needs and earthly functions as everyone else. The disciples were with him when he felt hunger and thirst, when he became tired and sometimes slept deeply, and they witnessed those periods when he needed a break and a place to go to get away from it all. At times he was troubled, at other times he was sad to the point of tears, and, at least on one occasion, he became very angry. For those first disciples, Jesus' humanity was never in question.

What was in question for them was the *significance* of this human being. They knew him as a "self," and they witnessed his remarkable interactions with themselves and others. Their experience raised for them the question, "Who can this be?" For in his presence, and in his words and his deeds, they found a window to the Spirit, to God, and to God's relationship with humankind. So this question of "Who?" was not a simple one about his place of honor in the social world of the time. Rather, it was a question of ultimate importance to them concerning his transcendent significance for their lives, for Israel, and for humanity.

That question was always in the background when they were with him. After all, they had left everything to follow him. But their wondering became consciously inescapable following Jesus' resurrection appearances. The resurrection left them thoroughly convinced that his life and work did indeed have transcendent significance, though they would spend much time and energy seeking to understand that meaning. After much reflection, they would adapt and employ an array of transcendent metaphors that expressed their faith that the human being they had known by the name of Jesus was also truly divine.

We began the journey of this book by asking what it might mean to see the particular relationships that constitute the experience of one's own personal reality today through the eyes of Jesus, and through the eyes of those who first had faith in him. In Part I we saw how Jesus the human being viewed his primary relationships and how each of these revealed aspects of his remarkable perspective. In Part II we addressed how the transcendent metaphors used by the post-resurrection followers of Jesus illumined the understanding of those who had faith in him. In this chapter I will attempt to summarize and sharpen our focus on these two related views, and we will examine how, behind the obvious differences between them, reality as viewed by Jesus the human being, and reality as viewed by faith in Jesus as the Christ, represent two relevant ways of viewing the same reality. Finally, we will explore briefly the implications of the Jesus Christ reality for lives of faith today.

Seeing Reality through the Eyes of Jesus

Jesus consciously defined the centerpiece of his own existence in terms of his relationship to the God of his experiential understanding. Yahweh, the God of his heritage, the Creator and Holy One, whose Name was sacred, was revealed to him as the intimate, personal, compassionate *Abba*, his spiritual

Father, and, at the same time, as the spiritual Parent of all humankind. Jesus experienced himself as radically loved by *Abba,* possessed by *Abba's* spirit, sustained by *Abba's* daily care, and guided by *Abba's* direction. This revelation and spiritual experience defined Jesus' relationship to human existence. And this relationship with *Abba* shaped his understanding of reality as inclusive of world and spirit, and the reality of all neighbors and their needs.

Reality as World and Spirit

To be oriented to reality in much contemporary thought, and in modern "realism" particularly, is to recognize the secular world, a world without "spirits," as the only existing world. Jesus, on the other hand, approached this world with at least as much seriousness as the most dedicated modern "realist" would today. Yet his attitude toward this world was neither that of a cynic nor a pragmatist, for Jesus was a person of the Spirit who perceived the world not only through his physical senses, but also with his spiritual eyes. Reality, for Jesus, was both world and Spirit.[1]

Jesus was up against what every human being was and is up against. He felt the serenity of seeing beautiful lilies in a field, and the pain of being pierced by thorns. He enjoyed the pleasure of aromas and tastes, and knew the discomforting conflict between bodily desire and social norms. He experienced the joy of weddings and feasts, and the humiliation of rejection and ridicule. He was comforted by the companionship of friends, and stressed by disagreements with his family. He found meaning in helping others, and was shamed by his enemies. And he faced the reality and certainty of his own death with the same anxieties that afflict all normal, life-loving human beings.

Human beings across time and cultures are confronted by the same mysteries of existence.[2] They are driven to secure their lives, yet are never able to do so. They are compelled to seek happiness, but moments of joy always pass. They desire to fulfill their obligations, but are continually missing

1. This statement is admittedly dualistic in that reality is said to consist of two dimensions, world and Spirit. But it also speaks of *one unified reality* that is inclusive of world and Spirit. From the perspective of the Jesus Reality it is spiritual blindness that tends to separate world from Spirit.

2. In this discussion of the mysteries of human existence I am indebted to an essay by Rudolf Bultmann (1955b) titled "The Crisis of Faith."

the mark amidst the ambiguities and competing duties of life. They long to be loved and appreciated, yet find themselves ultimately alone in their struggle with life and with death. They want to achieve something significant with their lives, yet even the most successful accomplishments in this world eventually become dust.

Jesus understood the mysterious realities of human longings, desires, and impulses toward duty as arenas where *Abba* manifests his loving care for his children. It is God who provides daily bread. It is God who bestows those special moments of joy. It is God who kindles love and devotion in human hearts. It is God who summons human beings to do what is good and never to neglect their duty to others. It is God who places the desire within human beings to do something meaningful and significant with their lives and fills their hearts with dreams.

And, yet, it is also God, as *Abba*, who establishes the boundaries that limit all those realities toward which human beings are driven. It is God who, in his mysterious love, guarantees that human beings cannot secure their futures, nor cause their moments of joy to last. It is God who assures that each human being ultimately must face his or her own death as a solitary being. It is God who has provided the voice of conscience that declares one "guilty" in the midst of the competing duties and responsibilities of one's life. It is God who makes life the way it is, with all its difficulties, and death the inescapable reality all must face.

For Jesus, "life as it is" was always a gift of *Abba*. As such, it was not to be denied or escaped, but to be embraced and lived robustly and with passion. The desert ascetics chose life-denying escape from the world through self-denial, rites of water purification, and apocalyptic fantasies. The Pharisees, while primarily focused on the issue of faithfulness to God in the world, clung to the illusions of certitude and personal purity through a legalism that attempted to avoid the realities of ethical ambiguities and human responsibility. The Zealots falsely believed that being God's chosen people assured that they could overcome the technology and military superiority of the Roman occupiers and usher in a new era of peace and independence. Even the disciples of Jesus, many of them social "nobodies," shared faulty dreams of worldly deliverance from their humble limitations in this life and trumped-up delusions of their own impending grandeur.

Each of these groups failed in differing ways to face reality and to accept "the way life is." Jesus, appropriating and innovatively reinterpreting the monotheism of his heritage, understood that refusal to accept "the way life is" was rebellion toward God as *Abba*.[3] To attempt to deny, escape, or defy "the way life is" was to miss the life for which one was created. That is why Jesus left the desert to carry out his ministry in the oasis of Galilee. And that is why Jesus did not run away and hide in the wilderness when he was faced with the inevitability of his death.

Jesus, as the revelation of what it means to be authentically human, demonstrated in his own life the possibilities for facing the reality of this world with honesty and courage. But Jesus did more than *face* reality. Jesus *embraced* reality. Reality was not simply "the way life is," those things he was up against in life and those circumstances that would ultimately take his life. Reality was "the way life is as *good*," as the gift of the Father.

The goodness of God's creation was transparent to Jesus as one who perceived in his vision of reality the activity of the Spirit in the midst of this world.[4] Through the eyes of his own faith, grounded in his own most personal experience, Jesus could see signs of the Spirit all about him. When he

---

3. The thoughtful reader may wonder at this point about the relationships among sin, evil, and "the way life is." While this is not the place for a systematic discussion of these relationships, a few brief comments may be in order. "The way life is" is understood by biblical faith to be God's good creation. But that faith also understands that "the way life is" has been corrupted by sin. Yet it is precisely "this good universe that has been corrupted by sin" that God is seeking to redeem and transform in Christ, who embraced those burdened by sin and who expended his life on their behalf. To enter the reality of Jesus, as the Ultimate Reality, is to be lucid about the corruption of the self and the world, yet, at the same time, to view that same self and world as radically loved by God. It is to acknowledge the depth of one's own sin, to surrender oneself to the process of transformation, and to become an instrument for change in the world that conforms to the reality of Christ. As one cannot change what one does not acknowledge, one cannot be an effective instrument for the transforming of humankind unless one is willing to see evil, and, at the same time, to see and trust with the eyes of faith the even greater reality that God is at work in the world turning that evil into good, and that the ultimate victory over evil is sure. To experience spiritual transformation in Christ, then, is to be given the grace to view each situation, no matter how it has been shaped by evil, as a gift from God and as an opportunity for service.

4. One does not have to accept the cosmology of the first century to see the spiritual activity of a Higher Power in the midst of everyday life. And one does not have to attribute disease to demons to see the struggle between cruel evil and compassionate good as a spiritual struggle. One does not have to have any particular map of the universe or the spirit world to experience the reality that relationships are by their very nature spiritual and that there is more to existence than that which can be experienced with the five senses. One may choose to embrace the prevailing cosmology of one's own time and through the eyes of faith still appropriate Jesus' understanding of the presence and power of transcendent reality in the midst of the observable world.

344

saw flowers blooming in a field, or birds flying through the air, or a lifeless sparrow on the ground, he was struck with the awesome reality of God's amazing care for each of his creatures. When it came to his attention that a poor widow had finally gotten justice from a corrupt judge who tired of her persistent efforts to get a favorable verdict, Jesus concluded that if this unjust judge showed mercy for all the wrong reasons, how much more can human beings count on their Spiritual Father, who alone is good, to show compassion toward those in need? When Jesus saw mustard weeds growing in a field of grain, or a woman making a loaf of bread, he also perceived the quiet miraculous activity of God's Spirit already being in charge in the world and the assurance of God's victory over evil.

For Jesus, the presence and power of the Spirit in this world was something he perceived and experienced every day. And because he lived and moved and had his being in that reality, he could speak with great clarity not only about the things of this world, but also about the things that cannot be seen with the eyes of the flesh. And because he always viewed the reality of this world as a world loved by *Abba*, whose care for the creatures of the earth was constantly transparent, everything in this world was a window to the world of the Spirit.

Reality as the Neighbor Loved by God

In Jesus' view of reality, there was no clearer manifestation of spiritual transparency than when a person encountered a neighbor in need. Jesus did not see his neighbors as human objects, but as *Abba*'s children. Jesus' relationships with the disabled, the destitute, and the despised disclosed not only a compassionate person, but one who viewed social outcasts and victims of discrimination and ridicule as being in reality spiritual beings, worthy of honor as children of God. Even Jesus' enemies among the religious leaders and the governing authorities were to be loved and forgiven, for they too were *Abba*'s children.

As we have seen, conventional social and religious beliefs often make a distinction between neighbors and non-neighbors. Non-neighbors may include foreigners, enemies, and unbelievers along with those who are social or religious outcasts. Most people agree that one is certainly to love one's neighbor, but they also believe that it is perfectly acceptable not to love, or even to hate, one's non-neighbors. Jesus would have no part in such distinctions.

For the most part, those who lived at the outer margins of society were ignored and invisible to those not personally affected by their suffering. But Jesus refused to divert his eyes in horror or disgust, or to pretend that suffering people do not exist in order to evade responsibility for them. He allowed his eyes to see the pain and misery of the world around him, even when others preferred to look away. He was willing to see a tormented psychotic, bruised and bleeding from self-injury among the tombs of a cemetery. He did not shut his ears to the desperate cries of blind and deaf beggars. Nor did he shrink back from touching an untouchable leper covered with putrid sores. He saw these suffering neighbors, and his heart filled with compassion and empathy. He reached out to them, and touched their diseased bodies. And, gifted healer that he was, he alleviated a great deal of suffering among the people of his land.

Jesus was also a gifted physician of the soul. He could look into the hearts of his fellow human beings and grasp their fundamental human struggles. He could see their indifference, their self-deceptions, the shame they tried to hide from the world, and the guilt that made them miserable. He could detect when they were losing their struggles to overcome their old destructive ways of living. He could see through their ludicrous attempts to enhance their own pride, their self-esteem, at the expense of others. And he could see the problem behind all these struggles of their souls.

The eyes of Jesus saw that the fundamental human problem, behind all other problems, was estrangement from God as *Abba*. The self could not know genuine peace, or find the blessedness of life for which it was created, until it was restored to its intended station as a beloved child of God. So Jesus' mission was always an evangelical one. But his evangelism was not a cynical effort to recruit followers and build an exclusive group, as frequently has happened with evangelists throughout history. The evangelism of Jesus was designed to address the fundamental relationship between his hearers and God.

Jesus understood that effectively addressing people's relationship with God required courage. He knew that love demanded that he call people's lives into question when they were missing the purposes for which they had been created. It meant that sometimes it was necessary to unveil the secrets of people's hearts and to address their character defects.

Jesus did not draw back from pointing out the hidden, self-centered motives that prevented his disciples from genuinely understanding the mission to which they were called. He did not hesitate to challenge those who lived in self-deception about their own righteousness. But as "tough" as this love sometimes was, it was not motivated by a desire to harm followers who could not seem to get discipleship right, or even to condemn his misguided critics. Even the despots, who were in the grip of cruel evil, were *Abba's* children and were entitled to Jesus' prophetic witness as an opportunity to turn from their spiritually rebellious and cruel ways.

Jesus understood that God did not desire any of his children to perish. He did not want to abandon them to a path of spiritual self-destruction. That is why Jesus was not an enabler.[5] That is why his compassion was never a shallow sentimentality. It was never permission for people to continue to do whatever they pleased, or to remain self-pitying victims of misfortune. Neither was it approval for people to persist in their attitudes of superiority toward others. It was out of authentic compassion that he challenged the worldly ambitions of his disciples, and out of genuine love that he criticized the self-righteousness of the Pharisees. He would deliver a prophetic word to those needing to be challenged, not in order to destroy them, but in order to offer them an opportunity to repent and be changed.

But that was not by any means the end of the matter. Recognition of one's estrangement from God was not an end in itself, but a prerequisite for experiencing forgiveness and restoration as children of the Father. Jesus' mission was not one of condemnation, but of forgiveness. When he encountered neighbors who were heavily burdened by their consciousness of spiritual and ethical failures, Jesus was swift to pronounce absolution. When he saw genuine repentance, he affirmed such spiritual honesty and declared salvation. And in doing so, he opened the door to a new and trusting relationship of child to *Abba*. He offered them transformed lives.

It was in this mission of inviting his neighbors to enter the reign of the Father that Jesus expended his life. Jesus ultimately would lay down his life for everyone, because the reality in which he understood his mission and purpose made no distinctions about who was worthy of his sacrifice. All were unworthy because of sin. But of far greater importance was the reality that all were God's greatly loved children.

---

5. The term *enabler* in this context is used similarly to the way it is used in twelve-step addiction programs where it refers to friends and family who, through misguided efforts to be kind, "enable" an addict to continue in addiction rather than taking the tough action the addict genuinely needs from them.

Seeing Jesus through the Eyes of Faith

Whenever an event of overwhelming importance in people's lives occurs, they immediately begin the struggle to find ways to conceptualize, understand, and make sense of it. They do this in order to know how to relate to it, what attitude to take toward it, how to cope with it and adapt to it. The resurrection was a momentous event that overwhelmed and transformed the lives of all who experienced it. It is not surprising that the disciples looked to the powerful metaphors and images of their religious history in order to appropriate this remarkable event into their consciousness and their relationships with God and neighbors.

By using the transcendent metaphors available to them, they not only clarified for themselves the significance of Jesus, they also reshaped the meaning of the metaphors themselves. To call Jesus the Messiah, for example, identified key elements of the significance of his life and work for Israel and humankind. But because Jesus was a Messiah contrary to expectations, the understanding of "Messiah" itself was altered in the process. The Messianic metaphor was no longer defined only by the tradition from which it came. The Messianic title would forever after be defined by Jesus, by the life he lived and the death he died. Christ and Jesus became, for the community of faith, inseparably linked in meaning. The same can be said for the metaphors of the Word, the Lamb of God, Savior, Lord, and all the symbolic expressions that became titles for Jesus. For Jesus was both the judgment of God on the expectations implied in the old symbols, and the authentic fulfillment of the primordial longing expressed in those images that God had placed in all human hearts.

Jesus as the Fulfillment of Human Longing

As we have seen, the hope for a Messiah can be understood as a concrete manifestation of the hopes of peoples in all cultures and eras. Faith came to realize that the universal longing for a hero had been revealed in Jesus as both illusion and fulfillment. To the degree that the universal hero, or the cultural Messiah, was an expression of the desire for rescue from "the way life is" so that human beings can have life on their own terms, Jesus is the "No" of God. To the extent that the universal hero myth is an immature fantasy of those who have an illusion of entitlement, and refuse to take responsibility for their

348

own lives, Jesus is the revelation of God's judgment. To those who live in such illusions, Jesus is not the one they are looking for, while those who have faith in him understand that there is no one else who is coming.

To the degree, however, that the longing for a universal hero is a yearning for authentic human existence, Jesus is seen by the eyes of faith as the fulfillment of that longing. Paul exhorted the Philippians to have the same mind, the same attitude toward life, as did Christ Jesus.[6] Mark pointed to Jesus as the model of what it means to live and die courageously and faithfully in times of persecution. Matthew presented Jesus as the instructor and exemplar of genuine discipleship, of radical obedience to God, and of mission to the world. Luke portrayed Jesus as the prototype of inclusiveness, compassion, and mercy. And John not only dramatized Jesus through the words of Pilate as "the man," he disclosed Jesus to be the revealer of what it means to be human. For John's Jesus is the Word of God. That Word of God brings every creature into being, and discloses that what it means to realize one's authentic humanity is to live in the light and in the reality of a world that is loved by God.

The longing for a universal hero also is the recognition of the limitations of human beings, their estrangement from their true nature and place in the universe, their tragic condition as living at enmity with the Creator and as having need for divine intervention. Faith understands that Jesus is the fulfillment of that longing as well.

Jesus as the Savior from Sin

To understand what it means to be human in the light of Jesus as the Christ is to see oneself as one who has "missed the mark," as one who lives in alienation from the origin and aim of one's existence, from that which brought one into being. Sometimes this alienation comes to light as denial of the possibilities of life. Some people, for example, consider themselves to be helpless victims in this world, and make excuses to justify their failure to live authentically. In Jesus' homeland, many of the disabled and destitute appear to have had the self-image of a victim.[7] Whether persons see themselves as victims of physical limitations, of neighborly neglect and abuse, of social conventions, of economic circumstances, or of cruel fate, the Jesus Christ

---

6. Phil. 2:5.

7. John 5 makes this explicit in the dialogue between Jesus and the paralytic by the pool.

Word bursts their illusions of self-doubt, of helplessness and hopelessness, and calls them to the possibilities inherent in a new life.

For others, however, in light of the sacrificial and generous nature of Jesus the Christ, this alienation from authentic existence is manifested as that of a predator. There is exposed within every human being a latent beast looking for opportunities to use others for its own benefit. For some persons, as was true of the tax collectors and despots in Jesus' day, the predator is manifested in obvious ways that are overtly cruel and vicious. For others, as was true for many of the religious authorities and landowning aristocrats in the first century, it is manifested in socially sanctioned forms of exploitation and self-serving at the expense of others. Even those who understand themselves to be victims become predators, when they seek to use their neediness as a means to gain unwarranted sympathy and benefits from others. Whatever the manifestation, in light of the one who became the self-emptying servant, the Christ, the Son of God, whose sacrifice was for every sin of every human being, the evil within human hearts has been exposed.

But to see oneself in light of Jesus as the Christ is not only to see the darkness within, but also to see oneself immersed in a world that is in disobedience to God, and as both a willing and unwilling participant in that disobedience. It is willing participation because each human being makes choices that violate conscience. It is unwilling participation because the world into which people come is a world that already has accommodated itself to the fact that all are sinners and that we live in a world full of "hearts of darkness." And to live in such a world is to live in ambiguity, to be frequently forced in this world and this life to choose not between good and evil, but between the lesser and the greater of evils.

The human condition, the struggle with sin and with the pervasive and persistent presence of evil in this world, has birthed a longing within humankind for divine intervention and deliverance. The heart cries out, "What a wretched human being I am! Who will rescue me from this body of death?"[8] When the consciousness of sin has created the awareness of spiritual imprisonment, one becomes desperate for deliverance.

The good news of Jesus Christ is that God has heard the cry of God's children, and has responded with saving intervention. The crucifixion of the Christ, the Son of God, is, for faith, an act of God's extravagant mercy. Christ died for the sins of the world, and in that death God was reconciling the sin-

8. Rom. 7:24.

ful world unto himself. And for a person of faith to believe that Christ died for his or her particular sins is to understand oneself as both culpable in that death and unworthy of that sacrifice. To accept God's Christ as the crucified one is to know oneself to stand before God, stripped of all pretensions and all claims of merit and all justifications for the way one has lived one's life.

Consequently, to experience the Jesus Christ event in one's own life is to experience the destruction of all reasons for boasting. The trumped-up self-images of entitlement and importance that are pervasive at every social level of society are revealed in Jesus Christ to be illusions. They are manifestations of the pride that separates people from God and neighbor. To know Christ is to know that those lies and half-truths about the self, which have provided human and social justification for one's existence in the world, have been forever penetrated and exposed. As the first converts were baptized naked, the state of their first birth, so Christ's coming into people's lives rips off the fig leaves of their self-deceit, so that they must stand uncovered before God and reveal themselves as the flawed, broken, inadequate, and sinful persons that they are.[9] But the miracle of Christ's coming is that the very life that is exposed is revealed to be the life that is loved and accepted by God.

To live "in Christ" is to live *in faith* as made possible and defined by Jesus Christ. It is to live one's life in the reality of the grace of God, rather than the illusions of one's own merits. It is to have one's spiritual eyes opened, to view oneself and the world with transformed eyes. When, for example, one sees through the eyes of faith, it becomes possible to grasp the spiritual meaning of the powerful emotional experiences of one's life. One is able to understand fear, fascination, joy, sorrow, love, anger, emptiness, exhilaration, and overwhelming awe, not simply as psychological dynamics within oneself, but as spiritual connections with God, with the universe, and with every human being. One learns to allow oneself to be sensitive to a Spiritual presence, at the birth of a child, the death of a parent, and at every life transition. One comes to understand one's personal talents, creativity, inspiration, and serendipity as gifts of the Spirit. And one grasps that within every accident and coincidence there is Spiritual guidance. A person is even able to see those dark nights of the soul that come to each human being as Spiritual

---

9. It is likely that most persons wore linen robes without any undergarments and removed their clothes for baptism. See Mark 14:51, where a follower of Jesus escaped naked from those who arrested Jesus by leaving his garment behind. That baptism was undergone while naked is widely accepted among scholars.

passages. And one becomes open to receiving the care and guidance that God's Spirit offers each day. *In faith* one is able to trust God for one's salvation, to trust God with one's care, to trust God with one's future.

To live "in Christ" is also to live *in hope*. It is to rely on the Lordship of Christ in the "now," despite all appearances to the contrary. And it is to rely on the reality that the future belongs to Christ, and that he is the hope that will not disappoint. To live "in Christ" is to live and act in the "now" as one who knows and trusts that the spiritual forces of evil in this world will be defeated, and that all will be held accountable according to the standard of judgment revealed in Christ. It is to live in the "now" as one who is immersed in the difficulties and challenges of this world, but as one whose true identity belongs to God's reign, to eternity.

To live "in Christ" in the "now" of this world is also to live *in love*. It is to live in the reality of God's love, and to be a loving spirit among all others. Love is the greatest of God's spiritual gifts. Love is an attitude toward life and others, and a style of living in which envy, boasting, pride, rudeness, selfishness, and resentments have no place.[10] It is a way of living in this world that sees and relates to every other human being as one whom God loves and for whom Christ has died. To love one's brother or sister is to live in the light, but to hate one's brother or sister is to expose that one still lives in darkness.[11] Love is defined by Jesus Christ, who laid down his life for humankind. Love comes from God, and that love makes possible genuine love for others who live in the reality of God's love.[12]

For the first-century Jesus movement, the Jesus Reality was not just one reality among many. For their pagan neighbors, reality consisted of many competing realities, personified in the pantheon of the gods. There were gods of weather, of wine, of erotic love, of grain, of music, of war, of disease, of earthquakes, and of any other perceived power experienced by human beings. It was common to pick and choose among them, according to one's personal needs at the time. But for the Jesus movement, grounded in monotheistic Judaism, there was only one way, one truth, and one life. Jesus was the pathway to the Father, the revelation of what is real, and the transforming power making possible authentic and eternal life. For faith, there was only *one* reality, the Jesus Reality. And the Jesus Reality was Ultimate Reality.

---

10. 1 Cor. 13:4-5.
11. 1 John 2:9-10.
12. 1 John 4:7-11.

The Faith *of* Jesus and Faith *in* Jesus as One Reality

Modern biblical scholarship long has distinguished between the Jesus of history and the Christ of faith.[13] This work has employed this distinction as a means of clarifying which words of the texts likely provide historical information about Jesus, and which ones speak to his transcendent significance, addressing the former in Part I and the latter in Part II. My separation of what traditionally has been referred to as the Jesus of history and the Christ of faith, however, has been a decision based less on the presuppositions of contemporary historical critical methodologies than on theological concerns.

The continued quest for the historical Jesus is important for faith because there is an ever-present tendency within the Christian community toward minimizing or even denying Jesus' full humanity. This problem was no stranger to the early church, as debates concerning Docetic and Apollinarian thinking about Jesus illustrate.[14] Docetism believed Jesus to be divine, but not a human being. Apollinarians also believed that Jesus was divine but believed that he was only partly human. Despite the decisive formulation of the Council of Chalcedon in 451 CE, affirming the full humanity *and* the full divinity of Jesus, the tendency has been persistent. Though fraught with difficulties, contemporary historical scholarship has emerged as a potent tool for countering the tendency of much popular Christianity to overemphasize the divinity and undermine the humanity of Jesus.

On the other hand, there also is an ever-present tendency, within our contemporary secular and pluralistic society, toward seeing Jesus as a very great and inspired human being, but as only a human being. For many outside the church and at the margins of the church today, Jesus is seen as an important and even decisive figure in Western civilization, but also as a very human man, limited by his culture and times, whose relevance today is confined to a few ethical principles that have inspired humanity. A similar view

13. The distinction has its roots in eighteenth-century philosophy and the terms are usually traced to D. F. Straus's critique of Schleiermacher's lectures on "The Life of Jesus" in 1865 titled "The Christ of Faith and the Jesus of History."

14. Docetism, an early Christian heresy that probably was present in the late first century CE and that came to prominence in the second century CE, held that Jesus only "seemed" to be human, but was not actually flesh, nor did he die on the cross. The Gnostics were proponents of Docetism, believing that the eternal Savior from the highest heaven only appeared to become flesh in order to share the secret knowledge of salvation. Apollinarism was a fourth-century heresy that held that Jesus had a physical body but a divine mind.

was held by the Ebionites in early church history.[15] The contemporary view, however, not only denies the divinity of Jesus, but also has employed, on occasion, the historical critical method as a polemical weapon for discrediting traditional Christian beliefs.

So, while the tools of modern scholarship can assist in the affirmation of Jesus' humanity, they may be misused to throw doubt on Jesus' divinity. It is a misuse, because the divinity of Jesus is outside the scope of such method. It has been the presupposition of this book that historical scholarship, using agreed upon methods, can be valuable in assisting with recovering important understandings about the human being Jesus. But such scholarship can clarify only who Jesus was as a human being; it cannot speak to the claims of faith. For the truth of faith is not empirical truth but the truth of decision and commitment.

Scholars who have debated the relationship between the Jesus of history and the Christ of faith largely have focused on the issue of Messianic consciousness.[16] Continuity or discontinuity appeared to ride on the question of whether Jesus thought himself to be the Christ, and if so, what he meant by that term. Was Jesus' view of the Messiah that of a human being called to a role in history, or was it in any way consistent with the notion of divinity? While the Messianic consciousness question is a relevant one, it is not the only way to approach the issue of continuity. What we have done in this work is to raise the question as one of continuity between Jesus' view of reality and the reality orientation of those who believed him to be the Christ, the Son of God. Within this approach Messianic consciousness is an important issue only to the degree that it informs Jesus' comprehensive view of reality.

On the surface, there are obvious differences between the Jesus of history and the Christ of faith. Jesus preached about the kingdom of God; the early missionaries preached that Jesus was the Christ, the Son of God. Jesus' primary relationship was a deeply personal and intimate relationship with *Abba,* while the missionaries spoke primarily of their new life "in Christ." Jesus spoke in parables and short pithy sayings about the nature of *Abba's*

15. The Ebionites were a second-century CE community (continuing into the fourth century) who rejected claims of Jesus' divinity, lived lives of asceticism, and believed that only those who had taken up a life of poverty would be saved.

16. The current debate, in which Crossan, Borg, and Funk are in the camp of those who have concluded that Jesus did not consider himself to be the Messiah, while Wright, Fredrickson, and Ehrman are spokespersons for those who do, reflects a longstanding discussion about the relationship between the Jesus of history and the Christ of faith.

reign. The post-resurrection faithful preached the *kerygma,* a message of a savior of humankind with a divine beginning, a descent to earth, a servant existence, a sacrificial death, a resurrection, an ascent to heaven, an exaltation, and a future coming. Jesus appears humbly to have denied any claim to be a good person, while the New Testament community declared Jesus to be without sin. Jesus went throughout his homeland healing the sick and pronouncing forgiveness of sins. The apostles went throughout the known world healing in Jesus' name and preaching the grace of God in his sacrifice on the cross. Jesus spoke of the last judgment as being decided by the way one treats the neighbors in greatest need. The apostles preached about a divide between those who believed in Jesus and those who rejected him. Jesus appears to have been primarily focused on discipleship as realization of the relationship between *Abba* and *Abba's* children in this era. The New Testament missionaries appear to have been preoccupied with the life of faith as preparation for the end times and the world to come.

Upon a closer look, however, these differences are not as significant as they might first appear. Some of these variances are more a matter of cultural translation than of substance, and of differing emphasis based on social context and historical roles. Preaching in the Aramaic language in his homeland of Galilee and around the Temple of Judea, Jesus brought a message of the kingdom that was a Messianic message. As I suggested in Part I, it probably was a message in which Jesus saw himself as a Messiah contrary to expectations, announcing and demonstrating that God was already in charge, and declaring that the day was coming when all things would be made right. When the apostles declared Jesus to be a crucified Messiah, they were also proclaiming him, as the crucified Christ, to be a Messiah contrary to expectations, and as the risen and exalted one, to be the divine manifestation of God's present and future victory over the forces of evil. To speak of forgiveness of sins on the one hand, and the grace of God as demonstrated in the death of the one who in life declared and mediated that forgiveness, on the other, are not to speak of two differing realities. To speak of the final judgment as a verdict based on a life of compassion is consistent with saying that Jesus, the one who spoke those words and demonstrated them with his life, is the judge of humankind.

This question of the relationship between the faith of Jesus and faith in Jesus can best be stated as one in which the reality that is revealed in the historical Jesus is, at its foundation, the same reality as that proclaimed by those who first had faith in him. The study of Jesus the human being as a self in relationship has revealed a view of reality that the early church declared to be the *Ultimate Reality*. It was Jesus the human being who had disclosed in his life with the disciples his transcendent significance. It was a significance confirmed in his resurrection and by the Holy Spirit. But there were not two different selves, the Jesus *before*, and the Jesus *after* the resurrection. It was Jesus the human being, whom they had known to be fully human, who was revealed to them to be the Son of God. While the rational doctrinal formulation would not occur for centuries, the apostolic community experientially knew that Jesus, their fully human brother, had been revealed to them as fully divine.

The faith *of* Jesus is one of trust in the goodness of the Father. Faith *in* Jesus is one of trust in the authenticity of the revelation of God's goodness. The faith *of* Jesus is one in which compassion trumps all rules and overcomes all barriers that pride and status create among human beings. Faith *in* Jesus is a life in which grace frees from the bondage of the Law, love is the greatest of spiritual gifts, and there is no distinction between male and female, or among those from varying ethnic backgrounds. The faith *of* Jesus is the realization that human beings are accountable for the way in which they treat the least of their neighbors. Faith *in* Jesus is the realization that Jesus the compassionate one, who gave himself in ministry to the disabled, the destitute, and the despised, is the judgment criteria upon which all will be held accountable. The faith *of* Jesus is one in which hope for God's ultimate victory is assured by the Spirit who is everywhere present and at work in the world. Faith *in* Jesus is the assurance of his resurrection that Jesus is Lord, who currently is present and at work in the world, and who ultimately will prevail over all evil. Faith declares that the Jesus Reality is one reality. And more than that, the Jesus Reality is Ultimate Reality.

The reality of the faith *of* Jesus and the reality of the faith *in* Jesus form a unified whole. Their relationship is not unlike the symbol of yin and yang in Eastern spiritual philosophy.[17] They struggle with each other as opposites, while a portion of each is found in the other. And, as they struggle, it is vitally important for those who participate in the reality to which they point, that the complementary opposites be kept in balance or restored to balance when they are out of kilter.

When the divinity of Jesus takes a back seat to his humanity in one's

17. See Smith (1966) for a clear discussion of the traditional Chinese yin and yang symbolism.

thinking, and Jesus is reduced to one gifted human being among others, one is in danger of failing to understand the depth of one's own estrangement from God, of the urgency of salvation, and of the radical nature of the Lordship of Christ over one's life and the world. When the role of Jesus the human being is reduced and even lost in one's thinking, because of a preoccupation with the presence and power of the eternal Christ to save from sin and death, there is likewise a danger that one will fail to grasp the true nature of that salvation, of the total transformation of one's humanity, and of the new life to which one is called in that saving event. Consequently, affirming the full humanity and full divinity of Jesus, while maintaining a balanced relationship between the Jesus of history and the Christ of faith is not simply a matter of good theology. It is essential for the life of faith, a life lived in the Jesus Christ Reality.

The Jesus Christ Reality and the Life of Faith

To be confronted by the claim that the Reality of Jesus is the Ultimate Reality is to encounter a decision about one's life. In the postmodern world, the Jesus Reality might be seen by many as one choice among a number of other ways one might view reality. In much contemporary thought, it is axiomatic that one cannot objectively establish one construct of reality as any better than another. Consequently, it is assumed that one could never prove that the Jesus Reality is Ultimate Reality. And this is true, as far as it goes, but this should not surprise us. Both Jesus and the apostolic community understood clearly that only faith is able to see and respond to the gospel. For the recognition of the Jesus Reality as Ultimate Reality is, and always has been, a matter of faith and faith alone, and not of evidential proof and rational certitude.

Yet that recognition should not obscure the equally true realization that the choice of what we consider to be "ultimate reality" for us truly matters. It is, quite urgently, a matter of life and death. For life demands a decision about which of the competing notions of reality one is going to live before. Which of the competing views is going to orient one's life, provide it meaning, purpose, and significance? Which reality is one to wager with one's existence to be true?

And this is no small decision. If one considers the competing versions of reality proclaimed by the cynic, the hedonist, the ascetic, and the Gnostic, to name only a few, it is obvious that the choice one makes, and commits to as one's own ultimate reality, makes a profound difference in the way in which one lives one's unique and unrepeatable life. And the collective impact of all personal commitments to varying constructs of "reality" also is no small matter. One lives and commits to future generations a world shaped by such "leaps of faith."

Furthermore, those other competing constructs do not lend themselves to proof any more than the Jesus Reality does. They, too, require faith. To assume that "reality," for example, is only about pleasure and pain, and that the purpose of life is to get as much pleasure as possible, may seem like an easy decision for some, but it also requires an ultimate commitment that takes for granted that this is a better way to be, and to expend one's life, than any other way. Such a decision must be made on faith, for there is no way objectively to prove it to be a truly authentic choice about one's existence in the world, although thoughtful persons probably will think of quite a few reasons to doubt the wisdom of such a lifestyle.

The person who takes life and such choices seriously might ask, "Is the leap of faith a leap into total darkness? Or is there a way at least to make an educated leap of commitment?" Although it is impossible to know fully what is in store until a leap has been made, it is clear that one can at least "look before one leaps," and one can consider the implications. This book has been written in part as an invitation to those seriously interested in taking a spiritual journey to "try on" the Jesus Reality, and to understand and consider what it might mean to commit oneself to that reality as Ultimate Reality.

To commit one's life to the Jesus Reality is far more than an intellectual undertaking. While the Reality of Jesus is a perspective, it is not a worldview in the sense of a particular cosmology or a body of doctrinal knowledge requiring assent. Rather, it is a Word that addresses our lives and speaks to our human condition. It demands that we examine our own hearts, take inventory of our human failings, and open our lives to forgiveness and grace. It breaks the illusions of our self-importance and self-reliance, and calls us to recognize the Spirit reality that already exists in our midst and already lives in our hearts. It lives in our hearts because the Christ Word is the universal Word that is present in the very creation, and thus in all experiences of finitude, and in all cultures and religions. It is already known to be the truth about "the way life is," at some level of our human consciousness. And this means that the leap of faith is not a leap into darkness but toward the light.

This leap of faith today is no different than the leap of faith taken by members of the Jesus movement in the first century. It is, as we have said, a leap into the reality of Jesus as the Ultimate Reality. It is the choice to live in the reality that God is for us, with us, and will never abandon us. And, it follows, to live in this reality is to live for those in need, with those in need, and never to abandon those in need. For the life of faith is not a life of good works in order to receive eternal life. It is a life that participates now, in anticipation of what is to come, in the eternal reality of God's love for this broken world and the pouring out of life in the ministry of reconciliation.

To live in the Jesus Reality is to die to all other constructs of reality, and to see them as illusions. It is to die to a life lived in defiance toward and estrangement from the origin and aim of existence. It is to die to self-will, the desire to have life on one's own terms and to use others for selfish means. And it is to be raised to new life, abundant and eternal, compassionate and self-giving. To live in the life of faith is to experience spiritual transformation, the resurrected life that lives in the Jesus Christ Reality.

For when Jesus is quoted in John's Gospel as saying, "I am the Resurrection and the Life," resurrection means far more than the past historical event and the hope of future salvation. Resurrection is a transcendent metaphor for a radical spiritual reality *in the present.* For the author of John's Gospel, Jesus and the life of faith are *one.* Jesus is the Way, the Truth, the Life, Abundant and Eternal. As Water, Bread, and Vine, Jesus is the amazing and awesome life-giving spiritual force of the universe. Jesus is the living Lord of history, and the personal Lord of those who live in his reality. It is Jesus' Spirit that is the Holy Spirit, the divine presence in the life of his people. He is the advocate, comforter, and friend of all who enter into relationship with him and his reality. To live in that reality is to live in that presence and to experience freedom, not as license, but as freedom fully to live life as it is, amidst all its difficulties, and genuinely to love and to expend one's life in responsible service to humankind.

Notes on Methodology

When teaching courses in the anthropology of religion, I have often begun a class by reciting a well-known nursery rhyme:

Humpty Dumpty sat on a wall.
Humpty Dumpty had a great fall,
And all the king's horses
And all the king's men
Couldn't put Humpty together again.

Then I would ask the class, "Is this story true?" Some students would look confused. Others, suspecting a trick question, would look suspicious. Still others complained that it was a ridiculous exercise. But there were students in every class who would respond by saying, "It depends on what you mean by *true*."

What often followed was a lively discussion of the possibility of the nursery rhyme being a coded story of an actual historical event, possibly involving the downfall of a king or prominent figure. The students could see in that case that it might represent a kind of historical truth. There would also be class discussion of an interpretation of the meaning of the story as a lesson about life, as in "Sometimes bad things happen and they cannot be undone." Students easily illustrated from their own experiences this reality. In this context the story represented existential truth, insight into "the way life is" for all of us.

Despite memories of the drawings that usually accompanied the nursery rhyme in children's books, no one argued that the story represented a literal event in which king's men and king's horses tried to reconstruct an anthropomorphic broken egg. The students understood that the narrative may not have been literally true, but it could be true nonetheless. As we explored during the semester the roles of myths and legends in various cultures, the point of the nursery rhyme discussion remained clear. Literal truth is only one kind of truth, and not necessarily the most interesting, useful, or relevant kind.

I. Differing Dimensions of Truth

What we mean by truth depends upon our context. Empirical truth is not the same as historical truth. Literary truth is not the same as literal truth. Existential truth is different from mathematical truth. Each type of truth has its own domain and its own criteria for validation. And each type of truth is primarily relevant within its own context. Of course, one kind of truth seeking can contribute to another type, as when DNA studies contribute to historical studies, or when historical fiction increases understanding of a previous era. But the search for truth often takes a wrong turn when it is assumed that the methods appropriate to determining what is true in one context can be applied to a very different realm. Whether it is the intrusion of theological method upon paleontology or the attempt to test religious belief in transcendent realities by the scientific method, there is a tendency of those who pursue a particular type of truth to extend their preferred method of truth seeking beyond its relevant boundaries.

One of the reasons the Bible represents an interesting interpretive challenge is that the text itself contains different types of statements intended to express different dimensions of truth. Of course, there are many statements in the Bible that were intended to describe historical events.[1] There are also many narratives and metaphors found in Scripture that were never intended by their originators as literal historical fact, but as expressions of the existential and spiritual truth of a transcendent faith.

1. Even these statements cannot be assumed on face value to be accurate representations of events, as the telling of such events may be shaped and reshaped over time in order to express existential and theological meaning. The establishment of probable facts by historians requires application of methods appropriate to the discipline of historical studies and a critical understanding of all historical texts as interpretive in nature.

It is important for those who study Scripture today to understand that the ancient writers did not conceive of truth in the modern scientific sense. They did not reduce all truth to facts supported by evidence obtained through rigorous methodologies, as many moderns do. Their faith, unlike the faith of some today, was not dependent upon a modern understanding of history. In contrast to the contemporary secular view, they assumed the reality of spiritual activity in the midst of historical events resulting in transcendent meaning.

Spiritual and transcendent realities by their very natures can only be articulated with the assistance of stories and metaphors grounded in human experience. Despite the obviousness of this point, many people, who would never understand Humpty-Dumpty as literal fact, think that a failure to assert the literal truth of all stories and images in the Bible is a failure of faith tantamount to sin. Furthermore, because they mistakenly think faith is a matter of intellectual belief in the factuality of such images, they often miss what faith is really all about. They are then hindered from authentically understanding, appropriating, and living their lives faithfully with regard to the transcendent and spiritual realities to which the narratives and metaphors are pointing.

That is why it is unfortunate that the study of the Bible over the centuries has often suffered from the failure to distinguish among literal fact, historical significance, existential meaning, and theological authenticity. And this confusion appears to remain equally true today for much of the reverent study that takes place in local churches on the one hand, and the critical examination of the Bible for the purpose of ridicule that occurs among secular skeptics on the other. Both have tended to create oversimplified caricatures of the faith witnessed by the biblical writers. It is a presupposition of this work that the Bible and the faith it discloses deserve to be studied with much greater seriousness.

II. Two Ways to Read the Bible

In general, there are two ways to read the Bible. The first is to read it critically as one would study any historical or literary set of materials. The second is to read it devotionally, as sacred writings through which transcendent truth is revealed. While academic and critical methods usually reside in university settings, devotional, or spiritual, interpretation has its home in churches and is the most common form of Bible study in local congregations. It is "spiritual" because it seeks the assistance of the Holy Spirit, usually within a community of faith, in disclosing the relevance of the sacred texts to the transcendent and relational concerns of those seeking to live by faith in the contemporary world.

Most academic scholars share the view that spiritual interpretation has no place in a literary, historical critical study of texts. For them, a spiritual hermeneutic is a particularly dangerous form of "bias" that seeks to establish facts and history not on the basis of evidence but on the basis of religious preconceptions and dogmas. Likewise, many church leaders and devotional students of the Bible are either oblivious to an academic approach, or see such critical efforts as threats to faith. For many, a literary and historical critical study is motivated by an attempt to undermine the authority and power of the Word of God, to reduce faith to superstition, and to subject believers to ridicule. Unfortunately, the suspicions on both sides have been demonstrated on many occasions to be well founded.

Nevertheless, both of these negative points of view are unacceptable to me. I share the concern of academics that religious beliefs should play no part in the establishment of historical facts.[2] I also share the criticism of faith communities that an interpretation of sacred texts that assumes any belief in spiritual reality to be an illusion is reductionistic and doomed to interpretive failure. It is important to remember that the critical methods can never disprove faith. Faith deals with matters that cannot be objectified, tested, and verified, or even expressed in probabilities. Likewise, for the same reason, faith can never prove itself by the establishment of probable historical facts. These two modes of understanding do not deal with the same types of "truth."

What I have attempted to do in this book is to employ critical and spiritual methods in a way that respects the rightful boundaries of each of these modes of understanding, while employing them in the search for a common goal. That goal has been the recovery of the full humanity of Jesus for our time using the scholarly methods discussed below, supplemented by the exploration of meaning from a faith perspective. What I have attempted to do is to seek to understand reality as the fully human Jesus understood and lived it and at the same time to ask the question of the relevance of that vision of reality for faith.

2. But faith can and should address the relative significance of those facts for believers.

III. Methods for Establishing Historical Probability

Historical method is not a hard science. Historical evidence is a matter of establishing historical probabilities along a continuum between that which probably did not happen and that which probably did. The historical methods appropriate to the establishment of the probable words, deeds, and relationships of Jesus include source criticism, form criticism, and redaction criticism and involve the application of generally accepted historical criteria for inclusion. Each of these methods utilizes a set of tools that have come to be more or less standard means for determining truth in the relevant contexts of their respective domains.[3]

Source Criticism

I have accepted the broad consensus in source criticism that there is little that can be relied upon for information about Jesus outside the New Testament Gospels.[4] The Dead Sea Scrolls provide useful information about the times, as does the work of the first-century historian Josephus. Aside from Josephus's confirmation that Jesus was a significant historical figure, there is no direct knowledge of Jesus available in those sources. The Gospel of Thomas and other non-canonical gospels and letters may in fact contain authentic fragments dating from Jesus, but their usefulness for that purpose is so controversial and limited that I have chosen not to rely upon them as historical sources in this book. It is the general consensus of most scholars that these works testify to the diversity within the church of the second century, but add little if anything to our knowledge of Jesus the human being.

---

3. The methods used in this work are widely recognized in scholarly circles. Much of this study of Jesus takes for granted broadly agreed upon conclusions arrived at by specialists far more qualified in these matters than I. Although in almost every instance there are interesting minority challenges to the prevailing opinions, I generally have chosen for practical purposes to embrace the majority views.

4. On the other hand, there are very respected scholars who have challenged this consensus. A number of members of the Jesus Seminar have embraced the Gospel of Thomas as a source alongside the canonical Gospels. Crossan (1991) is a particularly noteworthy example of newer scholars who rely significantly on sources not included in the New Testament writings, particularly using them to establish the principle of independent multiple attestation.

As for the Gospels themselves, I have accepted the broad scholarly consensus that Mark was the earliest Gospel, written between 65 and 75 CE. Matthew and Luke probably were written a decade or more later and relied heavily upon Mark for both structure and content. Matthew was likely written before Luke, but it is unlikely that Luke was familiar with Matthew. Matthew and Luke also used another common source that was probably a collection by the primitive church consisting of words of Jesus. That collection is referred to as Q, for *quelle*, a German word for "source." Q was probably written in the mid-50s CE. Matthew and Luke also appear to have had additional unique independent sources not used by Mark or one another. Matthew and Luke each adapted, edited, and created narratives to shape their sources for their own particular theological purposes, as Mark had done before them. The materials found in these three Synoptic Gospels are the texts that contain almost all of the useful information about the historical Jesus.

As for the Gospel of John, it probably was written between 90 and 100 CE, and the writer may have been familiar with Mark as well. Because of its late date and the overt theological style, John is seen by many scholars as containing limited useful information about the historical Jesus.[5] I have, however, assumed that it may be possible to decipher some earlier forms of narratives and sayings within the highly stylized Gospel of John that may support and enrich the picture of the historical Jesus derived from the Synoptic Gospels.

Paul, whose writings were earlier than any of these documents, with the possible exception of the hypothetical Q, is also a limited source for authentic material about Jesus. Only in a few important cases can we assume with confidence that Paul's writing indicates something that originated with "the Lord." However, it is reasonable to assume that Paul's very early message of grace was congruent with the message of Jesus about *Abba's* compassion.

Form Criticism

The units of text used in the composition of the Gospels had a history of transmission reaching back to an earlier and mostly oral period of develop-

---

5. Some find John's chronology of Jesus' ministry to be more likely than Mark's. While that is possible, I have remained unconvinced that it is possible to know which chronology, if either, is correct.

ment. Form criticism, as popularized by the New Testament scholar Rudolph Bultmann, is a type of literary criticism related to insights from the study of folklore.[6] Form critical methodology identifies and types the differing kinds of units of text. Types include miracle stories, parables, pithy sayings, and dialogues of challenge and response among other literary categories such as poetry, proverbs, and quotations. As folk studies have demonstrated, each type of material may be subject to patterns of memory and transmission over time. Some stories, for example, tend to change from their original forms during the transmission process to conform to culturally expected narrative patterns.[7] Hero stories tend to heighten the powers and accomplishments of the hero over time and parables and proverbs tend to change, particularly as to moral point, according to the circumstances in which they are transmitted and the relevant contextual issues faced at the time. By understanding these processes within their cultural context it is sometimes possible to approximate the form of such material in their original setting.

All of this is to say that form criticism approaches the texts as an archeologist would approach a dig. The assumption in the case of the Gospel passages is that Jesus may have spoken or done something in a particular context that was remembered and passed along orally. As these sayings and stories were handed down, the context of usage often changed and these historical materials were used by the primitive church to address new issues and problems. The materials were adapted in the process and "lessons" were often added to make them relevant to the circumstances at hand. Some stories about Jesus were heightened during the transmission process to express more dramatically his transcendent significance. Let me illustrate how I have employed form criticism in preparation for this book.

> Then Jesus told his disciples a parable to show them that they should always pray and not give up. *He said, "In a certain town there was a judge who neither feared God nor cared about men. And there was a widow in that town who kept coming to him with the plea, 'Grant me justice against my adversary.'*
>
> *For some time he refused. But finally he said to himself, 'Even though I don't fear God or care about men, yet because this widow keeps bothering*

6. See Bultmann (1934) and (1963).
7. See Propp (1968).

me, I will see that she gets justice, so that she won't eventually wear me out with her coming!'"

And the Lord said, "Listen to what the unjust judge says. **And will not God bring about justice for his chosen ones, who cry out to him day and night? Will he keep putting them off? I tell you, he will see that they get justice, and quickly.** However, when the Son of Man comes, will he find faith on earth?" (Luke 18:1-8)

Exegesis of such a passage depends on careful analysis of linguistic and contextual matters. But even the non-scholarly reader can easily be trained to see the possible layers in the story. At the core of this passage is the parable itself, indicated above by italics, that begins with "He said" and ends with the judge's statement about giving justice because the widow keeps bothering him. This is followed by an additional statement attributed to Jesus, "Listen to what the unjust judge says."[8]

This core unit was likely transmitted over several years with only the introduction of "Jesus said" or "He said" (as was evidently the case for much of what Jesus was reported to have spoken),[9] the story proper, and the conclusion consisting of the enigmatic charge to pay attention to the unjust judge. This is probably the entire story as it dates back to Jesus. If this was the original form of the parable, the question arises concerning what Jesus may have meant quite apart from what comes before and after this core material in the text.

It is easy to see that the focus of the parable without its surrounding interpretive comments is on the judge, not the widow. When examined in relation to Jesus' other parables and sayings about *Abba's* compassion for the destitute, the point is rather obvious. If such a hard-hearted judge can have mercy for all the wrong reasons, how much more does God show compassion on the destitute and needy?

What immediately follows the parable, in boldface type above, is a somewhat different message. It is an application of the parable that promises that God will hear those who are crying out to him and will soon give them justice. It is reasonable to speculate that this interpretive comment originated in the oral tradition during a time of persecution in the primitive church in which the final apocalypse that would set all things right was expected very soon.

8. The words "And the Lord said" are probably a literary construction of Luke.

9. The Gospel of Thomas uses this simple introduction many times without additional context.

What comes immediately before the core parable is a sentence that almost surely was written by Luke as a narrative introduction to the parable. The focus here is on the widow as an example to the faithful. This beginning sentence is an application of the parable suggesting that the purpose of the story was to encourage persistent prayer and hope. The final sentence in the passage, which challenges the reader with the question of whether, when the Son of Man comes, he will find faith on earth, is probably from Luke as well. It is consistent with Luke's stylistic peculiarities and it implies a delay in the "coming" of the Son of Man, in contrast to the imminent expectation implied in the verses that immediately precede the question. Together with his introductory sentence, it focuses on the widow's persistence as an example of persistent prayer and steadfastness in faith.

While certainty on any of these points is not achievable, such an analysis is consistent with the history of the transmission of folk material. In this case a core story is an emotionally charged memory passed to others devoid of any particular context. As the recipients of the tradition face new challenges over time, the story acquires interpretive statements of relevance. The Gospel writers continued this development by editing and adding interpretations to the material consistent with their own varying understandings of the gospel of Jesus.

Redaction Criticism

The study of the literary and theological composition and editing of the Gospels by their respective authors is called redaction criticism. By examining the narrative structure, the transitional language between units of text, and the ways in which the authors modified their sources, it is possible to identify a number of distinctive ways the evangelists shaped their works. Mark portrays Jesus as a misunderstood tragic hero facing danger and death with courage and faithfulness to God. For Matthew, Jesus is the new Moses who fulfills the Law and the Prophets and calls his followers to radical obedience and mission. Jesus, in Luke's Gospel, appears on the stage of world history as the compassionate Savior seeking out those who are lost. Other themes are present in these Gospels as well. In identifying the theological presuppositions of the authors and the literary techniques they used to convey them, light is thrown on the distinction between their work and the traditions upon which they relied, including the core material that probably dates back to Jesus.

Criteria for Establishing Authenticity

The archeological metaphor is useful in understanding the assumptions be-hind literary criticism because a typical "dig," as a Gospel literary unit, in-volves a number of levels. As we have seen, once this layering is understood, even a casual reader of the Gospels usually can begin to recognize likely stages of development. But even when the textual onionskin is peeled away, there can be no certainty that what was left originated with Jesus. For that determination, assumptions and criteria come into play.

Most scholars have general agreement on a few basic criteria that must be applied to those kernels of text that remain after the outer layers are peeled away. When any of these criteria are met there is an increased probability that the text authentically reflects a memory of the historical Jesus. When two or more of these criteria are met, the probability increases significantly.

The first such criterion states the commonsense notion that *the older the core text is determined to be, the more likely it approximately reflects something Jesus said or did.* A core text found in Q or in Mark is generally considered to be older than one uncovered in John. Most scholars today rely heavily on Q material and Markan texts for determining historical material since these sources precede the others. This does not, however, mean that narratives and sayings unique to Matthew or Luke, or the traditions behind the narratives in John's Gospel, must be ignored. It simply means that if such passages found in the later Gospels are to be used for the purposes of historical recon-struction, there is a greater need for the successful application of additional criteria and explanation.

The second criterion upon which most scholars agree is that of multi-ple independent attestations. This criterion means that *if two or more "in-dependent" sources contain approximately the same material, then the prob-ability of authenticity is increased. The more independent attestations, the greater are the probabilities of authenticity.*[10] For example, Mark does not appear to have been familiar with Q, or vice versa. Both Mark and Q sup-port the historical probability that Jesus was baptized by John, that he went into the wilderness to be tempted afterward, and that he began his

---

10. This criterion does not apply to those agreements where Matthew and Luke agree with Mark that are the result of the former two Gospels using Mark as a source. By defini-tion, Q is a single source and therefore agreements between Matthew and Luke cannot nec-essarily be seen as multiple independent attestations.

ministry soon after that. The probability of the historicity of that sequence of events is quite high.

The principle of multiple, independent attestations depends heavily on the results of source criticism. While Crossan and others have relied substantially on this principle, there are obvious limitations and problems in its application.[11] Those who find the Gospel of Thomas to be an early independent source of Jesus' sayings, for example, will find greater numbers of multiple attestations than those who see it as a late Gospel relying on one or more of the canonical writings.

The third widely accepted criterion is that of contextual congruence. This principle states that *only material that fits within the historical and cultural context of the first century prior to the destruction of the Second Temple can be considered authentic.* Archeological findings and various historical documents from the period are important resources in establishing contextual congruence.[12] This criterion has been primarily used to reject anachronistic materials. A number of passages in the Gospel of John, for example, appear to reflect a time when clear lines were drawn between Judaism and Christianity, a situation that did not yet exist during Jesus' ministry.

A recent trend among some scholars, however, appears to have taken contextual congruence to such an extreme that any suggestion of Jesus' unique and innovative perspective, which differed with or challenged traditional Judaism, was suspect. According to this perspective, Jesus was one devout Jew among other devout Jews whose historicity can only be understood as an expression of first-century Judaism that is consistent with that historical context. While I applaud the efforts of many scholars to place Jesus squarely within his historical and cultural context, there is a danger in this approach of reducing Jesus to a man of his times who lacked unique, creative, and innovative genius.

I have approached this issue affirming the need for contextual congruence without submitting to what I believe to be a simplistic notion of contextual conformity. Jesus lived "in" but was not altogether "of" his context. Material that is clearly anachronistic must be rejected. Core texts must be illuminated by cultural context as much as possible. But Jesus must be under-

11. Crossan (1991) was probably the first to apply this criterion rigorously, excluding material from consideration that did not meet the standard. Many of his assumptions about source independence are controversial.

12. Contextual methods also contribute to interpretation as discussed in Section IV below.

stood as a self in relation to his context, sometimes conforming to it, and sometimes openly challenging its assumptions.

The fourth generally accepted criterion is that of dissimilarity. This is probably the most controversial of the criteria. It states that *textual material that is dissimilar to the general portrait and theological proclamation presented by the Gospel writer, or early church source, has a high probability of being authentic.* This principle is based on the assumption that material was included in the text, even though it contradicted the author's intent, or represented a departure from the developing consensus in the early church, precisely because it came from a source that was considered by the author to be authentic. Perhaps the easiest to understand example is again the baptism of Jesus, a multiple attested event that probably would not have been included in the text by those who wanted to demonstrate that Jesus was superior to John the Baptist unless it was a well-established historical fact. The primary value of this criterion is in assuring serious consideration of the authenticity of material that appears out of place and contradictory to the author's intent.

While the criterion has some usefulness, it too may be carried to extremes. If only those things reported that are dissimilar to the intent of the Gospel writer are considered historical, a very fragmented and strange picture of Jesus would emerge.[13] I have attempted to take seriously this principle of dissimilarity, but have not found it nearly as authoritative for my work as have many scholars. On the contrary, I find it more helpful to distinguish between material that speaks of the transcendent significance of Jesus and material that reflects the life, work, teachings, and relationships of Jesus the human being. I assume that nearly all language that proclaims the transcendent significance of Jesus reflects post-resurrection theology.[14] But I also find it more credible for

13. Perhaps the weakness of this criterion can be seen in the example of Jesus' supposed prediction that people still alive would see the Son of Man coming on the clouds of heaven. Many scholars consider this, by the criterion of dissimilarity, to be authentic because it reflects a prediction that had already failed to come true by the time it appeared in the Gospel. But is the dissimilarity one between Jesus and the Gospel author, or between the Gospel writer and the persecuted church whose members retold the stories, and who attributed their hope for a speedy relief from their suffering to Jesus? Such a prediction may have been in the form of an elaboration on some less specific saying of Jesus that was reinterpreted to comfort the persecuted post-resurrection community.

14. While Jesus and his followers surely understood during his historical lifetime that there was some type of transcendent significance to Jesus' ministry, and Messianic speculation no doubt occurred during that period as well, faith in Jesus' transcendent significance as expressed in the many metaphors and symbolic narratives used by the early church are

the purpose of establishing authenticity, to find *thematic congruence* at the level of existential and spiritual meaning between the core texts about Jesus the human being and the post-resurrection language of transcendent significance, than to look at discontinuity. The tradition clearly testifies to the fact that the early Christians often misunderstood Jesus and sometimes got it wrong. But they also appear to have gotten the import of his perspective right in many, if not most, of their theological reflections and assertions.

I have, therefore, attempted to look in this work at material that could be considered independent of attributions about Jesus' transcendent significance, but I have not required, for the most part, that such material be dissimilar to the theology of the early church. It seems more probable to me that the earliest Christians grasped the mission and message of Jesus more or less accurately. For example, when John places in the mouth of Jesus that his kingdom is not of this world, it is unlikely that Jesus expressed himself in this way. But these words are consistent with everything he probably said and did as a "spiritual revolutionary" and "contrary-to-expectations Messiah."

I have also applied to the determination of authenticity what I call the principle of emotionally charged memory. Because of this criterion, I am somewhat less skeptical about what we can know about the historical Jesus than many of those of the Jesus Seminar and many mainstream scholars. Such confidence is rooted in studies of the psychology of memory and the dynamics of religious cults, as well as personal experiences. Disciples and followers of charismatic leaders retain and recall specific words and actions of those leaders for decades. The same phenomena of vivid memories occur when ordinary folk can recall in great detail interactions with celebrities. This intensification of memory increases even more when such encounters happen under circumstances of crisis.[15]

---

the result of the transformation in belief that came about as a result of resurrection experiences. Methodologically, it is important to make the distinction between the Jesus of history and the Christ of faith, since the Gospel writers wrote for the express purpose of convincing their readers that Jesus had ultimate transcendent significance. Historical method demands that one attempt to separate the perspectives of these authors from their subject matter.

15. I can recall in great detail a conversation with Coretta Scott King, wife of Dr. Martin Luther King, as we flew together from Montgomery to Atlanta following our participation in the first day of the Selma to Montgomery march in 1965. That was over forty years ago, but the memory is etched clearly in my consciousness. Do I remember it as accurately as it actually happened? I probably do not; but I am confident it is reasonably correct, because the circumstances made it an emotionally charged memory.

While I accept the majority view of scholars that the Gospel writers were not eyewitnesses, and probably did not receive their materials directly from eyewitnesses, many of the traditions behind the earliest sources represent emotionally charged experiences of followers of Jesus who knew him personally, if only for a brief encounter. Because of this, I generally assume some degree of historical authenticity for the core stories and sayings that do not make claims about Jesus' significance and that remain after later interpretations have been peeled away by form criticism, unless there is a compelling reason to reject them. Consequently, for example, while the core story of the Good Samaritan is found only in Luke, and Luke wrote after Mark and Matthew and represents a late tradition, thereby eliminating it for consideration as authentic by a narrow use of the criteria of "older is better" and "multiple independent attestation," I nonetheless accept it as an emotionally charged memory of a parable originating with the historical Jesus, because it is consistent with other historical materials and there is no compelling reason not to do so.[16]

Admittedly the principle of emotionally charged memory does little more than shift the burden of proof for contested passages to the skeptics. But that is no small shift. It provides a legitimate reason to accept as authentic core narratives and sayings that are congruent with materials for which there is greater consensus.

Establishing the authentic words and deeds of Jesus is a monumental and labor-intensive project. Rather than attempting to examine every unit of text in the Gospels, I have selected texts on the basis of their relevance to the subjects of the chapters, and have applied the methods and principles discussed above to them.

IV. Interpretive Methods

The methods discussed in Section III do not ensure agreement in outcome on the part of those who use them. And just as the anthropologist cannot escape the subjectivity of his or her own culture-bound person in the interpretation of ethnographic "texts," and the historian cannot step outside his or

16. Evidently, so do the voting members of the Jesus Seminar who have determined that this passage is authentic, despite the fact that it does not meet their own criteria. They have similarly included the "prodigal son" among the material that dates back to Jesus.

her historical moment to stand on some "objective ground," neither have I found a way to remain uninfluenced by my own cultural and historical assumptions. What I have striven for is not pure objectivity, but an inter-subjectivity that recognizes the tension between the objective and the subjective in both the interpreter and the texts. In the application of methods, established, adapted, and created, there has been a continuing sense of dialogue between the texts and my self as interpreter, between first-century presuppositions and twenty-first-century assumptions, between the culture of the ancient Jewish villages in which Jesus lived and ministered and that of the contemporary global village in which we all live today.

While interpretation is an admittedly subjective enterprise, I do not believe that it has to be purely subjective if appropriate methods are intentionally used. In this study, I have relied on contextual, existential, and spiritual methods in an effort to increase understanding and to increase the possibilities for relevance.[17]

Contextual Methods

I have spoken already of contextual congruence as a criterion for determining authenticity. But contextual methods are also critical for laying the groundwork for the interpretive process. Contextual data and the theories they generate are interpretive devices that allow persons from a distant time and culture to begin to understand the social and religious meanings of the ancient texts. *Non-biblical texts* that reveal the history of first-century Palestine as a subject territory of the Roman Empire, and those that throw light on first-century Judaism, obviously provide important contextual information. Sources such as the works of Josephus, a historian in the latter half of the first century, are extremely important. His writings were particularly relevant to chapter VII.[18]

---

17. Many scholars insist that the historical quest cannot be influenced by the desire for *relevance*. I agree that *relevance* must be "bracketed" while historical probabilities are established and, for the most part, while context is being determined. But it is disingenuous to pretend that the study of the historical Jesus is not motivated by various presuppositions about relevance. And relevance is always a consideration in the interpretive process. It seems appropriate to me to acknowledge that reality and to seek clarity of existential meaning and transcendent significance, rather than to pretend to ignore the "elephant in the room."

18. Nevertheless, Josephus's writings always must be read with caution, because of his

Archeology also has long played an important role in providing context for biblical interpretation. It is primarily useful in revealing the material culture of the time. It is particularly helpful for understanding the lifestyles of the rich and famous of the era. In order to leave behind valuable objects of material culture, one must be able to afford them. Archeology of the palaces of the House of Herod, and the Temple Mount in Jerusalem, have been particularly helpful in adding to our understanding of what life was like in and near the seats of power, and the context for much of what Jesus said and did in relation to the rich and powerful.[19]

Cultural anthropology with its emphasis on ethnographic meaning can also be an illuminating aid to interpretation. In discussing Jesus' relations with the desert prophets and ascetics in chapter II, and the poor and destitute in chapter IV, I have drawn specifically on insights from anthropological ethnographies of Mediterranean and Middle Eastern cultures utilizing the categories of "peril and refuge" and "honor and shame."

Of course, the obvious methodological question that comes to mind with regard to ethnographies is that of the relevance of studies based on cultural phenomena two thousand years after Jesus. While one must be extremely careful about imputing contemporary cultural phenomena to ancient settings, the assumption here is that some cultural preoccupations have been fundamentally resistant to change over time. They are often deeply rooted in the ecological experience, the linguistic patterns, and the traditional symbols and rituals of a region. They are taken-for-granted notions, and unquestioned assumptions, within the regional collective unconscious. As such, they are passed down relatively unchanged from generation to generation. One thinks of the harmonious tension of yin and yang in the

---

unbridled self-serving bias and the contradictions and inconsistencies within his own historical accounts. In general, one must approach all written history and literature of the period with a healthy skepticism. One compelling reason for that is that ancient history was almost always history from the perspective of the ruling classes. It is usually difficult to ascertain from them what life was like for ordinary people. That is particularly true where Greek and Roman historical materials, writings that are of critical significance to understanding the time in which Christianity emerged, are concerned.

19. Archeology can also support or call into question assumptions that have been made about the lives of more humble New Testament personalities. For example, discussion of the inner circle of fishermen in chapter VIII is in significant debt to the archeological work in and near the fishing village of Capernaum. Those efforts have identified a likely home for Simon Peter, ancient fishing equipment, a first-century boat, and boat docks on the Sea of Galilee.

Far East and the preoccupation with spiritual transcendence on the Indian subcontinent, preoccupations that continue after many centuries to influence important aspects of social relations and personality development.

Whether such cultural insights are appropriate for historical Jesus studies or not depends largely on their usefulness as heuristic (interpretive) devices. In particular, are they able, when applied to a text, to enrich understanding or throw new light on an enigmatic passage? Can they not only help us understand the externalities of our subject's life situation, but can they also assist us in exploring the attitudes, beliefs, and feelings of our subject's relation to that situation?

Existential Method

Multidisciplinary scholarship has affirmed with a high degree of probability that Jesus was a figure in history who lived in the social context of Second Temple Judaism and suffered and died on a cross. It has also demonstrated with significant probability that this human being spoke some of the words and engaged in some of the deeds attributed to him. And it has illuminated the social context and helped to clarify the meaning of those words and deeds.

It is not enough, however, to be able to know what a historical figure said, and what he did, and how he interacted with his historical and cultural context, if we are to understand the core reality of that person. To see reality as another sees it, it is necessary to see through the cultural manifestations to the underlying truths about human existence that transcend all cultural variations. In order genuinely to see through the eyes of another, as I have attempted to do in this book, it is necessary to go beyond all of the literary, historical, and contextual approaches discussed above. *For only when we find commonality on a basic and universal human level do we genuinely begin to understand another human being.*

As we have seen, every human being is up against a set of realities about life that transcend time and space. The ways in which people understand and cope with these realities are cultural in nature. But beneath the cultural forms are basic human attitudes about life and life's challenges that are universal, existential options within every culture. Even when a culture has shown preference for and encouraged a particular response to an existential challenge, other choices are presumed and have been available. So I have asked not only the question of what Jesus was up against in his culture, but also what the evidence tells us about how he dealt with what every human being is up against in life. For example, Jesus' decision, as explored in chapter II, to reject the asceticism of desert theology and to participate in the robust life of the Galilean oasis and its peasantry, was an existential choice not only about cultural options, but also about life affirmation versus life negation.

The existential method involves establishment of the basic challenges of human living across all cultural times and places and exploration of the possible relationships human beings can take to those realities. The anthropological quest for human universals, human physiology, cross-cultural psychiatry, and comparative philosophy have provided important clues to the understanding of "the way life is" for all human beings.

The existential method is also an approach to understanding that depends upon the interpreter's ability to ask and answer questions about the nature of reality with regard to texts and symbols. Just as Humpty Dumpty conveys the truth about life that sometimes bad things happen that cannot be undone, so parables and metaphors used by Jesus can also carry similar truth about life. That rain falls upon the just and the unjust as Jesus said, for example, is a truth about life. It is a truth that cannot be denied despite the human desire to create the illusion of justice in this world by maintaining that good deeds will inevitably be rewarded by good fortune, and that evil will be punished by misfortune.

This example leads us to another critical insight. It is important to understand that *existential truth is not the same as moral truth.* Existential truth may sometimes imply or suggest that a wise person will behave in a particular way, but the existential insight is ontological rather than prescriptive. Existential truth confronts human beings with questions and choices about life. It does not answer them. The answers come from those confronted as they decide how to respond to these challenges and questions. We can learn, however, from the ways in which wise people before us have chosen to deal with those realities. And such wise people can clarify for us the existential choices we have for relating to our own life circumstances. That Jesus can clarify for us such choices has been a presupposition of this book.

The philosopher Paul Ricoeur has written that one must understand in order to believe, but one must believe in order to understand.[20] In practical

---

20. Ricoeur (1978, p. 45) refers to this as the "hermeneutic circle."

terms, this means that one must "try on" the understanding of reality disclosed by the interpreted phenomena and embrace it in order to understand it. To clarify choices is "to try them on" theoretically. And such a "trying on" is a beginning of wisdom. In fact, it is no doubt a sign of wisdom that one looks before one leaps in faith. Failure to do so can lead to serious mistakes in one's life. But not to decide is also to decide. And to truly understand a choice about relating to reality requires commitment of one's own life to a chosen hypothesis about the true meaning of one's life.

To be specific, one can certainly advance understanding by theoretically trying on Jesus' view of reality and asking if one believes this to be reality for oneself. This requires, among other things, a willingness to open oneself to the potential validity of transcendent meaning. But understanding is more than an intellectual enterprise. It also requires that leap of faith and a vulnerability to spiritual experience. When a decision is made to live one's life in relation to reality, as Jesus perceived it, this is a "trying on" that has consequences and is determinative for one's own existence. But should one make this choice, a level of understanding will be achieved through living that could never have been achieved through thought alone.

Spiritual Method

Spiritual method is a profound extension of existential method. It is characterized by a prayerful opening of oneself to experience transcendent meaning. In traditional terms, it is receptivity to enlightenment by the Holy Spirit in which the relevance of a particular passage of Scripture becomes transparent to one's life of faith. Spiritual method is a reading of the text with the eyes of faith, in which the faith of the interpreter enters into dialogue with the faith that brought the text into being. It is a reading of the text within the context of a community of faith, whether physically present or represented by the "meditative counsel" of witnesses to faith and transcendent meaning in the mind of the reader. It is, therefore, a theological and spiritual conversation between the text, the reader, and other spiritual interpreters as well. In the midst of such study, the experience of faith may be created, supported, judged, and transformed by what is revealed and learned.

Until an interpreter of Scripture moves beyond those critical and interpretive methods that are limited to non-transcendent meaning, the results cannot disclose the richness of ancient meaning and the profound relevance of the texts for contemporary faith. That does not mean, however, that critical scholarship is irrelevant to the life of faith.

Both the critical approach and the spiritual method can serve a greater purpose if their respective boundaries and limitations are respected and they are employed alongside each other and in dialogue with one another according to some relevant guidelines. For example, the academic study of the Bible can "prepare the way" for spiritual study by transforming texts from one-dimensional narratives and writings to multidimensional witnesses to faith. The historical and literary criticism of the Bible has uncovered diversity not only between canonical books, but also between the layers of tradition within those writings. Far from being a threat to faith, this diversity bears witness to the richness of the biblical tradition and cries out for a more profound spiritual interpretation than has been historically demonstrated where the emphasis has been on harmonization.

A spiritual interpretation that respects the diversity within the Bible itself, including the diversity of ways of expressing various types of truth, creates fresh opportunities to discern the Word of God in our own age of diversity. By applying spiritual interpretation to the faith struggles determined by critical scholarship to be transmitted in various times and contexts, new possibilities for hearing and responding to God's Word are uncovered for those on a spiritual quest today. Spiritual study can, in turn, assist with discerning the unity of transcendent meaning and spiritual experience that underlies the testimony of diverse witnesses. And it can provide interpretive insights that increase historical understanding by translating meaning in ways that reveal the profundity of the historical faith.

In Part I of this book I have looked at the New Testament materials relevant to Jesus the human being. But the New Testament is also filled with rich confessions of faith in the significance of that human being that occurred over the next several decades following his death. In Part II I have explored the transcendent significance of Jesus for persons of faith in New Testament times. While Part I is about seeing through the eyes of Jesus the human being, Part II is about what it means to see Jesus through the eyes of faith and to confess his divinity in today's world.

Writing this book has been at once a scholarly study and a spiritual journey. It has been a quest for the core, objective truth about a historical human being, and, at the same time, a search for a subjective understanding of the depth of the existential spiritual reality of that person and his significance for faith. It has been an intentional cross-disciplinary approach designed to lessen the reductionism inherent in any single discipline. Such an interdisciplinary method is at the same time a scientific pursuit, a quest for meaning, and the creation of an art form. The truth of its outcome lies as much with the ability of the reader's heart to grasp spiritual reality as it does with the ability of the rational mind to grasp evidence and rational argument.

REFERENCES

Achtemeier, Paul J., ed. *HarperCollins Bible Dictionary.* The Society of Biblical Literature. New York: HarperCollins, 1996.

Allison, Dale C., Jr. *The New Moses: A Matthean Typology.* Minneapolis, Minn.: Fortress, 1993.

American Psychiatric Association. *Diagnostic and Statistical Manual of Mental Disorder: DSM-IV-TR.* Washington, D.C.: American Psychiatric Association, 2000.

Aulén, Gustaf. *Christus Victor: An Historical Study of the Three Main Types of the Idea of Atonement.* New York: Macmillan, 1969.

Barnouw, Victor. *An Introduction to Anthropology: Ethnology.* Homewood, Ill.: Dorsey, 1978.

Barrett, C. K. *The New Testament Background: Selected Documents.* London: SPCK, 1956.

Bartchy, S. S. *First Century Slavery and 1 Corinthians 7:21.* Eugene, Ore.: Wipf & Stock, 2003.

Beattie, John. *Other Cultures: Aims, Methods, and Achievements in Social Anthropology.* New York: The Free Press, 1964.

Benedict, Ruth. *Patterns of Culture.* Boston: Houghton Mifflin, 1934.

Bierhorst, John. *The Mythology of Mexico and Central America.* New York: William Morrow, 1990.

Biven, David. "Jerusalem Perspective Article: Jesus Education." www.jerusalem perspective.com, 1987-2004.

Bleicher, Josef. *Contemporary Hermeneutics: Hermeneutics as Method, Philosophy and Critique.* Boston: Routledge & Kegan Paul, 1980.

Bonhoeffer, Dietrich. *Ethics.* New York: Macmillan, 1955.

———. *Christ the Center.* San Francisco: HarperSanFrancisco, 1960.

————. "Paper on the Historical and Pneumatological Interpretation of Scripture." In *Dietrich Bonhoeffer Works,* vol. 9, *The Young Bonhoeffer, 1918-1927.* Minneapolis, Minn.: Fortress, 2003.

Borg, Marcus J. *Jesus A New Vision: Spirit, Culture, and the Life of Discipleship.* San Francisco: HarperCollins, 1987.

————. *Meeting Jesus Again for the First Time: The Historical Jesus and the Heart of Contemporary Faith.* San Francisco: HarperCollins, 1994.

Borg, Marcus J., and N. T. Wright. *The Meaning of Jesus: Two Visions.* San Francisco: HarperCollins, 1999.

Boring, M. Eugene. "The Gospel of Matthew: Introduction, Commentary and Reflections." In *The New Interpreter's Bible,* vol. VIII, edited by Leander E. Keck. Nashville: Abingdon Press, 1995.

Bourguignon, Erika. "World Distributions and Patterns of Possession States." In *Trance and Possession States,* edited by R. Prince. Montreal: R. M. Bucke Memorial Society, 1968.

Bradley, Keith. *Slavery and Society at Rome.* Cambridge: Cambridge University Press, 1994.

Brant, Jo Ann A. *Dialogue and Drama: Elements of Greek Tragedy in the Fourth Gospel.* Peabody, Mass.: Hendrickson, 2004.

Brown, Raymond E. *An Introduction to New Testament Christology.* New York: Paulist, 1994.

Bultmann, Rudolf. *Form Criticism, Two Essays on New Testament Research.* New York: Harper & Row, 1934.

————. *Theology of the New Testament.* Vol. I. New York: Scribners, 1951.

————. *Theology of the New Testament.* Vol. II. New York: Scribners, 1955a.

————. "The Crisis of Faith." In *Essays — Philosophical and Theological.* London: SCM, 1955b.

————. *The History of the Synoptic Tradition.* New York: Harper & Row, 1963.

Campbell, Joseph. *The Hero with a Thousand Faces.* Princeton, N.J.: Princeton University Press, 1972.

Chilton, Bruce. *Rabbi Jesus: An Intimate Biography.* New York: Image, Doubleday, 2000.

Collins, Francis S. *The Language of God.* New York: The Free Press, 2006.

Crossan, John Dominic. *The Historical Jesus: The Life of a Mediterranean Jewish Peasant.* San Francisco: HarperCollins, 1991.

————. *Jesus: A Revolutionary Biography.* San Francisco: HarperCollins, 1994.

Crossan, John Dominic, and Jonathan L. Reed. *Excavating Jesus: Beneath the Stones, Behind the Texts.* San Francisco: HarperCollins, 2001.

————. *In Search of Paul: How Jesus's Apostle Opposed Rome's Empire with God's Kingdom.* San Francisco: HarperSanFrancisco, 2004.

De Souza, Phillip. *Piracy in the Graeco-Roman World.* Cambridge: Cambridge University Press, 1999.

Dorsey, Larry. *Prayer Is Good Medicine.* San Francisco: HarperSanFrancisco, 1997.

Douglas, Mary. *Purity and Danger: An Analysis of Concepts of Pollution and Taboo.* London: Routledge & Kegan Paul, 1966.

Durkheim, Emile. *The Elementary Forms of the Religious Life.* New York: The Free Press, 1915.

Ehrman, Bart D. *Jesus: Apocalyptic Prophet of the New Millennium.* New York: Oxford University Press, 1998.

Eisenman, Robert. *The Dead Sea Scrolls and the First Christians.* New York: Barnes and Noble, 2004.

Eliade, Mircea. *Shamanism: Archaic Techniques of Ecstasy.* Translated by Willard R. Trask. Bollingen Series LXXVI. Princeton, N.J.: Princeton University Press, 1964.

Eusebius, Pamphilus. *Ecclesiastical History.* Translated by C. F. Cruse. Peabody, Mass.: Hendrickson, 1999.

Evans-Prichard, E. E. *The Nuer.* Oxford: Clarendon Press, 1940.

Foster, George M. "Peasant Society and the Image of Limited Good." *American Anthropologist* 67 (1965): 293-315.

———. "The Anatomy of Envy: A Study in Symbolic Behavior." *Current Anthropology* 13 (1972): 165-86, 198-202.

Fredriksen, Paula. *From Jesus to Christ.* New Haven, Conn.: Yale University Press, 1988.

———. *Jesus of Nazareth: King of the Jews.* New York: Vintage, 2000.

Freud, Sigmund. *Totem and Taboo.* New York: W. W. Norton & Company, 1950.

Geertz, Clifford. "Thick Description." In *The Interpretation of Cultures.* New York: Basic Books, 1973.

Gilmore, David D. *Honor and Shame and the Unity of the Mediterranean.* American Anthropology Association Paperback (January), 1987.

Gulick, John. *The Middle East: An Anthropological Perspective.* Lanham, Md.: University Press of America, 1983.

Hagedorn, Anselm C. (with Jerome H. Neyrey). "'It Was Out of Envy that They Handed Jesus Over' (Mark 15:10): The Anatomy of Envy and the Gospel of Mark." *Journal for the Study of the New Testament* 69 (1983): 15-56.

Hanson, K. C. "How Honorable! How Shameful! A Cultural Analysis of Matthew's Makarisms and Reproaches." *Semeia* 68 (1996): 83-114.

———. "The Galilean Fishing Economy and the Jesus Tradition." *Biblical Theology Bulletin* 27 (1997): 99-111.

Harland, Philip A. "The Economy of First Century Palestine: The State of Scholarly Discussion." In *Handbook of Early Christianity: Social Science Approaches,* edited by Anthony J. Blsi, Paul-André Turcotte, and Jean Duhaime, pp. 511-27. Walnut Creek, Calif.: Alta Mira, 2002.

Harner, Michael. "The Enigma of Aztec Sacrifice." *Natural History* 86, no. 4 (April 1977): 46-51.

Harris, Marvin. *Cannibals and Kings: The Origin of Culture.* New York: Random House, 1977.

Horsley, Richard A., ed. *Paul and Empire: Religion and Power in Roman Imperial Society.* Harrisburg, Pa.: Trinity Press International, 1997.

Hultkranzz, Ake. *Native Religions of North America.* New York: HarperCollins, 1988.

Hurtado, Larry W. *How on Earth Did Jesus Become a God? Historical Questions about Earliest Devotion to Jesus.* Grand Rapids, Mich.: Eerdmans, 2005.

Janzen, John M. *The Quest for Therapy in Lower Zaire.* Berkeley and Los Angeles: University of California Press, 1978.

Jensen, Adolf E. *Myth and Cult Among Primitive Peoples.* Chicago: University of Chicago Press, 1951.

Jeremias, Joachim. *The Central Message of the New Testament.* New York: Charles Scribners' Sons, 1965.

———. *Jerusalem in the Time of Jesus: An Investigation into Economic and Social Conditions During the New Testament Period.* Minneapolis, Minn.: Augsburg Fortress, 1979.

Johnson, Luke Timothy. *Sharing Possessions: Mandate and Symbol of Faith.* Minneapolis, Minn.: Fortress, 1981.

———. *The Real Jesus: The Misguided Quest for the Historical Jesus and the Truth of the Traditional Gospels.* San Francisco: HarperSanFrancisco, 1997.

Josephus, Flavius. *The Works of Flavius Josephus.* Introduction by Paul L. Maier and translated by William Whiston. Grand Rapids, Mich.: Kregel, 1999.

Jung, C. G. *Symbols of Transformation: An Analysis of the Prelude to a Case of Schizophrenia.* Princeton, N.J.: Princeton University Press, 1956.

———. *Psyche and Symbol.* Garden City, N.Y.: Doubleday Anchor, 1958.

———. *Man and His Symbols.* New York: Dell, 1964.

Keck, Leander E., ed. *The New Interpreter's Bible.* Vols. I-XIII. Nashville: Abingdon, 1994-2000.

Kerenyi, Carl. *Dionysos: Archetypal Image of Indestructible Life.* Princeton, N.J.: Princeton University Press, 2003.

Kierkegaard, Søren. *The Sickness Unto Death: A Christian Psychological Exposition for Upbuilding and Awakening.* Edited and translated by Howard V. Hong and Edna H. Hong. Princeton, N.J.: Princeton Paperbacks, 1980.

Kiev, Ari. *Magic, Faith, and Healing.* New York: The Free Press, 1964.

Klass, Morton. *Mind Over Mind: The Anthropology and Psychology of Spirit Possession.* Lanham, Md.: Rowan & Littlefield, 2004.

Kleinman, Arthur. *Patients and Healers in the Context of Culture.* Berkeley: University of California Press, 1979.

Kohler, Kaufmann. "Pharisees" in *JewishEncyclopedia.Com*. www.jewishencyclo pedia.com., 2002a.

———. "Zealots" in *JewishEncyclopedia.Com*. www.jewishencyclopedia.com, 2002b.

Kroeber, Alfred L. "Totem and Taboo in Retrospect." In *Reader in Comparative Religion: An Anthropological Approach,* edited by William A. Lessa and Evon Z. Vogt. New York: Harper & Row, 1979.

Kuhn, Thomas. *The Structure of Scientific Revolutions.* Chicago: University of Chicago Press, 1970.

Lakoff, George, and Mark Johnson. *Metaphors We Live By.* Chicago: University of Chicago Press, 1980.

Lamsa, George. *The New Testament According to the Eastern Text.* Philadelphia: A. J. Holman, 1940.

Levine, Amy-Jill. *The Misunderstood Jew: The Church and the Scandal of the Jewish Jesus.* San Francisco: HarperSanFrancisco, 2006.

Levi-Strauss, Claude. *Structural Anthropology.* New York: Basic Books, 1963.

Lewis, C. S. *Mere Christianity.* San Francisco: HarperOne, 2001.

Malina, Bruce J. (with Jerome H. Neyrey). *Calling Jesus Names: The Social Value of Labels in Matthew.* Sonoma, Calif.: Polebridge, 1988.

———. *New Testament World: Insights from Cultural Anthropology.* Louisville: Westminster John Knox, 2001.

Malinowski, Bronislaw. *Argonauts of the Western Pacific.* London: Routledge & Kegan Paul Ltd., 1922.

———. *Magic, Science, and Religion and Other Essays.* New York: Doubleday Anchor, 1954.

Meier, John P. *A Marginal Jew: Rethinking the Historical Jesus.* Vol. 1. New York: Random House, 1991.

———. *Mentor, Message and Miracles* (*A Marginal Jew,* vol. 2). New York: Random House, 1994.

———. "The Historical Jesus and the Historical Samaritans: What Can Be Said?" *Biblica* 81 (1999): 202-32.

———. *Companions and Competitors* (*A Marginal Jew,* vol. 3). New York: Random House, 2000.

Mowery, Robert L. "Son of God in Roman Imperial Titles and Matthew." *Biblica* 83 (2002): 100-110.

Murphy, Jane M. "Psychotherapeutic Aspects of Shamanism on St. Lawrence Island, Alaska." In *Magic, Faith and Healing,* edited by Ari Kiev. New York: The Free Press, 1964.

Neusner, Jacob. *From Politics to Piety.* Englewood Cliffs, N.J.: Prentice-Hall, 1973.

Neyrey, Jerome H. "A Symbolic Approach to Mark 7." *Forum* 4, no. 3 (1988a): 63-91.

——— (with Bruce J. Malina). *Calling Jesus Names: The Social Value of Labels in Matthew*. Sonoma, Calif.: Polebridge, 1988b.

———. "Josephus' *Vita* and the Encomium: A Native Model of Personality." *Journal for the Study of Judaism* 25 (1994): 177-206.

——— (with Anselm C. Hagedorn). "'It Was Out of Envy that They Handed Jesus Over' (Mark 15:10): The Anatomy of Envy and the Gospel of Mark." *Journal for the Study of the New Testament* 69 (1998): 15-56.

———. *Honor and Shame: Matthew and the Great Code*. Louisville: Westminster John Knox, 1999.

———. "Who Is Poor in the New Testament?" *Scripture from Scratch*. American Catholic.org, October 2002.

———. "God, Benefactor and Patron: The Major Cultural Model for Interpreting the Deity in Greco-Roman Antiquity." *Journal for the Study of the New Testament* 27 (2005): 465-92.

Niebuhr, H. Richard. *The Purpose of the Church and Its Ministry*. New York: Harper & Row, 1956.

Oakman, Douglas E. *Jesus and the Economic Questions of His Day*. Queenston: Edwin Mellen, 1995.

Ozturk, Orhan M. "Folk Treatment of Mental Illness in Turkey." In *Magic, Faith, and Healing*, edited by Ari Kiev. New York: The Free Press, 1964.

Peace, Richard V. *Conversion in the New Testament: Paul and the Twelve*. Grand Rapids, Mich.: Eerdmans, 2000.

Peristiany, J. G., ed. *Honor and Shame: The Values of Mediterranean Societies*. The Nature of Human Society Series. Chicago: University of Chicago Press, 1965.

Perkins, Pheme. "The Gospel of Mark: Introduction, Commentary, and Reflections." In *The New Interpreter's Bible*, vol. VIII, edited by Leander E. Keck. Nashville: Abingdon, 1995.

Philo, Judaeus. *The Works of Philo: Complete and Unabridged*. Translated by C. D. Yonge. Peabody, Mass.: Hendrickson, 1996.

Pitt-Rivers, Julian. "Honor and Social Status." In *Honor and Shame: The Values of Mediterranean Societies*, edited by J. G. Peristiany. The Nature of Human Society Series. Chicago: University of Chicago Press, 1996.

Pitulac, Sebastian, and Sebastian Nastuta. "Choosing to be Stigmatized: Rational Calculus in Religious Conversion." *Journal for the Study of Religions and Ideologies* 16 (Spring 2007).

Poston, Larry. *Islamic Da'wah in the West. Muslim Missionary Activity and the Dynamics of Conversion to Islam*. New York and Oxford: Oxford University Press, 1992.

Powelson, Mark, and Ray Riegert. *The Lost Gospel Q: Original Sayings of Jesus*. Berkeley, Calif.: Ulysses, 1999.

Propp, Vladimir. *Morphology of the Folktale*. Austin: University of Texas Press, 1968.

Rambo, L. *Understanding Religious Conversion*. New Haven, Conn.: Yale University Press, 1993.

Ricoeur, Paul. *The Symbolism of Evil*. Boston: Beacon, 1967.

———. *The Rule of Metaphor: Multi-Disciplinary Studies of the Creation of Meaning of Language*. Toronto: University of Toronto Press, 1975.

———. *The Philosophy of Paul Ricoeur: An Anthology of His Work*. Edited by Charles E. Reagan and David Stewart. Boston: Beacon, 1978.

Schwartz A. J. "The Nature of Spiritual Transformation: A Review of the Literature." Metanexus Institute, http://www.metanexus.net, 2001.

Schwarz, Hanz. *Christology*. Grand Rapids, Mich.: Eerdmans, 1998.

Seeley, David. "The Background of the Philippians Hymn (2:6-11)." *Journal of Higher Criticism* 1 (Fall 1994).

Shaw, Brent. "Bandits in the Roman Empire." *Past & Present* 105 (1984): 5-52.

Smith, Houston. *The Religions of Man*. New York: Harper & Row, 1966.

Snell, Daniel C. *Life in the Ancient Near East 3100-332 B.C.E.* New Haven, Conn.: Yale University Press, 1997.

Specter, A., S. Davies, B. Woods, and M. Orrell. "Reality Orientation for Dementia: A Systematic Review of the Evidence for its Effectiveness." *Gerontologist* 40 (2001): 206-12.

Stark, Norman. "Normal Revelations: A Rational Model of 'Mystical' Experiences." In *Religion and the Social Order,* vol. 1, edited by David G. Bromiley, pp. 239-51. Greenwich: JAI, 1991.

Strong, James. *The New Strong's Exhaustive Concordance of the Bible*. Nashville: Thomas Nelson, 1984.

Strupp, H. H., and S. W. Hadley. "Specific Versus Nonspecific Factors in Psychotherapy." *Archives of General Psychiatry* 36 (1980): 1125-36.

Tillich, Paul. *Biblical Religion and the Search for Ultimate Reality*. Chicago: University of Chicago Press, 1963.

Torrey, E. Fuller. *Witchdoctors and Psychiatrists: The Common Roots of Psychotherapy and Its Future*. New York: Harper & Row Perennial Library, 1972.

Turner, Victor. *The Forest of Symbols*. Ithaca: Cornell University Press, 1967.

Uberoi, J. P. Singh. *Politics of the Kula Ring*. Manchester, England: University of Manchester Press, 1962.

Varner, William C. "Jesus and the Pharisees: A Jewish Perspective." Saint Louis, Mo.: Personal Freedom Outreach. http://www.pho.org, 1998.

Vermes, Geza. *Jesus the Jew*. Minneapolis, Minn.: Augsburg Fortress, 1981.

———. *The Complete Dead Sea Scrolls*. New York: Penguin Group, 1998.

———. *The Authentic Gospel of Jesus*. New York: Penguin Group, 2005.

Vieten, Cassandra, Tina Amorok, and Marilyn Schiltz. "Many Paths, One Mountain: A Cross-Traditional Model of Spiritual Transformation." www.ions.org, Petaluma, Calif., Institute of Noetic Sciences.

Vine, W. E. *Vine's Concise Dictionary of the Bible.* Nashville: Thomas Nelson, 2007.

Wallace, Anthony. "Revitalization Movements." *American Anthropologist* 56, no. 2 (1956): 264-81.

Webber, George W. *God's Colony in Man's World: Christian Love in Action.* Nashville: Abingdon, 1960.

Wiedemann, Thomas. *Greek and Roman Slavery.* New York: Routledge, 1989.

Worsley, Peter. *The Trumpet Shall Sound: A Study of Cargo Cults in Melanesia.* New York: Schocken, 1967.

Yamaouchi, Edwin M. *Pre-Christian Gnosticism.* Grand Rapids: Baker, 1983.

Zias, Joe. "Health and Healing in the Land of Israel: A Paleopathological Perspective" (www.joezias.com/HealthHealingLandIsrael.htm). From *Mikhmanim* (Spring 2002).

Zinnbauer, Brian, and Kenneth Pargament. "Spiritual Conversion: A Study of Religious Change Among College Students." *Journal for the Scientific Study of Religion* 37 (1998): 161-80.

INDEX OF SUBJECTS

389